LUCRETIUS

Selections from DE RERUM NATURA

LUCRETIUS

Selections from
DE RERUM NATURA

Bonnie A. Catto

With a Foreword by Kirk Summers

BOLCHAZY-CARDUCCI PUBLISHERS, INC.
Wauconda, Illinois

General Editor
Laurie Haight

Contributing Editors
Aaron Baker
Gilbert Lawall

Cover Design
Anne May

Typography and Page Design
Charlene Hernandez

Cover Illustration
after the cosmic egg design
on a fifth-century BC dish
from Hotnica, Bulgaria

© Copyright 1998

Bolchazy-Carducci Publishers, Inc.
1000 Brown Street
Wauconda, Illinois 60084 (USA)
http://www.bolchazy.com

ISBN 0-86516-399-5

Printed in the United States of America
by Thomson-Shore

Library of Congress Cataloging-in-Publication Data

Lucretius Carus, Titus
    [De rerum natura. English & Latin. Selections]
    Selections from De rerum natura / Lucretius ; edited for students
by Bonnie A. Catto.
        p.   cm.
    Includes bibliographical references.
    ISBN 0-86516-399-5 (softcover : alk. paper)
    1. Didactic poetry, Latin--Translations into English.
2. Philosophy, Ancient--Poetry. 3. Latin language--Readers.
I. Catto, Bonnie A., 1951-   . II. Title.
PA6483.E5C3852 1998
187--dc21

∽ CONTENTS ∾

❦ Acknowledgments ❧

This book is the result of the efforts of many people, to whom I am deeply grateful. First I would like to thank Assumption College for granting me a fully-funded, year-long sabbatical to work on the book. By their letters of support William Borowski, Charles Bradshaw, Marie Cleary, Philippa Goold, Andrea Warren Hamos, Gilbert Lawall, George Ryan, and Nell Wright were instrumental in the success of my sabbatical proposal. Initial discussions with Gilbert Lawall and Sally Murphy were most helpful in organizing my thoughts and plan of approach. During the sabbatical year, the advice and help of the Assumption computer support staff, especially Robert Fry and Mimi Royston, and of the library staff were invaluable. My friend Michael Lyons came to my rescue when I first attempted, unsuccessfully, to type the notes into the proper word-processing format. Roberta Adams and Bruce Plichta listened sympathetically for many hours to my mutterings and complaints. Matthew Deady and William Shaheen answered my pleas for help in understanding the relationship between ancient and modern physics. Tom Dennis introduced me to many scientific sources and explained many concepts when we co-taught a course entitled "Atoms: Ancient to Modern" at Mount Holyoke College. My students in Latin 22 in Spring 1995, Jerry Bissonette, Tara Kelly, Beth Vincent, Jon Volpe, and Jill Zalieckas, offered helpful suggestions on a preliminary version of notes on several passages and seemed to forgive me for seeing everything through Lucretian eyes. Of course, I would like to thank all the many students who have read Lucretius with me over the years at Mount Holyoke, Middlebury, and Assumption Colleges; each has contributed something to this text. While I was an undergraduate at Mount Holyoke College, Betty Quinn and Dargan Jones opened my eyes to the joys of scholarship. In a seminar on Lucretius Philippa Goold truly inspired my appreciation and love for the poet. She also guided my first efforts at serious scholarship during her supervision of my undergraduate thesis on the elegiac poets. During graduate school at the University of Pennsylvania, Douglas Minyard furthered my understanding of Lucretius and his sources, and Phillip DeLacy, even after his retirement, graciously supervised my doctoral dissertation on Lucretius. During work on this book, Gilbert Lawall, editor of the CANE series, was indefatigable, and his keen eye for detail and precision is much appreciated. Of course, any errors that may remain are solely mine. Finally, I would like to thank my parents, Lina and Harold MacNeill, who have unfailingly and lovingly supported all my efforts. My husband Alistair, as always, was most supportive as I spent countless hours pounding the computer keyboard. Thanks to him, I finished this book with my sanity intact and memories of an enjoyable year spent at home despite the snowiest winter on record.

"If something could come from nothing," Lucretius wrote, "then anything could arise from anything, and there would be no need for seed." These simple words, the heart and soul of the Epicurean philosophy, mask a complex web of ideas, and transport us to the center of the intellectual debate in the Hellenistic world. Can we rely on our senses to investigate the material world, or should we look beyond matter to the metaphysical for the ultimate truth about reality? Lucretius insists that the universe is knowable through scientific inquiry alone, that even the soul and the gods are material, and furthermore that we can determine the nature of things that are invisible to our eyes through analogy with the visible. His confidence in calm reflection and observation of natural phenomena is at the same time a rejection of spiritual meditation, religion, and faith, at least as those activities are commonly conceived. And it is from this materialistic outlook that Lucretius, as Epicureans did before him, proceeds to address the most pressing issues that touch us all as human beings: the nature of justice and society; free will versus determinism; the chief end of our existence; the ways in which we should conduct ourselves; the value of love and relationships; the problem of death.

Whether Lucretius came up with satisfactory answers to all the questions inherent in these issues is another matter. What Lucretius does do, and what makes his work so compelling, is to demand with all the passion he can muster that we confront these issues head on. One can feel with every sweaty line of his hexameters the urgency with which he advocates the Epicurean way of life: fear of the unknown and unexplained can strike at the heart and tear down the life of a human being; ambition for power and fame grinds down humanity and renders it chaotic; obsession with death destroys any hope for present happiness. In contrast, the truth about nature frees the mind to live in pleasure and peace. Lucretius' missionary zeal was unprecedented in his day. For him, Epicureanism is nothing less than a critical message of comfort and salvation.

Precisely because Lucretius charges headlong into all that matters to us as human beings he deserves to be introduced early in the curriculum of a classical education. Certainly Caesar, Cicero, and Vergil all vie for first place in our intermediate Latin reading courses. Caesar offers readability, Cicero historical intrigue, and Vergil myth and heroism. But Lucretius too belongs in their company, not because we can trace the fall of the republic or the rise of the empire through his writings, but because he so easily transcends that time and space. Students, who are often themselves introspective and searching for answers, will find Lucretius challenging and profound. The problems being bantered about in Lucretius' day, the ones for which he is ready with an answer, are the same ones today.

But until now we have faced a dearth of suitable Lucretian textbooks that would make it possible to read him early on. The present volume remedies that problem admirably. Rather than confining herself to one book, thereby giving an incomplete picture of Epicurean philosophy, Professor Catto has made selections from all six books. As she herself says, these selections are a mixture of the purple passages and the essence of the philosophy. With the vocabulary added on the facing pages, in the style of *Ecce Romani III*, the students can keep their eyes fixed on the flow of the argument rather than the Latin dictionary. By the end of the course the students will have the basic outline of Epicureanism, a knowledge of the basic questions of Hellenistic philosophy, and an introduction to epic/didactic poetry.

Even so, we may recoil from the notion of teaching a philosophical text in the intermediate stages. Aeneas, Catiline, and Caesar all do things. Philosophy, on the other hand, is by nature plodding and dry. But Lucretius appears to have recognized the problem. In his own words, he administers the bitter medicine of philosophical doctrine in a honey-rimmed cup. With a flare for the dramatic, a love-hate relationship with myth, and vivid vignettes from everyday life, Lucretius achieves a kind of clarity and charm never before found in philosophical writing. He can at one moment turn gruesomely dark, as when describing the Athenian plague, then bizarre, especially as he expounds his views on sex, and then suddenly be touching and sentimental, as when he describes scenes from family life. In short, he suits the present generation of students more than we give him credit.

Given, then, that Lucretius' pen ranges over a myriad of pivotal issues, and that he presents his case with passion and conviction, still we are left with a nagging question: Does Lucretius have any insights that will enrich our students' lives? Does his message still ring true today? Without a doubt, Lucretius believed ardently in the doctrines of Epicureanism, and wanted his readers to believe them also. Epicurus was almost a god to him. At the same time, Lucretius did not pretend to have comprehended the workings of the universe. He followed Epicurus in asserting that in many cases we can surmise numerous causes for any given phenomenon (5.526–533; 6.703–711). The reasons why the Nile overflows its banks in the summer, for example, can be attributed to any number of natural causes, but the correct one awaits further study. What causes the celestial bodies to move also admits several explanations, only one of which can be the right one. For Lucretius, nature is always calling us to unlock her mysteries, and he is certain that in the very quest for knowledge beauty, peace, and purpose lie. The person who is not curious, who lazily makes assumptions on the basis of superficial investigation, must live in fear and ignorance. This is a message worthy of our times. And few would disagree that this insistence on the liberating power of knowledge should be at the heart of any humanistic, liberating education.

Kirk Summers
University of Alabama

∞ INTRODUCTION ∞

∞ Methodology ∞

Vocabulary

This text is designed so that it can be used by students who have completed any standard Latin program. The running notes that face the text gloss vocabulary that is not included in *Ecce Romani* I and II (including Review Readings), published by Longman. If a word is used in an unusual way or in a sense different from the definition in *Ecce Romani*, it is also glossed in the notes. Words whose meaning can easily be deduced are not given in the running vocabularies but are included in the end vocabulary. All words that occur two or more times are included in the end vocabulary. Thus, if a word occurs only once, it is glossed in the running notes but not included in the end vocabulary.

Ideally students will be able to read all the passages; however, this may not be possible in a particular course. Therefore, to help students in reading selected passages, rather than the entire text, many words that have been glossed in the running notes for an earlier passage are glossed again in a passage on a new topic. Of course it is assumed that, as students read, they will become familiar with the Lucretian style, so that the most frequent words need not be glossed repeatedly.

Selections

Any group of selections is, by necessity, subjective. Lucretius has suffered more than most authors from this subjectivity, since editors have generally focused on the "purple passages" and excluded the more scientific portions. This approach is problematic, since to ignore the science is to violate the poet's clearly stated purpose to free man from his fears by educating him in the scientific truth. Moreover, such an approach gives students an erroneous impression of the epic's content and its influence on later writers and thinkers. Therefore, I have tried to assemble a group of selections that (1), by including the most famous poetic passages, reveals the beauty and power of Lucretius' poetry, and (2) also covers at least the bare bones of the scientific theory. I have also included some personal favorites. Since Book 1 acts as the foundation of the epic, there are necessarily more selections from this book. The passages occur in Lucretius' order of presentation. The text includes 1291 lines in all (about 17% of the epic) with some repeated passages. Since each passage has its own introduction, teachers should be able to skip over several passages without undue confusion, although it would be helpful to summarize the omitted passages to maintain the flow of argumentation. I have tried to present continuous passages, without any cuts if possible, to maintain the integrity of the thought and imagery.

In the preparation of the text I consulted Bailey (1947), Costa (1984), Godwin (1986, 1991), Kenney (1984), Leonard and Smith (1968), Merrill (1907), and Munro (1928) (see Bibliography). The textual readings for the most part follow Bailey's 1947 edition with some changes in punctuation and with capitalization at the beginning of sentences. In instances where Bailey left a crux in the text, I have printed the reading which to me seemed most reasonable (e.g., **gnātīs** for **magnīs**, 3.962); in the accompanying commentary I have noted the corruption of the manuscripts and have sometimes provided alternate readings. In a number of instances, however, in the light of more recent scholarship I have chosen a reading different from Bailey's (e.g., **plācāta** for **pācāta**, 5.1203).

ଓ Introduction to Lucretius ଓ

The *De rerum natura* of Lucretius is a marvelous and unique blend of poetry, physics, and philosophy, in which Lucretius celebrates the awesome power of nature both for creation and destruction. The epic speaks powerfully to us across the centuries as it propounds with apostolic fervor the philosophy of Epicurus and depicts with loving attentiveness the intricacies of nature. But what do we know about the poet himself? Sadly, very little. His name was Titus Lucretius Carus, and he lived from approximately 94 to 55 B.C. Although he was a contemporary of Catullus, Caesar, and Cicero, the only mention of him by his contemporaries is a passing comment by Cicero in a letter to his brother Quintus: **Lucrētī poēmata, ut scrībis, ita sunt—multīs lūminibus ingenī multae tamen artis**: "the poems of Lucretius, as you write, are thus—with many lights of talent, many still of skill."[1] That is all. Donatus in the fourth century A.D. tells us Lucretius died in 55 B.C., but his account is somewhat fanciful. Still later St. Jerome provides a birthdate of 94, but adds other material that is probably unreliable and indeed seems prejudicial (such as his implausible statement that Lucretius wrote the poem in intervals between fits of insanity). Does the poem itself offer any evidence for his dates? Possibly. In 6.1106 Lucretius refers to the climate of Britain, which may indicate that he was aware of Caesar's invasion of the island in 55. If so, we have a **terminus post quem** for his death. Lucretius' place of birth has also been a matter for debate. Though generally considered to be a Roman, one scholar, on the basis of linguistic evidence, has suggested that, like Catullus, he was a Transpadane (from across the Po River).[2] From his name it can be assumed that Lucretius was a member of the aristocratic **gēns Lucrētia**. Certainly the breadth of his education (i.e., his knowledge of Greek and of archaic Latin) and his familiarity with the details of the lives of the wealthy indicate a privileged upbringing. Moreover, he dedicated his poem to Gaius Memmius, praetor in 58 and governor of Bithynia in 57, ironically the same Memmius whom Catullus so vehemently insulted (poems 10 and 28). Lucretius' informal manner of address to Memmius suggests shared aristocratic status. Why, then, if Lucretius was a member of a prominent Roman family, does his name never occur in contemporary records of office-holders or of the courts? Why, in short, do we hear nothing about him? We know of many Epicureans in Italy during this period, such as the Greek author Philodemus, whose library has been discovered at Herculaneum, and who actively influenced many Romans of the day. There were also Roman Epicureans who were active in political life: the consul in 58 L. Calpurnius Piso Caesoninus, the patrician praetor L. Manlius Torquatus, who in Cicero's *De finibus* expounds the Epicurean view, and even the infamous praetor T. Albucius, who went into voluntary exile in Athens after conviction for corruption. Nonetheless, we also know of Roman Epicureans who seem to have followed their master's precept: λάθε βιώσας, "live unnoticed," and thus chose to lead private lives. Among these are Cicero's great friend T. Pomponius Atticus, the poet Vergil, and possibly the poet Horace.[3] Perhaps Lucretius belongs in this number. What then was this Epicurean philosophy that advocated withdrawal from society?

ଓ The First Philosophers ଓ

In order to understand Epicureanism, we must place it in its philosophical context. Let us then begin our examination with a very brief history of the origins of Greek philosophy. In the sixth century B.C. many Greeks, particularly in Ionia, began to question the traditional mythological explanation of the world in which the Olympian gods created and controlled all nature. They began to seek a rational explanation for the workings of nature and to search

---

[1] *Ad Quintum fratrem* 2.9.3–4 (February, 54 B.C.)

[2] Louise Adams Holland, *Lucretius and the Transpadanes* (Princeton: Princeton University Press, 1979).

[3] For a complete list of known and possible Roman Epicureans see Catherine Castner, *Prosopography of Roman Epicureans, from the Second Century B.C. to the Second Century A.D.*, Studien zur klassischen Philologie, vol. 34 (Frankfurt am Main: Verlag Peter Lang, 1988).

for a simplicity underlying the world's variety. The fundamental question they asked was: "What is the primary substance from which everything is made?" Their word for the primary substance was φύσις (*physis*, **nātūra** in Latin). Thus the first philosophers were really physicists. In Greek *physis* has a variety of meanings ranging from (1) what is primary, permanent, and fundamental, to (2) the laws and principles of nature, to (3) the nature of an individual thing, to, finally, (4) the universe as a whole. This one word thus illustrates the idea that the microcosm and macrocosm are in essence the same. Of course there was much disagreement about the identity of the primary substance. Thales, generally considered to be the first scientist because of his prediction of a solar eclipse in 585 B.C., believed that everything was water in various manifestations. On the other hand, Heraclitus (floruit c. 500) chose fire as the primary substance. These two thinkers are called monists. Others, however, saw obvious defects in the monistic approach. First, how could one substance account for the incredible variety of the world? Secondly, monism violates sense perception since if, for instance, everything is fire, it makes no sense that everything does not burn. If fire can lose such a fundamental property as heat, is it then still fire? In answer to such objections, other philosophers developed pluralistic theories. The most famous of these pluralists is Empedocles (493–33), who chose four elements—fire, air, water, and earth—as the primary substances, which by their interaction, in a conflict controlled by the two opposing impulses of love and strife (attraction and repulsion), create the world around us. Both monists and pluralists believed that the universe was completely full of matter with no empty space, and in fact the monist Parmenides even denied that change or motion was possible. Since the world seems to be composed of a myriad of substances and seems to be in constant motion, neither the monists nor pluralists could satisfactorily answer concerns about variety and the validity of sense perception, or indeed about the permanence of the primary substance itself.

ෆ The Atomists ಬಿ

In about 440 B.C. Leucippus solved these problems by inventing the atomic theory, an extreme form of pluralism. According to this theory, the world is composed of "atoms," literally "uncuttables," permanent bits of matter which are unlike ordinary, visible substances. The atoms are absolutely solid and homogeneous in substance, though they differ in shape and size. It is by differences in their shapes and sizes and by their differing arrangements with one another that the variety evident in our world can be explained. Secondly, and equally importantly, Leucippus posited the existence of void: absolutely empty space in which the atoms can move with self-generated motion. Leucippus himself is a somewhat shadowy figure, and it is unclear how fully he developed the atomic theory. His pupil, Democritus (c. 460–370), is generally believed to have elaborated the theory, particularly with respect to atomic motion and its results. According to Democritus, "All things happen according to necessity, the whirl [of atoms] being the cause of the birth of everything" (Diels, A1). In the Democritean system there are no random occurrences; absolute determinism prevails: "The causes of those things now coming into existence have no beginning, but altogether from the beginning from boundless time absolutely all things that were and are and will be are preordained by necessity" (Diels, A39). On the human level, of course, this determinism precludes free will.

The denial of free will troubled many. Perhaps it is one reason why Socrates (469–399), having expressed an initial interest in natural science, turned instead to an examination of the good, and thus forever changed the course of philosophy from the study of nature to ethics.[4] In modern times, those Greek thinkers who had investigated the constituents of nature became known as Pre-Socratic philosophers; later investigators are, of course, called

---

4   "When I was young . . . I had an extraordinary passion for that branch of learning which is called natural science; I thought it would be marvellous to know the causes for which each thing comes and ceases and continues to be. . . . At last I came to the conclusion that I was uniquely unfitted for this form of inquiry. . . . I was so befogged by these speculations that I

physicists. There was another man to whom the denial of free will was deeply troubling—Epicurus. Epicurus formulated his philosophy in reaction to determinism; after all, what is the point of an ethical system if everything is ruthlessly predetermined? Epicurus wrote in the *Letter to Menoeceus*: "It would be better to follow the myths of the gods than to enslave yourself to the destiny of the natural philosophers. For the first adds the hope of supplication to the gods through worship, but the second has implacable necessity" (134, tr. Bailey).

☙ Epicurus ❧

Epicurus, in revulsion from determinism, created a new atomic philosophy, which combined both an ethical system and an understanding of nature that allowed for free will. This combination was unique because science and ethics were interdependent: the science both generated and served the ethics. What do we know about Epicurus and the development of his philosophy? The son of Athenian parents, Epicurus was born, probably on the island of Samos, in 341 and died in Athens in 270. In his youth he studied philosophy and was introduced to the theories of Democritus. In 319 he started his own school in Mytilene on the island of Lesbos and then in Lampsacus on the Hellespont, but soon (306) he moved to Athens and established a permanent school in a quiet garden not too far from the agora, the city center. Hence his school has been called "the garden." At his school he welcomed all who were interested, including even women and slaves. This inclusiveness, in contrast to other philosophical schools, together with the school's isolation from politics and business, was probably responsible for some of the gossip that rivals of the school, such as the Stoics, spread. Moreover, the stated goal of Epicureanism, ἡδονή (*hēdonē*, **voluptās** in Latin), "pleasure," surely contributed to misunderstanding of the true nature of the school. Epicurus wrote in the *Letter to Menoeceus*: "Pleasure is the beginning and end of the blessed life" (128, tr. Bailey); however, he soon clarified his meaning: "When, therefore, we maintain that pleasure is the end, we do not mean the pleasures of profligates and those that consist in sensuality, as is supposed by some who are either ignorant or disagree with us or do not understand, but freedom from pain in the body and from trouble in the mind" (131–32, tr. Bailey). Let us, therefore, examine the fundamental points of Epicurean philosophy in order to understand the system that Lucretius so enthusiastically embraced.

☙ Epicurean Philosophy ❧

Epicurus believed that men generally led miserable lives because, in continual fear of vengeful gods and of punishment after death, they could not enjoy even the simplest pleasures. By freeing men from these fears, Epicurus hoped to enable men to lead an ideal life, which he called ἀταραξία, (*ataraxiā*), "calm," "tranquillity," which could also be described as freedom from pain of mind and body. Indeed, it is crucial to emphasize that to Epicurus pleasure, *hēdonē*, meant the absence of pain. Epicurus clearly distinguished pleasure, which is always good, from the desires, which he divided into categories. Some desires, such as for food, are natural and necessary, some merely natural but unnecessary, while others are actually harmful and thus to be avoided. One must therefore evaluate choices and decide whether, if one indulges in a certain activity, the end result will be pleasure or pain. Furthermore, there is a limit to pleasure, which is the satisfaction of desire; beyond that limit pleasures can only be varied, not increased. So, instead of promoting what we might erroneously call hedonism, Epicurus in fact advocated a rather ascetic lifestyle, which he called αὐταρκεία (*autarkeia*),

---

unlearned even what I had thought I knew. . . . So I reject it altogether, and muddle out a haphazard method of my own. . . . Therefore if anyone wishes to discover the reason why any given thing came or ceased or continued to be, he must find out how it was best for that thing to be, or to act or be acted upon in any other way. On this view there was only one thing for a man to consider, with regard both to himself and to anything else, namely the best and highest good" (Socrates in *Phaedo* 96a–97d, tr. Tredennick).

"self-sufficiency." He believed that the only way for men to attain peace was through a true understanding and acceptance of the universe and man's place in it. With that knowledge men should be able to enjoy the simple pleasures of nature, friendship, philosophy, and the study of nature but to avoid things, such as politics, greed, and infatuation, that produce anxiety.

How did Epicurus hope to free men from the fears that so sullied their pleasure? By atomic theory. By adopting the materialist theories of Leucippus and Democritus, Epicurus explained, first, that the gods, though they exist, can have no direct influence on us; second, that the human soul itself is material and therefore cannot survive after death; and third, that man has free will. How did Epicurus adapt the atomic theory to reach these conclusions? He accepted the basic premise that the universe consists of two elements: (1) the imperishable atoms, which have weight, mass, and motion, and (2) void. His fundamental addition to the theory is the invention of the swerve (**clīnāmen** in Latin; the Greek term is unknown). The theory of atomic motion proposed by Leucippus and Democritus is not well understood, but it seems they believed that atoms possessed self-generated motion and could move in all directions. Epicurus, however, relying on the evidence of the senses, believed that atoms moved downwards. If, however, the atoms had always moved directly downwards in parallel lines, no collisions would ever have taken place to create larger aggregates of matter. By the principle of the swerve, any atom, at a completely unpredictable time and place, could move ever so slightly from true vertical. This swerve would cause it to collide with another atom, which in turn would hit another, which would rebound, and a chain reaction would ensue. Thus the random nature of the swerve at the atomic level caused the formation of aggregates (what we would call molecules); at the level of human behavior, the swerve permitted free will. For many centuries the Epicurean swerve was thought to be a rather ridiculous, desperate invention to justify the philosopher's belief in free will. Recently, however, the new science of chaos has discovered a paradoxical ordered randomness, a randomness within limits evident in all natural phenomena. It is intriguing to speculate that in his invention of the swerve Epicurus prefigured this breakthrough in modern scientific understanding.[5] In fact, when studying ancient philosophy and science, one realizes that the ancient thinkers were often asking the same questions about the world as modern scientists, and, in some cases, the answers too are remarkably similar.

In his atomic theory Epicurus emphasized the idea of natural limitations. Although the universe is infinite in extent and the number of atoms is infinite, nevertheless there is a finite number of types of atoms. Moreover, not all atomic combinations are possible. The universe operates under a system of fixed, natural laws, which result solely from the nature of its constituent parts and that are applicable everywhere. Finally, although the atoms themselves are eternal, any aggregation of atoms is ultimately subject to destruction. The atoms of a decaying object will then be used to create a new object in an endless and perfectly balanced process of creation and dissolution. Lucretius states that even the earth itself will one day fall in ruin, a radical idea in antiquity. Furthermore, Epicurus believed that the human body and soul, joined together, are born and grow and feel. The soul is thus a material thing and therefore mortal. Consequently it is foolish to fear punishment after death, when we will no longer exist. Similarly, we should not fear the gods, since, by the laws of their own nature, they are unable to affect us. According to Epicurus, the gods are made of very fine substances, which could not survive the blows of our world. They live, therefore, in the spaces between worlds (in Latin, **intermundia**), which he describes in idyllic terms. The gods' delicate nature prevents them from having any contact with our world, other than passively through their images (in Latin, **simulācra**) which come to us. Instead of mistakenly fearing their wrath, we should admire them as beings who have attained the Epicurean goal of *ataraxiā*.

---

5   Similarly, if one studies the *De rerum natura* carefully from a scientific perspective, it is evident that it foreshadows many modern scientific theories, albeit in rudimentary form. For instance, we find discussions of the extinction of species, genetics, geology, bacterial transmission of disease, some anthropological views of man's evolutionary development, cosmology (the birth and death of worlds), and the existence of other worlds.

Moreover, Epicurus argues that we should cease to believe that the gods created the world for us, a feat that would have been impossible for them, or that we have a privileged place in it, a theory that its many faults clearly refute.

How did Epicurus reach his conclusions about the composition and working of the universe? Ancient science did not rely upon experimentation; there were no labs or grants for research. It is astonishing to think how much the ancients discovered about our world by relying purely on the power of the mind to reason. What kind of reasoning did Epicurus employ? Primarily he believed that one should rely on the evidence of the senses; otherwise there will be no firm foundation upon which to base any knowledge. Thus in the *De rerum natura* Lucretius anchors his proofs in the world of everyday life, particularly with illustrations from nature; these illustrations are a major part of the beauty of the poem. For instance, he uses the example of a flock of sheep grazing on a hillside seen from a great distance to illustrate how distant motion can be invisible. Moreover, he draws on the realm of ordinary experience, so that the poem provides many glimpses of daily life, from the hustle-bustle of the city to the tranquillity of the countryside. One might ask, if one relies on sensory evidence, how one can draw any firm conclusions about matters below the threshold of our senses. Here analogy is a powerful tool which allows one, for instance, to draw inferences about things that are invisible from those that are visible. Lucretius proves the existence of invisible particles of wind by making an analogy between the actions of wind and water. Once the existence of this one type of invisible particle is proved, it is much easier to prove the existence of invisible atoms. Our senses and powers of inference, however, do not permit us to draw definite conclusions about all phenomena. Therefore, when no one explanation can be proven to the exclusion of all others, until we find further evidence, multiple explanations must be accepted. Epicurus wrote: "Whenever someone accepts one theory, but rejects another that is likewise consistent with the phenomenon, it is clear that he completely departs from scientific investigation and comes to myth" (*Letter to Pythocles* 87, tr. Bailey). Thus Lucretius provides multiple explanations for phenomena such as eclipses and the phases of the moon. Readers are left to come to their own conclusions based upon the evidence.

In the *De rerum natura* Lucretius expounds the findings of Epicurus. But how, some two hundred years after Epicurus' death, was he so familiar with Epicurus? Epicurus was a prolific writer, whose main work, Περὶ φύσεως (*Peri physeōs*), *On Nature*, covered thirty-seven books. There was also an epitome of this work. Sadly, neither of these survives to us. We do, however, have summaries of his philosophy in three letters—to Herodotus (not the historian) on atomic theory, to Pythocles on astronomy, and to Menoeceus on ethics. In addition, there is a series of principal docrines, literally *The Master's Sayings* (*Kuriai doxai*), and a Life of Epicurus, all preserved by the third-century A.D. author Diogenes Laertius. Finally, there are eighty sayings preserved in a manuscript now housed in the Vatican, thus called **sententiae Vaticānae**. Scholars have argued about how many of Epicurus' writings were available to Lucretius. The consensus is that the epitome was Lucretius' main source, but that he consulted the full work when necessary, and that he relied heavily on the *Letter to Herodotus*. The question that then arises is: how original was Lucretius? Did he merely report the findings of Epicurus, or did he develop or refine them in any way?

☙ Lucretian Originality ❧

It is interesting that Epicurus himself disapproved of poetry as an educational tool, since he believed its elaborate language and imagery led to confusion and misunderstanding of the truth. Indeed Epicurus recommended clarity as the primary quality of good writing (Diogenes Laertius 10.14). Diogenes Laertius also reports Epicurus' belief that "only the wise man could discourse rightly on music and poetry, but in practice he would not compose poems" (10.121b). Why, then, did Lucretius choose seemingly to violate his master's precepts by expounding Epicurean philosophy in poetic form? First, Epicurus did allow that one could enjoy poetry as entertainment. From this acceptance later Epicureans, particularly Philodemus, then reconsidered the relationship between poetry and philosophy. They believed that philosophy could "form an alliance with poetry, in which both pursuits achieve their own ends."[6] The philosopher could even, in an amateur way, enjoy composing poetry for entertainment. Lucretius takes this new attitude one step further by combining the enjoyment of poetry with the educational function of philosophy. Indeed, Lucretius compares his poetry to honey on the rim of a cup of bitter medicine (1.937–38) and explains: "since this philosophy generally seems to be rather bitter to those by whom it is not practiced, and the crowd recoils from it, I have wanted to expound our philosophy to you with sweet-sounding Pierian poetry and to touch it, as it were, with the sweet honey of the Muses, in the hope that by chance in such a way I could hold your mind on my verses, until you see clearly all the nature of things, with what shape it is arranged" (1.943–50). Lucretius begins his epic by beguiling his reader with an entrancingly beautiful picture of creative Venus in springtime. Although the poetry acts as a lure, Monica Gale argues that "the poetry is much more than an external sweetener applied to the philosophy of Epicurus"; rather, every poetic device is deliberately adapted to create a clear and persuasive presentation of Epicurean philosophy.[7] Similarly, Elisabeth Asmis concludes that "Lucretius does not regard poetry simply as a necessary device, dictated by the antipathy of his audience. Instead, what makes him so enthusiastic about his work is that poetry makes a positive contribution to the presentation of philosophy."[8] In fact, when one carefully compares Lucretius' poem with the writings of Epicurus, it is clear that Lucretius faithfully followed the precepts of his master; he was not an original philosopher. While he concentrated on a systematic exposition of Epicurean scientific principles, he also included within this scientific framework all the fundamental ethical principles, although not in a methodical fashion. Furthermore, Lucretius closely adhered to his master's precepts in using words in their most basic sense to achieve clarity.[9] This plainness is certainly evident in Lucretius' technical vocabulary. Is Lucretius then a mere translator or reporter? Not at all. When one compares the rather dry writing of Epicurus with the charm of Lucretian poetry, Lucretius' originality is abundantly clear. Certainly Lucretius was intimately familiar with the writings of Epicurus, but his understanding of nature is largely self-taught and resulted from long hours of patient and keen observation of its intricacies. Thus his originality lies in his choice of the poetic medium and in his inventive and vivid illustrations. He has a very visual way of expressing his thoughts, so that he can explain even a very obscure point, such as the velocity of the atoms, with a lively illustration from the world of ordinary experience. Many of his illustrations also have a particularly Roman flavor, and we find a Roman perspective in his depictions of politics, family life, and other areas. In fact, Lucretius himself is keenly aware and proud of his originality in elucidating the principles of his master in Latin verse. He declares that he is traversing ground never before trodden by the foot of man, and thus he lays claim to a crown from the Muses (1.925–30).

❃ Poetic Predecessors ❧

Poets, however, rarely work in complete isolation; rather, they derive inspiration from earlier poets. So too with Lucretius. From the narrative epics of Homer, Lucretius adapted techniques such as formulae (see below under Lucretian Style, II.3) and extended similes to suit his new topic. Although narrative epic was the most common form of epic, there was also a long and noble tradition of didactic epic, beginning with the poet Hesiod in his *Theogony* and *Works and Days*. Moreover, some of the Pre-Socratic philosophers wrote didactic epic and can be seen as models for Lucretius. Both the pluralist Empedocles, whom Lucretius

---

6   Elisabeth Asmis, "Epicurean Poetics," *Philodemus and Poetry*, ed. Dirk Obbink (Oxford: Oxford University Press, 1995), 30.
7   Monica Gale, *Myth and Poetry in Lucretius* (Cambridge: Cambridge University Press, 1994), 2.
8   Asmis, op. cit., 33.
9   "It is essential that the first mental image associated with each word should be regarded, and that there should be no need of explanation" (Epicurus, *Letter to Herodotus* 38, tr. Bailey).

praises at 1.716–33, and his predecessor, the monist Parmenides, composed didactic poems on nature. Finally, Alexandrian poets, such as Aratus (c. 315–240), expanded the scope of didactic epic to include such specialized topics as astronomy. Interestingly, Aratus' epic *Phaenomena* was translated by Cicero as part of his youthful poetic efforts. Cicero's translation provides an intriguing parallel to Lucretius' work in his use of archaisms and poetic devices. The Roman epic tradition was much less rich than the Greek. The major Roman epic poet before Lucretius was Ennius (239–169), who in his *Annales* described Roman history up to his own time. In Lucretius we find numerous echoes from the extant fragments of Ennius. Nonetheless, despite all these poetic predecessors, Lucretius did indeed create something new. His epic combines the features of both narrative and didactic epic. From the realm of didactic epic we find much technical vocabulary, repetition of key concepts, and the orderly marshalling of evidence. Nevertheless the epic also has a hero—nature herself. Indeed what more magnificent subject could one find than the entire universe, including the foundation of the world and the history of mankind? Lucretius created a lively sense of narrative by employing poetic techniques such as the personification of nature herself and also, frequently, of the atoms, which meet in combat or unite in harmony.

☙ The Plan of the Poem ❧

How did Lucretius manage to structure a poem that encompasses the entire universe? He began by expounding the fundamental principles of Epicurean science and then turning to discuss the specific results of these principles. Books 1 and 2 give the principles of the atomic system. Books 3 and 4 treat the atomic system in human terms: Book 3 discusses the soul, while Book 4 examines the operation of the senses. Book 5 then turns to the formation and working of the world and, in particular, the rise of human civilization. Book 6 continues to discuss the phenomena of our world and concludes with a horrific description of the great plague at Athens. Each book begins with a proem, or prelude, which presents a beautiful picture of the glories of nature and of Epicurean philosophy. These proems contrast strongly with the conclusions of the books, which feature destruction and dissolution. Thus in the structure of his poem Lucretius has mirrored the cyclical reality of nature itself. Unfortunately, we cannot fully analyze Lucretius' overall poetic scheme, since the epic is incomplete, or at least was never fully revised. For instance, there are doublets of explanations, passages which seem out of place, awkward references forward and backward within the text and, most significantly, a missing passage. At 5.155 Lucretius promises that he will provide a complete picture (**largō sermōne**) of the life of the gods, but the epic closes without such an account. Finally, many critics have found difficulty with the end of the epic as it has come down to us. It is possible that a few lines of conclusion have been lost, but it seems unlikely that Lucretius intended to write another book, since at the close of the proem to Book 6 he pictures himself as speeding toward the finish line (**mihi suprēmae . . . calcis / currentī**, 6.92–93). Nor is a much longer sixth book probable, since at 1286 lines the sixth book is one of the longest, containing more than seventeen percent of the entire epic. Therefore we must read and enjoy the epic as we find it, as generations of readers have done before us.

☙ Lucretian Influence ❧

It is ironic to note how much influence Lucretius, who seems to have been nearly unknown in his own lifetime, has exerted on other writers and thinkers. The poet Vergil acknowledged his debt to Lucretius in the famous lines from his didactic epic, *The Georgics* (2.490–92):

fēlīx quī potuit rērum cognōscere causās
atque metūs omnīs et inexōrābile fātum
subiēcit pedibus strepitumque Acherontis avārī.

Blessed is he who was able to know the causes of things
and all fears and inexorable fate
trod underfoot and the roar of greedy Acheron.

The passage clearly echoes Epicurus' victory over religion in *De rerum natura* 1.78–79. Throughout the *Georgics* and the *Aeneid* Vergil employs Lucretian language, oftentimes while refuting his Epicurean message in a process one scholar has termed polemical allusion.[10] Lucretius also influenced the poetry and thoughts of Ovid and Horace; indeed, it would be hard to find a Roman poet who did not fall under his spell. What is more, his influence on both poets and scientists has continued well beyond the limits of the Roman Empire. Throughout this text there are numerous quotes from both classical and modern literature that attest to Lucretius' pervasive influence and to his important role in both the literary and scientific traditions. There are illustrative quotations from authors as diverse as Milton and Marx, Shakespeare and Einstein. Thus, by studying Lucretius one can attempt to bridge the articifial divide that currently exists between the arts and the sciences. To conclude, Lucretius truly possessed an all-encompassing view of the world; to study Lucretius is to think deeply of the world in all its aspects.

℃ Lucretian Style ℰ

Lucretius developed a unique Latin style characterized by archaisms, didactic repetition, ordered argumentation, the love of compound words, and alliteration and other poetic devices. Several factors contributed to his unique style. First, Lucretius represents a transitional point in the Latin language between the archaic poets, such as Ennius (239–169) and Plautus (c. 255–184), and Vergil and the Augustan poets. Lucretius' contemporary Cicero is generally credited with standardizing Latin spelling and grammar to create what is known as the classical style, but it is clear that in Lucretius' lifetime the language was still very fluid. Secondly, Lucretius was writing on a subject new to Latin, Greek philosophy, which required him to develop a philosophical vocabulary and to use Latin terms in new ways. Indeed, he comments in Book 1.136–39:

Nec mē animī fallit Graiōrum obscūra reperta
difficile inlūstrāre Latīnīs versibus esse,
multa novīs verbīs praesertim cum sit agendum,
propter egestātem linguae et rērum novitātem.

Nor does it escape me that it is difficult to illustrate the dark findings of the Greeks in Latin verses, especially since one must treat many concepts with new words because of the poverty of the [Latin] language and the newness of the concepts.

Finally, Lucretius' choice to "compose poetry, touching all with the muses' charm" (1.933–34) subjected him to a great number of metrical constraints. We have seen above that Lucretius could turn to a number of poetic predecessors, both Greek and Latin, for inspiration, but it is also interesting to picture his literary struggles as he "watch[es] through the calm nights, searching with what words and with what song [he] can at last spread before your mind bright lights, with which you can see deeply into hidden things" (1.142–45).

The following discussion of forms, grammar, meter, and style will not mention all features of the Lucretian style, but those that are most prominent. Less frequent features will be treated in the notes where they occur. Each prominent feature will be illustrated by at least

---

10   Benjamin Farrington, "Polemical Allusions to the *De Rerum Natura* of Lucretius in the Works of Vergil," *Geras: Studies Presented to G. Thompson on the Occasion of His 60th Birthday*, ed. L. Varcl and R. F. Willets (Prague: Charles University, 1963), 87–94.

one example from the selections in the text, with emphasis on examples from the first passages. When a feature occurs for the first time in the text, it is discussed in some detail in the notes. For subsequent occurrences only a brief note is given, and students should consult the definitions given below. It is therefore important that students soon familiarize themselves with these terms, since they will be used frequently in the notes.

I. Archaic Forms

Lucretius has a fondness for archaisms. They produce an air of solemnity and elevate the language of the epic. Moreover, archaisms are often metrically convenient by allowing the poet flexibility in scansion. The most frequent archaisms are given below:

Nouns and Adjectives

1) First declension genitive singular in **-āī**. This ending occurs very frequently, particularly at the line-end, since it gives the poet an extra long syllable in scansion. For instance, **māteriāī** alone occurs 41 times, always at the line-end, whereas **māteriae** only occurs three times.

2) Second declension genitive plural in **-um**, instead of **-ōrum**. Lucretius prefers this old form, particularly in words such as **dīvum** (1), **deum** (68), and **virum** (95).

3) The third declension during this period was in a transitional state, particularly between consonant stems and i-stems, and Lucretius' usage mirrors this fluctuation.

   a) Third declension genitive plural is usually **-um**, rarely **-ium**. Example: the participle **meantum** (1.318).

   b) Third declension accusative plural is almost always **-īs** (not **-ēs**). This helps to differentiate it from the nominative plural. Beware, however, of confusing this ending with the genitive singular ending **-is**, which always has a short vowel. Examples: **frugiferentīs** (1.3), **suāvīs** (1.7), and **amnīs** (1.15).

4) With certain nouns there is a variance between two declensions. This is most frequent with **māteria / māteriēs**; there are 47 examples of **māteria**, first declension, and 31 of **māteriēs**, fifth declension.

5) Lucretius forms certain adjectives that are normally third declension in the first and second declensions: **imbēcillus, -a, -um** (5.1023), **exanimus, -a, -um** (6.1256), **sēmanimus, -a, -um** (6.1268).

6) There is also a fluidity of gender. For instance we find **caelōs**, masculine rather than neuter, in 2.1097, **fīnis** as feminine in 5.1433, and **Tartara**, neuter, in 3.42, but **Tartarus**, masculine, in 3.1012.

7) Lucretius generally scans the pronoun **hīc, haec, hōc** with a long vowel, representing the archaic forms **hicce, haecce, hocce**. Thus the neuter nominative, accusative, and ablative singular all scan as **hōc**.

Verbs

Lucretius generally prefers shorter forms wherever possible.

1) Alternate second singular passive ending **-re**, rather than **-ris**: **cōnfiteāre** (1.270, 2.1074). This ending allows for elision into the following syllable.

2) Alternate third plural perfect active ending **-ēre**, rather than **-ērunt**: **pepigēre** (1.1023), **fuēre** (1.234, 3.836). Here the alternate ending gives a final short rather than a long syllable.

3) Syncopated perfect forms: Lucretius frequently drops the **-ve** or **-vi** of the perfect and pluperfect in both the indicative and subjunctive. The syncopation is by far the most frequent with the third plural perfect indicative: **turpārunt** (1.85) = **turpāvērunt** and **locārunt** (1.1022) = **locāvērunt**; but we also find **irrītāt** (1.70) = **irrītāvit**, **dōnārat** (1.94) = **dōnāverat**, **vēlārint** (1.930) = **vēlāverint**, **creāsset** (2.224) = **creāvisset**. There are even syncopated infini-

tives: **cōnsūmpse** (1.233) = **cōnsūmpsisse** and **cognōsse** (1.331) = **cognōvisse**.

4) Passive Infinitives in **-ier** rather than **–i**: examples: **mīrārier** (2.1029), **vertier** (5.1199). This ending provides two short syllables rather than the two longs of the usual ending.

5) Similar to nouns, there is also a variance between conjugations. The verb **tueor** is found in the second conjugation at 1.152 (**tuentur**) but in the third at 1.300 (**tuimur**). One verb, **ciere**, varies so often between the second and fourth conjugation that the relevant principal parts are given each time in the notes. Some other verbs which experience such fluctuation are **queō**, **nequeō**, **potior**, and **cupiō**.

6) Variable verb forms: Lucretius fluctuates between the archaic and classical forms of the imperfect subjunctive of **esse**: we find **foret** (18), **forent** (9) but **esset** (16) and **essent** (4). Here the fluctuation may be a response to metrical considerations. The verb **posse** also fluctuates, particularly in the third person singular. We find **potis est** 11 times, **potest** 31 times.

7) Governance of cases: a verb frequently governs an unusual case. Examples: verbs taking an unusual accusative: **īnstō** (1.406), **potior** (2.653), **parcō** (2.1163), **fruor** (3.940); verbs taking the genitive: **egeō** (3.45), **potior** (2.13).

Other Archaisms

1) The Formation of Adverbs: Lucretius is very inventive in his use of adverbs. He prefers the archaic termination **-tim**, which is found in classical Latin in **partim**, **passim**, and **praesertim**. In Lucretius we find numerous other such adverbs: **generātim** (20), **minūtātim** (7), **raptim** (5), and rarer formations such as **catervātim** (6.1144), **pedetemptim** (5.1453), **turmātim** (2.119), and **virītim** (2.1172).

Lucretius also uses adverbs with the termination **-us**: **dīvīnitus** (8), **funditus** (20, all but once as the fifth foot dactyl), and **penitus** (24).

Lucretius also creates adverbs with the termination **-(i)ter** from first and second declension adjectives (rather than strictly the third): **ūniter** (5), **dūriter** (5.1402), and his coinage **moderanter** (2.1096).

2) Emphatic terminations: Lucretius appends the emphatic termination **-te** to personal pronouns, particularly **tū**: **tūte** (8). We even find the emphatic termination **-met** added to the already emphatic **tūte** at 1.102: **tūtemet**. Lucretius also adds **-ī** to a variety of conjunctions for metrical reasons. Examples: **utī** (83), **velutī** (10).

3) Other spelling changes: Lucretius uses the archaic **reddunda** for **reddenda** (1.59) and **experiundō** for **experiendō** (1.1026). We also find **ollīs** for **illīs** (2.1003), and **artubus** for **artibus** (1.260, 3.7). Many changes are a response to metrical constraints. For instance, Lucretius uses both the consonantal and vocalic forms of the verb **solvo** (**dissoluat** 1.216, but **exsolvere**, 1.220). We find **alid** rather than **aliud** six times, always in the phrase **alid ex aliō** (e.g., 1.263); elsewhere Lucretius writes **aliud**. Similarly, Lucretius often uses forms shortened by syncope: **nīl** and **nīlum** for **nihil** and **nihilum**. We also find the older, shortened from **perīclī** for **perīculī** and **saeclum** for **saeculum**. Perfect passive participles are also sometimes shortened: **reposta** (1.35), **disposta** (1.52). Lucretius also uses archaic doubled consonants in **reddūcit** and **redductum** in 1.228 to create long syllables; similarly **rellātum** (2.1001). With the noun **cupīdō** Lucretius uses both the classical forms and the archaic forms **cuppēdine** (3.994, 4.1090) and **cuppēdinis** (5.45). Sometimes Lucretius adds an archaic infix, such as **-du** in **indugredī** (1.82) and **indu** for the preposition **in** (2.1096), which gives him an extra syllable.

4) Dative for genitive of possession or objective genitive, often for metrical convenience. The dative of possession usually occurs with the verb **esse**. Lucretius extends this use particularly with verbs that are equivalent in force to **esse**, e.g., **cōnstāre**. Examples: **rēbus** (1.58), **arboribus** (1.165).

II. Other Features of Lucretian Style

1) **Technical vocabulary**: Since Lucretius was writing a didactic work on a scientific subject, he needed to devise a number of technical terms. The number of synonyms that he developed for the sake of variety and metrical convenience is remarkable. Moreover, like a good teacher, he is careful to define his terms. In Book 1, after Lucretius has introduced his main word for atoms, **prīmōrdia**, in line 55, he then provides a list of synonyms in lines 58–61: **māteriem et genitālia corpora . . . sēmina rērum . . . corpora prīma**. In addition, he will also use the terms **prīncipia, exōrdia, elementa**, and **figūrae**. For the other constituent of the universe, void, he uses the words **ināne, locus, spatium, vacāns**, and **vacuum**.

Other technical terms are: **clīnāmen** = *the swerve*, **mundus** = *the world, earth*, **plāgae** = *blows* (from atoms), **(rērum) summa** = *the universe*, **simulācra** = *films* (which objects constantly shed), and **animus** = *soul* (synonyms **mēns, cōnsilium**), which is inextricably united with **anima** = *the vital principle* (spread throughout the body).

2) **Ordered argumentation**: Lucretius presents his ideas and their proofs in an orderly fashion. First he states a principle and then offers multiple proofs of it. One can easily follow the order of his argument by paying attention to the introductory words. The various stages of an argument are typically introduced as follows: **prīmum** or **prīncipium, praetereā, dēnique, postrēmō**. For the first argument Lucretius also often uses **nam**; other phrases connecting his argumentation are **nec porrō, tum porrō, hūc accēdit (utī),** and **adde quod**.

A favorite Lucretian argumentative device is the contrary-to-fact condition. Lucretius asks the reader to imagine what the world would be like if a certain proposition were not true—such as that nothing can come from nothing. The result of this speculation is generally a *reductio ad absurdum*, e.g., that men would spontaneously arise in the sea. Lucretius then concludes that his proposition must be true, since its opposite is patently false.

3) **Formulae**: A feature of the Homeric epic style is the repetition of phrases and even whole lines and sections. Lucretius makes liberal use of this poetic device, since it particularly suits his didactic purpose. Formulaic phrases introduce sections (**quod superest**, 1.50, 921; 2.39; 4.1283; 5.64; **nunc age**, 1.265, 921; 2.333), and point out conclusions (**quāre etiam atque etiam,** 1.295; 2.1064). More poetically we find line-end phrases such as **in lūminis ōrās** (1.22, 170; 5.224, 1455) and the closely related phrases **lūmina sōlis** (1.5, 2.114, 162, 654) and **lūmina vītae** (1.227). The descriptive **pābula laeta** occurs in 1.14, 257; 2.317, 364, and 1159. Lucretius also uses formulaic phrases to reinforce his message: **aequō animō** describes the tranquillity of the Epicurean at 1. 42, 3.939 and 962. His formulaic phrase for independent action is **sponte suā**, found at 2.1059, 1092, 1158; 5.212, 938 and 961. Sometimes Lucretius, having created a phrase that he felt was the best way of expressing a point, repeated it several times, often in quick succession. To describe the indivisibility of the atoms, he uses the phrase **solidō corpore** three times in five lines (1.486, 488, 500), again in 518, and several times subsequently. Finally, Lucretius repeats entire passages to remind us of a proposition already proven or to emphasize a point. In 1.146–48 he describes in vivid imagery how man's terrors can be conquered. The same passage is repeated, with a new preface (2.55–58), in 2.59–61, and again with the new preface in 3.87–93 and 6.35–41.

4) **Periphrasis**: Lucretius often uses the nominative of a noun plus a dependent genitive to express nothing much more than the genitive noun itself. For example, **aquae . . . nātūra** in 1.281 means little more than **aqua**. This device is most frequent with the noun **nātūra**, especially in book 3 with the phrase **nātūra animī**, but also occurs with many other nouns, such as **genus omne animantum** (1.4) meaning *all living things* and **strāta viārum** (1.315) meaning simply *pavements*.

5) **Love of compound words**: Lucretius seems inordinately fond of compound words, especially from the roots **-fer, -gen**, and **-ger**, often in adjectives beginning with a dactylic pattern. Some of these he found in his predecessor Ennius (**suāviloquentī**, 1.945), but many appear to be his own inventions: **frūgiferentis** (1.3), **terriloquīs** (1.103), **silvifragīs** (1.275), **flūctifragō** (1.305), **multigenīs** (2.335), **tūricremās** (2.353), **flōriferīs** (3.11), **innūbilus** (3.21), **vulvivagō** (5.932), and the magnificently descriptive fourth declension adjective for elephants

anguimanūs (2.537). He also uses compound nouns such as **squāmigerum** (1.162, 2.343) and the participial substantive **aedituentēs** (6.1275). His love of compounds is also found in the tremendous number of words prefixed by the preposition **per** used intensively; examples: **pervulgāre, pervincere, perfacilis**.

6) **Coinages**: Lucretius appears to have coined many words, some of which have been noted above. In addition to adjectives we find nouns such as **mactātus** (1.99), **conciliātus** (1.575), **clīnāmen** (2.292), **disiectus** (3.928), and **luella** (3.1015). There are also diminutives such as **querella** (9), **loquella** (1.39, 5.71, 230), and **muliercula** (4.1279).

7) **Substantive use of the adjective**: In Latin it is common to use adjectives such as **bonum, malum**, and **suum** as substantives (nouns), and Lucretius follows this practice. In addition he uses many other adjectives substantively, such as **pinguī** (1.257) = *richness*, **commoda** (3.2, 3.937, 4.1154), **vērum** (1.409), **īnfestum** (4.1150), and **altum** (5.1434) = *the sea*.

8) **Infinitive as substantive**: again this is a normal Latin practice, but Lucretius seems particularly fond of it. For instance, **cognōsse** as the subject in 1.331: **quod tibi cognōsse in multīs erit ūtile rēbus**, and the infinitives **pāscere** and **explēre**: **ingrātam nātūram pāscere semper / atque explēre bonīs rēbus satiāreque numquam, . . . hōc . . . est** (3.1003–08). Lucretius also frequently uses an accusative and infinitive construction as the subject of an impersonal verb.

9) **Partitive Genitive**: closely related to categories 4 and 7 above. Lucretius frequently uses a dependent genitive after a substantive use of an adjective: **prīma virōrum** (1.86), *the first men*; **tantum malōrum** (1.101), *so much evil*; **tantundemst . . . corporis** (1.360–01), *so much body*.

10) **Ablative of Description**: To describe the characteristics of something, Lucretius generally uses the ablative of description, such as **solidō corpore**, noted above in 3. The construction generally occurs with a form of **esse**.

11) **Fondness for fourth declension abstract nouns**: Lucretius regularly uses, and in many instances appears to have invented, fourth declension forms, frequently in place of third declension words ending **-tiō**, which would not scan in dactylic hexameter. There are 59 such words, including 11 which occur nowhere else. For instance, we often find **fluctus**, **frūctus**, and **cōnsēnsus**, but we also find **disiectus** (3.928) and **mactātus** (1.99), which occur nowhere else.

12) **Neuter gender and *rēs* used interchangeably**. Probably for metrical reasons, Lucretius habitually switches from the neuter to **rēs** and sometimes back again. For instance, at 1.56 we first find **omnīs . . . rēs**, whereas in line 57 the neuter **perēmpta** is used.

13) **Postponed Linking Conjunctions and Relatives**: Frequently the linking conjunction or relative is delayed by one, two, or even more words in the clause that it governs. Examples: **in gremium quī** (1.33) and **undique māteriēs quoniam stīpāta quiēsset** (1.345).

14) **Devices to Create Emphasis**:

a) The repetition of pronouns and modifiers: **per tē tūte ipse vidēre / . . . poteris** (1.407–08); **ipsa suā per sē sponte** (2.1092).

b) Word order: Lucretius uses the line-beginning and line-end as places of particular emphasis. Enjambement, delay of an important word until the beginning of a line (see below under III, Poetic Devices), is used by all poets to emphasize a word. Lucretius also uses the line-end as a place of stress; for instance, emphasizing the power of Venus, he closes 1.13 with **tuā vī**. Also Lucretius often emphasizes the verb *to be*, which is normally weak, by positioning it at the beginning of a line or a phrase: **est igitur** (1.368, 1002); **sunt igitur** (1.277, 510, 574), or sometimes at the end: **cum summa locī sit / īnfīnīta** (2.1044–45).

15) **Use of verbs in a middle sense**: Lucretius uses the passive forms to express the middle voice, in which the subject acts upon itself. See **summissa** (1.92), where Iphigenia sinks to the ground, **moventur** (1.421) where the atoms move themselves, and **rigantur** (2.262) where motions spread themselves through the limbs.

16) **Passive forms of vidēre are true passives**, *it is seen* rather than *it seems*. Examples: **vidērī** (1.224), **videntur** (1.262), **visumst** (1.308), and **vidētur** (1.935).

17) Although Lucretius was translating Greek philosophy into Latin verse, he avoided using Greek words and forms when possible and preferred to invent or redefine a Latin word. Greek words are generally only found in the context of decadence (**lampadas**, 2.25; **anadēmata, mitrae**, 4. 1129), in describing astronomical phenomena, or as proper mythological names (**Tityon . . . Acherunte**, 3.984).

III. Poetic Devices (in alphabetical order)

Alliteration: the repetition of sounds, especially initial consonants, in successive words. Lucretius' extreme fondness for alliteration, sometimes for emphasis, but often for its own sake, is a primary characteristic of his style. Lucretius creates alliteration most often with the letters *p, v,* and *c,* but also with *m* and *t,* and occasionally with other letters such as *l, d, s,* and *f.* Examples:

> With *p*: **petēns placidam . . . pācem** (1.40); **pecudēs pinguī per pābula laeta** (1.257).
> With *v*: **vīvida vīs animī pervīcit** (1.72).
> With *c*: **cum loca cursū / campōrum complent bellī simulācra cientēs** (2.323–24).
> With *m*: **multa modīs multīs . . . movērī** (1.341).

Often the alliteration also occurs medially (within a word) as in **pervīcit** (1.72) and **simulācra** (2.324). See also **flammantia moenia mundī** (1.73) and **variae volucrēs nemora āvia pervolitantēs** (2.145).

Lucretius creates innummerable short alliterative pairs, such as **mōmen mūtātum, ponderibus propriīs, dēlūbra deum, fātī foedera,** and **cōpia concīrī.** He even likes to link such alliterative pairs: **sēdāre sitim fluviī fontēsque** (5.945), **lūdit lacte merō mentis** (1.261), and often interweaves alliteration of two letters: e.g., *v* and *f*: **silvifragīs vexat flābrīs** (1.275).

Lucretius often uses alliteration to create an onomatopoeic effect. The most memorable examples mimic the whistling of the wind: **ventī vīs verberat** (1.271), **ventōrum violentō . . . vexant** (5.217), **verbera ventōrum vītāre** (5.957). Sometimes the letter *s* gives the effect of the sizzling of the sun: **dispānsae in sōle serēscunt** (1.306) and **subitō soleat sōl** (2.147). Lucretius uses *p* to replicate the pounding of atomic blows: **plāgīs . . . / possunt nec porrō penitus penetrāta** (1.528–29), and *c* to imitate the hard sound of water dripping on stone: **stīlicidī cāsus lapidem cavat** (1.313) and the clang of armor in battle (see 2.323–24 above).

Anaphora: the repetition of words or phrases for emphasis. Examples: **tē . . . tē . . . tē** (1.6), **hinc . . . hinc. . . hinc** (Book 1, beginning lines 254, 255 and 257), **adde quod . . . adde quod** (4.1121–22).

Anastrophe: the reversal of normal word order, most frequently with the preposition following its object: **hunc propter** (1.90), **portās propter** (1.316). Lucretius often likes to put the preposition immediately following the adjective modifying the object: **dīās in lūminis ōrās** (1.22), **tūricremās propter . . . ārās** (2.353).

Assonance: the repetition of vowels or syllables to create an effect: **omnī / omnibus ōrnātum** (1.26–27). Lucretius generally combines assonance with alliteration, such as in the repeated sounds of the vowel *i* combined with the consonant *v* in **vīvida vīs animī pervīcit** (1.72) and *a* and *o* sounds with *v* in **variae volucrēs nemora āvia pervolitantēs** (2.145).

Asyndeton: the omission of conjunctions. This is very frequent in Lucretius both between phrases (**ex omnibu' rēbus / omne genus nāscī posset, nīl sēmine egēret**, 1.159–60) and particularly in a series: **āēr aqua terra vapōrēs** (1.567), **caelum mare terrās flūmina sōlem / . . . frūgēs arbusta animantīs** (2.1015–16).

Chiasmus: a change in the relative order of two phrases to create the order ABBA, which when arranged vertically can be compared to the Greek letter chi (χ). Examples: **vacuās aurīs animumque sagācem** (1.50), **ō miserās . . . mentīs, ō pectora caeca** (2.14).

Embedded Order: one adjective-noun phrase is embedded in another. Examples: **suāvīs** *daedala tellūs* / . . . **flōrēs** (1.7–8), **plācātumque** . . . *diffūsō lūmine* **caelum** (1.9).

Enjambement: the delay of a word or phrase to the beginning of the next verse. This technique both emphasizes the delayed word and prevents the style from becoming too choppy and monotonous, as it would be if each line contained one idea. Examples: **quae terrās frūgiferentīs / concelebrās** (1.4), **nam tū sōla potes tranquillā pāce iuvāre / mortālīs** (1.32). Lucretius uses this device frequently, on average in nearly 28% of the epic, but even more frequently in the proems.

Hendiadys: two nouns joined by a conjunction but really representing a singular concept. Examples: **rēligiōnibus atque minīs . . . vātum** (1.109), **īnfīnīta aetās . . . anteācta diēsque** (1.233), **spatiō atque anteācta aetāte** (1.234), **nātūrae speciēs ratiōque** (1.148, 2.61).

Interlocking Word Order: alternating arrangement of pairs of words in the pattern ABAB, often used with dramatic effect. Examples: **dōna . . . studiō disposta fidēlī** (1.52), **īnfula virgineōs circumdata cōmptūs** (1.87), **sāncta . . . tranquillā pectora pāce** (2.1093).

Metaphor: an implied comparison in which one thing is described with the characteristics of another. Examples: **laetās urbīs puerīs flōrēre** (1.255; cities are like flowers, since they bloom with children); **plāgās in amōris nē iaciāmur** (4.1146; love is compared to a hunting-net, since we can be ensnared by love).

Metonymy: a figure of speech in which the name of a person or thing is substituted for the thing it represents. Lucretius refers to the use of metonymy with the names of the gods in 2.655–659, and throughout the poem Venus is a metonymy for the creative power of nature (see especially the first proem and 4.1058ff.).

Number: Verbal Flexibility: partly as a result of hendiadys (see above), compound subjects sometimes govern singular verbs, but Lucretius also readily switches from a plural verb to a singular (**At nunc sēminibus quia certīs quaeque creantur, / inde ēnascitur atque ōrās in lūminis exit**, 1.169–70), or he uses a singular verb even when he appends another subject to the line-end (**māteriēs ubi inest cuiusque et corpora prīma**, 1.171).

Oxymoron: the juxtaposition or use of opposites for dramatic effect. Examples: **casta inceste** (1.98), **discidium parere** (1.220), **strāgemque propāgant** (1.280), **innumerō numerō** (2.1054), **cadāveribus caelestum** (6.1274), **cōnsanguineōs aliēna** (6.1283), **vulnera . . . aluntur** (3.64), **novitāte . . . vetustās** (3.964), **Acherūsia . . . vīta** (3.1023).

Pleonasm or Redundancy: Lucretius is very fond of repetition and frequently piles up words of similar meaning to make his point. Examples: **validāsque vīrīs** (1.576) and **validīs . . . viribus** (1.971), **fīne modōque** (1.964), **iūcunda voluptās** (2.3), **anteācta priorque** (3.935), **grandior . . . seniorque** (3.952). This becomes most extreme when Lucretius tries to illustrate the random nature of events: **sponte suā forte . . . temerē incassum frūstrāque** (2.1059–60).

Poetic Plural for Singular: for metrical convenience Lucretius often prefers a plural noun when a singular would be logical. Examples: **lūmina sōlis** (1.5), **avidōs . . . vīsūs** (1.36).

Repetition: Lucretius frequently likes to juxtapose two forms of the same word or root: **genus generātim** (1.227), **īnsignibus īnsignis** (3.1015), **tūte tibi** (4.1150), **omnibus omnia** (5.233).

Transferred Epithet (Hypallage): the transference of an adjective to a noun when in meaning it applies to another. Examples: **speciēs . . . vērna diēī** (1.10), **impia . . . ratiōnis . . . elementa** (1.81), **puerōrum aetās imprōvida** (1.939), **equōrum / vim cupidam** (2.264–65), **Nemeaeus . . . hiātus / . . . leōnis** (5.24–25).

Word Play (Figura Etymologica): the use of the same root or sequence of syllables in different words to create a sort of pun. This device has sometimes been referred to as "atomology" in Lucretius, who believes that there is a natural connection between the name of a thing and the thing itself. Examples: **māter cum terra** (2.993); it is not by chance that the syllable **ter** occurs in both and contains echoes of **māteriēs**, the basic substance. See also **officium . . . / officere** (1.336–37), **funditus . . . / fundāmentī** (1.572–73), **deceptaque nōn capiātur** (1.941), **effugiumque fugae** (1.983), **summa** (*the universe*) **. . . summā** (*the greatest*) (2.310), and **mōmenque movētur** (3.144).

IV. Meter

It is assumed that the student is familiar with the basic principles of scansion and of the dactylic hexameter, the meter of epic. It is important to be able to read Lucretius aloud metrically, since the beauty of his poetry is revealed by the sounds created by various metrical effects. The student will be greatly helped in scansion since this text includes macrons (long marks) over all vowels that are long by nature. As a reminder to the student, here follows a brief summary of the scheme of the dactylic hexameter and the rules of meter.

Metrical scheme for dactylic hexameter: – ‿‿ / – ‿‿ / – | ‿‿ / – ‿‿ / – ‿‿ / – x

The x at line-end indicates that the syllable is anceps, in other words that its quantity can be either long or short, since it is not affected by the letters beginning the next line.

The fifth foot is almost always a dactyl, but occasionally Lucretius uses a spondee, as in 1.60, which ends with the quadrisyllabic **ūsurpāre**.

The caesura (a break between words within a foot) is here indicated by | in the strong position, after the first long of the third foot. It can also occur in a weak position, after the first short syllable of the third foot or after the first long of the fourth foot, in which case there is usually also a caesura in the second foot. Lucretius is not nearly as careful about the caesura as Vergil, and there are 13 lines which have no caesura at all.

Summary of Rules for Scansion

1) A syllable is long if it contains a vowel that is long by nature (marked here with a macron), if it is a diphthong, or if it is followed by two or more consonants.

2) The letters *x (= ks)* and *z (= ds)* are counted as double consonants.

3) The letter *h* counts neither as a consonant nor a vowel. Therefore a vowel short by nature will scan as a short syllable if it is followed by only one consonant and *h*. Example: the word **inhiāns** (1.36) scans a two short syllables plus a long—**in** + **hi** + **āns**; similarly **et haec** scans as a short plus a long.

4) The letter *i* acts as both a consonant and a vowel. For instance, *i* is vocalic in the preposition **in** but consonantal in the verb **iungō**. A good rule of thumb is that, if the derivative in English begins with *j* (e.g., junction, judge), then the *i* is consonantal.

5) In most instances the letter *u* is a vowel, but following certain other letters it is consonantal and so does not scan: e.g., after *q*, after *g* in **sanguen**, **unguentum**, **lingua**, and **languidus**; after *s* in **suāvis** and **suēscō** and its compounds. Also, Lucretius varies between vocalic and consonantal *u* in the verb **solvō** and its compounds.

6) Rules for elision: when one word ends in a vowel and the next begins with a vowel, the first vowel is dropped or elided: e.g., **omne animantum** (1.4) elides to **omn' animantum**.

Since the letter *h* does not count in scansion, elision will take place if one word ends with a vowel and the next begins with *h* plus a vowel: e.g., **agere hōc** (1.41) elides to **ager' hōc**.

The letter *m* is also weak in the final position (ending a word) so that if a word ends with a vowel + *m* and the next word begins with a vowel or *h* plus a vowel, the closing vowel + *m* will elide. Examples: **incipiam et** (1. 55) elides to **incipi' et**; **prīmum hominēs** (1.161) elides to **prīm' hominēs**.

7) One aspect of scansion that is frequently ignored is the mute (or stop) plus liquid option, which grants the poet great flexibility. Lucretius takes advantage of this option with

considerable frequency (63 in these selections, about 5% of the lines), so the student who forgets this option will find the scansion of a particular line impossible. The option: when a mute (the letters *b, p, d, t, c, k, g*, and rarely *f*) is followed by a liquid (the letters *l* and *r*), the poet may choose to scan the preceding syllable as short if it contains a naturally short vowel. This occurs most frequently (21) with a short vowel followed by *pr*, as in **saecla propāgant**, where the final *a* of **saecla** scans as short, or within a word such as **proprium**, so that the *o* remains short. There are 17 instances with *cr* (e.g., **sacrōrum** (1.96), 8 with *tr* (e.g., **patriō**, 1.94), 4 with *gr* (e.g., **peragrāvit**, 1.74), 2 with *br* (**tenebrīs**), and 6 of a mute plus the liquid *l* (e.g., **percita plāgīs**, 1.1025 , **mare flūminis**, 1.1031, **nōta cluēre**, 2.351). Most interesting is where the poet scans the same word differently: in 5.1163 the first *a* of **sacra** scans as a long; in the very next line it is short.

Lucretian Metrical Style

All the features noted below occur in other poets, but most are more noticeable in Lucretius, probably because of difficulties he encountered in adapting Greek scientific and philosophical subjects to Latin meter.

Aphaeresis (Prodelision): the converse of elision. When a vowel closes one word and is followed by a word beginning with another vowel, the second vowel drops out. Unlike elision, in aphaeresis the vowel is actually dropped from the text. This device occurs most frequently with **est**: e.g., **patefactast** (1.10), **profūsast** (1.88), and very frequently **necessest**. Since the consonant *m* is weak, aphaeresis also occurs after a closing *m*: **vīsumst** (1.308).

Bucolic Diaeresis: word break between the fourth and fifth feet. This feature occurs so frequently in Lucretius (58.9% of the lines) that it will not be mentioned in the notes. The diaeresis helps the poet secure coincidence or correspsion between the verse ictus (stress) and the natural word accent in the last three feet of the line. A word break after the fourth foot ensures that the usual fifth-foot dactyl will be in correspsion. Lucretius prefers a spondaic fourth foot containing a single word (10.7% of lines, e.g. **quae mare / nāvige/rum, quae /terrās //frūgife/rentīs**, 1.3), but he also creates dactylic fourth feet in diaeresis using one or more words: (e.g., one word: **quem neque / fāma de/um nec / fulmina// nec minitantī** (1.68); two words: **concele/brās per /tē quoni/am genus // omne ani/mantum** (1.4).

Diastole: the short final vowel of a word is lengthened to fit the meter. Examples: **tibī** (1.104, 3.899), **fulgēt** (2.27). Lucretius also sometimes alters the quantity of other syllables to fit his meter; for instance, **religiō** normally scans with a short *e*, but Lucretius consistently writes **rēligiō**.

Suppression of Final *S*: an archaism comparable to elision, but not found in the Augustan poets. A final *s* in a syllable with a naturally short vowel drops before a consonant to maintain a short syllable. Examples: **omnibu' rēbus** (1.159), **quōminu' quō** (1.978); interestingly, there are two such suppressions at 2.53: **quid dubitās quin omni' sit haec ratiōni' potestās?**

Syncopation: see 3 above under I, Archaic Forms, Verbs.

Synizesis: adjacent vowels within a word are counted as one syllable for scansion, similar to diphthongs. Examples: **cuius** (1.149), resulting in a monosyllable; **anteācta** (1.233 and 234), **deorsum** (1.362), **deinde** (1.933), and **suō** (1.1022).

Tmesis: the separation of a compound word into its parts: with prepositional prefixes (e.g., **praeterque meantum**, 1.318); with pronouns (**quae . . . cumque** , 2.21, 3.940).

Vowel Shortening in Hiatus: the opposite of diastole above. Here a normal long vowel which closes a word before a word beginning with a vowel shortens rather than elides. Examples: **si** rather than **sī** in 4.1061 and 5.7.

Verbal Separation: Lucretius often separates by one or more words the parts of a perfect passive form. Examples: **est . . . ausus** (1.67), **sit . . . reperta** (1.318), **genita . . . fuissent** (1.344).

Metrical Effects: As noted above, Lucretius uses meter for dramatic effect. The use of monosyllabic line-endings has been mentioned above. Lucretius also uses pentasyllabic endings to stress a point (**lūdificētur, 1.939**. Moreover, the relative length of a metrical line contributes to the imagery. For instance, when Lucretius writes of the relief one feels in being free from troubles, he composes a purely dactylic line: **sed quibus ipse malīs careās quia cernere suāve est** (2.4). Conversely, he composes heavily spondaic lines to stress labor and trouble. An interesting contrasting group of lines can be found at 3.999–1002, when Lucretius describes the labors of Sisyphus. The meter is heavily spondaic as Sisyphus struggles to push the rock up the hill: **semper dūrum sufferre labōrem / hōc est adversō nixantem trūdere monte / saxum quod**. As the rock then rushes back down the hill, the meter turns to quick dactyls: **tamen ē summō iam vertice rūrsum / volvitur et plānī raptim petit aequora campī**. Lucretius also creates special effects through elision. As the water flows out of the Danaids' leaky vases, the three elisions emphasize their loss: **commoda perflūxēre atque ingrāta interiēre** (3.937). The water leaks out just as the vowels drop from the line.

Lucretius employs many other special effects, but I will leave it to the reader to discover these pleasures.

❧ Some Personal Favorite Passages ❧
(not included in the text)

❧ The Succession of Life:

Augēscunt aliae gentēs, aliae minuuntur,
inque brevī spatiō mūtantur saecla animantum
et quasi cursōrēs vitāī lampada trādunt.

2.77–79
Some races increase, others decrease,
and in a brief time the generations of animals are changed
and like runners pass on the torches of life.

❧ Regarding Thunder and Lightning:

Cūr etiam loca sōla petunt frūstrāque labōrant?
An tum bracchia cōnsuēscunt firmantque lacertōs?

6.396–97
Why also do they [the gods] seek deserted places and work in vain?
Or are they then practicing and strengthening their arms and forearms?

☙ SELECT BIBLIOGRAPHY ❧

☙ Texts and Commentaries

Bailey, Cyril. *Epicurus*. Oxford: The Clarendon Press, 1926.

————. *Titi Lucreti Cari De Rerum Natura Libri Sex*. 3 vols. Oxford: The Clarendon Press, 1947.

————. *Lucreti De Rerum Natura Libri Sex*. Oxford: The Clarendon Press, 1922.

Benfield, G.E. and R. C. Reeves. *Selections from Lucretius*. Oxford: Oxford University Press, 1978.

Brown, P. Michael. *Lucretius: De Rerum Natura I*. Bristol: Bristol Classical Press, 1984.

Brown, Robert D. *Lucretius on Love and Sex: A Commentary on* De Rerum Natura *IV, 1030–1287*. Leiden: E.J. Brill, 1987.

Costa, C.D.N. *Lucretius: De Rerum Natura V*. Oxford: The Clarendon Press, 1984.

Cox, A.S. *Lucretius on Matter and Man*. London: G. Bell and Sons, 1970.

Godwin, John. *Lucretius: De Rerum Natura IV*. Warminster, England: Aris & Phillips, 1986.

————. *Lucretius: De Rerum Natura VI*. Warminster, England: Aris & Phillips, 1991.

Kenney, E.J. *Lucretius: De Rerum Natura. Book III*. Cambridge: Cambridge University Press, 1984.

Leonard, William Ellery and Stanley Barney Smith. *T. Lucreti Cari De Rerum Natura Libri Sex*. Madison: University of Wisconsin Press, 1968.

Merrill, William Augustus. *T. Lucreti Cari De Rerum Natura Libri Sex*. New York: American Book Company, 1907.

Munro, H.A.J. *T. Lucreti Cari De Rerum Natura Libri Sex*. London: G. Bell and Sons, 1928.

Roberts, Louis. *A Concordance of Lucretius*. New York: Garland Publishing, 1968.

☙ Translations

Bailey, Cyril. *Lucretius on the Nature of Things*. Oxford: The Clarendon Press, 1910.

Copley, Frank O. *Lucretius: The Nature of Things*. New York: W.W. Norton, 1977.

Esolen, Anthony M. *Lucretius: On the Nature of Things*. Baltimore: The Johns Hopkins University Press, 1995.

Latham, R.E. *Lucretius: On the Nature of the Universe*. Harmondsworth, England: Penguin Books, 1951.

Leonard, William Ellery. *Of the Nature of Things by Lucretius*. New York: E.P. Dutton, 1957.

Rouse, W.H.D.; Rev. Smith; Martin Ferguson. *Lucretius: De Rerum Natura*. Cambridge: Harvard University Press, 1982.

☙ Selected Secondary Sources

Bailey, Cyril. *The Greek Atomists and Epicurus*. Oxford: The Clarendon Press, 1928.

Castner, Catherine. *Prosopography of Roman Epicureans, from the Second Century B.C. to the Second Century A.D.*, Studien zur klassischen Philologie, vol. 34. Frankfurt am Main: Verlag Peter Lang, 1988.

Clay, Diskin. *Lucretius and Epicurus*. Ithaca: Cornell University Press, 1983.

Dudley, D.R. *Lucretius*. New York: Basic Books, 1965. [A collection of essays by various authors]

Gale, Monica. *Myth and Poetry in Lucretius*. Cambridge: Cambridge University Press, 1994.

Hadzits, George Depue. *Lucretius and His Influence*. New York: Longmans, Green, 1935.

Minadeo, Richard. *The Lyre of Science: Form and Meaning in Lucretius'* De Rerum Natura. Detroit: Wayne State University Press, 1969.

Nussbaum, Martha. *The Therapy of Desire: Theory and Practice in Hellenistic Ethics.* Princeton: Princeton University Press, 1994. Chapter 5 ("Beyond Obsession and Disgust: Lucretius on the Therapy of Love"), Ch. 6 ("Mortal Immortals: Lucretius on Death and the Voice of Nature"), Ch. 7 ("'By Words, Not Arms': Lucretius on Anger and Agression").

Obbink, Dirk, ed., *Philodemus and Poetry.* Oxford: Oxford University Press, 1995. Elisabeth Asmis, "Epicurean Poetics," 15–34; David Sider, "Epicurean Poetics: Response and Dialogue," 35–41; Michael Wigodsky, "The Alleged Impossibility of Philosophical Poetry," 58–68.

Rist, J.M. *Epicurus: An Introduction.* Cambridge: The University Press, 1972.

Segal, Charles. *Lucretius on Death and Anxiety: Poetry and Philosophy in* De rerum natura. Princeton: Princeton University Press, 1990.

West, David. *The Imagery and Poetry of Lucretius.* Edinburgh: Edinburgh University Press, 1969.

cs Selected Sources on Science for the General Reader

Ferris, Timothy. *Coming of Age in the Milky Way.* New York: William Morrow, 1988.

———. *The Creation of the Universe,* 1985. [60 minute video, sponsored by Texas Instruments, with teacher's manual and suggestions for further reading]

Flamsteed, Sam. "Crisis in the Cosmos," *Discover,* March 1995. [The universe is younger than the stars it contains]

Freedman, David. "Beyond Einstein," *Discover,* Feb. 1989 (particles faster than light).

Gleick, James. *Chaos. Making a New Science.* New York: Penguin, 1987.

Greenstein, George. *Frozen Star: Of Pulsars, Black Holes, and the Fate of Stars.* New York: New American Library, 1983.

———. *The Symbiotic Universe: Life and Mind in the Cosmos.* New York: William Morrow, 1988. Chapter 10 ("The Moment of Creation"), Ch. 11 ("Grand Unification and the Inflationary Universe").

Hawking, Stephen W. *A Brief History of Time.* New York: Bantam Books, 1988.

Lorenz, Edward N. *The Essence of Chaos.* Seattle: University of Washington Press, 1993.

Mann, Charles C., "The Massive Search for Mass," *Smithsonian,* March 1989. [The search for the source of weight in the form of the Higg's boson.]

Pagels, Heinz R. "Before the Big Bang," *Natural History,* April 1983. [Inflationary universe and bubble theory]

Steward, Ian. *Does God Play Dice? The Mathematics of Chaos.* London: Blackwell, 1990.

Trefil, James. Numerous articles on physics in *Smithsonian:* "'Nothing' May Turn Out to Be the Key to the Universe" (Dec. 1981), "How the Universe Began" (May 1983), "How the Universe will End" (June 1983), "Quantum Physics' World: Now You See It, Now You Don't" (Aug. 1987), "Using Chaos to Make Order" (Dec. 1987), "Dark Matter" (June 1993), "Life on Earth: Was it Inevitable?" (Feb. 1995).

von Baeyer, Christian. *Taming the Atom: The Emergence of the Visible Microworld.* Random House: 1992.

Weinberg, Steven. *Dreams of a Final Theory: The Search for the Fundamental Laws of Nature.* Pantheon, 1992.

———. *The First Three Minutes: A Modern View of the Origin of the Universe.* New York: Bantam Books, 1977.

LUCRETIUS

Selections from DE RERUM NATURA

1   **Aeneadēs, -ae**, m., *descendant of Aeneas;* pl., *Romans.*
        Aeneadum: = gen. pl.
    genetrīx, genetrīcis, f., *mother.*
    dīvus, -ī, m., *god.*
        divum: = **divōrum**, as always in Lucretius.

2   **almus, -a, -um**, *kindly, gracious, nurturing.*
    subter, prep. + acc., *beneath.*
    signum, -ī, n., here = *constellation, stars.*

3   **quae**: delayed relative pronoun introducing the clause beginning with **caelī** in line 2; the verb is
        concelebrās (4); the antecedent is **Venus** (2).
    nāviger, nāvigera, nāvigerum [a compound adjective apparently coined by Lucretius], *ship-bearing, navigable.*
    frūgiferēns, frūgiferentis [another coinage of Lucretius], *fruit-bearing, fruitful.*
        frūgiferentīs: the ending **-īs** is accusative plural, third declension, as throughout Lucretius.
        The pentasyllabic line-ending is unusual.

4   **concelebrō, -āre, -āvī, -ātus**, *to fill with living things, enliven.*
        concelebrās: an instance of enjambement: the word that ends a phrase is delayed until the
        next line. This technique both emphasizes the delayed word and prevents the style from
        becoming too choppy and monotonous, as it would be if each line contained one idea.
    animāns, animantis, m., f., n., *living thing, animal.*

5   **concipiō, concipere, concēpī, conceptus**, *to conceive.*
    vīsō, vīsere, vīsī, vīsus [frequentative], *to look upon, see, behold.*
    exorior, exorīrī, exortus sum, *to come into existence, spring to life, arise.*
        exortum: modifying **genus** (4), *once arisen.*
    lūmen, lūminis, n., *light.*
        lūmina: here, as often, poetic plural for singular.

6   **tē . . . tē . . . tē**: the anaphora effectively emphasizes Venus' power.
    nūbila, -ōrum, n. pl., *clouds.*

7   **adventus, -ūs**, m., *approach, arrival.*
        adventumque tuum: expanding on **tē**.
        tuum, tibi: emphatic repetition continuing that in line 6.
    suāvīs: the *u* of **suāvis** is consonantal, as if it were a *w*. The **-īs** ending is accusative plural.
    daedalus, -a, -um, *variegated, skillful, inventive.*
    tellūs, tellūris, f., *earth.*
        suāvīs daedala tellūs . . . flōrēs: adjective-noun phrase embedded within another adjective-noun phrase.

Sing to me, O Muse, of the works of golden Aphrodite
The Cyprian, who stirs sweet longing in gods
and subdues the races of mortal men as well as
the birds that swoop from the sky and all the beasts
that are nurtured in their multitude on both land and sea.
    Homeric Hymn to Aphrodite 5.1–5 (tr. Athanassakis)

CB BOOK 1 &C

1. Proem: Invocation and Dedication

In conventional fashion Lucretius opens his poem with an invocation to bountiful Venus, who creates springtime's plenty. As the epic progresses, the reader will soon learn to view this Venus not as the traditional Roman goddess, but as a representation of the creative power of Nature. Lucretius then dedicates the poem to the patrician Memmius. Returning to the picure of Venus, he asks that she work her charms on Mars to assure that there will be peace, so that Memmius can approach his work with tranquil attentiveness. The depiction of the infatuation of Mars with Venus has been interpreted as an allusion to the Greek philosopher Empedocles, who used the figures of Aphrodite and Ares to symbolize the two operative principles of the universe: love and strife. In a more directly Roman reference, Venus is mother, through her son Aeneas, and Mars is father, through Romulus and Remus, of the Roman race.

1   Aeneadum genetrīx, hominum dīvumque voluptās,
2   alma Venus, caelī subter lābentia signa
3   quae mare nāvigerum, quae terrās frūgiferentīs
4   concelebrās, per tē quoniam genus omne animantum
5   concipitur vīsitque exortum lūmina sōlis;
6   tē, dea, tē fugiunt ventī, tē nūbila caelī
7   adventumque tuum, tibi suāvīs daedala tellūs

CB Discussion Questions

1.   Why does Lucretius include the word **voluptās** in line 1? What might it represent?

2.   What fundamental concept of Epicurean philosophy does Lucretius include in the first line?

3.   In mythology how is Venus associated with the sea? (3)

4.   Into how many parts does Lucretius divide the physical universe in lines 2–4?

5.   With what is the sun's light (**lūmina sōlis**) equated in line 5?

6.   What happens to the natural landscape as Venus approaches?

She wings her way through the air; she is in the sea,
in its foaming billows; from her everything
that is, is born. For she engenders us
and sows the seed of desire whereof we're born,
all we her children, living on the earth.

   Euripides, *Hippolytus* 447–51 (tr. Grene)

8 **summittō, summittere, summīsī, summissus**, *to send up, put forth.*
 tibi: in anaphora with line 7.
 aequor, aequoris, n. [here, as often, poetic plural for singular], *smooth/level surface, plain*
 pontus, -ī, m., *sea.*
9 **plācātus, -a, -um**, *peaceful, calm.*
 niteō, -ēre, -uī, *to be radiant, shine.*
 diffundō, diffundere, diffūdī, diffūsus, *to spread widely, diffuse.*
  plācātum . . . diffūsō lūmine caelum: adjective-noun phrase embedded within another
   adjective-noun phrase.
10 **simul ac**: = **simulac**, *as soon as.*
 speciēs, -ēī, f., *sight, appearance; face.*
 patefaciō, patefacere, patefēcī, patefactus, *to make visible, reveal; to open.*
  patefactast: = **patefacta est**, a normal aphaeresis of the *e* in **est** in Lucretius.
 vērnus, -a, -um, *occurring in spring, vernal.*
  speciēs . . . vērna diēī: an instance of transferred epithet; **vērna**, though agreeing in sense
   with **diēī**, modifies **speciēs**.
11 **reserō, -āre, -āvī, -ātus**, *to unbar a door, unseal.*
  reserāta: the breeze is personified and thought of as released from the imprisoning cave of
   Aeolus, god of the winds.
 vigeō, -ēre, -uī, *to thrive, flourish.*
 genitābilis, -is, -e, *generative, creative, fruitful.*
  genitābilis: nominative modifying **aura** or genitive modifying **favōnī**.
 aura, -ae, f. , *breeze.*
 favōnius, -ī, m., *west wind, zephyr.*
12 **āerius, -a, -um**, *existing in air, airy.*
 volucris, volucris, f., *bird.*
13 **significō, -āre, -āvī, -ātus**, *to indicate, show, make known.*
 initus, -ūs, m., *approach, arrival.*
  tuumque . . . initum: echoing **adventumque tuum** (7).
 percello, percellere, perculī, perculsus, *to strike.*
 corda: accusative of respect with **perculsae**, *struck through the hearts.*
 vī: closing the line on a monosyllable. Such line-endings occur with far greater frequency in
   Lucretius than in Vergil.
14 **fera, -ae**, f., *animal, wild beast.*
 pecus, pecudis, f., *herd.*
  pecudēs: in asyndeton with **ferae** as compound subject, *wild beasts and herds.*
 persultō, -āre, -āvī, -ātus, *to leap over.*
 pābulum, -ī, n., *pasture.*
 laetus, -a, -um: here, *fertile, productive.*
15 **trānō, -āre, -āvī -ātus**, *to swim across.*
 amnis, amnis, m., *river.*
 capta: modifying understood subject, **fera**, *animal*, to which **quamque** then refers.
 lepos, lepōris, m., *charm, grace.*
16 **cupidē**, adv., *eagerly, desirously.*
 quisque, quaeque, quidque, *each, each one.*
 indūcō, indūcere, indūxī, inductus, *to lead on, urge, entice.*
 pergō, pergere, perrēxī, perrēctus, *to proceed, continue.*
17 **dēnique**, adv., here, *then.*
 rapāx, rapācis, *apt to seize or tear away, tearing, rushing.*
18 **frondifer, frondifera, frondiferum**, *leaf-bearing, leafy.*
 domōs: = **domūs**, accusative plural feminine.
 vireō, -ēre, -uī, *to be green with vegetation; to be vigorous, thrive.*

8   summittit flōrēs, tibi rīdent aequora pontī
9   plācātumque nitet diffūsō lūmine caelum.
10   Nam simul ac speciēs patefactast vērna diēī
11   et reserāta viget genitābilis aura favōnī
12   āeriae prīmum volucrēs tē, dīva, tuumque
13   significant initum perculsae corda tuā vī.
14   Inde ferae pecudēs persultant pābula laeta
15   et rapidōs trānant amnīs: ita capta lepōre
16   tē sequitur cupidē quō quamque indūcere pergis.
17   Dēnique per maria ac montīs fluviōsque rapācēs
18   frondiferāsque domōs avium campōsque virentīs

ɔ3 Discussion Questions

1.   What metaphorical language do you find in the description of the sea in line 8?

2.   What image associated with love does the phrase **perculsae corda** (13) bring to mind?

3.   How does Lucretius create a sense of motion and activity in lines 14–16?

4.   What poetic device do you notice in line 14?

5.   How does Lucretius establish the universal nature of Venus' appeal? (17–18)

Ay, but I meant not thee; I meant not her
Whom all the pines of Ida shook to see
Slide from that quiet heaven of hers, and tempt
The Trojan, while his neatherds were abroad;
Nor her that o'er her wounded hunter wept
Her deity false in human-amorous tears;
Nor whom her beardless apple-arbiter
Decided fairest. Rather, O ye Gods,
Poet-like, as the great Sicilian called
Calliope to grace his golden verse—
Ay, and this Kypris also—did I take
That popular name of thine to shadow forth
The all-generating powers and genial heat
Of Nature, when she strikes thro' the thick blood
Of cattle, and light is large, and lambs are glad
Nosing the mother's udder, and the bird
Makes his heart voice amid the blaze of flowers;
Which things appear the work of mighty Gods.
     Tennyson, *Lucretius* (1868), 85–102

19 **omnibus**: dative with **incutiēns**, but also as dative of possession with **per pectora**.

    incutiō, incutere, incussī, incussus, *to strike, dash* (one thing [acc.] on another [dat.]).

      incutiēns: modifying an understood **tū** (Venus).

    blandus, -a, -um, *charming, alluring, enticing.*

20 **efficiō, efficere, effēcī, effectus** [with **ut** plus subjunctive], *to bring about, accomplish.*

    generātim, adv., *by species, according to kind/race.*

    saeclum, -ī, n., *breed, race, generation.*

    propāgō, -āre, -āvī, -ātus, *to reproduce, propagate.*

21 **Quae quoniam**: linking **quī**, *And since you.*

    gubernō, -āre, -āvī, -ātus, *to pilot, control, govern.*

22 **quisquam, quicquam**, *anyone, anything.*

    dīus, -a, -um, *with the brightness of day, bright, divine.*

    in lūminis ōrās: a formulaic phrase equating light with life, from the early Latin poet Ennius. Here **ōrās** continues the nautical image established in lines 3 and 8 which is reinforced by **gubernās** (21).

23 **exoritur**: enjambement; repeating the verb from line 5 where it occurred in a very similar context: **vīsitque exortum lūmina sōlis**. Such repetition is a prominent feature of Lucretius' style.

24 **socia, -ae**, f., *ally.*

    studeō, -ēre, -uī, *to desire.*

    scrībendīs versibus: dative of purpose, *for the writing of my verses.*

    versus, -ūs, m., *verse.*

25 **dē rērum nātūrā**: the title of the epic, modeled on the Greek Περὶ φύσεως (*About Nature*), the title of Epicurus' great work.

    pangō, pangere, pepigī, pactus, *to arrange, compose.*

"Great Venus! Queen of beauty and of grace,
The joy of gods and men, that under sky
Dost fairest shine, and most adorn thy place;
That with thy smiling look dost pacify
The raging seas, and mak'st the storms to fly;
Thee, goddess, thee the winds, the clouds do fear;
And, when thou spread'st thy mantle forth on high
The waters play, and pleasant lands appear,
And heavens laugh, and all the world shows joyous cheer:

Then doth the daedal earth throw forth to thee
Out of her fruitful lap abundant flow'rs;
And then all living wights, soon as they see
The Spring break forth out of his lusty bow'rs,
They all do learn to play the paramoúrs:
First do the merry birds, thy pretty pages,
Privily prickéd with thy lustful pow'rs,
Chirp loud to thee out of their leavy cages,
And thee their mother call to cool their kindly rages.

(continued on next page)

19   omnibus incutiēns blandum per pectora amōrem
20   efficis ut cupidē generātim saecla propāgent.
21   Quae quoniam rērum nātūram sōla gubernās
22   nec sine tē quicquam dīās in lūminis ōrās
23   exoritur neque fit laetum neque amābile quicquam,
24   tē sociam studeō scrībendīs versibus esse
25   quōs ego dē rērum nātūrā pangere cōnor

♋ Discussion Questions

1.   What common image of love is found in line 19?

2.   How extensive is the power attributed to Venus in lines 21–23?

3.   What image does the verb **gubernās** (21) create? What is the basic meaning of the verb?

4.   Why does Lucretius appeal to Venus for help rather than more traditionally to the Muses? (24–25)

Then do the savage beasts begin to play
Their pleasant frisks, and loathe their wonted food:
The lions roar; the tigers loudly bray;
The raging bulls rebellow through the wood,
And breaking forth dare tempt the deepest flood
To come where thou dost draw them with desire:
So all things else, that nourish vital blood,
Soon as with fury thou dost them inspire,
In generation seek to quench their inward fire.

So all the world by thee at first was made,
And daily yet thou dost the same repair:
Ne aught on earth that merry is and glad,
Ne aught on earth that lovely is and fair,
But thou the same for pleasure didst prepare:
Thou art the root of all that joyous is:
Great god of men and women, queen of th' air,
Mother of laughter, and well-spring of bliss,
O grant that of my love at last I may not miss!"
        Spenser, *Fairie Queen* (1596), Book IV, Canto X, 44–47

Throned in splendor, deathless, O Aphrodite,
child of Zeus, charm-fashioner, I entreat you . . . .
standing by me . . . come even again. . . appear and
        stand by my shoulder.
            Sappho 1.1–2, 5, 25, 27–28 (tr. Lattimore)

26   **Memmiadēs, -ae**, m., *descendant of the patrician Memmian family,* i.e., Gaius Memmius, who is probably also the Memmius of Catullus' poems. Venus was the patron deity of this distinguished family. Throughout the poem Lucretius will use the second person to refer both to Memmius and to his reader.

   Memmiadae: Lucretius uses the patronymic instead of the dative **Memmiō**, which would not scan in dactylic hexameter.

   tempore in omnī: the preposition **in** is optional with the temporal ablative.

27   **omnibus**: ablative modifying **rēbus**, describing how Memmius is **ōrnātum**. The adjective **omnibus** and its noun **rēbus** emphatically frame the line.

   ōrnātus, -a, -um, *distinguished, illustrious.*

   excellō, excellere, excelluī, *to be pre-eminent; to excel.*

28   **quō**, adv., *for which reason, therefore.*

   aeternus, -a, -um, *eternal, immortal.*

29   **Effice**: Lucretius rather boldly gives a second direct command (cf. **dā**, 28) to Venus, and places the imperative in an emphatic position at the beginning of the line. **Effice** governs an **ut** plus subjunctive clause.

   intereā, adv., *meanwhile,* i.e., while he is composing his poem.

   ferus, -a, -um, *fierce, rough, harsh.*

   moenera: archaic spelling for **mūnera**, *duties.*

   mīlitia, -ae, f., *military service, warfare, soldiery.*

   mīlitiāī: the -āī ending is an archaic genitive singular, first declension. This ending is frequent in Lucretius and gives an extra long syllable in scansion, which is particularly convenient at the end of a line, as here creating a pentasyllabic ending.

30   **per maria ac terrās**: note the similar phraseology here to **per maria ac montīs** in line 17.

   sōpītus, -a, -um, *lulled to sleep, asleep.*

31   **Nam tū sōla potes**: reiterating the idea of Venus' supreme authority, as seen in line 21: **quae quoniam rērum nātūram sōla gubernās**.

   tranquillus, -a, -um, *calm, quiet, tranquil.*

   tranquillā pāce: such mental peace is the Epicurean moral ideal, for which the Greek term is ἀταραξία (*ataraxiā*).

   iuvō, -āre, iūvī, iūtus, *to please, delight.*

32   **mortālīs**: enjambement.

   fera moenera: note the repetition of the phrase from line 29.

   Māvors, Māvortis, m., *Mars* (god of war). This is another archaic spelling.

33   **armipotēns, armipotentis**, *powerful in arms, valiant.*

   regit: Venus may rule **rērum nātūram** (21), but Lucretius acknowledges that she is not omnipotent; Mars is in charge of war.

   gremium, -ī, n., *lap.*

   quī: the relative has been delayed.

   tuum: separated from its noun **gremium**. The phrase **in gremium . . . tuum** wraps around **quī**, just as Venus enfolds Mars.

   sē: again the line closes on a monosyllable.

34   **rēiciō, rēicere, rēiēcī, rēiectus**, here, *to let (himself, sē) sink into.*

   dēvictus, -a, -um, *completely overcome, subdued.*

   aeternō dēvictus vulnere amōris: by the word-order, Mars is completely encompassed by his love, **aeternō . . . vulnere amōris**.

35   **suspiciēns, suspicientis**, *looking up.*

   teres, teretis: here, *shapely.*

   cervīx, cervīcis, f., *neck.*

   repōnō, repōnere, reposuī, repositus, *to place back, lay back.*

   repostā: = **reposită**: by syncope the form is shortened for metrical convenience.

   teretī cervīce repostā: ablative absolute.

26   Memmiadae nostrō, quem tū, dea, tempore in omnī

27   omnibus ōrnātum voluistī excellere rēbus.

28   Quō magis aeternum dā dictīs, dīva, lepōrem.

29   Effice ut intereā fera moenera mīlitiāī

30   per maria ac terrās omnīs sōpīta quiēscant.

31   Nam tū sōla potes tranquillā pāce iuvāre

32   mortālīs, quoniam bellī fera moenera Māvors

33   armipotēns regit, in gremium quī saepe tuum sē

34   rēicit aeternō dēvictus vulnere amōris,

35   atque ita suspiciēns teretī cervīce repostā

36   pascit amōre avidōs inhiāns in tē, dea, vīsūs,

37   ēque tuō pendet resupīnī spīritus ōre.

ᘓ Discussion Questions

1.   What do Venus and Mars respectively represent? (31–33)

2.   In the relationship between Venus and Mars who appears to dominate? (33–39) How does Lucretius make this domination clear?

3.   It has been suggested that the depiction of Venus and Mars may have been derived from a sculptural group. Imagine such a sculpture. Compare also the paintings of Mars and Venus by Botticelli (1444–1510) in the National Gallery, London, and by Nicolas Poussin (1628) in the Boston Museum of Fine Arts.

Demodokos struck the lyre and began singing well the story
about the love of Ares and sweet-garlanded Aphrodite,
. . . [how] he entered the house of glorious Hephaistos,
lusting after the love of sweet-garlanded Kythereia.
    Homer, *Odyssey* 8.266–67, 287–88 (tr. Lattimore)

---

36   **avidus, -a, -um**, *greedy.*
     inhiāns, inhiantis, *gaping at, gazing at with longing.*
       inhiāns in tē: *longingly gazing at you.*
     vīsus, -ūs, m., *sight, vision.* Here again poetic plural for singular.
37   **ēque**: = the preposition **ē** and the enclitic **-que**.
     tuō: again this possessive adjective is separated from its noun, **ōre** (cf. 33).
     resupīnus, -a, -um, *lying on (one's) back, supine.*
       resupīnī: genitive singular modifying the understood noun **Māvortis**, *Mars.*
     spīritus, -ūs, m., *breath.*
       spīritus: nominative. Lucretius has changed the subject from Mars himself to his breath.

38 **Hunc**: direct object of **circumfūsa** (39); also modified by **recubantem**.
　　Hunc tū: note the verbal juxtaposition of the two lovers.
　　recubāns, recubantis, *reclining*.
　　tuō . . . corpore sānctō: ablative of means with **circumfūsa** (39).
　　　　tuō recubantem corpore sānctō: again the word order intertwines Mars and Venus; see line
　　　　34 above.

39 **circumfūsus, -a, -um**, *having embraced*, literally, *poured around*, *draped around*, showing how
　　　　Venus has totally mastered Mars.
　　super, adv., *from above*.
　　suāvīs: accusative plural feminine with **loquellās**. Again, as in line 7, the *u* is consonantal and
　　　　so does not scan.
　　loquella, -ae, f. [diminutive], *speech, words*.
　　　　suāvīs . . . loquellās, *sweet little nothings*, the typical language of love. For a disdainful treat-
　　　　ment of romantic love, see the selections from Book 4.

40 **fundō, fundere, fūdī, fūsus**, *to pour out, pour forth*.
　　funde: repeating the root and thus the image of **circumfūsa** above.
　　placidus, -a, -um, *quiet, calm, serene*.
　　inclutus, -a, -um, *celebrated, illustrious*.
　　　　incluta: vocative, referring to Venus.
　　　　　　petēns placidam . . . pācem: alliteration. Also, the phrase **placidam . . . pācem** reminds the
　　　　　　reader of **tranquillā pāce**, the Epicurean ideal, in line 31.

41 **Nam**: giving the reason why Lucretius prays to Venus for peace. Lucretius lived in a time of
　　　　great civil turmoil in the first half of the first century B.C.
　　nōs: nominative plural; emphatic; also an editorial plural: Lucretius is referring to himself.
　　hōc: accusative singular with archaic spelling.
　　　　agere hōc: i.e., to work on his poem.
　　patriāī: archaic genitive singular.
　　inīquus, -a, -um, *unfavorable, adverse*.
　　　　patriāī tempore inīquō: referring to the civil and social unrest that characterized Roman
　　　　society as the Republic crumbled.

42 **aequus, -a, -um**, *even, calm*.
　　　　aequō animō: ablative of manner; a favorite Lucretian phrase to describe the Epicurean ideal,
　　　　in contrast to the phrase **tempore inīquō** (41).
　　Memmius, -ī, m., *Memmius*, father or ancestor of the Memmius to whom the poem is dedicated.
　　clārus, -a, -um: here, *illustrious*.
　　propāgō, propāginis, f., *offspring*.
　　　　Memmī clāra propāgō: Gaius Memmius, the dedicatee of the poem, was only one in a long
　　　　succession of sons of this patrician house.

43 **dēsum, dēesse, dēfuī** + dat., *to fail (in respect of), be neglectful in one's duty (to)*.
　　dēsse: a poetic contraction of **dēesse**; understand **potest** (from **possumus**, 42).
　　salūs, salūtis, f.: here, *safety*.
　　　　commūnī . . . salūtī: the safety of the state.

38   Hunc tū, dīva, tuō recubantem corpore sānctō
39   circumfūsa super, suāvīs ex ōre loquellās
40   funde petēns placidam Rōmānīs, incluta, pācem.
41   Nam neque nōs agere hōc patriāī tempore inīquō
42   possumus aequō animō nec Memmī clāra propāgō
43   tālibus in rēbus commūnī dēsse salūtī.

☙ Discussion Question

1.   Can you think of any specific Roman historical events that the phrase **patriāī tempore inīquō** (41) might describe?

Appearedst thou not to Paris in this guise?
Or to more deeply blest Anchises? or,
In all thy perfect goddess-ship, when lies
Before thee thy own vanquished Lord of War?
And gazing in thy face as toward a star,
Laid on thy lap, his eyes to thee upturn,
Feeding on thy sweet cheek!
        Lord Byron, *Childe Harold* (1811), Canto IV, 51

50   **supersum, superesse, superfuī, superfutūrus**, *to remain.*
       Quod superest: a formulaic phrase, literally, *as to what remains,* simply meaning *next.*
    vacuus, -a, -um, *empty;* here, *free.*
    auris, auris, f., *ear.*
    sagāx, sagācis, *keen, sharp, wise.*
       vacuās aurīs animumque sagācem: chiasmus (see Introduction).

51   **sēmoveō, sēmovēre, sēmōvī, sēmōtus**, *to remove, separate.*
    adhibeō, adhibēre, adhibuī, adhibitus, *to apply, direct.*
    ratiō, ratiōnis, f., *reason, explanation; way; system, philosophy;* a key word in Lucretius with a
       variety of meanings; here *reason.*

52   **dispōnō, dispōnere, disposuī, dispositus**, *to order, arrange.*
       disposta: = **disposita**, by syncope.
          dōna . . . studiō disposta fidēlī: another example of interlocking word order.

53   **prius quam**, comparative, *before.*
    contemnō, contemnere, contempsī, contemptus, *to despise, scorn.*
       contempta: modifying **dōna**; predicative.

54   **ratiōne**: here, *workings.*
    deum: = **deōrum**; this older genitive plural is usual in Lucretius.

55   **disserō, disserere, disseruī, dissertus**, *to set out in words, discuss.*
    prīmōrdia, -ōrum, n. pl., *first-beginnings, beginnings, elements* (the main Lucretian word for the
       basic substance, the atoms).
    pandō, pandere, passus (or **pansus**) **sum**, *to spread out, reveal, make known.*

56   **unde**: = **ē quibus**, i.e., **ē prīmōrdiīs**.
    omnīs: accusative plural.
    auctō, -āre, -āvī, -ātus, *to increase, cause to grow.*

57   **quōve**: = **quō** plus enclitic **-ve**, *or to where,* or *into which,* in opposition to **unde** (56).
    eadem: ambiguous; nominative singular feminine with **nātūra** or accusative plural neuter with
       perēmpta.
    rūrsum: = **rūrsus**, adv., *again, in turn.*
    perimō, perimere, perēmī, perēmptus, *to destroy.*
       perēmpta: accusative plural neuter; Lucretius has switched to the neuter from **rēs**, as he
         frequently does.
    resolvō, resolvere, resolvī, resolūtus, *to loosen, unfasten, release.*

58   **quae**: accusative plural neuter, the antecedent is **prīmōrdia** (55).
    nōs: nominative plural; its verb, **suēmus**, is postponed until line 60.
    māteriēs, -ēī, f., *matter.*
    genitālis, -is, -e, *concerned with creation/growth; generative.*
    rēbus: archaic use of the dative for genitive of possession.

59   **reddunda**: = **reddenda**.
       reddundā ratiōne, idiom, *in giving an account/explanation.*
    sēmen, sēminis, n., *seed.*

60   **suēscō, suēscere, suēvī, suētus**, *to be accustomed.*
       suēmus: syncopated perfect = **suēvimus**; here the *u* is vocalic and so scans.
    ūsūrpō, -āre, -āvī, -ātus, *to call habitually; to name, term.*
       ūsūrpāre: note the unusual spondaic ending of the line.

61   **prīmīs**: the primacy of the atoms is emphasized by the line-end position, the bisyllabic line
       ending, and the displacement from **illīs**.

2. His Topic: Technical Terms

After asking for his reader's undivided attention, Lucretius summarizes his topic and offers a number of synonymous terms for the particles, or atoms, that constitute the universe.

50   Quod superest, vacuās aurīs animumque sagācem
51   sēmōtum ā cūrīs adhibē vēram ad ratiōnem,
52   nē mea dōna tibi studiō disposta fidēlī,
53   intellecta prius quam sint, contempta relinquās.
54   Nam tibi dē summā caelī ratiōne deumque
55   disserere incipiam et rērum prīmōrdia pandam,
56   unde omnīs nātūra creet rēs auctet alatque
57   quōve eadem rūrsum nātūra perēmpta resolvat,
58   quae nōs māteriem et genitālia corpora rēbus
59   reddundā in ratiōne vocāre et sēmina rērum
60   appellāre suēmus et haec eadem ūsūrpāre
61   corpora prīma, quod ex illīs sunt omnia prīmīs.

∽ Discussion Questions

1.   How does Lucretius describe his efforts for his reader? (52)

2.   How does Lucretius involve his reader? (54)

3.   What topic will Lucretius discuss first? Why? (54)

4.   How does the idea expressed in the phrase **unde omnīs nātūra creet rēs** (56) contrast with the thought of passage 1?

5.   What process does line 57 describe, and how does it compare with the process of line 56?

6.   List the synonyms that Lucretius uses for the atoms. (58–61)

62   **Hūmāna ... vīta**: human life is depicted as a creature prostrate in fear of a personified religion, which menaces mankind from the sky.

     ante oculōs: *before the eyes* (of all); with **iacēret** connotes the humiliation of utter subjugation.

     foedē, adv., *foully, basely.*

     cum: the conjunction is delayed; translate *when.*

63   **rēligiō, rēligiōnis**, f., *religion.*

64   **regiō, regiōnis**, f., *region, area, direction.*

     ostendēbat: unusual spondaic line-ending.

65   **horribilis, -is, -e**, *fearful, dreadful.*

     super, adv., *from above.*

     aspectus, -ūs, m., *appearance, expression.*

     īnstō, īnstāre, īnstitī + dat., *to stand over, press upon.*

66   **prīmum**, adv., *first.*

     Grāius, -a, -um, *Greek.*

       Grāius homō: Epicurus (see Introduction iv–vii).

     mortālīs: accusative plural with **oculōs** (67).

67   **est ... ausus**: separation, here with transposition of **ausus est** from **audeō, audēre**.

     prīmusque: the repetition after **prīmum** (66) stresses Epicurus' originality.

     obsistō, obsistere, obstitī, *to stand before, oppose, resist.*

     contrā: the repetition of the adverb in the same line-end position in successive lines is extremely emphatic in conveying Epicurus' fearless resistance.

68   **deum**: = **deōrum**.

     fulmen, fulminis, n., *thunderbolt.* The Romans conceived that a thunderstorm consisted of three parts: the lightning (**fulgur**), the thunder (**tonitrus**, here **murmur**), and the thunderbolt, allegedly wielded by an angry and vindictive Jupiter, who might strike one dead. Naturally, therefore, the thunderbolt was the most fearsome part of a storm.

     minitor, minitārī, minitātus sum, *to threaten.*

       minitantī murmure: effective alliteration to describe the rumblings of a stormy sky, followed by the hard *c*s of **compressit caelum** which may mimic the crack of thunder.

69   **comprimō, comprimere, compressī, compressus**, *to curb, constrain, suppress.*

     compressit: with three alternative subjects, **fāma, fulmina**, and **caelum**.

     eō magis: signaling the result clause with **ut** and **cupīret** in lines 70–71.

70   **irrītō, -āre, -āvī, -ātus**, *to provoke, rouse, excite.*

     irrītāt: syncopated perfect = **irrītāvit**. Take as the subject the singular nouns of the preceding clause, which were the subject of **compressit** (69).

     virtūs, virtūtis, f., *strength, excellence.*

     effringō, effringere, effrēgī, effrāctus, *to break open.*

     artus, -a, -um, *close, tightly-fastened.*

71   **claustrum, -ī**, n., *lock, bolt, bar for a door.*

     effringere ... arta nātūrae ... portārum claustra: the secrets of nature are metaphorically locked in a closely-barred prison, which Epicurus desired to break open.

     cupīret: = **cuperet**; a change of conjugation indicating the fluidity of language in Lucretius' time.

72   **ergō**, conj., *therefore.*

     vīvidus, -a, -um, *lively, vigorous.*

     pervincō, pervincere, pervīcī, pervictus, *to win a complete victory, prevail.*

       vīvida vīs animī pervīcit: a characteristic instance of alliteration combined with assonance of the vowels *i* and *a*.

     extrā: governing **flammantia moenia** (73).

3. Philosophy Prevails over Religion: The Sacrifice of Iphigenia

Only one man, Epicurus, dared to challenge the oppressive power of traditional religion and thereby discovered the true workings of nature. Through the poignant depiction of the sacrifice of Iphigenia, Lucretius shows the evils that religious superstition causes.

62	Hūmāna ante oculōs foedē cum vīta iacēret
63	in terrīs oppressa gravī sub rēligiōne
64	quae caput ā caelī regiōnibus ostendēbat
65	horribilī super aspectū mortālibus īnstāns,
66	prīmum Grāius homō mortālīs tollere contrā
67	est oculōs ausus prīmusque obsistere contrā,
68	quem neque fāma deum nec fulmina nec minitantī
69	murmure compressit caelum, sed eō magis ācrem
70	irrītāt animī virtūtem, effringere ut arta
71	nātūrae prīmus portārum claustra cupīret.
72	Ergō vīvida vīs animī pervīcit, et extrā
73	prōcessit longē flammantia moenia mundī
74	atque omne immēnsum peragrāvit mente animōque,

∽ Discussion Questions

1.   In line 66 why does Lucretius include the descriptive adjective **mortālīs**?

2.   To what is Lucretius referring in the phrase **fāma deum** (68)?

The solid vault of the heaven is cleft asunder. Our eyes and thoughts plunge into the infinite abysses of the heavens. Beyond the planets, we discover . . . a hundred millions of suns rolling through space, escorted each by its own procession of dim satellites, invisible to us.

   Anatole France, *The Garden of Epicurus* (1894), Ch. 1

The philosopher's mind "is borne in all directions," as Pindar says "both below the earth," and measuring the surface of the earth, and "above the sky," studying the stars, and investigating the universal nature of everything that is, each in its entirety.

   Plato, *Theaetetus* 173e (tr. Fowler)

---

73   **flammō, -āre, -āvī, -ātus**, *to flame, blaze.*
   mundus, -ī, m., *world, earth.*
      flammantia moenia mundī: the Epicureans believed that the earth was surrounded by an envelope of fiery ether, which here is described as a bordering wall. Note also the alliteration of *m*, which begins medially in **flammantia** and then continues initially.

74   **immēnsus, -a, -um**, *infinite, boundless.*
      immēnsum: here a neuter accusative noun governed by **per** of the verb **peragrāvit**; *infinite space, the universe.*
   peragrō, -āre, -āvī, -ātus, *to traverse.*
      mente animōque: Epicurus traversed the reaches of the universe by sheer mind-power!

75 **refert**: the objects of this verb are the indirect questions: **quid possit orīrī** (75), **quid nequeat** (76), **fīnīta potestās . . . quānam sit ratiōne** (76–77), and **(quānam ratiōne sit) altē terminus haerēns**.

76 **nequeō, nequīre, nequīvī,** *to be unable* (to).
 fīnītus, -a, -um, *limited.*
  fīnīta: predicate adjective modifying **potestās**; reorder this clause: **dēnique quānam ratiōne cuique potestās sit fīnīta**.
 dēnique, adv., *and then, finally.*
 quisque, quaeque, quidque, *each, each one.*
 cuique: dative of possession.

77 **quīnam, quaenam, quodnam,** interrog. adj., *what kind of, what indeed?*
  quānam . . . ratiōne: *in what way, how.*
 altē, adv., *deeply.*
 terminus, -ī, m., *boundary post/stone.*
  terminus: here Lucretius creates a very Roman metaphor, which shows concern for property rights. By this image he conveys the idea that all things are bound by natural limits.
 haerēns: (*deeply*) *clinging.*

78 **quāre,** adv., *by which means, wherefore, therefore.*
 subiciō, subicere, subiēcī, subiectus, *to place underneath/below.*
  subiecta: governing the dative **pedibus**. Lucretius has reversed the imagery of the beginning of the passage; now religion is trampled underfoot and man is uppermost.
 vicissim, adv., *in turn.*

79 **obterō, obterere, obtrīvī, obtrītus,** *to crush, tread upon, trample.*
 exaequō, -āre, -āvī, -ātus, *to make x* (acc.) *equal to y* (dat.).

80 **Illud**: explained by the **nē** clause.
 reor, rērī, ratus sum, *to think.*

81 **impius, -a, -um,** *irreligious, impious.*
  impia: the epithet is transferred to **elementa** from **ratiōnis**.
 elementum, -ī, n., *basic principle, element.*

82 **indugredī**: archaic form of **ingredī**. Lucretius always uses the archaic form of this verb.
   inīre . . . viamque indugredī: Lucretius metaphorically pictures the reader's fears that he is on the road to ruin.
 Quod contrā: *Whereas on the contrary.*
 saepius, comparative adv., *more often.*

83 **pariō, parere, peperī, partus,** *to give birth to, produce, create.*
 scelerōsus, -a, -um, *wicked.*
 factum, -ī, n., *deed.*

84 **Aulis, Aulidis,** f., *Aulis* (coastal city in Greece from which Agamemnon led the Greeks against Troy).
  Aulide: locative.
 pactum, -ī, n., *way, manner.*
 Trivia, ae, f., *the goddess of the crossroads, Diana* (the Greek Artemis).
  Triviāī: archaic genitive singular. See also **Iphianassāī** (85).

85 **Īphianassa, -ae,** f., *Iphigenia* (the eldest daughter of Agamemnon; Diana, the Greek Artemis, demanded her sacrifice so that the Greek fleet could sail).
 turpō, -āre, -āvī, -ātus, *to pollute, defile.*
  turpārunt: syncopated perfect = **turpāvērunt**.
 sanguine: the *u* is consonantal, as if it were a *w*, for the purposes of scansion, as also in **suāvīs** (7).
   Īphianassāī . . . foedē: a most unusual line composed of only four words.

75	unde refert nōbīs victor quid possit orīrī,
76	quid nequeat, fīnīta potestās dēnique cuique
77	quānam sit ratiōne atque altē terminus haerēns.
78	Quārē rēligiō pedibus subiecta vicissim
79	obteritur, nōs exaequat victōria caelō.
80	Illud in hīs rēbus vereor, nē forte reāris
81	impia tē ratiōnis inīre elementa viamque
82	indugredī sceleris. Quod contrā saepius illa
83	rēligiō peperit scelerōsa atque impia facta.
84	Aulide quō pactō Triviāī virginis āram
85	Īphianassāī turpārunt sanguine foedē
86	ductōrēs Danaum dēlectī, prīma virōrum.

☙ Discussion Questions

1. What particularly Roman image would the phrase **unde refert nōbīs victor** (75) elicit in a Roman audience?

2. How does Lucretius immediately bias our opinion in his description of the sacrifice of Iphigenia? (84–86)

Fēlīx quī potuit rērum cognōscere causās,
atque metūs omnīs et inexōrābile fātum
subiēcit pedibus strepitumque Acherontis avārī.

Blessed is he who has been able to learn the causes of things
and has trampled underfoot all fears and relentless fate
and the roar of greedy Acheron.
    Vergil, *Georgics* 2.490–92

---

86 **ductor, ductōris**, m., *leader.*
     Danaī, -ōrum or **-um**, m. pl., *Danaans, Greeks.*
     dēlectus, -a, -um, *select, picked for excellence.*
     prīma, -ōrum, n. pl., *the flower or cream (of), the best, first.*
         prīma virōrum: periphrasis. The neuter plural has a somewhat ironic flavor, especially in the
             context of the preceding harsh alliteration of *d*: **ductōrēs Danaum dēlectī.**

87   **Cui**: referring to Iphigenia.

    simul: = **simulac**, adv., *as soon as.*

    īnfula, -ae, f., *fillet* (a head-band of twisted wool worn by priests as well as sacrificial victims, whereas a simple headband, **vitta**, was worn by brides). Throughout this passage Lucretius highlights the many similarities between the rites of a sacrifice and of a wedding. Iphigenia thought she had come to Aulis to be the bride of Achilles. She discovered her true fate only moments before her death, when she was decorated with an **īnfula** rather than a **vitta**.

    circumdō, circumdare, circumdedī, circumdatus, *to put/place around.*

    cōmptus, -ūs, m., *hair, tress.*

        cōmptūs: accusative plural governed by the **circum** of **circumdata**, *placed around her maidenly hair.*

    īnfula virgineōs circumdata cōmptūs: interlocking word order, suggesting a sense of entrapment.

88   **pār, paris**, *equal, matching.*

    ex utrāque parī . . . parte: take **parī** with **parte**, *in equal length on each side.*

    māla, -ae, f., *cheek.*

    profundō, profundere, profūdī, profūsus, *to pour forth*; here, *to cause to hang down.*

        profūsast: = **profūsa est**, *was made to hang down.*

89   **maestus, -a, -um**, *sad.*

    maestum . . . adstāre parentem: this indirect statement and the two following are governed by **sēnsit** (90), for the subject of which supply *Iphianassa.*

90   **propter**: the postponed position (anastrophe) strengthens the force of **hunc**, which it governs; *next to him, near him.*

    ferrum, -ī, n., *sword.*

    minister, ministrī, m., *attendant (of a priest).*

91   **aspectus, -ūs**, m., *appearance.*

    suō: reflexive, referring to Iphigenia, subject of the verb.

    cīvīs: accusative plural, subject of the infinitive **effundere**, in indirect statement.

92   **genu, -ūs**, n., *knee.*

    summissa: here in a middle sense, i.e., Iphigenia acts upon herself, *having sunk to her knees.*

93   **prōsum, prōdesse, prōfuī** + dat., *to be of use, benefit* (to).

    queō, quīre, quīvī or **quiī, quitus**, *to be able.*

        quībat: contracted form; its subject is the following **quod** clause (94), (*the fact that . . . .*

94   **prīnceps, prīncipis**, m., *first*; here as adjective.

    dōnārat: syncopated pluperfect = **dōnāverat**.

87   Cui simul īnfula virgineōs circumdata cōmptūs
88   ex utrāque parī mālārum parte profūsast,
89   et maestum simul ante ārās adstāre parentem
90   sēnsit et hunc propter ferrum cēlāre ministrōs
91   aspectūque suō lacrimās effundere cīvīs,
92   mūta metū terram genibus summissa petēbat.
93   Nec miserae prōdesse in tālī tempore quībat
94   quod patriō prīnceps dōnārat nōmine rēgem.

Iphigenia to Agamemnon:

I was first to call you father,
You to call me child. And of your children
First to sit upon your knees. We kissed
Each other in our love. "O child,"
You said, "surely one day I shall see you
Happy in your husband's home. And like
A flower blooming for me and in my honor."
. . . . But you, forgetting,
Have willed it in your heart to kill me.
       Euripides, *Iphigenia in Aulis* 1220–25, 1231–32 (tr. Walker)

95   **sublāta**: perfect passive participle from **tollō, tollere, sustulī, sublātus**.

        virum: = **virōrum**.

        tremibundus, -a, -um, *trembling.*

96   **dēdūcō, dēdūcere, dēdūxī, dēductus**, *to escort, lead away.*

        dēductast: = **dēducta est. Dēdūcō** is the verb customarily used to describe the escort of a bride from her house to the groom's house.

        sollemnis, -is, -e, *formal, ceremonial, solemn.*

        sollemnī mōre sacrōrum perfectō: ablative absolute.

97   **clārus, -a, -um**: here, *clear-sounding, resounding, loud.*

        comitō, -āre, -āvī, -ātus, *to accompany.*

        Hymenaeus, -ī, m., *wedding song.* For examples see Catullus' poems 61 and 62.

98   **casta incestē**: note the marked antithesis.

        incestē, adv., *impurely.*

        nūbendī: genitive gerund.

99   **hostia, -ae**, f., *victim.*

        hostia: the position at the beginning of the line emphasizes the jarring contrast with **nūbendī tempore in ipsō** at the previous line's end.

        concideret: the **ut** of line 96 governs this purpose clause. By juxtaposing the negative clause (**non ut**, 96) with the positive purpose clause, Lucretius effectively contrasts Iphigenia's expectations and the horrific reality.

        mactātus, -ūs, m., *sacrificial slaying, slaughter.*

        maesta: nominative singular feminine with **hostia**.

100   **exitus, -ūs**, m., *departure.*

        classis, classis, f., *fleet.*

        faustus, -a, -um, *fortunate, of good omen, favorable.*

        fēlīx faustusque: this phrase is deeply ironic in the context of human sacrifice.

101   **Tantum . . . malōrum**: a partitive genitive, *so much evil.* This line, perhaps the most famous in Lucretius, summarizes his argument and points out the significance of the myth.

        suādeō, suādēre, suāsī, suāsus, *to urge, induce.*

        suādēre: the *u* is consonantal and so does not scan.

95 Nam sublāta virum manibus tremibundaque ad ārās
96 dēductast, nōn ut sollemnī mōre sacrōrum
97 perfectō posset clārō comitārī Hymenaeō,
98 sed casta incestē nūbendī tempore in ipsō
99 hostia concideret mactātū maesta parentis,
100 exitus ut classī fēlīx faustusque darētur.
101 Tantum rēligiō potuit suādēre malōrum.

CS Discussion Questions

1. What imagery does Lucretius interweave with the sacrifice? (95–100)

2. How does Lucretius use alliteration in this passage?

Her supplications and her cries of father
were nothing, nor the child's lamentation
to kings passioned for battle.
Her father prayed, called to his men to lift her
with strength of hand swept in her robes aloft
and prone above the altar, as you might lift
a goat for sacrifice.
    Aeschylus, *Agamemnon* 227–34 (tr. Lattimore)

102   **tūtemet**: a very emphatic **tū**, addressed here to Memmius as well as his reader; *you yourself.*
     Tūtemet ā nōbīs: note the juxtaposition of the pronouns and the displacement of **nōbīs** from **dēscīscere** (103).
   quīvīs, quaevīs, quodvīs, *any (one/thing) you like.*
   vātēs, vātis, m., *prophet, seer.*
     vātum: genitive with **terriloquīs . . . dictīs** (103).

103   **terriloquus, -a, -um**, *fear-speaking, fear-inspiring.*
   dēscīscō, dēscīscere, dēscīvī, dēscītus, *to defect, revolt, desert.*

104   **quippe**, adv., *surely, indeed.*
   etenim, conj., *for.*
   quam: exclamatory, *how.*
     quam multa: with **somnia** (105).
   tibī: the final *i* is long by diastole. Lucretius sometimes changes the quantity of syllabes for metrical convenience.
   fingō, fingere, fīnxī, fictus, *to invent, devise, imagine.*
   possunt: supply **vātēs** as subject.

105   **quae**: introducing a relative clause of characteristic.
   ratiōnēs: here, *principles.*
   vertere: here, *to overturn.*

106   **turbō, -āre, -āvī, -ātus**, *to confuse, disturb, alarm.*

107   **meritō**, adv., *deservedly, with reason.*
   vidērent: imperfect subjunctive in a present contrary-to-fact condition, a frequent conditional construction in Lucretius.
   fīnem: here feminine in gender.

108   **aerumna, -ae**, f., *trouble, affliction.*
     aerumnārum: genitive with **fīnem** (107).

109   **rēligiōnibus**: here, *religious fears.*
   minae, -ārum, f., *threats, menaces.*
   obsistere: + dative.

110   **restō, restāre, restitī**, *to stand firm in opposition; to resist.*
     restandī: gerund, genitive.
   facultās, facultātis, f., *power, ability.*

111   **timendum**: understand **est**; impersonal use of the gerund as a verb governing a direct object, *one must fear. . . .*

112   **ignōrō, -āre, -āvī, -ātus**, *not to know, to be ignorant of.*
     Ignōrātur: impersonal, *it is not known*, i.e., *men do not know.*
   animāī: archaic genitive singular.

113   **nāta sit**: supply **utrum**, also understand **cum corpore**. Here Lucretius gives alternative views of the nature of the soul: (1) it develops with the body (**nāta sit cum corpore**), (2) it is inserted whole into the body.
   nāscentibus: supply **nōbīs**.
   īnsinuō, -āre, -āvī, -ātus + dat., *to insert by sinuous means, to work one's way in.*

114   **et simul**: now Lucretius presents three views of the fate of the soul.
   intereō, interīre, interiī, interitūrus, *to perish, be destroyed.*
   dirimō, dirimere, dirēmī, dirēmptus, *to pull apart, break up.*
     dirēmpta: nominative singular feminine modifying **anima**, understood from line 112.

115   **tenebrae, -ārum**, f., *darkness.*
   Orcus, -ī, m., *Orcus*, god of the underworld (here a personification of death).
   lacūna, -ae, f., *hollow, chasm.*

116   **pecudēs**: supply **in**. Here Lucretius refers to the theory of metempsychosis, according to which the human soul at death can pass into an animal's body.
   dīvīnitus, adv., *by divine agency, power.*
   sē: the line ends with an emphatic monosyllable.

4. Beware of False Prophets

The seers, with threats of retribution after death, will try to frighten you from the investigation of nature. They can succeed only because man is ignorant of the soul's true nature.

102   Tūtemet ā nōbīs iam quōvīs tempore vātum
103   terriloquīs victus dictīs dēscīscere quaerēs.
104   Quippe etenim quam multa tibī iam fingere possunt
105   somnia quae vītae ratiōnēs vertere possint
106   fortūnāsque tuās omnīs turbāre timōre!
107   Et meritō. Nam sī certam fīnem esse vidērent
108   aerumnārum hominēs, aliquā ratiōne valērent
109   rēligiōnibus atque minīs obsistere vātum.
110   Nunc ratiō nūlla est restandī, nūlla facultās,
111   aeternās quoniam poenās in morte timendum.
112   Ignōrātur enim quae sit nātūra animāī,
113   nāta sit an contrā nāscentibus īnsinuētur,
114   et simul intereat nōbīscum morte dirēmpta
115   an tenebrās Orcī vīsat vāstāsque lacūnās
116   an pecudēs aliās dīvīnitus īnsinuet sē.

&#x08; **Discussion Questions**

1.   What motivates the seers to mislead men? (102–09)

2.   What sort of dreams do the seers invent? Why are they frightening?

3.   What is the **certam fīnem . . . aerumnārum**? (107–08)

4.   What is the effect of the anaphora **nūlla . . . nūlla** and the alliteration of *n* in line 110?

My own opinion at least is that the Romans have adopted this course of propagating religious awe for the sake of the common people. . . . As every multitude is fickle, full of lawless desires, unreasoned passion, and violent anger, the multitude must be held in by invisible terrors and suchlike pageantry.
     Polybius, *Universal History* 6.56.9 (tr. Paton)

Cotta the Academic: "There are those who have argued that all our beliefs about the gods have been fabricated by wise men for reasons of state, so that men whom reason could not persuade to be good citizens might be persuaded by religion. Have not these also totally destroyed the foundations of belief?"
     Cicero, *De natura deorum* 1.118–19 (tr. McGregor)

146   **Hunc . . . terrōrem . . . tenebrāsque**: direct object of **discutiant** (148).

    necessest: = **necesse est**, with the subjunctive clause (**discutiant**) as its subject.

147   **radius, -ī**, m., *ray*.

    lūcidus, -a, -um, *bright, shining*.

    tēlum, -ī, n., *spear, shaft, missile*. Here Lucretius metaphorically describes the sun's ability to defeat darkness.

148   **discutiō, discutere, discussī, discussus**, *to dispel, scatter*.

    speciēs, -ēī, f.: here, *outer appearance*.

      nātūrae speciēs ratiōque: *the outer appearance and inner workings of nature*. In Epicurean philosophy there is a close correspondence between external appearance and inner, atomic reality.

146   Hunc igitur terrōrem animī tenebrāsque necessest
147   nōn radiī sōlis neque lūcida tēla diēī
148   discutiant, sed nātūrae speciēs ratiōque.

❧ Discussion Question

1.   What effect does the placement of **animī** in line 146 create?

So in the very beginning we must persuade our citizens that the gods are the lords and rulers of all things, and that what is done, is done by their will and authority; that they are likewise great benefactors of man, observing the character of every individual, what he does, of what wrong he is guilty, and with what intentions and with what piety he fulfills his religious duties; and that they take note of the pious and the impious. For surely minds imbued with such ideas will not fail to form true and useful opinions.

    Cicero, *De legibus* 2.7.15 (tr. Keyes)

If we were not troubled by our suspicions of the phenomena of the sky and about death, fearing that it concerns us, and also by our failure to grasp the limits of pains and desires, we should have no need of natural science.

    Epicurus, *Principal Doctrines* 11 (tr. Bailey)

A man cannot dispel his fear about the most important matters if he does not know what is the nature of the universe but suspects the truth of some mythical story. So that without natural science it is not possible to attain our pleasures unalloyed.

    Epicurus, *Principal Doctrines* 12 (tr. Bailey)

149   **prīncipium, -ī**, n., *first principle.*

        cuius: referring to the hendiadys **nātūrae speciēs ratiōque** of line 148, with emphasis on **ratiō**; **cuius** scans as a monosyllable by synizesis.

        hinc, adv., *from here,* i.e., from the first principle, which is given in line 150.

        nōbīs: ethical dative, *for us.*

        exōrdium, -ī, n., *starting point, beginning.*

150   **nūllam rem . . .**: the principle is expressed as an indirect statement. The heavily spondaic line adds emphasis. Additionally, the phrasing of the principle within one metric line increases its impact, since the reader can easily remember it.

        nīlum, -ī, n., a contraction of **nihilum**, *nothing.*

        gignō, gignere, genuī, genitus, *to create.*

        umquam: the bisyllabic ending of the line stresses the word.

151   **quippe**, adv., *surely, indeed.*

        formīdō, formīdinis, f., *fear.*

        mortālīs: accusative plural as substantive, *mortal men.*

        continet: here, *constrains, dominates.*

152   **multa**: accusative plural neuter; supply **opera**, which is found attracted into the genitive case in the following relative clause (153). **Multa (opera)** is the subject of the indirect statement governed by **tuentur**.

        tueor, tuērī, tuitus sum, *to see, observe.*

        tuentur: supply **mortālēs** as subject.

154   **nūmen, nūminis**, n. *divine power, will.*

        dīvīnō nūmine: the adjective may seem redundant but is instead emphatic, and the phrase may mean *by the power of the gods.* The phrase contrasts with **nūllā ratiōne** (153); when men can find no rational explanation for a phenomenon, they attribute it to the gods.

155   **Quās ob rēs**: the preposition is displaced (anastrophe); *because of which things; wherefore.*

        vīderimus: future perfect.

156   **quod sequimur**: i.e., our goal = the understanding of the universe; direct object of **perspiciēmus** (157).

157   **perspiciō, perspicere, perspexī, perspectus**, *to see clearly, thoroughly; to perceive.*

        perspiciēmus: this verb also introduces the following indirect questions: **unde queat. . .** and **quō quaeque modō. . . .** (158).

158   **quō**: take with **modō**.

        quaeque: Lucretius switches to the neuter plural, giving an equivalent to **quaeque rēs**.

        operā sine dīvum: again emphasizing that there is a rational explanation of events; the gods have no influence on seemingly mysterious phenomena.

159   **Nam sī dē nīlō fierent. . . .**: here Lucretius offers proof of the first principle in a present contrary-to-fact condition: he imagines what would happen if things did come from nothing.

        fierent: supply **rēs** as subject.

        omnibu': the suppression of the final *s* is an archaism, which Lucretius often employs for metrical convenience.

161   **prīmum**: introducing the first example of the consequences of something coming from nothing.

        hominēs: supply the potential subjunctive **possent** from the following clause and **orīrī** from the end of this line..

162   **squāmigerī, -ōrum** or **-um**, m. pl., *scale-bearing creatures, fish.*

        squāmigerum: genitive plural with **genus**.

        volucrīs: supply **possent**.

        ērumpō, ērumpere, ērūpī, ēruptus, *to burst forth/out.*

        caelō: ablative governed by the prepositional prefix **ē** of **ērumpere**.

5. First Principle: Nothing Comes from Nothing: First Proof

If men can understand that nothing comes from nothing, they will cease falsely to attribute the creation and control of the universe to gods. In his first proof Lucretius typically employs a contrary-to-fact argument to create a colorful *reductiō ad absurdum*. He imagines the consequences if the reverse of the principle were true: that something *could* arise from nothing. In subsequent proofs Lucretius discusses the limitations placed upon growth: things only grow at appropriate times and at fixed rates.

149   Prīncipium cuius hinc nōbīs exōrdia sūmet,
150   nūllam rem ē nīlō gignī dīvīnitus umquam.
151   Quippe ita formīdō mortālīs continet omnīs,
152   quod multa in terrīs fierī caelōque tuentur
153   quōrum operum causās nūllā ratiōne vidēre
154   possunt ac fierī dīvīnō nūmine rentur.
155   Quās ob rēs ubi vīderimus nīl posse creārī
156   dē nīlō, tum quod sequimur iam rēctius inde
157   perspiciēmus, et unde queat rēs quaeque creārī
158   et quō quaeque modō fīant operā sine dīvum.
159   Nam sī dē nīlō fierent, ex omnibu' rēbus
160   omne genus nāscī posset, nīl sēmine egēret.
161   Ē mare prīmum hominēs, ē terrā posset orīrī
162   squāmigerum genus et volucrēs ērumpere caelō;

⅓ Discussion Questions

1. Why does Lucretius include the adverb **dīvīnitus** in line 150?

2. Why did men believe that the gods were responsible for celestial phenomena? (151–54)

3. What is the effect of the oxymoronic image in lines 161–62?

Furthermore, we must believe that to discover accurately the cause of the most essential facts is the function of the science of nature, and that blessedness for us in the knowledge of celestial phenomena lies in this and in the understanding of the nature of the existences seen in these celestial phenomena, and of all else that is akin to the exact knowledge requisite for our happiness.

     Epicurus, *Epistle to Herodotus* 78 (tr. Bailey)

163   **armenta, -ōrum**, n. pl., *herds, cattle.*

          genus omne ferārum: in asyndeton with **armenta atque aliae pecudēs**.

164   **incertus, -a, -um** *not fixed, uncertain.*

          partus, -ūs, m., *birth.*

          cultus, -a, -um, *cultivated.*

          dēsertus, -a, -um, *deserted, uninhabited.*

              culta ac dēserta: supply **loca**.

165   **frūctus, -ūs**, m., *fruit.*

          arboribus: archaic use of dative for genitive of possession (see Introduction, Other Archa-isms, 4).

          cōnstō, cōnstāre, cōnstitī, *to remain constant, be fixed.*

              frūctūs īdem arboribus cōnstāre solērent: Lucretius now turns from animals to plants in examining the consequences of something coming from nothing.

166   **mūtō, -āre, -āvī, -ātus**, *to change.*

              mūtārentur: in the passive voice this verb often expresses an intransitive, active idea; here, *would change.*

          omnēs: nominative plural feminine; supply **arborēs**.

          omnia: Lucretius switches to the neuter (rather than the masculine with **frūctūs**), since it would cause unnecessary confusion if he had written **omnēs (arborēs) omnēs (frūctūs)**. The repetition of the **omn-** root is emphatic.

167   **Quippe**: beginning the explanation of why these results would ensue, *For.*

          ubi: here equivalent to **sī** in introducing another present contrary-to-fact idea.

          nōn: the emphatic position of the negative stresses the unreality of the proposition.

          genitālia corpora: see line 58, where Lucretius introduced his terms for the atoms.

168   **quī**: archaic ablative used as an interrogative, *how?*

          cōnsistere: here, *to remain fixed.*

          certa: the adjective, in the line-end position, displaced from its noun, should be taken closely with **cōnsistere**, *to remain fixed and certain.*

              quī posset māter rēbus cōnsistere certa: the line is completely spondaic, except for the usual fifth-foot dactyl. The heaviness of the line audibly stresses the fixity of natural production. Lines 164 and 166 are similarly spondaic.

169   **At nunc**: Lucretius turns to the true situation of nature; note that all the verbs are now indicative.

          sēminibus . . . certīs: ablative of source, *out of fixed seeds.*

          quia: the conjunction has been postponed.

          quaeque: nominative plural neuter.

          certīs: reinforcing the concept of the fixity of natural law.

170   **inde**: anticipating **ubi** in the next line.

          ēnāscor, ēnāscī, ēnātus sum, *to arise out of something by natural growth; to spring forth.*

              ēnāscitur: supply a subject (**quidque**) from **cuiusque** in line 171.

          ōrās in lūminis: a reworking of the formulaic phrase **in lūminis ōrās**, found in line 22.

171   **māteriēs**: a technical term in Lucretius (cf. 58), but used here with a word-play on **māter** (168), with which it is etymologically related. Lucretius enjoys this sort of **figūra etymologica**.

          īnsum, inesse, īnfuī, *to be present.*

172   **hāc rē**: ablative of means, *because of this fact, therefore.*

          nequeunt ex omnibus omnia gignī: here Lucretius paraphrases the first principle of line 150.

173   **quod certīs . . . facultās**: a final, heavily spondaic restatement of the fixed limits imposed on the growth of things.

          sēcrētus, -a, -um, *distinct, special.*

          certīs . . . sēcrēta: another instance of word-play with *cert-* and *-cret-*.

163	armenta atque aliae pecudēs, genus omne ferārum,
164	incertō partū culta ac dēserta tenērent.
165	Nec frūctūs īdem arboribus cōnstāre solērent,
166	sed mūtārentur, ferre omnēs omnia possent.
167	Quippe ubi nōn essent genitālia corpora cuique,
168	quī posset māter rēbus cōnsistere certa?
169	At nunc sēminibus quia certīs quaeque creantur,
170	inde ēnāscitur atque ōrās in lūminis exit,
171	māteriēs ubi inest cuiusque et corpora prīma;
172	atque hāc rē nequeunt ex omnibus omnia gignī,
173	quod certīs in rēbus inest sēcrēta facultās.

⠶ Discussion Questions

1. Is Lucretius' contrary-to-fact argumentation convincing? (159–66)

2. In this passage Lucretius uses the phrases **genitālia corpora** (167), **sēminibus certīs** (169), and **corpora prīma** (171). To what is he referring?

Modern views of creation and nothingness:

[Describing the "Standard Model" of creation]: In the beginning there was an explosion . . . which occurred simultaneously everywhere, filling all space from the beginning, with every particle of matter rushing apart from every other particle.
    Steven Weinberg, *The First Three Minutes* (1977), 2

These particles—electrons, positrons, neutrinos, photons—were continually being created out of pure energy, and then after short lives being annihilated again. Their number was not preordained, but fixed instead by a balance between processes of creation and annihilation.
    Steven Weinberg, *The First Three Minutes* (1977), 4

One bewildering outcome of quantum theory has led some scientists to speculate that the entire universe, including the time in which it exists, may have been created by a spontaneous quantum fluctuation—a "twitch" in the nothingness that preceded it. Could a twitch in the opposite direction convert the universe back into non-existence?
    Malcom W. Browne, "Reality: A Grand Illusion?," *New York Times*, February 26, 1986

[The anthropic principle] operates in the realm of alternative realities, asking what the universe would have been like had some feature of reality been different, and whether life could have been possible in such circumstances. If the answer is no, we can be sure that feature could not have been other than it is.
    George Greenstein, *The Symbiotic Universe* (1988), 48.

215 **accēdō, accēdere, accessī, accessūrus**, *to go/come to, approach.*
　　Hūc accēdit: a formulaic phrase of transition, *it comes to this, here it follows, (there is) added to his that . . .*, introducing an additional argument.
　utī: = **ut**.
　sua: referring to **quidque**, the object.

216 **dissoluō, dissoluere, dissoluī, dissolūtus**, *to break up, dissolve.*
　　dissoluat: the u is vocalic for metrical reasons, but see later **exsolvere** (220).
　interimō, interimere, interēmī, interēmptus, *to destroy.*
　rēs: monosyllabic line ending.

217 **Nam sī quid mortāle. . . .**: first proof. Lucretius begins with his typical contrary-to-fact proof: imagine what the consequences would be if the doctrine were *not* true: things would literally vanish from our sight. Note the heavily spondaic meter.
　quid: = **aliquid**, as usual after **sī, nisi**, etc.

218 **rēs**: Lucretius again switches from the neuter gender (**quidque**) to the word **rēs**.
　repente, adv., *suddenly.*
　ērepta: from **ēripiō, ēripere**; take closely with **ex oculīs**.
　perīret: imperfect subjunctive of **pereō, perīre**.

219 **foret**: alternative form of **esset**, imperfect subjunctive of **sum, esse**.
　ūsus, -ūs, m., + abl. + form of **sum**, *to need, be necessary.*
　　Nullā vī foret ūsus, *no force would be necessary.*
　quae: introducing relative clause of characteristic.
　partibus: dative with **discidium**, *dissolution for the parts.*
　eius: referring to **rēs quaeque** (218).

220 **discidium, -ī**, n., *separation, sundering, dissolution.*
　parere: from **pario**, *to give birth to, create*; an ironic oxymoron here with **discidium**.
　nexus, -ūs, m., *bond, fastening, intertwining.*
　exsolvō, exsolvere, exsoluī, exsolūtus, *to unloosen, release, unravel.*

221 **Quod**: here *Whereas*; cf. line 82, **quod contrā**.
　aeternō . . . cōnstant sēmine: **aeternō** and **sēmine** frame the verb **cōnstant**.
　sēmine: here *matter*; ablative of source.

222 **obeō, obīre, obiī, obitus**, *to meet, encounter, come up against.*
　quae: introducing a compound relative clause of characteristic.
　rēs: accusative plural, here referring to bodies compounded from atoms.
　dīverberō, -āre, -āvī, -ātus, *to cause to part by hitting; to cleave, split.*
　ictus, -ūs, m., *blow.*

223 **intus**, adv., *within, inside.*
　　intus: amplified by the prepositional phrase **per inānia**.
　penetrō, -āre, -āvī, -ātus, *to penetrate.*
　ināne, inānis, n., *empty space, void*; a key word for Lucretius, which he introduces for the first time here. He will describe the necessity for and characteristics of void in 329ff.

224 **nūllius**: genitive singular; the negative is in an emphatic position at the line-beginning.
　exitium: accusative singular.
　vidērī: a true passive infinitive, *to be seen.*

225 **Praetereā quaecumque. . . .**: beginning the second proof, which is phrased as a question. If matter is completely destroyed, how do we explain the continuing fertility of nature?
　quīcumque, quaecumque, quodcumque, *whoever, whatever, whichever.*
　　quaecumque: accusative plural neuter, *whatever parts.*
　vetustās, vetustātis, f., *old age.*
　āmoveō, āmovēre, āmōvī, āmōtus, *to remove.*
　aetās, aetātis, f., *time, age.*

226 **penitus**, adv., *from within, deeply.*
　perimit: the subject is **aetās**, its direct object , the phrase **quaecumque . . . aetās**, line 225.
　cōnsūmō, cōnsūmere, cōnsūmpsī, cōnsūmptus, *to destroy, consume, reduce to nothing.*
　　cōnsūmēns: modifying **aetās**.

6. Second Principle: Nothing Returns to Nothing

When something dies, nature dissolves it into eternal first-bodies, which she then re-uses to create other things. Lucretius again proves his point by contrary-to-fact argumentation. Two proofs are included here.

215   Hūc accēdit utī quidque in sua corpora rūrsum
216   dissoluat nātūra neque ad nīlum interimat rēs.
217   Nam sī quid mortāle ē cūnctīs partibus esset,
218   ex oculīs rēs quaeque repente ērepta perīret.
219   Nūllā vī foret ūsus enim quae partibus eius
220   discidium parere et nexūs exsolvere posset.
221   Quod nunc, aeternō quia cōnstant sēmine quaeque,
222   dōnec vīs obiit quae rēs dīverberet ictū
223   aut intus penetret per inānia dissoluatque,
224   nūllius exitium patitur nātūra vidērī.
225   Praetereā quaecumque vetustāte āmovet aetās,
226   sī penitus perimit cōnsūmēns māteriem omnem

␣ Discussion Questions

1.   In lines 219–20 what are the compound bodies to which Lucretius refers? What would we call them?

2.   What are the methods by which something can be dissolved into its parts?

Fools! — for they have no long-sighted thoughts, since they imagine that what previously did not exist comes into being, or that a thing dies and is utterly destroyed.
    Empedocles, *On Nature* 11 (tr. Freeman)

All these [Elements] are equal and of the same age in their creation . . . and besides these, nothing else comes into being, nor does anything cease. For if they had been perishing continuously, they would be no more; and what could increase the Whole? And whence could it have come? In what direction could it perish, since nothing is empty of these things?
    Empedocles, *Fragment* 17 (tr. Freeman)

First of all, . . . nothing is created out of that which does not exist: for if it were, everything would be created out of everything with no need for seeds. And again, if that which disappears were destroyed into that which did not exist, all things would have perished, since that into which they were dissolved would not exist. Furthermore, the universe always was such as it is now, and always will be the same. For there is nothing into which it changes: for outside the universe there is nothing which could come into it and bring about the change.
    Epicurus, *Epistle to Herodotus* 38–39 (tr. Bailey)

227   **animālis, -is, -e**, *living, live; of a living creature, animal.*

        genus generātim: note the effective etymological repetition.

        in lūmina vītae: a paraphrase of the formula **in lūminis ōrās** (22, 170).

228   **reddūcit**: = **redūcit**. Lucretius use the archaic doubled *d* for metrical reasons. So also
        redductum.

        Venus: the subject of the clause is placed in an unusual final position. Venus here represents
        the creative power of the universe, as in the proem to Book 1.

        redductum: modifying **genus** (227) and acting as direct object of **alit** and **auget** (229).

        daedala tellūs: the phrase is repeated from line 7. Once Venus has created living things, the
        earth is responsible for their nourishment, hence the new subject **daedala tellūs**.

229   **unde alit atque auget**: for similar phrasing see line 56: **unde nātūra . . . auctet alatque**.

        generātim: take with **pābula praebēns**. By repeating this word from line 227, Lucretius
        emphasizes the richness of **daedala tellūs**, which offers food individually suitable for each
        species.

        pābula: here, *food.*

232   **Omnia**: neuter plural accusative, object of **cōnsūmpse** (233).

        dēbet: the subject is the hendiadys **infīnīta aetās . . . anteācta diēsque** (233), which is under-
        stood as a singular concept.

        mortālī corpore: ablative of description.

233   **īnfīnītus, -a, -um**, *limitless, infinite.*

        īnfīnīta aetās . . . anteācta diēsque: hendiadys, *infinite time of days gone by.* Note also that
        the heavily spondaic line drags, almost as if to replicate the slow passage of time.

        cōnsūmpse: syncopated perfect infinitive = **cōnsūmpsisse**.

        anteāctus, -a, -um, *past, gone before.*

        anteācta: synizesis; the two successive vowels in the interior of a word scan as one long
        syllable. The same synizesis is found in line 234.

        diēs: here feminine.

234   **Quod**: here, *whereas.*

        spatium, -ī, n., *time, period.*

        spatiō atque anteāctā aetāte: another hendiadys, similar to that in the previous line.

        fuēre: alternate third plural perfect = **fuērunt**. The subject, the antecedent for **quibus** in the
        next line, has been ellipsed; supply **haec corpora**.

           Quod sī . . . fuēre: a line full of elisions—four in all!

235   **summa, -ae**, f., *sum, whole.*

          haec rērum . . . summa: *this sum of things, our world.*

        refecta: predicative; here referring to its present state, which has been created from the matter
        reused from previously existing states.

236   **immortālī . . . nātūrā**: ablative of description contrasting with **mortālī corpore** (232).

        praeditus, -a, -um + abl., *endowed with, possessing.*

        certē: the line-end position and the bi-syllabic ending are emphatic.

          immortālī . . . certē: the almost exclusively spondaic line again mirrors the slowness of
          eternity.

227 unde animāle genus generātim in lūmina vītae
228 reddūcit Venus, aut redductum daedala tellūs
229 unde alit atque auget generātim pābula praebēns?
232 Omnia enim dēbet, mortālī corpore quae sunt,
233 īnfīnīta aetās cōnsūmpse anteācta diēsque.
234 Quod sī in eō spatiō atque anteāctā aetāte fuēre
235 ē quibus haec rērum cōnsistit summa refecta,
236 immortālī sunt nātūrā praedita certē.

❧ Discussion Question

1.   Why does Lucretius believe the primary substance must be immortal?

We may lay it down as an incontestible axiom that, in all the operations of art and nature, nothing is created; an equal quantity of matter exists both before and after the experiment; the quality and quantity of the elements remain precisely the same and nothing takes place beyond changes and modifications in the combination of elements.

Antoine Lavoisier, *Elements of Chemistry* (1789), Part I, Ch. 13 (tr. Kerr)

Until Einstein, it was thought that Mass was conserved. . . . Then along comes $E=mc^2$. Mass is now considered a form of energy, and it is ENERGY which is conserved in toto. . . . For the most part, mass is conserved as far as we can measure it. But in our heart of hearts, we physicists know that mass is just a particular form of energy, available to be changed into other forms of energy under the right conditions.

Matthew Deady, Professor of Physics, Bard College, personal communication

250   **postrēmō**, adv., *finally.*

         pereunt: here, *vanish, i.e., seem to disappear.*

         aether, aetheris, m., *ether, sky.*

251   **gremium, -ī**, n., *lap.*

         praecipitō, -āre, -āvī, -ātus, *to hurl.*

           praecipitāvit: a violent image for precipitation; an unusual pentasyllabic line-ending.

252   **nitidus, -a, -um**, *bright, shining, gleaming.*

           nitidae: here connoting the gleam or sheen of healthy crops.

         frūgēs, frūgum, f. pl., *produce, crops, fruit.*

         virēscō, virēscere, *to become green/verdant.*

253   **arboribus**: archaic use of dative of possession for genitive.

         crēscō, crēscere, crēvī, crētūrus, *to grow.*

         ipsae: modifying **arborēs**, understood as the subject of the two verbs **crēscunt** and **gravantur**.

         fētus, -ūs, m., *fruit, produce.*

         gravō, -āre, -āvī, -ātus, *to make heavy, weigh down.*

254   **hinc**: the anaphora of **hinc** here and at the beginning of lines 255 and 257 as well as in the middle of 259 reinforces Lucretius' point: that the fertility of earth results from the invisible interaction of rain with earth. This example acts as an introduction to the next section, in which Lucretius proves the existence of invisible particles.

         porrō, adv., *moreover.* A very frequent adverb in Lucretius, which he uses to tie his arguments together.

         genus: is modified by **nostrum** and then has the genitive **ferārum** dependent upon it.

255   **urbīs**: accusative plural.

         flōreō, flōrēre, flōruī, *to flourish, blossom.*

         laetās urbīs puerīs flōrēre: a vivid metaphor: the cities bloom with children.

         vidēmus: governing two indirect statements: **urbīs . . . flōrēre** and **frondiferās . . . canere . . . silvās** (256).

256   **frondiferās**: Lucretius has used the same compound adjective before in the context of birds: **frondiferāsque domōs avium** (18).

           frondiferāsque novīs avibus . . . silvās: embedded word order; the birds are contained within the forest.

         canere: the descriptive word is transferred: the forests are singing rather than the birds!

257   **fessus, -a, -um**, *tired, weary.*

         pecudēs pinguī per pābula: strong alliteration.

         pinguī: substantive, *with the richness*; ablative of means with **fessae**.

         per pābula laeta: a lively formulaic phrase; cf. 14.

258   **corpora**: accusative plural neuter.

         candēns, candentis, *gleaming white.*

         lacteus, -a, -um, *milky, of milk.*

         ūmor, ūmōris, m., *moisture, liquid.*

           candēns lacteus ūmor: an unusual double modifier, although **lacteus ūmor** is really no more than a rephrasing of **ūmor lactis**.

259   **ūber, ūberis**, n., *udder.*

         mānat: from **mānō, -āre**, *to drip.*

         distentus, -a, -um, *distended, swollen.*

           ūberibus distentīs: ablative of source, *from swollen udders.*

         prōlēs, prōlis, f., *offspring.*

7. Father Rain and Mother Earth

Lucretius gives an illustration of his second doctrine by drawing attention to a readily observable natural phenomenon: raindrops seem to disappear into the ground, but in fact their particles are incorporated into living creatures. Nature recycles matter. In his description Lucretius relies on the mythological picture of a creative union between Father Sky and Mother Earth.

250 Postrēmō pereunt imbrēs, ubi eōs pater aether
251 in gremium mātris terrāī praecipitāvit;
252 at nitidae surgunt frūgēs rāmīque virēscunt
253 arboribus, crēscunt ipsae fētūque gravantur;
254 hinc alitur porrō nostrum genus atque ferārum,
255 hinc laetās urbīs puerīs flōrēre vidēmus
256 frondiferāsque novīs avibus canere undique silvās;
257 hinc fessae pecudēs pinguī per pābula laeta
258 corpora dēpōnunt et candēns lacteus ūmor
259 ūberibus mānat distentīs; hinc nova prōlēs

○ Discussion Questions

1. What alliterative effects do you find in lines 250–51?

2. What season is described in this passage? Does the description remind you of an earlier passage?

The holy heaven yearns to wound the earth
And yearning seizes earth to mate in wedlock.
From the bed-loving heaven falls the rain
And makes the earth swell. She brings forth for men
The food sheep feed on and Demeter's life;
And from this drenching wedlock is fulfilled
The forests' bloom. Of this I [Aphrodite] am the cause.
    Aeschylus, *Fragment* 25 (from *Danaids*), ed. Smyth

The Heaven, the Father almighty, comes down in fruitful showers into the lap of his joyous spouse, and his might, with her mighty frame commingling, nurtures all growth. Then pathless copses ring with birds melodious, and in things abounds soft moisture.
    Vergil, *Georgics* 2.325–31 (tr. Fairclough)

260   **artus, -ūs**, m., *limb.*
> **artubus**: archaic spelling for **artibus**; ablative of description.

> **tener, tenera, tenerum**, *tender, delicate.*

> **lascīvus, -a, -um**, *playful, frisky, frolicsome.*
>> **lascīva**: modifying **prōlēs**; its placement between **tenerās** and **per herbās** indicates that the new shoots of spring have occasioned this playfulness.

> **herba, -ae**, f., *grass.*

261   **lac, lactis**, n., *milk.*
> **lacte merō**: a wonderful image; the young animals are almost intoxicated by the pure, "neat" milk they have drunk.

> **mentīs . . . novellās**: accusative of respect or Greek accusative, indicating the respect in which they are **perculsa**.

> **percellō, percellere, perculī, perculsus**, *to strike.*
>> **perculsa**: modifying **prōlēs** (258).

> **novellus, -a, -um** [diminutive], *young little, new little.*

> **lūdit lacte merō mentīs perculsa novellās**: an interesting line with alliteration of *l* and *m*; also the line begins with four bisyllabic words.

262   **Haud igitur penitus pereunt**: Lucretius restates his main point: things do not perish into nothing.

> **penitus pereunt**: the alliteration is emphatic and echoes the similar phrase **penitus perimit** in his earlier discussion (226).

> **videntur**: a true passive, *are seen.*

263   **quandō**, adv., *since.*
> **alid**: = **aliud**, accusative singular neuter.

264   **patitur**: here, *allows.*

> **adiuvō, adiuvāre, adiūvī, adiūtus**, *to aid, help, assist.*
>> **adiūta**: modifying **nātūra**.

> **aliēnus, -a, -um**, *of another, another's.*

260 artubus īnfirmīs tenerās lascīva per herbās

261 lūdit lacte merō mentīs perculsa novellās.

262 Haud igitur penitus pereunt quaecumque videntur,

263 quandō alid ex aliō reficit nātūra nec ūllam

264 rem gignī patitur nisi morte adiūta aliēnā.

As is the generation of leaves, so is that of humanity.
The wind scatters the leaves on the ground, but the live timber
burgeons with leaves again in the season of spring returning.
So one generation of men will grow while another dies.
     Glaukos in Homer's *Iliad* 6.146–50 (tr. Lattimore)

265 **Nunc age, rēs ... nīl revocārī** (266): Lucretius summarizes his first two principles before
continuing with the proof of the existence of invisible particles.
  nunc age: a common phrase in Lucretius, which demands the reader's attention.
rēs: Lucretius uses **rēs** as the equivalent of a neuter plural (see 1.56–57 for this equivalence).
docuī: Lucretius reminds us that he is the teacher by using the first person singular. Such a
personal voice is very rare in other epic poets.

266 **item**, adv., *likewise, similarly, in turn*.
genitās: modifying **rēs** (265), *things once created*.

267 **quā forte**: **forte** is a substantive so can be modified, *by any chance*.
coeptō, -āre, -āvī, -ātus, *to begin*.
diffīdō, diffīdere, diffīsus sum+ dat., *to lack confidence* (in), *distrust*.
dictīs: supply **meīs**.

268 **quod ... cernī**: stating why the reader might distrust Lucretius' words: because the fundamental particles are invisible.
oculīs: ablative of means.
cernō, cernere, crēvī, crētus, *to see, discern, perceive*.

269 **accipe**: here, *take, learn about*; the imperative is the main verb of this rather complex sentence,
taking **corpora** as its direct object.
quae: accusative plural neuter; its antecedent is **corpora**, which is the direct object of **accipe**.
tūte: emphatic form of **tū** (see also **tūtemet**, 102); subject of **confiteāre**.
necessest: the same construction as in lines 146–48; the impersonal verb has a subjunctive
clause as its subject. Reorder: **quae necessest tūte confiteāre esse in rēbus**, *which you must
confess exist in things*.

270 **cōnfiteor, cōnfitērī, cōnfessus sum**, *to confess, admit*.
  cōnfiteāre: alternative second person singular passive = **cōnfiteāris**, which would scan
differently.

271 **Prīncipiō = Prīmum**.
  Prīncipiō ventī vīs: Lucretius first uses the powerful effects of the wind to prove that it
consists of invisible particles. He envisions a storm at sea (271–72), then in the mountains
(273–75).
ventī vīs verberat: wonderful onomatopoeic alliteration replicating the whistling of the wind.
incitus, -a, -um, *set in rapid/violent motion, roused, stirred up*.

272 **ruō, ruere, ruī**, *to drive headlong, ruin, destroy*.
differō, differre, distulī, dīlātus, *to scatter, disperse*.

273 **percurrō, percurrere, per(cu)currī, percursus**, *to rush over/through*.
turbō, turbinis, m., *whirl, whirlwind, tornado*.

274 **sternō, sternere, strāvī, strātus**, *to strew*.
suprēmus, -a, -um, *highest, top (of)*.

275 **silvifragus, -a, -um**, *forest-cracking*; apparently a Lucretian invention, found only here. The
reader will by now have noticed that Lucretius is innovative in his language and particularly likes to coin compounds, usually adjectives, in which the first three syllables form a
dactyl. See **nāviger** (3), **frūgiferēns** (3), **frondifer** (18, 256), and **squāmiger** (162). In most
instances these compounds occur at the beginning of the line.
flābra, -ōrum, n. pl., *blasts*.
  silvifragīs vexat flābrīs: onomatopoeia replicating the whistling and cracking of the wind.
perfurō, perfurere, *to rage, storm*.

276 **fremitus, -ūs**, m., *roar*.
saeviō, saevīre, saeviī, saevītūrus, *to rage*.
mināx, minācis, *menacing, threatening*.
  minācī murmure: compare **minitantī murmure** (68–69) for similar alliteration.

8. Invisible Particles Exist

Lucretius overcomes disbelief in invisible particles (atoms) by drawing an analogy between the actions and effects of wind, which is invisible, and water, which is clearly visible.

265   Nunc age, rēs quoniam docuī nōn posse creārī
266   dē nīlō neque item genitās ad nīl revocārī,
267   nē quā forte tamen coeptēs diffīdere dictīs,
268   quod nequeunt oculīs rērum prīmōrdia cernī,
269   accipe praetereā quae corpora tūte necessest
270   cōnfiteāre esse in rēbus nec posse vidērī.
271   Prīncipiō ventī vīs verberat incita pontum
272   ingentīsque ruit nāvīs et nūbila differt,
273   interdum rapidō percurrēns turbine campōs
274   arboribus magnīs sternit montīsque suprēmōs
275   silvifragīs vexat flābrīs: ita perfurit ācrī
276   cum fremitū saevitque mināci murmure ventus.

☙ Discussion Questions

1.   Why else, other than because of the invisibility of the **prīmōrdia**, might Lucretius fear that the reader will distrust his belief that nothing comes from or returns to nothing? (267)

2.   How does the imagery of lines 271–76 contrast with that of the preceding passage 7?

3.   What would Lucretius think now that atoms have been seen by the scanning-tunneling microscope invented in 1981? (For pictures, see James Trefil, "Seeing Atoms," *Discovery*, June 1990, 55–60.)

Describing the existence of "dark matter" Trefil draws an analogy between its effects on other matter and that of hypothetically invisible water moving twigs in a stream:
> You would have to accept that there was something exerting force, something which you couldn't see directly, but the influence of which was manifest in the movement of twigs.
> James Trefil, "Dark Matter," *Smithsonian*, June 1993, 28

277   **Sunt**: in a very emphatic position at the beginning of the line and the sentence, emphasizing that these particles *do* exist.

     nīmīrum, adv., *without doubt, certainly.*

     caecus, -a, -um, *blind; unseen, invisible.*

279   **verrō, verrere, verrī, versūrus**, *to sweep.*

     vexantia: modifying **corpora caeca** (277).

     raptō, -āre, -āvī, -ātus, *to drag violently away; to sweep along.*

280   **nec ratiōne fluunt . . .**: Lucretius now makes the comparison between the actions of invisible wind and visible water.

     fluō, fluere, flūxī, flūxūrus, *to flow, stream.*

       fluunt: Lucretius begins his analogy by using a word normally applicable to water to describe the wind. For the subject understand **ventī**.

     strāgēs, strāgis, f., *destruction, devastation.*

     propāgō, -āre, -āvī, -ātus, *to produce, cause.*

       strāgemque propāgant: an oxymoron, similar to **discidium parere** (220).

281   **et**: here acting as a comparative, *than*, with **aliā** (280).

     mollis: ambiguous; could be genitive modifying **aquae** or nominative with **nātūra**, but probably applicable to both, especially in the context of periphrasis.

       mollis aquae . . . nātūra: a typical Lucretian periphrasis, **nātūra aquae = aqua**.

     repente: speed is a major point of comparison between the natures of wind (**subitō . . . turbine**, 279) and water.

282   **flūmen, flūminis**, n., *river, stream, flow.*

     abundāns, abundantis, *overflowing.*

       flūmine abundantī: ablative of manner.

     quam: antecedent **aquae** (281).

     largus, -a, -um, *plentiful, copious.*

     auget: the subject is **magnus dēcursus aquāī** (283).

283   **dēcursus, -ūs**, m., *descent, downward rush.*

284   **frāgmen, frāgminis**, n., *fragment, broken piece.*

     cōniciēns: modifying **nātūra aquae** (281), not **dēcursus**.

       frāgmina cōniciēns silvārum: reminding the reader of the actions of the wind described by **silvifragīs . . . flābrīs** (275).

     arbusta, -ōrum, n. pl., *trees, woods, orchards.*

     tōta: here, *whole, entire.*

295   **Quārē etiam atque etiam**: a very frequent and emphatic formula which Lucretius uses to introduce his conclusion.

     sunt ventī corpora caeca: note how Lucretius repeats his phrasing from line 277. Such repetition is an effective didactic technique.

296   **factīs et mōribus**: ablatives of respect with **aemula**.

     aemulus, -a, um + dat., *equal* (with), *comparable* (to), *rivaling.*

297   **apertus, -a, -um**, *open* (to view), *visible*; the opposite of **caeca** (277, 295).

       apertō corpore: ablative of description with **sunt**; cf. **mortālī corpore** (232), **immortālī nātūrā** (236).

277   Sunt igitur ventī nīmīrum corpora caeca
278   quae mare, quae terrās, quae dēnique nūbila caelī
279   verrunt ac subitō vexantia turbine raptant,
280   nec ratiōne fluunt aliā strāgemque propāgant
281   et cum mollis aquae fertur nātūra repente
282   flūmine abundantī, quam largīs imbribus auget
283   montibus ex altīs magnus dēcursus aquāī,
284   frāgmina cōniciēns silvārum arbustaque tōta.

                                    . . .

295   Quārē etiam atque etiam sunt ventī corpora caeca,
296   quandoquidem factīs et mōribus aemula magnīs
297   amnibus inveniuntur, apertō corpore quī sunt.

☙ Discussion Questions

1.   What is the effect of the anaphora of **quae** and the asyndeton in line 278?

2.   Why does Lucretius include the descriptive adjective **mollis** (281)? What actions of **mollis aquae . . . nātūra** are here detailed?

3.   What specific words and phrases connect the description of the actions of wind and water?

298   **Tum porrō**: a phrase, similar to the adverb **praetereā**, which Lucretius uses to introduce additional illustrations of his point, here the effects of invisible particles on the senses of smell, touch, and hearing.

    varius, -a, -um, *different, various, varied.*

    odor, odōris, m., *smell, odor.*

299   **nec tamen**: the phrase has an adversative effect, *and yet . . . not.*

    nārēs, nārium, f. pl., *nostrils, nose.*

    venientīs: modifying **odōrēs** (298).

    umquam: in its usual line-end position; cf. 150.

300   **aestus, -ūs**, m., *heat.* Almost always in the plural in Lucretius; translate as singular.

    tueor, tuērī, tuitus sum, *to see, observe.*

        tuimur: Lucretius here conjugates the verb in the third conjugation; see line 152 for a second conjugation form. Such variation of conjugation reflects the fluidity of the Latin language during Lucretius' lifetime.

    frīgus, frīgoris, n., *cold.*

        frīgora: the plural may be translated as singular, as was **aestūs**.

    quīmus: from **queō, quīre**.

301   **ūsūrpō, -āre, -āvī, -ātus**, here, *to grasp with the senses, perceive.*

    cernere: understand with **oculīs**.

    suēmus: syncopated perfect of **suēvimus**. Again the *u* is consonantal = *w*.

302   **quae**: accusative neuter plural; the neuter refers to the various sensations described above; accusative in an accusative and infinitive construction, subject of **necessest**, which before has taken a subjunctive (146, 269).

    corporeā . . . nātūrā (303): ablative of source or material.

    cōnstāre: *to exist, be formed.*

303   **sēnsus, -ūs**, m., *sensation, sense.*

        sēnsūs: accusative plural.

    impellō, impellere, impulī, impulsus, *to strike/beat against, stir.*

304   **Tangere enim et tangī, nisi corpus, nūlla potest rēs**: a succinct, one-line statement of a fundamental Epicurean principle: only material things can affect and be affected by other material objects. Epicurus, unlike some other philosophers, insisted on reliance on the material evidence of the senses. All knowledge ultimately derives from the senses.

    rēs: again Lucretius uses **rēs** for the neuter. Also, Lucretius has again placed the monosyllable **rēs** in the emphatic line-end position; cf. similarly **neque ad nīlum interimat rēs** (216).

305   **Dēnique**: here, *Furthermore,* introducing further examples of the hidden actions of invisible particles.

    flūctifragus, -a, -um, *wave-beaten.* The compound adjective, similar to **silvifragīs** in 275, is a vivid Lucretian invention.

306   **ūvēscō, ūvēscere**, *to become wet.*

    eaedem: nominative plural feminine of **īdem**; the letters *eae* scan as one long syllable by synizesis.

    dispandō, dispandere, dispānsus, *to spread out.*

    serēscō, serēscere, *to become dry.* Lucretius has apparently coined this word as an antonym for **ūvēscō**.

        dispānsae in sōle serēscunt: the sibilant alliteration reproduces the sizzling effect of the sun.

307   **persīdō, persīdere, persēdī**, *to seep through, penetrate.*

    persēderit: perfect subjunctive in indirect question with **quō pactō**.

    ūmor, ūmōris, m., *moisture, liquid.*

        ūmor aquāī: periphrasis.

9. Additional Proofs of Invisible Matter

Invisible particles are also responsible for sense perception, since, by a fundamental tenet of Epicurean philosophy, only something corporeal can affect a physical object. The acuity of Lucretius' observation is revealed in his description of commonplace occurrences that demonstrate the operations of invisible matter.

298	Tum porrō variōs rērum sentīmus odōrēs
299	nec tamen ad nārīs venientīs cernimus umquam,
300	nec calidōs aestūs tuimur nec frīgora quīmus
301	ūsūrpāre oculīs nec vōcēs cernere suēmus;
302	quae tamen omnia corporeā cōnstāre necessest
303	nātūrā, quoniam sēnsūs impellere possunt.
304	Tangere enim et tangī, nisi corpus, nūlla potest rēs.
305	Dēnique flūctifragō suspēnsae in lītore vestēs
306	ūvēscunt, eaedem dispānsae in sōle serēscunt.
307	At neque quō pactō persēderit ūmor aquāī
308	vīsumst nec rūrsum quō pactō fūgerit aestū.

ℭℨ Discussion Questions

1. Of what does Lucretius perceive heat and cold to be composed? (300)

2. How does Lucretius' conception of the operation of sense perception compare to the modern understanding?

We must suppose that smell too, just like hearing, could never bring about any sensation, unless there were certain particles carried off from the object of suitable size to stir this sense-organ, some of them in a manner disorderly and alien to it, others in a regular manner and akin in nature.
    Epicurus, *Epistle to Herodotus* 53 (tr. Bailey)

---

308   **vīsumst** := **vīsum est**; a true passive form with an indefinite subject, *is it seen*; governing the indirect question of the previous line as well as **quō pactō fūgerit aestū**.
      fūgerit: the subject is **ūmor aquāī**.
      aestū: ablative of means, *in the heat*.

309   **dispergō, dispergere, dispersī, dispersus**, *to scatter, disperse.*

311   **quīn**, adv., *but.*

      quīn etiam, idiom, *but also, furthermore;* introducing further examples.

   multīs sōlis redeuntibus annīs: ablative absolute.

   sōlis: genitive singular of **sōl, sōlis**, m.

   annus, -ī, m., *year;* here, *cycle.*

312   **ānulus, -ī**, m., *ring.*

   subter: here possibly, *inside.*

   tenuō, -āre, -āvī, -ātus, *to wear thin, diminish.*

   habendō: gerund in ablative of means, *by holding, wearing.*

313   **stīlicidium, -ī**, n., *dripping water.*

   cāsus, -ūs, m., *fall.*

   cavō, -āre, -āvī, -ātus, *to make hollow, to hollow out.*

   stīlicidī cāsus lapidem cavat: the alliteration of *c* and other hard consonants replicates the pinging sound of dripping water.

   uncus, -a, -um, *curved, hooked.*

      uncus: very displaced from its noun, **vōmer** (314).

   arātrum, -ī, n., *plow.*

314   **ferreus, -a, -um**, *made of iron, iron.*

   occultus, -a, -um, *invisible, secret.*

   dēcrēscō, dēcrēscere, dēcrēvī, dēcrētūrus, *to diminish, decrease.*

   vōmer, vōmeris, m., *plowshare.*

      uncus arātrī ferreus . . . vōmer: unusual phrase; the noun is modified by two adjectives (cf. **candēns lacteus ūmor**, 258), but also the position of **uncus** almost makes it a transferred epithet for **arātrī**, despite the difference in cases.

   arvum, -ī, n., *plowed field.*

315   **strātum, -ī**, n., *sheet, covering;* here, *pavement.*

      strāta . . . viārum: common periphrasis of neuter plural plus genitive, *paved streets.*

   iam: take closely with **cōnspicimus** (316). Reorder entire clause for translation: **iam cōnspicimus saxea strāta viārum dētrīta pedibus vulgī**. At Pompeii one can see paving stones hollowed by the constant press of feet as well as the rutting of roads by wagon wheels.

   vulgus, -ī, n., *crowd.*

   dēterō, dēterere, dētrīvī, dētrītus, *to wear away.*

316   **saxeus, -a, -um**, *made of stone, stony.* Roman roads were paved with large cobbles.

   tum: introducing the final example.

   propter: in anastrophe following the word it governs, **portās**.

   aēnus, -a, -um, *made of bronze, bronze.*

317   **signum, -ī**, n., *sign;* here, *statue.*

   ostendunt: a vivid image personifying the statues. Here they "show" their worn hands, almost in a gesture asking for pity. Roman statues often had their right hands outstretched and uplifted with the palms forward. For instance, see the Augustus of the Prima Porta.

   attenuō, -āre, -āvī, -ātus, *to wear away, diminish.*

      manūs dextrās . . . attenuārī saepe salūtantum tactū: perhaps travelers were giving high-fives to the statues! For a similar phenomenon, see the foot of the statue of St. Peter in the Vatican, which is very worn by the kissing of pilgrims.

309 In parvās igitur partīs dispergitur ūmor
310 quās oculī nūllā possunt ratiōne vidēre.
311 Quīn etiam multīs sōlis redeuntibus annīs
312 ānulus in digitō subter tenuātur habendō,
313 stīlicidī cāsus lapidem cavat, uncus arātrī
314 ferreus occultē dēcrēscit vōmer in arvīs,
315 strātaque iam vulgī pedibus dētrīta viārum
316 saxea cōnspicimus; tum portās propter aēna
317 signa manūs dextrās ostendunt attenuārī
318 saepe salūtantum tactū praeterque meantum.
319 Haec igitur minuī, cum sint dētrīta, vidēmus;
320 sed quae corpora dēcēdant in tempore quōque,
321 invida praeclūsit speciem nātūra videndī.

ℭ Discussion Questions

1. What terms do we use for the processes described in lines 311–18?

2. Can you think of other examples of the invisible processes of particles?

3. Consider what discoveries Lucretius might have made if he had had a microscope.

4. What would Lucretius think of particles such as photons with no mass or charge but that still affect our senses?

---

318 **salūtō, -āre, -āvī, -ātus**, *to greet.*
    tactus, -ūs, m., *touch.*
    praeter: here adverbial, *by*; in tmesis with **meantum** = *passers-by.*
    meō, -āre, -āvī, -ātūrus, *to pass, travel.*
      meantum: the usual genitive plural for Lucretius (instead of **meantium**, which would not scan in dactylic hexameter).
319 **Haec**: referring to all the previous examples of attrition: the ring, the hollowed stone, the plow, and the statues' hands.
    cum: *because.* We understand that they are diminished, because they have lost parts.
320 **dēcēdō, dēcēdere, dēcessī, dēcessūrus**, *to go away, depart.*
    dēcēdant: subjunctive in an indirect question which is dependent on the noun **speciem** (321), *the appearance (of) what bodies. . . .*
321 **invidus, -a, -um**, *envious, jealous, grudging.*
    invida . . . nātūra videndī: perhaps **invida** is a pun on **videndī**; sight is "un-seeing," blind.
    dēcēdō, dēcēdere, dēcessī, dēcessūrus, *to depart.*
    praeclūdō, praeclūdere, praeclūsī, praeclūsus, *to prevent, deny, shut out.*
    nātūra videndī: not simply another periphrasis. If the nature of our sight were different, we could see smaller things. Of course modern technology has accomplished this.

329 **corporeā**: with **nātūrā**, ablative of means.

stīpō, -āre, -āvī, -ātus, *to compress, pack tight.*

   stīpāta: predicative, *(held) tightly packed.*

330 **omnia**: nominative plural neuter as subject of clause, *all things.*

namque: **-que** here meaning *also* (in addition to the **prīmōrdia**).

est: the position of the verb is emphatic; Lucretius used the same technique to stress the existence of invisible particles (cf. **sunt**, 277).

ināne, inānis, n., *empty space, void.*

   namque est in rēbus ināne: heavily spondaic, which stresses the importance of Lucretius' point.

331 **Quod**: accusative singular neuter; its antecedent is the previous clause: the fact that void exists.

tibi: ethical dative with **ūtile**.

cognōsse: syncopated perfect infinitive = **cognōvisse**, *to know.*

   Quod . . . cognōsse: this infinitive phrase is the subject of **erit** and of **sinet** (332).

rēbus, here, *situations, connections.* Lucretius has no qualms about using **rēs** (and other words) with quite different meanings in successive lines, as here in contrast with **rēs**, *things*, in line 330. The two different meanings even follow the same preposition, **in**.

332 **errantem**: agreeing with an understood **tē**, an accusative and infinitive construction dependent on **sinet**.

dubitō, -āre, -āvī, -ātus, *to be in doubt; to hesitate.*

333 **summa, -ae**, f., *sum, whole.*

   summā rērum: indicating the whole universe; cf. 235 for the same usage.

diffīdō, diffīdere, diffīsus sum + dat., *to lack confidence (in), mistrust.*

   diffīdere dictīs: the phrase is repeated from line 267, where Lucretius expressed the same concern that his reader would not believe him.

334 **quāpropter**, adv., *because of which, therefore.*

intactus, -a, -um, *not touched, intangible.*

   intacta: in Epicurean theory only corporeal things can touch and be touched (cf. 304); therefore intangibility is an essential characteristic of void. It acts as the perfect non-interfering medium for the actions of the atoms.

vacāns, vacantis, *empty.*

   ināne vacānsque: both words are adjectival, with **ināne** in asyndeton with **intacta**; i.e., *intangible, void, and empty.*

335 **Quod**: the relative pronoun has been attracted from **locus** into the neuter case by the presence of **ināne**, Lucretius' favorite word for void.

   Quod sī nōn esset: once again Lucretius uses a contrary-to-fact argument to prove his point.

336 **rēs**: another use of this noun as equivalent to a neuter plural, *things.*

officium, -ī, n., *duty, function.*

corporis: genitive of possession.

exstō, exstāre, exstitī, *to be, exist.*

   quod corporis exstat, *which is of the body, belongs to the body.*

337 **officiō, officere, offēcī, offectus**, *to block the path, check, impede.*

   officere: Lucretius creates a word-play with **officium** in the previous line. This infinitive and **obstāre** are verbal nouns.

obstō, obstāre, obstitī, obstātūrus, *to stand in the way, obstruct, block.*

id: = **officium** (336), defined by **officere atque obstāre** (337).

   officere atque obstāre, id in omnī tempore adesset: the four elisions in the line, particularly the third elision, which crosses the caesura, make the line hard to pronounce and imitate the obstructive effect of body.

338 **omnibus**: supply **rēbus**. The importance of **omnibus** is enhanced by the enjambement.

haud igitur quicquam: Lucretius now reaches the conclusion to his conditional clause: what would happen if void did not exist.

10. The Existence of Void

The universe does not consist wholly of matter. Void is an equally important constituent. If void or empty space did not exist, motion would be impossible, since matter would be too densely packed. Here Lucretius refutes philosophers such as Aristotle, who believed that the universe consisted wholly of matter with no empty space.

329   Nec tamen undique corporeā stīpāta tenentur
330   omnia nātūrā; namque est in rēbus ināne.
331   Quod tibi cognōsse in multīs erit ūtile rēbus
332   nec sinet errantem dubitāre et quaerere semper
333   dē summā rērum et nostrīs diffīdere dictīs.
334   Quāpropter locus est intactus ināne vacānsque.
335   Quod sī nōn esset, nūllā ratiōne movērī
336   rēs possent; namque officium quod corporis exstat,
337   officere atque obstāre, id in omnī tempore adesset
338   omnibus; haud igitur quicquam prōcēdere posset,

---

cs   **Discussion Questions**

1.   A Rubik's cube has no empty square. Therefore how is it possible to change the positions of the small cubes?

2.   What adjectives does Lucretius use to describe the void?

3.   What is the effect of the repetition of the prefix **ob-** in **officium**, **officere**, and **obstāre** (336–37)?

Contrasting views on void:

The revolution of the All, since it comprehends them all, compresses them all . . . and thus it suffers no void place to be left.
      Plato, *Timaeus* 58a (tr. Bury)

Inasmuch as no void exists into which any of the moving bodies could enter.
      Plato, *Timaeus* 79b (tr. Bury)

A modern view:

The existence of atomic structure meant that [physical objects] and human beings, like Hamlet's "too solid flesh," consisted mostly of empty space. My thumb, in other words, is a void in which infinitessimal packages of energy whirl and vibrate giving a gross semblance of substance.
      Malcom W. Browne, "Reality: A Grand Illusion?," *New York Times*, February 6, 1980

339 **prīncipium, -ī**, n., here, *beginning;* governing **cēdendī**.

   cēdendī: genitive gerund, *of yielding*.

   rēs: another monosyllabic ending with this noun; see also line 216.

340 **At nunc**: Lucretius now turns to what he regards as the truth: we see movement everywhere.

   sublīmus, -a, -um, *high, lofty*.

   sublīma: here a substantive accusative plural neuter in a periphrasis with **caelī**, *lofty places of the sky, heights of heaven*.

341 **multa**: accusative neuter plural as subject of accusative and infinitive construction with **cernimus** (342).

   multa modīs multīs . . . movērī: strong alliteration. **Multa modīs multīs** recurs frequently. The repetition of the root **mult-** matches the many possibilities that Lucretius is describing. This richness is further reinforced by the phrase **variā ratiōne**.

342 **ante oculōs**: Lucretius appeals to the physical senses for direct evidence of his point.

   quae, sī nōn esset ināne: Lucretius returns to his contrary-to-fact argumentation, which here is a mixed present contrary-to-fact condition in the protasis (**sī** clause) and past contrary-to-fact in the apodosis (the conclusion).

343 **nōn tam . . . quam** (344), *not so much . . . as, not merely . . . but also*.

   sollicitus, -a, -um, *restless*.

   mōtus, -ūs, m., *motion*.

   prīvō, -āre, -āvī, -ātus + abl., *to deprive* (of.)

   sollicitō mōtū: the ablative is governed both by **prīvāta** and **carērent**; *deprived, they would lack restless motion*.

344 **quam**, comparative, *as*.

   genita: with **fuissent**, pluperfect passive subjunctive in past contrary-to-fact apodosis, *would have been born*.

   omnīnō, adv., *at all;* take closely with **nūllā ratiōne**, *in no way at all, not in any way*.

345 **quoniam**: the conjunction connecting the clauses has been considerably delayed.

   quiēsset: syncopated pluperfect subjunctive = **quiēvisset**; with **stīpāta**, *would have lain piled up at rest*.

339   prīncipium quoniam cēdendī nūlla daret rēs.
340   At nunc per maria ac terrās sublīmaque caelī
341   multa modīs multīs variā ratiōne movērī
342   cernimus ante oculōs, quae, sī nōn esset ināne,
343   nōn tam sollicitō mōtū prīvāta carērent
344   quam genita omnīnō nūllā ratiōne fuissent,
345   undique māteriēs quoniam stīpāta quiēsset.

❧ Discussion Question

1.   Would anything recognizable as a compound body exist if void did not exist?

More contrasting views on void:

Now the void is thought to be place in which there is nothing. (The reason for this is that people think that what is, is body, and that every body is in a place, and that void is a place in which there is no body; so that, if anywhere there is no body, then there is nothing there. Further, they think that every body is tangible, and that of such a kind is whatever has heaviness or lightness. Hence it results by syllogism that that is void, in which there is nothing heavy or light). . . . But it is absurd, if a point is to be void; for [void] must be [place] in which there is an extension between tangible body. . . . It is manifest that . . . there is no void, whether separated or inseparable.
    Aristotle, *Physics* 213b30–214a (tr. Hussey)

Some people, then, think that if there is to be change in respect of place, there is a void which is in itself distinct. This is the same thing as to say that place is something separated, and that this is impossible has been said before.
    Aristotle, *Physics* 216a (tr. Hussey)

Can you really suppose that any such thing as empty void exists, when the universe is so completely filled and packed that whenever a bodily object is set in motion it gives place and another object at once moves into the place that it has left?
    Cicero, *Academica* 2.40.125 (tr. Rackham)

According to modern theory, a vacuum is not exactly nothing but is teeming with quantum particles that fluctuate between being and nothingness. These tiny particles can come into existence for a fraction of a second before they annihilate each other leaving nothing behind.
    Heinz R. Pagels, "Before the Big Bang," *Natural History*, April 1983, 26

358   **aliās**: modifying **rēs** (359); juxtaposed with **aliīs** to replicate the comparison that Lucretius is illustrating, as the reader weighs two things side by side. Similarly he juxtaposes **rēs** and **rēbus** in the next line.

       aliīs: modifying **rēbus** (359).

       praestō, praestāre, praestitī + dat. and abl. of measure, *to excel, surpass; to be greater* (in).

359   **pondus, ponderis**, n., *weight*.

       pondere: ablative of measure, *in weight, by weight*.

       nīlō: ablative of degree of difference with **maiōre**, *by nothing*.

       figūra, -ae, f., *shape, size*.

         maiōre figūrā: ablative of description.

360   **tantusdem, tantadem, tantundem**, *just as much*.

       tantundemst: = **tantundem est**. For similar elision see also in this passage **officiumst** (362) and **magnumst** (364). **Tantundem** is a nominative neuter substantive with the partitive genitive **corporis** (361) dependent upon it, *so much of body, so much body*.

       glōmus, glōmeris, n., *ball*.

       quantum: nominative singular neuter substantive, correlative with **tantundem** and taking the same partitive genitive construction: **quantum corporis**, *as much of body, as much body*.

361   **plumbum, -ī**, n., *lead*.

       in plumbō: Lucretius has altered the construction; the exact parallel to the phrase in line 360 would be **in glōmere plumbī**.

       pendō, pendere, pependī, pēnsus, *to weigh*.

       pār, paris, *equal; fitting, reasonable*.

         pār est: **pār** is neuter, *it is fitting, it ought* (to) + infinitive. The line ends most unusually with two monosyllables.

362   **corporis**: note the anaphora with line 361.

       corporis officiumst: for the phrase, see line 336.

       quoniam: the linking conjunction has been postponed to mid-line, as Lucretius often does (lines 4, 32, 111, 303, 339, 345, and especially line 265).

       premō, premere, pressī, pressus, *to press*.

       deorsum, adv., *downwards*. By synizesis the two vowels *eo* scan as one long syllable.

363   **contrā autem**: having defined the duty of weight, Lucretius now turns to the duties of void.

       nātūra . . . inānis: a typical periphrasis with nominative and dependent genitive.

364   **quod**: nominative singular neuter, with no expressed antecedent, *a thing which, what*.

       aequē: take closely with **magnum**.

365   **plūs . . . inānis**: another periphrasis, *more of void, more void*.

       sibī: dative of possession. The final syllable is long by diastole for metrical reasons; cf. **tibī** (104).

       dēclārō, -āre, -āvī, -ātus, *to declare, reveal, show*.

         dēclārat: a vivid personification of the subject **quod**; it actually speaks to us by its weight.

366   **at contrā gravius . . . dēdicat**: Lucretius uses a parallel construction to show the opposite situation.

       gravius: supply **quod est**.

367   **dēdicō, -āre, -āvī, -ātus**, *to make clear, proclaim, declare*.

       dēdicat: synonymous with **dēclārat** (365).

       multō: ablative of degree of difference, *by much, much*; cf. **nīlō** (359).

       vacuī: here a substantive, *empty space, void*; partitive genitive with **minus**, *less void*. Earlier Lucretius used the same root in **vacāns** to describe the void (334).

       intus, adv., *within, inside*.

368   **Est igitur**: emphatic phraseology with the verb **esse** (cf. 277, **Sunt igitur**, and 330).

369   **admixtus, -a, -um** + dat., *mixed* (in), *intermingled* (in).

       quod ināne vocāmus: Lucretius again, as a good teacher, defines his terms.

11. Relative Weights Prove Void's Existence

If two objects of the same size have different weights, the lighter encloses more void. Lucretius closes his proofs about void by comparing his reader to a keen-scented hunting dog who can sniff out the truth for himself.

358 Dēnique cūr aliās aliīs praestāre vidēmus
359 pondere rēs rēbus nīlō maiōre figūrā?
360 Nam sī tantundemst in lānae glōmere quantum
361 corporis in plumbō est, tantundem pendere pār est,
362 corporis officiumst quoniam premere omnia deorsum,
363 contrā autem nātūra manet sine pondere inānis.
364 Ergō quod magnumst aequē leviusque vidētur,
365 nīmīrum plūs esse sibī dēclārat inānis;
366 at contrā gravius plūs in sē corporis esse
367 dēdicat et multō vacuī minus intus habēre.
368 Est igitur nīmīrum id quod ratiōne sagācī
369 quaerimus, admixtum rēbus, quod ināne vocāmus.

. . .

400 Multaque praetereā tibi possum commemorandō
401 argūmenta fidem dictīs corrādere nostrīs.

ℭ℈ Discussion Question

1. What do we call the fundamental force to which Lucretius refers in line 362?

---

400 **Multa**: modifying **argūmenta** (401); very emphatic in this position.
   commemorandō: gerund in ablative of means. Also note the pentasyllabic line-ending.
401 **argūmentum, -ī**, n., *fact, proof, argument.*
   argūmenta: accusative plural, direct object of **commemorandō** (400).
   dictīs: dative.
   corrādō, corrādere, corrāsī, corrāsus, *to scrape together.*
   fidem corrādere: a colloquialism borrowed from the comic poets, usually in the context of scraping together some cash.
   nostrīs: editorial plural.

402   **vērum**, adv., *but*.

         satis: acting as predicate of the phrase **haec vēstīgia parva . . . sunt**.

         vēstīgia: an image from hunting, which will be elaborated upon below.

         sagācī: modifying **animō** and recalling **ratiōne sagācī** (368). The primary meaning of the adjective is *keen-scented*, and thus this image anticipates the hunting-dog comparison which follows in lines 404–9.

403   **per**: introducing a relative clause of characteristic, *through which*.

         tūte: the emphatic form of **tū** in a particularly emphatic position, almost as if concluding the sentence *"yes you can."*

404   **Namque**: = **nam**.

         ut: with indicative, introducing a simile.

         montivagus, -a, -um, *mountain-ranging*.

           montivagae: modifying **ferāī**, genitive of possession with **quiētēs** (405).

         persaepe, frequentative adverb, *very often*.

405   **nārēs, nārium**, f. pl., *nostrils, nose*.

         integō, integere, intēxī, intēctus, *to cover, cover over*.

         frōns, frondis, f., *leaf, foliage*.

           fronde: ablative of means with **intēctās**.

         quiētēs: here, *dens*; poetic plural for singular.

406   **semel**, adv., *once*.

         īnstiterunt: perfect of **īnstō, īnstāre, īnstitī**; here with the accusative, an archaic usage, *to set foot on the traces*. Also the short *e* of the ending is an archaism.

407   **sīc**: beginning the conclusion of the comparisons.

         alid: = **aliud**.

         per tē tūte ipse: it would be hard to find a more emphatic expression or one that more involves the reader.

408   **latebra, -ae**, f., *hiding-place, lair*.

409   **īnsinuāre**: here with accusative, *to wriggle into*.

         vērum: here a substantive neuter, *the truth*.

         prōtrahō, prōtrahere, prōtrāxī, prōtrāctus, *to drag forward/out*.

         inde: i.e., from the beast's lair.

402 Vērum animō satis haec vēstīgia parva sagācī
403 sunt per quae possīs cognōscere cētera tūte.
404 Namque canēs ut montivagae persaepe ferāī
405 nāribus inveniunt intēctās fronde quiētēs,
406 cum semel īnstiterunt vēstīgia certa viāī,
407 sīc alid ex aliō per tē tūte ipse vidēre
408 tālibus in rēbus poteris caecāsque latebrās
409 īnsinuāre omnīs et vērum prōtrahere inde.

❧ **Discussion Questions**

1. Why doesn't Lucretius add more examples? What advantage is to be gained by assuring his reader that he can now discover the truth for himself? (402–03)

2. Why does Lucretius use **cētera** rather than **alia** in line 403?

3. Why does Lucretius compare the truth to a beast hidden in its lair? What does the comparison imply?

4. The lair, from which the reader will drag out the truth, is described as hidden by foliage. Into what will the reader drag the truth? What commonly-used contrasting imagery underlies this description?

For I drag into light many things which no one who was not proceeding by a regular and certain way to the discovery of causes would have thought of inquiring after.
    Sir Francis Bacon, *Magna Instauratio* (1620), 261

419 **Omnis**: separated from its noun, **nātūra**, by the intervening **ut** clause.

igitur: should be taken to apply to the whole sentence, although it has been postponed until the dependent clause.

duābus: ablative plural feminine with **rēbus** (420).

420 **cōnstitit**: perfect of **cōnstō, cōnstāre, cōnstitī** with a present sense; literally *has taken up position* (in), *has stood* (in). Translate: *is made up of, consists of.*

rēbus: = atoms and void.

421 **haec**: = **corpora**.

situs, -a, -um, *placed, situated.*

sita: predicative adjective with **sunt**, *are placed, situated.*

quā, adv., *where.*

dīversus, -a, -um, *in different directions.*

moventur: middle/passive in force: the atoms generate their own motion and are also moved when struck by other atoms.

422 **Corpus**: accusative singular in indirect statement; placed at the beginning of the line as the first consitutent of the universe.

per sē: probably to be construed with **corpus esse**, *body exists in and of itself.* For a similar usage see line 419.

commūnis . . . sēnsus (423): not our "common sense," but the sensation which is shared by all of us — the five bodily senses.

dēdicat: again personifying an abstraction; our sense *proclaims.*

423 **sēnsus**: enjambement.

cui: dative with **fidēs**, on the analogy of **crēdō**, which takes the dative.

prīma: almost adverbial, *first of all.*

fundō, -āre, -āvī, -ātus, *to base, found, establish; to ground.*

fundāta: a favorite Lucretian metaphor from laying the foundation of a building.

424 **erit**: the subject is the clause **quō referentēs . . . queāmus** (425).

quō: the antecedent is unexpressed; understand "any standard," or, drawing on the imagery of the previous line, "any foundation," *to which referring.*

425 **animī**: genitive with **ratiōne**. Again Lucretius stresses that the investigation of nature should be based upon logical inference from sensory evidence, not guess-work or superstition.

queāmus: subjunctive from **queō, quīre**, in relative clause of characteristic.

426 **Tum porrō locus**: now Lucretius turns to void, the second constituent element.

spatium, -ī, n., *space.*

locus . . . spatium . . . ināne: synonyms for the void (cf. 334), just as Lucretius uses multiple terms for the atoms.

427 **nūllum**: nominative singular neuter, agreeing with the last of the words for void, **ināne**.

foret: = **esset**, imperfect subjunctive in another present contrary-to-fact condition.

usquam, adv., *anywhere.*

sita: predicative adjective with **esse** (428), as above in line 421.

428 **quōquam**, adv., *to anywhere.*

430 **Praetereā**: here not, as usual, indicating a transition, but literally *Besides these, In addition to these* (i.e., body and void).

possīs: subjunctive in relative clause of characteristic.

431 **sēiungō, sēiungere, sēiūnxī, sēiūnctus**, *to separate.*

ab omnī corpore sēiūnctum sēcrētumque . . . ab ināne: chiastic phrasing which, by the juxtaposition of the two synonyms, is very emphatic.

Praetereā nīl . . . . ab ināne: lines 430–31 are metrically interesting; both are heavily spondaic and follow exactly the same metrical pattern.

432 **sit**: with **reperta**; subjunctive in relative clause of characteristic.

numerō: take closely with **tertia**, *third in number.*

reperiō, reperīre, repperī, repertus, *to find.*

12. Summation on Matter and Void; Sensory Evidence; Solidity of the Atoms

Only matter and void exist; there is no third element. Our beliefs must be based upon the evidence of the senses, which we all share. Finally, the atoms must be eternal.

419 Omnis, ut est igitur per sē, nātūra duābus
420 cōnstitit in rēbus; nam corpora sunt et ināne,
421 haec in quō sita sunt et quā dīversa moventur.
422 Corpus enim per sē commūnis dēdicat esse
423 sēnsus; cui nisi prīma fidēs fundāta valēbit,
424 haud erit occultīs dē rēbus quō referentēs
425 cōnfirmāre animī quicquam ratiōne queāmus.
426 Tum porrō locus ac spatium, quod ināne vocāmus,
427 sī nūllum foret, haud usquam sita corpora possent
428 esse neque omnīnō quōquam dīversa meāre.

. . .

430 Praetereā nīl est quod possīs dīcere ab omnī
431 corpore sēiūnctum sēcrētumque esse ab inānī,
432 quod quasi tertia sit numerō nātūra reperta.

[Reply of the senses to the intellect]: Miserable mind, you get your evidence from us, and do you try to overthrow us? The overthrow will be your downfall.
  Democritus, *Fragment* 125 (tr. Freeman)

If you fight against all sensations, you will have no standard by which to judge even those of them which you say are false.
  Epicurus, *Principal Doctrines* 23 (tr. Bailey)

We must keep all our investigations in accord with our sensations, and in particular with the immediate apprehensions whether of the mind or of any one of the instruments of judgement, and likewise in accord with the feelings existing in us, in order that we may have indications whereby we may judge both the problem of sense-perception and the unseen.
  Epicurus, *Epistle to Herodotus* 38 (tr. Bailey)

For we must not conduct scientific investigations by means of empty assumptions and arbitrary principles, but follow the lead of phenomena: for our life has not now any place for irrational belief and groundless imaginings, but we must live free from trouble.
  Epicurus, *Epistle to Pythocles* 86–87 (tr. Bailey)

In contrast: Is there any certainty in human sight or hearing, or is it true, as the poets are always dinning into our ears, that we neither hear nor see anything accurately? Yet if these senses are not clear and accurate, the rest can hardly be so, because they are all inferior to the first two.
  Plato, *Phaedo* 65b (tr. Tredennick)

485   **Sed quae sunt rērum prīmōrdia. . . .:** Lucretius now turns to a fuller description of the essential characteristic of the atoms: their indestructibility.

         quae: there is no expressed antecedent; understand an accusative plural neuter **ea** to act as the direct object of **stinguere** (486).

         nūlla. . . vīs: Lucretius returns in language and thought to his earlier argumentation about the permanence of matter (215–24). There he argued that if matter were mortal, no force (**vīs**) would be necessary to bring about destruction.

         vīs: note the monosyllabic ending and enjambement into the next line.

486   **stinguō, stinguere, stīnxī, stīnctus,** *to extinguish, annihilate, destroy.*

         stinguere: the *u* is consonantal (as also in **sanguen** and **suāvis**) and so does not scan.

         vincunt: in an absolute sense, *prevail.*

         dēmum, adv., *indeed, in the end.*

487   **etsī**, conj., *even if, although.*

         difficile: predicate adjective modifying the subject clause.

         vidētur: the subject is the clause **crēdere quicquam . . . corpore posse**; *to believe . . . seems to be difficult.* Again Lucretius addresses the reader's potential doubts; cf. 267.

488   **in rēbus**: i.e., in nature, in the world.

Further views on the evidence of the senses:

What do you say to the main philosophers of our school, who . . . never wanted to see the planets, the moon or the telescope? . . . Really, as some have shut their ears, these have shut their eyes towards the light of truth. . . . This sort of person thinks . . . that one has not to search for truth in the world of nature but in the comparisons of texts.

    Letter from Galileo to Johannes Kepler, August 19, 1610

Being convinced that the human intellect makes its own difficulties, not using the true helps which are at man's disposal soberly and judiciously, whence follows manifold ignorance of things, and by reason of that ignorance mischiefs innumerable, [Bacon] thought that all trial should be made, whether that commerce between the mind of man and the nature of things . . . might by any means be restored. Whence it follows that the entire fabric of human reason, which we employ in the inquisition of nature, is badly put together and built up, and like some magnificent structure without any foundation.

    Sir Francis Bacon, *Prooemium to Magna Instauratio* (1620)

Then the way is still to be made by the uncertain light of the sense, sometimes shining out, sometimes clouded over, through the woods of experience and particulars. . . . Our steps must be guided by a clue, and the whole way from the very first perception of the senses must be laid out upon a sure plan.

    Sir Francis Bacon, *Magna Instauratio*, 248

485   Sed quae sunt rērum prīmōrdia, nūlla potest vīs
486   stinguere; nam solidō vincunt ea corpore dēmum.
487   Etsī difficile esse vidētur crēdere quicquam
488   in rēbus solidō reperīrī corpore posse.

CS Discussion Questions

1.   Examine the word order of line 486. What effects are created?

2.   Why might it be difficult to believe that anything has an absolutely solid body?

I frame no hypotheses; for whatever is not deduced from the phenomena is to be called an hypothesis; and hypotheses, whether metaphysical or physical, whether of occult qualities or mechanical, have no place in experimental philosophy.
    Sir Isaac Newton, *Letter to Robert Hoyle*, February 5, 1675 or 1676

The main business of natural Philosophy is to argue from Phaenomena without feigning Hypotheses, and to deduce Causes from Effects.
    Sir Isaac Newton, *Opticks* (1704) 3.1

James Boswell reports Ben Johnson's memorable illustration of the existence of matter:
    After we came out of the church, we stood talking for some time together of Bishop Berkeley's ingenious sophistry to prove the non-existence of matter, and that every thing in the universe is merely ideal. I observed, that though we are satisfied his doctrine is not true, it is impossible to refute it. I never shall forget the alacrity with which Johnson answered, striking his foot with mighty force against a large stone, till he rebounded from it. 'I refute it *thus*.'
    James Boswell, *Life of Johnson*, vol. 1, 6 Aug. 1763

499   **cōgit**: by hendiadys the phrase **vēra . . . ratiō nātūraque rērum** (498) forms a singular subject, which governs this verb. In Lucretius' mind true reasoning or philosophy (Epicureanism) is a perfect mirror of **nātūra rērum**.

        ades: singular imperative of **adsum**; a very direct address to the reader to wake him up and demand his attention, *come on, pay attention!*

        dum, conj. + subjunctive, *until*.

        expediō, expedīre, expedīvī or **expediī, expedītus**, *to explain*.

500   **esse**: emphatic position.

        cōnstent: subjunctive in relative clause of characteristic *and* subordinate clause in indirect statement.

501   **quae**: the relative has been delayed.

        sēmina. . . prīmōrdia: accusative subjects of indirect statement governed by **docēmus**.

        docēmus: indicative to emphasize that this is a statement of fact.

502   **unde**: = **ē quibus**, i.e., from the atoms.

        cōnstet: Lucretius returns to the subjunctive as a subordinate clause in indirect statement after **expediāmus** (499).

           omnis rērum cōnstet summa creāta: for very similar phrasing see 235: **ē quibus haec rērum cōnsistit summa refecta**.

528   **dissoluī**: passive infinitive governed by **possunt** (529).

        plāga, -ae, f., *blow*.

        extrīnsecus, adv., *from outside*.

        īciō, īcere, īcī, īctus, *to strike*.

           īcta: nominative plural neuter modifying **haec**.

529   **penitus**, adv., *from within, inside*; directly contrasted with **extrīnsecus** (528).

        possunt . . . porrō penitus penetrāta: interesting alliteration following the *p* of **plāgīs** (528). Does it reproduce the harsh sound of the blows?

        retexō, retexere, retexuī, retextus, *to unravel, unweave*.

           dissoluī plāgīs extrīnsecus īcta . . . penitus penetrāta retexī: an aggregate of atoms can be destroyed in one of two ways: (1) by external blows, when something hits it, or (2) from within, in the spaces, by the force of heat or cold, etc. (cf. 223, **intus penetret per inānia dissoluatque**). The solid atoms themselves, however, are truly impervious to any and all assaults.

530   **ratiōne . . . aliā**: a hypothetical option only; there is no third way in which things can be destroyed.

        temptāta: here, *assailed, attacked*.

        labō, -āre, -āvī, *to totter, give way, break down*.

498   Sed quia vēra tamen ratiō nātūraque rērum
499   cōgit, ades, paucīs dum versibus expediāmus
500   esse ea quae solidō atque aeternō corpore cōnstent,
501   sēmina quae rērum prīmōrdiaque esse docēmus,
502   unde omnis rērum nunc cōnstet summa creāta.

. . .

528   Haec neque dissoluī plāgīs extrīnsecus icta
529   possunt nec porrō penitus penetrāta retexī
530   nec ratiōne queunt aliā temptāta labāre.

❦ Discussion Questions

1.   What is the **vēra ratiō** to which Lucretius refers in line 498?

2.   *Atoma* in Greek means "uncuttables." What would Lucretius think now that the atom has been split into sub-atomic particles?

We now know that neither the atoms nor the protons and neutrons within them are indivisible. So the question is: What are the truly elementary particles, the basic building blocks from which everything is made?

     Stephen W. Hawking, *A Brief History of Time* (1988), 65

Quarks were unknown and unimagined as recently as the 1960s, and their discovery ranks as one of the paramount accomplishments of twentieth century science. They are the smallest indivisible units of heavy matter. Each proton or neutron is made of three quarks bound together. The Standard Model calls for six kinds (or "flavors") of quarks.

     Curt Siplee, *The Washington Post*, March 3, 1995

565   **Hūc accēdit utī**: a formulaic phrase repeated from line 215, *(there is) added to this that.*

       utī: = **ut** governing a subjunctive clause with **possint** (566).

       māteriāī: here Lucretius uses the first declension form of the noun; with this noun he switches declensions regularly from first to fifth.

566   **cum**: in a concessive clause, *although*, here with the indicative, as sometimes in early Latin. As a linking conjunction **cum** has been severely postponed. Reorder the clause: **cum corpora māteriāī cōnstant solidissima.**

       cōnstant: essentially = **sunt.**

       omnia: defined by the relative clause **mollia quae fīunt** (567).

       reddī: here, *to be explained.*

567   **fīunt**: here, *are made.*

       āēr, āeris, m., *air.*

       vapōrēs: poetic plural for singular.

         āēr aqua terra vapōrēs: a list of the four Empedoclean elements. Note the asyndeton, which Lucretius generally employs when creating lists.

568   **quō pactō . . . quā vī . . .**: indirect questions dependent on **reddī** (566).

569   **admixtum**: predicate adjective modifying, but very separated from, **ināne.**

       quoniam: here, *when.*

570   **At contrā**: introducing a mixed condition: future less vivid, then future more vivid.

       sint, here, *should be*, in ideal or future less vivid condition.

571   **queant**: present subjunctive in indirect question with **non poterit ratiō reddī** (572).

       validus, -a, -um, *strong, powerful.*

       silex, silicis, m., *rock.*

       ferrum, -ī, n., *iron.*

572   **poterit**: future as the conclusion of the mixed condition.

       ratiō reddī: idiom (cf. 59), *an explanation (will not be able) to be given.*

       funditus, adv., literally, *from the foundation*; here, *utterly*; modifying **carēbit** (573).

       omnis: nominative singular with **nātūra** (573).

573   **prīncipiō**: ablative with **carēbit.**

       fundāmentum, -ī, n., *foundation.*

         prīncipiō fundāmentī: *the beginning of a foundation.* A word-play with **funditus** (572). The building metaphor is a favorite with Lucretius; see line 423, **prīma fidēs fundāta valēbit.**

574   **Sunt**: emphatic position (cf. 277, 368). The subject is understood as **prīmōrdia**, *the atoms* (570).

       pollēns, pollentis, *powerful, strong.*

       simplicitās, simplicitātis, f., *singleness of nature, unity.*

         solidā . . . simplicitāte: ablative of description. Note the alliteration with **sunt.**

575   **condēnsus, -a, -um**, *dense, tightly packed.*

       magis: take closely with **condēnsō.**

       omnia: referring to all hard compounds.

       conciliātus, -ūs, m., *union, aggregate, assemblage.* This fourth declension noun appears to have been coined by Lucretius and is used by no one else.

         condēnsō magis . . . conciliātū: ablative of means.

576   **artō, -āre, -āvī, -ātus**, *to fix firmly/closely together.*

       ostendere: a personification of the atoms.

       vīrīs: accusative plural of **vīs.**

         validās . . . vīrīs: intentionally and emphatically redundant, *strong strengths.*

The atoms do not change at all, since there must needs be something which remains solid and indissoluble at the dissolution of compounds, which can cause changes . . . effected by the shifting of position of some particles, and by the addition or departure of others.

    Epicurus, *Epistle to Herodotus* 54 (tr. Bailey)

13. Solid Atoms Together with Void Can Form Soft Objects

Solid atoms, by the admixture of void in their aggregation, can produce soft substances, but soft atoms could never produce hard substances. In the passage that follows these lines, Lucretius describes the atoms as composed of **cacūmina**, *points* or *least parts*, which can never be separated from their union. The **cacūmina** are essential in explaining how atoms can have different shapes and sizes, and thus how the atoms, by varying combinations, create all different substances.

565 Hūc accēdit utī, solidissima māteriāī
566 corpora cum cōnstant, possint tamen omnia reddī,
567 mollia quae fīunt, āēr aqua terra vapōrēs,
568 quō pactō fīant et quā vī quaeque gerantur,
569 admixtum quoniam semel est in rēbus ināne.
570 At contrā sī mollia sint prīmōrdia rērum,
571 unde queant validī silicēs ferrumque creārī
572 non poterit ratiō reddī; nam funditus omnis
573 prīncipiō fundāmentī nātūra carēbit.
574 Sunt igitur solidā pollentia simplicitāte
575 quōrum condēnsō magis omnia conciliātū
576 artārī possunt validāsque ostendere vīrīs.

A contrasting view, describing how the Many arises out of One:
     Fire and Water and Earth and the boundless height of Air.... All these [elements] are equal and of the same age in their creation; but each presides over its own office, and each has its own character, and they prevail in turn in the course of time. And besides these, nothing else comes into being, nor does anything cease. For if they had been perishing continuously, they would Be no more; and what could increase the Whole? And whence would it have come? In what direction could it perish, since nothing is empty of these things? No, but these things alone exist, and running through one another they become different things at different times, and are ever continuously the same.
     Empedocles, *On Nature* 17 (tr. Freeman)

It seems probable to me, that God in the Beginning, form'd Matter in solid, massy, hard, impenetrable, moveable Particles, of such Sizes and Figures, and with such other Properties, and in such Proportion to Space, as most conduced to the End for which he form'd them; and that these primitive particles being Solids, are incomparably harder than any porous Bodies compounded of them; even so very hard as never to wear or break in pieces. While the particles continue entire, they may compose Bodies of one and the same Nature and Texture in all Ages.... And therefore that Nature may be lasting, the Changes of Corporeal Things are to be placed only in the various Separations and new Associations and Motions of these permanent Particles.
     Sir Isaac Newton, *Opticks* (1704), 375–76.

921   **Nunc age quod superest**: a very formulaic beginning. For **nunc age** cf. 265.
        quod superest: repeated from line 50; here direct object of **cognōsce** and **audī**.
    clarius: here, *more clearly*.

922   **animī**: *in my mind*; an archaic usage, either a genitive of relation or locative.
    fallō, fallere, fefellī, falsus, *to escape (the notice of), elude*.
        fallit: the following indirect question, **quam sint obscūra**, acts as the subject.
    quam: here, *how*.
    obscūrus, -a, -um, *dark, obscure*.
        obscūra: modifying the understood phrase **Grāiōrum reperta**, *the findings of the Greeks*,
            which occurs in the same context in lines 136–37: **nec mē animī fallit Grāiōrum obscūra
            reperta / difficile inlūstrāre**. Here **obscūra** contrasts with **clārius** (921).
    ācrī: modifying **thyrsō** (923) and indicating the sharpness of the thyrsus, whose end was a
            spear-point.

923   **percutiō, percutere, percussī, percussus**, *to strike*.
    thyrsus, -ī, m., *wand, goad* (carried by devotees of Bacchus, which indicated their inspiration
            by the god).
    laus, laudis, f., *praise, fame*.
        laudis: objective genitive with **spēs**.
    spēs, speī, f., *hope*.
    cor: emphatic monosyllabic line-ending in an extraordinarily spondaic line.

924   **incutiō, incutere, incussī, incussus**, *to strike into, instill*.
        incussit: repeating the root from **percussit** (923) and echoing line 19 in imagery: **incutiēns
            blandum per pectora amōrem**.
    mī: contracted form of **mihi**, dative of reference.

925   **mūsārum**: enjambement. Indeed this whole passage moves freely across the borders of the
            lines; see especially **ācrī / percussit** (922–23) and, below, lines 926–27.
    īnstīnctus, -a, -um, *excited, roused*.
    vigeō, -ēre, -uī, *to be active/lively/vigorous; to flourish, thrive*.
        mente vigentī: ablative of manner.

926   **āvius, -a, -um**, *out of the way, unfrequented*.
    Pīeridēs, Pīeridum, f. pl., *the Muses* (by one account, daughters of Pierus).
    peragrō, -āre, -āvī, -ātus, *to traverse*.
        āvia Pīeridum peragrō loca. . . .: note the assonance, particularly of *a*. Also the word order
            is flexible, with **loca** very separated from its two modifiers, **āvia** and **trīta** (927).
    nūllius: possessive genitive singular with **solō** (927).
    ante: adverbial.

927   **trītus, -a, -um**, *worn, trodden*.
    solum, -ī, n., *sole* (of the foot).
    Iuvat: the subject is the infinitive clause **integrōs accēdere fontīs atque haurīre** (928); supply
            mē as direct object.
    integer, integra, integrum, *pure, untouched, untasted*.
    fōns, fontis, m., *spring, the water of a spring*.

928   **hauriō, haurīre, hausī, haustus**, *to draw* (water); *to drink*.
    iuvatque: note the emphatic anaphora with the line above.
    dēcerpō, dēcerpere, dēcerpsī, dēcerptus, *to pluck, pick*.

929   **īnsignis, -is, -e**, *conspicuous, glorious*.
    inde: with a double reference; first to the **flōrēs** with which he will make his wreath; second,
            anticipating **unde** in 930 and referring to his poetic originality in presenting Epicurean
            philosophy in verse.
        īnsignemque . . . corōnam: embedded word order; the phrase surrounds the poet's head
            just as the wreath.

14. Poetic Originality

Lucretius strives for recognition of his poetic originality. Realizing that many people may find his new ideas distasteful, Lucretius decides to sweeten his philosophy and attract the reader by writing his philosophy in poetry. Indeed, this passage itself has always been acclaimed for the exceptional beauty of its poetic imagery.

921   Nunc age quod superest cognōsce et clārius audī.
922   Nec mē animī fallit quam sint obscūra; sed ācrī
923   percussit thyrsō laudis spēs magna meum cor
924   et simul incussit suāvem mī in pectus amōrem
925   mūsārum, quō nunc īnstīnctus mente vigentī
926   āvia Pīeridum peragrō loca nūllius ante
927   trīta solō. Iuvat integrōs accēdere fontīs
928   atque haurīre, iuvatque novōs dēcerpere flōrēs
929   īnsignemque meō capitī petere inde corōnam

᧯ Discussion Questions

1.   Explain why Lucretius describes his findings as **obscūra** (922).

2.   Examine the vivid metaphorical personification implicit in the verb **percussit** (923).

3.   Why is it important to Lucretius that he is traversing places that are **āvia** (926)? What is the significance of the phrase **nūllius ante trīta solō** (926–27)?

4.   What does the wreath of new flowers signify? (928–29)

And well I know how hard it is to win with words a triumph herein, and thus to crown with glory a lovely theme. But sweet desire hurries me over the lonely steps of Parnassus; joyous it is to roam o'er heights, where no forerunner's track turns by a gentle slope down to Castalia.
    Vergil, *Georgics* 3.289–93 (tr. Fairclough)

This too I bid you: tread a path which carriages do not trample; do not drive your chariot upon the common tracks of others, nor along a wide road, but on unworn paths, though your course be more narrow.
    Callimachus, *Aetia* 25–28 (tr. Trypanis)

930   **nūllī**: = **nēminī**, possessive dative.
   vēlō, -āre, -āvī, -ātus, *to cover, veil.*
    vēlārint: syncopated perfect subjunctive = **vēlāverint**; subjunctive in a relative clause of
     result introduced unusually by **unde**: the location is such that the Muses have crowned
     no one there before.
   tempus, temporis, n., *time*; here, *temple, side of the head.*

931   **artus, -a, -um**, *close, tightly-fastened.*
    artīs: modifying **nōdīs** (932) and in the context echoing lines 62–79, where Epicurus over-
     came the threats of religion and opened the closely-fastened gates of nature (**arta nātūrae**
     . . . portārum claustra, 70–71).

932   **rēligiōnum**: poetic plural possibly indicating the many exacting rites which Roman religious
   ritual entailed.
   nōdus, -ī, m., *knot.*

933   **deinde**, adv., *then, next.* The two vowels *ei* scan as one long syllable by synizesis.
    prīmum (931) **. . . dēinde**: the sequence indicates the relative importance with which
     Lucretius views his efforts and his claim to originality. His first priority is, through
     philosophy, to free man from his fears. The creation of new and beautiful poetry, of
     which he is proud, is also, as he himself states, a pragmatic ploy to gain the reader's
     attention.
    obscūra dē rē: see line 922 for his acknowledgment that Greek philosophy is **obscūra**. The
     phrase also parallels **magnīs . . . dē rēbus** above (931).
   lūcidus, -a, -um, *bright, shining, clear.*
    obscūra . . . lūcida: a clear antithesis.

934   **carmen, carminis**, n., *song; poetry.*
   musaeus, -a, -um, *of the Muses.*
   contingō, contingere, contigī, contactus, *to touch.*
   lepos, lepōris, m., *charm, grace.*

935   **Id**: referring to Lucretius' decision to write in poetry.
   nōn ab nūlla ratiōne, *not for no reason; with reason, intentional*; here **ab** literally means *proceed-*
    ing from.
   vidētur: a true passive; supply **esse**, *is seen to be.*

936   **velutī**: = **velut**, introducing one of the most famous images in Lucretius, in which he compares his reader to a young child who needs to swallow bitter medicine.
   puerīs: dative of indirect object; here, *children.*
   absinthium, -ī, n., *wormwood* (a particularly bitter medicine with a greenish color). The
    French liqueur, *absinthe*, is made from wormwood and is actually toxic.
   taeter, taetra, taetrum, *foul.*
    absinthia taetra: poetic plural.
   medēns, medentis, m., *healer, doctor.*

937   **ōra, -ae**, f., *shore*; here, *rim.*
    ōras: governed by the preposition **circum** in anastrophe.

938   **contingunt**: echoing the touching (**contingēns**, 934) of his philosophy with poetry.
   mel, mellis, n., *honey.*
   dulcis, -is, -e, *sweet.*
   flāvus, -a, -um, *golden.*
   liquor, liquōris, m., *liquid.*
    mellis . . . liquōre: another periphrasis = *sweet and golden honey.*
     contingunt . . . liquōre: the slow progression of the line imitates the slow movement of
     the honey.

930   unde prius nūllī vēlārint tempora mūsae;
931   prīmum quod magnīs doceō dē rēbus et artīs
932   rēligiōnum animum nōdīs exsolvere pergō,
933   deinde quod obscūrā dē rē tam lūcida pangō
934   carmina, mūsaeō contingēns cūncta lepōre.
935   Id quoque enim nōn ab nūllā ratiōne vidētur;
936   sed velutī puerīs absinthia taetra medentēs
937   cum dare cōnantur, prius ōrās pōcula circum
938   contingunt mellis dulcī flāvōque liquōre,

CB Discussion Questions

1.   Where have you seen similarly imprisoning imagery applied to religion? (931–32)

2.   What contrasting image system occurs in line 933?

... I thence
Invoke thy aid to my advent'rous song,
That with no middle flight intends to soar
Above th' Aonian mount, while it pursues
Things unattempted yet in prose or rhyme.
      John Milton, *Paradise Lost* (1667), 1.12–16

A spoonful of sugar makes the medicine go down.
      The film *Mary Poppins* (1964) based on the P.L. Travers series of books

939   **puerōrum**: again, *children*.

            imprōvidus, -a, -um, *unsuspecting*.

               imprōvida: transferred epithet; it is the children who are unsuspecting, not their age.

            lūdificō, -āre, -āvī, -ātus, *to delude, deceive*.

940   **labrum, -ī**, n., *lip*.

            tenus, prep. always placed after its noun + gen., *up to, as far as*.

               labrōrum tenus: significant instance of enjambement. Line 939 seems to imply that the doctors are deceiving the children, but line 940 reassures us that the trick is only up to the lips. Moreover, the trick is ultimately beneficial, as the following lines show.

            perpōtō, -āre, -āvī, -ātus, *to drink up*.

               perpōtet: the subject remains **puerōrum aetās**. The prepositional prefix **per** conveys the idea that the medicine is drunk to the last drop.

            amārus, -a, -um, *bitter*.

941   **latex, laticis**, m., *liquid*.

               absinthī laticem: periphrasis.

            dēcipiō, dēcipere, dēcēpī, dēceptus, *to deceive, cheat, trick*.

            capiātur: *be harmed*.

               dēcepta nōn capiātur: a pun (**dēcepta** = **dē-**+ **capta**) that is difficult to replicate in English; Cyril Bailey translates "and though charmed be not harmed," which at least gives the sound effect.

942   **recreō, -āre, -āvī, -ātus**, *to restore, revive*.

            valēscō, valēscere, *to grow strong, thrive*.

943   **sīc**: after the extensive description, Lucretius reaches his main point of comparison.

            haec ratiō: i.e., Epicurean philosophy.

            plērumque, adv., *generally, often*.

944   **trīstior**, *rather bitter*.

            quibus: no antecedent is expressed; understand **eīs** (dative after **vidētur**, 943); dative of agent in a passive construction, (*to those) by whom*.

            tractō, -āre, -āvī, -ātus, *to try, investigate, practice*.

            retrō, adv., *backwards*.

945   **vulgus, -ī**, n., *crowd, common people*.

            abhorreō, -ēre, -uī, *to shrink back from, recoil from*.

            hāc: supply **ratiōne**.

               retrōque vulgus abhorret ab hāc: a very vivid image, as if the crowd had suddenly seen a snake.

            voluī: perfect of **volō**.

            suāviloquēns, suāviloquentis, *sweet-sounding*.

               suāviloquentī: a characteristic Lucretian compound with an onomotopoeic effect; here ablative singular in a pentasyllabic line-ending with enjambement to the next line.

946   **carmine**: surrounded by an unusual double epithet: **suāviloquentī** and **Pīeriō**.

            Pīerius, -a, -um, *of the Muses, Pierian* (from Pieria, a region of Macedonia where the Muses were worshiped).

            expōnō, expōnere, exposuī, expositus, *to set forth, expound, explain*.

947   **quasi**: reminding the reader of the previous comparison of Epicurean philosophy to a cup of bitter medicine.

            mūsaeō dulcī contingere melle: closely echoing the imagery of line 938 (**contingunt mellis dulcī . . . liquōre**), which described the smearing of honey on the rim of the cup. Again an unusual double epithet for **melle**, as for **carmine** in line 946.

948   **sī**, here, *to see whether, in the hope that*; governing the subjunctive in remote intention, a type of purpose clause.

            tibi: dative of reference with **animum**. Lucretius personalizes the description of his methodology by consistently reminding the reader that he is acting on his behalf. See also **tibi** (945) and the second person verb **perspicis** in line 949.

            tālī ratiōne: = **tālī pactō** or **modō**, *in such a way*, i.e., by writing in poetry.

939   ut puerōrum aetās imprōvida lūdificētur

940   labrōrum tenus, intereā perpōtet amārum

941   absinthī laticem dēceptaque nōn capiātur,

942   sed potius tālī pactō recreāta valēscat,

943   sīc ego nunc, quoniam haec ratiō plērumque vidētur

944   trīstior esse quibus nōn est tractāta, retrōque

945   vulgus abhorret ab hāc, voluī tibi suāviloquentī

946   carmine Pīeriō ratiōnem expōnere nostram

947   et quasi mūsaeō dulcī contingere melle,

948   sī tibi forte animum tālī ratiōne tenēre

949   versibus in nostrīs possem, dum perspicis omnem

950   nātūram rērum quā cōnstet cōmpta figūrā.

☙ Discussion Question

1.   What about Epicurean philosophy might seem bitter to those unfamiliar with it? (943–44)

---

949   **possem**: imperfect subjunctive idiomatically used in primary sequence after the main verb
         voluī (945), not *I wished*, but *I have wished*.

950   **quā**: modifying **figūrā** and introducing an indirect question.
         cōnstet: again, *exists, is*.
         cōmptus, -a, -um, *adorned, arranged, composed*.

958   **Omne quod est**: i.e., the universe, which consists of matter and void.

        nūllā regiōne viārum: literally, *in no direction of its ways*, i.e., *in no direction*.

959   **fīnītumst**: = **fīnītum est**, *is bounded, limited*.

        namque, conj.; here, *for indeed*.

        extrēmum, -ī, n., *extreme point, edge, limit, boundary*.

        dēbēbat: a potential use of the imperfect indicative, analogous to the imperfect subjunctive in a contrary-to-fact condition; if the universe were limited, *it ought (to have a boundary)*.

963   **Nunc**: returning to the true situation.

        summam: *the universe*.

        quoniam: as often, the linking conjunction has been delayed.

        fateor, fatērī, fassus sum, *to concede, admit*.

          fatendum: supply **est**; **nīl esse** is its subject, *that nothing exists must be admitted*.

964   **habet**: for subject understand **summa**, the universe, from line 963.

        fīne modōque: an emphatic redundancy, *a boundary and a limit*.

965   **rēfert, rēferre, rētulit**: impersonal, *makes a difference, matters*.

          rēfert: the subject is the indirect question **quibus . . . eius**.

        adsistō, adsistere, adstitī, *to take up position, stand, stop*.

          adsistās: here governing the dative **quibus . . . regiōnibus** in an indirect question, *in what regions you stand*.

        eius: = **summae**, *the universe*.

966   **usque**, adv., *all the way* (to), *as far as*.

          usque adeō: idiom, *to such an extent*; here amplifying the phrase **in omnīs . . . partīs**.

        quem: here, *whatever*; the clause is made general by **quisque**, since each person would probably choose a different place.

        quisque: a change from the second person subject of **adsistās**, perhaps implying *each one (of you)*.

        possideō, possidēre, possēdī, possessus, *to occupy*.

          possēdit: perfect with present sense in present general condition.

967   **tantundem**: here adverbial, *just so much, equally*.

        īnfīnītum: predicative, *infinite*, i.e., so that it is unbounded.

968   **iam**: *at this point*, i.e., for the sake of argument.

        fīnītum: predicative with **esse** understood; modifying **omne quod est spatium** (969).

        cōnstituātur: present subjunctive in future less vivid condition, *should be decided*. The subject is the clause **omne quod est spatium**, i.e., **omne spatium** (969).

969   **prōcurrō, prōcurrere, prō(cu)currī, prōcursūrus**, *to run forward*.

        ōrās: *borders, limits*.

970   **ultimus, -a, -um**, *farthest, at the end*.

        extrēmus, -a, -um, *at the end, uttermost, extreme*.

          ultimus extrēmās: emphatic juxtaposition.

        volātilis, -is, -e, *flying, swift*.

          sī quis prōcurrat ad ōrās . . . iaciatque volātile tēlum: Lucretius seems to be using the imagery of the Roman declaration of war, in which a fetial (a special priest) went to the border of the enemy and, after a formulaic declaration, threw a spear into the enemy's territory.

15. Infinite Space

A boundary implies something beyond it. Since there can be nothing outside the universe, it can have no boundary. Space is therefore infinite, unbounded in every direction. Lucretius illustrates the infinity of space and the absence of a boundary by asking what would happen to a javelin thrown from the hypothetical limit of the universe.

958   Omne quod est igitur nūllā regiōne viārum
959   fīnītumst; namque extrēmum dēbēbat habēre.

            . . .

963   Nunc extrā summam quoniam nīl esse fatendum,
964   nōn habet extrēmum, caret ergō fīne modōque.
965   Nec rēfert quibus adsistās regiōnibus eius;
966   usque adeō, quem quisque locum possēdit, in omnīs
967   tantundem partīs īnfīnītum omne relinquit.
968   Praetereā sī iam fīnītum cōnstituātur
969   omne quod est spatium, sī quis prōcurrat ad ōrās
970   ultimus extrēmās iaciatque volātile tēlum,

✑ **Discussion Questions**

1.   Explain or paraphrase the argumentation of lines 958–64.

2.   Does the universe have a center? (965–67)

A similar demonstration for a different purpose:

      But to return to our Idea of Space. If Body be not supposed infinite, which I think no one will affirm, I would ask, whether, if God placed a Man at the extremity of corporeal beings, he could not stretch his Hand beyond his Body? If he could, then he would put his Arm where there was before Space without Body; and if there he spread his Fingers, there would still be Space between them without Body: If he could not stretch out his Hand, it must be because of some external hindrance. . . . Where nothing hinders (as beyond the utmost bounds of all bodies) a Body put into motion may move on.

      John Locke, *An Essay Concerning Human Understanding* (1690), 2.13.21

971 **id**: = **tēlum**.

    validīs . . . vīribus: intentionally and emphatically redundant, *strong strengths;* cf. **validās . . . vīrīs** (576).

    utrum: introducing, together with **an** in line 973, the two alternative results.

    contortus, -a, -um, *hurled.*

    īre: infinitive in accusative and infinitive construction with **māvīs** (972).

972 **quō**: *where, to where.*

    fuerit missum: = **missum sit**, perfect subjunctive in subordinate clause in indirect statement. Here Lucretius uses **fuerit** as an extension from instances in which the participle is primarily adjectival.

    māvīs: second person singular present of **mālō, mālle**, *to prefer.* Lucretius returns to the second person, with which he began the sentence (965), and thus actively involves his reader.

    volō, -āre, -āvī, -ātūrus, *to fly.*

973 **prohibeō, -ēre, -uī, -itus**, *to prevent, hinder.*

    aliquid: accusative singular neuter subject of accusative and infinitive construction with **cēnsēs**; the *something* must be matter, since matter alone has the capability to obstruct.

974 **alteruter, alterutra, alterutrum**, *one or the other, one of the two.*

    Alterutrum . . . sūmāsque: the substantive clauses are the subject of **necessest**.

    fateāris . . . sūmās: subjunctives with **necessest**.

975 **Quōrum**: referring to the two alternative results of the javelin experiment.

    effugium, -ī, n., *escape.*

    praeclūdō, praeclūdere, praeclūsī, praeclūsus, *to shut off, bar.*

    omne: neuter as substantive, accusative subject of accusative and infinitive construction with **concēdās patēre** (976), *the all, the universe.* The word is severely displaced from its grammatical position, probably for emphasis at the line-end.

976 **exēmptā**: perfect passive participle of **eximō**, modifying **fīne** in an ablative absolute.

    concēdō, concēdere, concessī, concessūrus, *to admit, concede.*

977 **sīve . . . sīve**, conjs., *if . . . or if, whether . . . or.*

    prōbeat: contracted form of **prohibeat**, subjunctive in relative clause of characteristic expressing purpose.

978 **quōminus**, conj. + subjunctive, *so that not.* The final *s* has here been suppressed, as in **omnibu'** (159).

    quō: *where, to where.*

    missum est veniat . . . locet the subject of these verbs is **tēlum**.

        quō missum est: i.e., to its goal.

    fīnī: locative use of ablative with archaic ending, *at its goal.*

    sē: monosyllabic line-ending. Brown has suggested that "the staccato effect . . . fits the description of a spear thudding to its mark."

979 **sīve**: introducing the second alternative result.

    forās fertur: *if it is borne outside,* i.e., if it goes beyond the hypothetical limit.

    est . . . profectum: separation of **profectum est** (from **proficīscor**).

980 **Hōc pactō**, i.e., by this method of testing to see if the universe is limited.

    sequar: future; an interesting image in which Lucretius almost hounds the reader.

    ubicumque, relative adv., *in whatever place, wherever.*

    locāris: syncopated future perfect = **locāveris**.

981 **extrēmās**: emphatic enjambement, almost as if he were saying, *no matter how far;* modifying **ōrās** (980).

    tēlō: dative, *to the spear.*

    dēnique: *finally, in the end.*

    fīat: subjunctive in indirect question with **quid**; translate as future, *what will happen.*

971   id validīs utrum contortum vīribus īre

972   quō fuerit missum māvīs longēque volāre,

973   an prohibēre aliquid cēnsēs obstāreque posse?

974   Alterutrum fateāris enim sūmāsque necessest.

975   Quōrum utrumque tibi effugium praeclūdit et omne

976   cōgit ut exēmptā concēdās fīne patēre.

977   Nam sīve est aliquid quod prōbeat efficiatque

978   quōminu' quō missum est veniat fīnīque locet sē

979   sīve forās fertur, nōn est ā fīne profectum.

980   Hōc pactō sequar atque, ōrās ubicumque locāris

981   extrēmās, quaeram quid tēlō dēnique fīat.

982   Fīet utī nusquam possit cōnsistere fīnis

983   effugiumque fugae prōlātet cōpia semper.

ᴄꜱ Discussion Questions

1.   What sort of demonstration or mini-drama does Lucretius create to illustrate the infinity of space?

2.   How persistent is Lucretius as a teacher?

3.   In the warp of space-time as understood by Einstein, what would happen to the javelin?

---

982   **Fīet**: the bold juxtaposition with **fīat** closing the previous line stresses Lucretius' certainty about the outcome: *it will happen*.

     utī: = **ut**.

     nusquam, adv., *nowhere*.

     fīnis: nominative singular, *end, boundary* (of the universe).

983   **fuga, -ae**, f., *flight*.

     fugae: genitive with **cōpia**, *the opportunity for flight*.

       effugium fugae: interesting assonant word-play contributing to the ambiguity of the line. The line can be interpreted as describing how the infinite opportunity for flight endlessly prolongs the escape of the javelin; or one can conclude that the ongoing flight of the javelin prolongs the reader's escape from acceptance of Lucretius' argumentation. Or both interpretations may have been intended.

     prōlātō, -āre, *to extend, prolong*.

     cōpia, -ae, f., *supply, opportunity*.

     semper: in line-end position stressing the endlessness of space. It extends—always.

1021 **cōnsiliō**: ablative of means, *by plan, design.*

certē neque cōnsiliō: alliteration of hard *c* and *q* producing a sarcastic tone.

1022 **ōrdō, ōrdinis**, m., *order, position.*

ōrdine: ablative of place; understand **in**.

suō: modifying **ordine**; meaning the appropriate place for each atom, in order to constitute the world as we know it. **Suō** scans as one long syllable by synizesis.

sagācī: the adjective emphasizes the absurdity of believing that the atoms themselves have consciousness and thus could formulate plans.

locārunt: syncopated perfect = **locāvērunt**.

sē suō . . . sagācī: sibilant alliteration enhancing the sound effects of line 1021, which are continued in **nec quōs quaeque** (1023).

1023 **quōs**: introducing an indirect question governed by **pepigēre**; modifying **mōtūs**.

quaeque: i.e., **prīmōrdia**; subject of **darent**, *what motions each would give.*

mōtus, -ūs, m., *motion, movement.*

pepigēre: alternate third plural ending, perfect of **pangō**, *did they arrange, agree upon.*

profectō, adv., *indeed, certainly.*

1024 **multa**: i.e., **prīmōrdia**.

mūtāta: the atoms have changed in position and combination only; as atoms they cannot fundamentally change.

multa modīs multīs mūtāta: strong alliteration, recalling line 341, which also described variety in motion (**multa modīs multīs . . . movērī**). Note also the embedded word order.

omne: again as a substantive, *the universe.*

1025 **īnfīnītō**: understand **tempore**.

vexantur, *are harried.*

ex īnfīnītō vexantur: the slow pounding of the spondees stresses the vastness of time.

percieō, perciēre, perciī, percitus, *to propel.*

plāga, -ae, f., *blow.*

percita plāgīs: more hard alliteration; cf. 529 for a similar instance.

1026 **genus**: *type, kind;* accusative of repect or specification, equivalent to a genitive, *of every type.*

coetus, -ūs, m., *union, combination.*

mōtūs and **coetūs**: accusatives.

experiundō: gerund, ablative of means; interesting pentasyllabic line-ending here *and* in the line below, both preceded by spondaic fourth feet.

1027 **tandem**: i.e., after experimentation over infinite time.

dēveniō, dēvenīre, dēvēnī, dēventūrus, *to come, arrive.*

dēveniunt: present tense here and in **vexantur** (1025) for generalization. In Book 2.1023–76. Lucretius will show that our world is not unique; the process he describes has happened countless times throughout the universe.

dispositūra, -ae, f., *arrangement.*

1028 **haec rērum . . . summa**: our world; cf. 235 **haec rērum cōnsistit summa refecta**.

1029 **etiam**: *also.* It is important that the atoms, once they have come into a proper arrangement to create the world, then are able to maintain the arrangement.

magnōs: *long.*

1030 **ut**, here, *when.*

coniectast: = **coniecta est**; the subject is **rērum summa** (1028).

convenientīs: modifying **mōtūs**; here, *appropriate, harmonious,* i.e., those motions that permit the newly formed unions to continue. Note also the pentasyllabic ending, the third in this short passage!

16. Infinite Atoms

The universe was not created by design; rather, the atoms, by an interminable series of accidental collisions, eventually created the world we see around us. This creation would have been impossible if infinite matter were not present.

1021	Nam certē neque cōnsiliō prīmōrdia rērum
1022	ōrdine sē suō quaeque sagācī mente locārunt
1023	nec quōs quaeque darent mōtūs pepigēre profectō,
1024	sed quia multa modīs multīs mūtāta per omne
1025	ex īnfīnītō vexantur percita plāgīs,
1026	omne genus mōtūs et coetūs experiundō
1027	tandem dēveniunt in tālīs dispositūrās,
1028	quālibus haec rērum cōnsistit summa creāta,
1029	et multōs etiam magnōs servāta per annōs
1030	ut semel in mōtūs coniectast convenientīs

ᴏ⃝ Discussion Questions

1. Lucretius denies that the atoms arranged themselves in their order by a plan (**cōnsiliō**, 1021). To whom or what might such a **cōnsilium** belong?

2. Examine the word order in line 1029. What effects do the placement of **multōs** and **magnōs** create?

The contrary view of the Stoic Balbus:

My belief is that the universe and everything in it has been created by the providence of the gods and is governed by their providence through all eternity. The philosophers of our school usually divide the proof of this into three parts. The first derives from the same argument by which we prove that the gods exist. If you grant their existence, you must admit that the world is governed by their providence. In the second part we show that all things are ordered by a sentient natural power, impelling them towards their own perfection. When this has been established, it follows that in everything from the beginning there have been the seeds of life. Our third proof we derive from all the wonders of the earth and sky. So you must either deny that the gods exist at all, as Democritus and Epicurus did in their own way by reducing them to "phantom images": or else, if you admit their existence, you must also admit that they are active in the highest sense. What could be better than that their activity should be the government of the world? Therefore the world is governed by the wisdom of the gods. . . . God is not subject to obey the laws of nature. It is nature that is subject to the laws of God.

Cicero, *De natura deorum* 2.75–77 (tr. McGregor)

The biblical view:

In the beginning God created the heaven and the earth. And the earth was without form, and void; and darkness was upon the face of the deep. And the Spirit of God moved upon the face of the waters. And God said, Let there be light: and there was light.

Genesis 1.1–2

1031   **efficit ut**: Lucretius, in describing the enduring creativity of the earth, follows the usual division into sea, land, and air.

        avidum mare: direct object governed by **integrent amnēs** (1032). Here Lucretius refers to a natural phenomenon that puzzled the ancients. They saw that rivers perpetually drain into the sea, yet the sea never seems to increase. In Book 6.608–38 Lucretius solves the mystery by explaining the process of evaporation.

        flūminis: here in its root sense, *stream, flow*; singular because each river contributes its own stream.

        largis . . . flūminis undīs: ablative of means, *with the copious waves of the stream.*

1032   **integrō, -āre, -āvī, -ātus**, *to replenish.*

        sōlis: genitive singular with **vapōre**.

1033   **foveō, fovēre, fōvī, fōtus**, *to warm.*

        novō, -āre, -āvī, -ātus, *to renew, replenish.*

        summissa: *arisen from earth.* The use of this root, found also in line 8 (**tellus / summittit flōrēs**), shows that Lucretius believes the same natural processes apply to plants and animals.

1034   **flōreō, -ēre, -uī**, *to flourish.*

        vīvant: *thrive*, i.e., continue to shine. The subject is **ignēs**.

        lābentēs: describing the gliding motion of the stars; cf. line 2, **lābentia signa**.

1035   **quod**: accusative singular neuter relative, referring to line 1027, the fact that the atoms eventually reached arrangements that allowed for the earth's creation.

        facerent: the subject is the trio of natural forces: the sea, the earth with its living creatures, and the sky.

        māteriāī: genitive singular with **copia** (1036).

1036   **ex īnfīnītō**: supply **spatiō**.

        suborior, suborīrī, subortus sum, *to spring up; to come into being; to be provided.*

1037   **āmittō, āmittere, āmīsī, āmissus**, *to lose.*

        āmissa: accusative plural with **quaeque**. The idea is that each thing that has been created constantly sheds atoms, which must be replaced if the thing is to continue to survive.

        solent: again the subject is the trio of sea, earth, and sky.

        reparō, -āre, -āvī, -ātus, *to replace, restore.*

        in tempore: *at the right time.*

        quaeque: placed as it is at the line-end, gives the effect that the lost atoms are replaced—*one by one.*

1031   efficit ut largīs avidum mare flūminis undīs
1032   integrent amnēs et sōlis terra vapōre
1033   fōta novet fētūs summissaque gēns animantum
1034   flōreat et vīvant lābentēs aetheris ignēs;
1035   quod nūllō facerent pactō, nisi māteriāī
1036   ex īnfīnītō suborīrī cōpia posset,
1037   unde āmissa solent reparāre in tempore quaeque.

❧ Discussion Question

1.   Has Lucretius here offered sufficient proof that matter must be infinite in order to explain the existence and longevity of the universe familiar to us?

If . . . the void were boundless, and the bodies limited in number, the bodies could not stay anywhere, but would be carried about and scattered throughout the infinite void, not having other bodies to support them and keep them in place by means of collisions.
    Epicurus, *Epistle to Herodotus* 42 (tr. Bailey)

1   **Suāve**: understand **est**; predicate of the sentence, governing **spectāre** (2). As usual the *u* is consonantal and so does not scan.

      Suāve, marī magnō: note assonance giving the effect of peace and pleasure, which is then abruptly changed by the hard sounds of **turbantibus aequora ventīs**.

   marī magnō: ablative of place. **Magnum** is Lucretius' usual alliterative epithet for **mare**.

   turbantibus . . . ventīs: a descriptive ablative absolute.

   aequora: almost oxymoronic here, since during a storm the sea would certainly not be level, as the root **aequ-** implies.

2   **alterius**: genitive singular.

   labōrem: *struggle*.

      Suāve . . . ē terrā . . . alterius spectāre labōrem: the thought was a commonplace in antiquity, and the image reflects the ancient fear of the sea.

3   **quemquamst** : = **quemquam est**.

   vexārī quemquam: the accusative and infinitive construction is the subject of **est**.

   voluptās: predicate nominative with **est**. **Voluptās** itself is the Epicurean goal of pleasure through tranquillity. Here, however, Lucretius is careful to avoid the impression that his pleasure comes from callously delighting in another's misfortune (the German term for this is *Schadenfreude*).

      iūcunda voluptās: another instance of apparent redundance, which is in fact emphasis.

4   **quibus**: ablative interrogative in indirect question governed by **cernere**.

   malīs: here a substantive, *evils*.

   careās: the second person address involves the reader, as Lucretius likes to do.

   quia: the conjunction is delayed.

   cernere: the subject of **est**; **suāve** is the predicate adjective.

      sed quibus . . . suāve est: the purely dactylic line conveys a sense of lightness and relief.

5   **Suāve**: again, understand **est**. The construction parallels that of lines 1–2; in addition, the repetition of **suāve** three times in five lines is emphatic.

   magna: the third occurrence of this adjective in five lines is also emphatic!

   tueor, tuērī, tuitus sum, *to see, observe*.

6   **īnstructus, -a, -um**, *drawn up, arranged, ordered*.

   īnstructa: modifying **certāmina**, and going closely with **per campōs**.

   perīclī: = **perīculī**.

      tuā sine parte perīclī: this is the essential point—the enjoyment of one's own freedom from pain, rather than pleasure in another's suffering.

7   **bene**: take closely with **mūnīta**.

   quam, comparative *than* with **dulcius**.

   mūnīta: modifying **templa serēna** (8) and separated from it by the intervening adjective and ablative of means.

8   **ēditus, -a, -um**, *high, lofty*.

   doctrīna, -ae, f., *teaching, instruction, learning*.

   sapientum: genitive plural., as always in Lucretius, rather than the i-stem ending **-ium**.

      doctrīnā sapientum: i.e., Epicureanism; ablative of means with **mūnīta** (7).

   templa: *quarters, dwelling places*, but the word perhaps also anticipates Lucretius' claim that man can, through philosophy, live a life worthy of the gods (3.322).

   serēna: *tranquil, serene*.

      bene quam . . . templa serēna: reorder for translation: **quam tenēre ēdita serēna templa bene mūnīta doctrīnā sapientum**.

9   **dēspiciō, dēspicere, dēspexī, dēspectus**, *to look down on*.

   unde: again the linking word has been delayed.

   queās: potential subjunctive.

   passim, adv., *everywhere, in every direction*.

      passim . . . vidēre errāre: the adverb applies to both verbs.

   vidēre: governing a series of accusative and infinitive constructions with the infinitives **errāre, quaerere, certāre, contendere** and **nītī**.

ᘖ BOOK 2 ᘇ

17. Proem: The Sweet Tranquillity of Philosophy

Lucretius contrasts the sweetness of Epicurean tranquillity with the travails of other men, who vainly labor because they do not understand that human nature only requires a body free from pain and a mind released from worry and fear. Men should find pleasure in simplicity rather than in the excesses of wealth and power.

1	Suāve, marī magnō turbantibus aequora ventīs,
2	ē terrā magnum alterius spectāre labōrem;
3	nōn quia vexārī quemquamst iūcunda voluptās,
4	sed quibus ipse malīs careās quia cernere suāve est.
5	Suāve etiam bellī certāmina magna tuērī
6	per campōs īnstructa tuā sine parte perīclī.
7	Sed nīl dulcius est, bene quam mūnīta tenēre
8	ēdita doctrīnā sapientum templa serēna,
9	dēspicere unde queās aliōs passimque vidēre
10	errāre atque viam pālantīs quaerere vītae,

ᘖ Discussion Questions

1. How does the phrasing of line 1 elicit a sense of surprise?

2. In the three situations described, where does Lucretius place the man who is experiencing pleasure?

The direct survey of another's pleasure naturally gives us pleasure; and therefore produces pain when compar'd with our own. His pain, consider'd in itself, is painful: but augments the idea of our own happiness, and gives us pleasure. . . . Suppose I am now in safety at land, and wou'd willingly reap some pleasure from this consideration: I must think on the miserable condition of those who are at sea in a storm, and must endeavor to render this idea as strong and lively as possible, in order to make me more sensible of my own happiness. But whatever pains I may take, the comparison will never have an equal efficacy, as if I were really on the shore, and saw a ship at a distance, tost by a tempest, and in danger every moment of perishing on a rock or sand-bank.
    David Hume, *A Treatise of Human Nature* (1739–40), III.3.2

I am conscious that we have a degree of delight, and that no small one, in the real misfortunes and pains of others.
    Edmund Burke, *Of the Sublime and Beautiful* (1757), 51

---

10   **viam . . . vītae**: i.e., a way of life such as Epicurean philosophy teaches.
      pālor, -ārī, -ātus, *to wander aimlessly, stray.*
        pālantīs: accusative plural with **aliōs**, *as they wander aimlessly.*

11   **certō, -āre, -āvī, -ātūrus,** *to strive.*

     contendō, contendere, contendī, contentus, *to compete, contend.*

     nōbilitās, nōbilitātis, f., *nobility of rank/ birth.*

       ingeniō . . . nōbilitāte: a contrast. **Ingenium** is innate ability, whereas **nōbilitās** is social distinction, which was determined by birth and the political stature of one's family (which, with a few exceptions such as Marius and Cicero, was also dependent on birth).

     certāre . . . nōbilitāte: an unusual, and thus memorable, line containing only four words.

12   **noctēs atque diēs:** accusatives of duration of time.

     nītor, nītī, nīxus sum + infin., *to strive, strain, exert oneself* (to).

     praestāns, praestantis, *exceptional, extraordinary.*

       praestante: ablative singular in **-e** rather than the usual **-ī,** probably for metrical convenience.

13   **ēmergō, ēmergere, ēmersī, ēmersūrus,** *to come forth, arise, emerge.*

       ēmergere: a vivid image, suggesting rising out of water, as if from a murky swamp.

     ops, opis, f., *power;* pl., *wealth.*

     potīrī: here with the genitive **rērum,** *to be master of.*

       rērumque potīrī: referring to political power. There were many contemporary examples of such aspirants, such as Caesar and Catiline. Epicurus believed that one should avoid political life, since it is particularly stressful and thus precludes tranquillity.

14   **Ō miserās . . . mentīs, ō pectora caeca:** accusatives of exclamation. Also note the chiasmus.

15   **tenebrae, -ārum,** f. pl., *darkness.*

16   **dēgō, dēgere,** *to live, spend* (one's time).

     hōc: nominative singular neuter, subject of **dēgitur.**

     aevum -ī, n., *life.*

       aevī: genitive of the whole after a neuter substantive, *this life.*

     quodcumque: here adding a diminutive effect, *however small it is.*

       hōc aevī quodcumquest: a phrase intended to evoke pity at the short span of man's years, *this our life, however small it is.*

     vidēre: idiomatic use of an exclamatory infinitive with **nōnne,** *not to see that . . . ?*

17   **nīl aliud:** accusative, direct object of **lātrāre.**

     nātūram: accusative subject of accusative and infinitive construction; here referring to *human nature.*

     lātrō, -āre, *to bark, bark for;* here, *to cry out for.*

       nātūram lātrāre: a very vivid personsification, in which Lucretius conveys the intensity with which human nature demands attention to its needs by making a comparison to the insistent barking of a dog.

     utquī: strengthened form of **ut,** *that indeed.*

18   **sēiungō, sēiungere, sēiūnxī, sēiūnctus,** *to separate.*

     corpore: ablative of separation with **sēiūnctus** and **absit.**

     dolor, here, *pain.*

     mente: ablative of specification, *in the mind.*

     fruor, fruī, frūctus sum + abl., *to enjoy.*

       fruātur: the subject is understood as (human) **nātūra.** Also note the asyndeton (absence of a conjunction connecting to the previous idea).

19   **iūcundō sēnsū:** object of **fruātur.**

     cūrā . . . metū: ablatives of separation with **sēmōta.**

     sēmōta: perfect passive participle, nominative singular feminine, modifying the understood noun **nātūra.**

11   certāre ingeniō, contendere nōbilitāte,
12   noctēs atque diēs nītī praestante labōre
13   ad summās ēmergere opēs rērumque potīrī.
14   Ō miserās hominum mentīs, ō pectora caeca!
15   Quālibus in tenebrīs vītae quantīsque perīclīs
16   dēgitur hōc aevī quodcumquest! Nōnne vidēre
17   nīl aliud sibi nātūram lātrāre, nisi utquī
18   corpore sēiūnctus dolor absit, mente fruātur
19   iūcundō sēnsū cūrā sēmōta metūque?

ᘒ Discussion Questions

1.   Where and in what context have you seen the noun **tenebrae** before? (15)

2.   Paraphrase the goal of human nature as expressed in lines 16–19.

The things needed by the body are available to all without toil and trouble. But the things which require toil and trouble and which make life disagreeable are not desired by the body but by the ill-constitution of the mind.
    Democritus, *Fragment* 223 (tr. Freeman)

We must release ourselves from the prison of affairs and politics.
    Epicurus, *Vatican Sayings* 58 (tr. Bailey)

It is true that one man plants vineyards larger
than his neighbor's; that in the Campus
one candidate for office is of nobler blood;
another of greater reputation
and worth; another has a bigger crowd
of retainers; but with impartial justice
Necessity chooses from high and low,
the capacious urn shuffles every name.
    Horace, *Odes* 3.1.9–16 (tr. Shepherd)

A constrasting view:
    It is asserted, for example, that political life attracts in general only utterly worthless men, to be compared with whom is disgusting, and to contend with whom, especially when the mob is aroused is deplorable and dangerous. Therefore, it is said, a wise man does not grasp the reins of government, since he cannot restrain the mad lunges of the untamed rabble, nor does a free man strive against vile and savage opponents, or submit to the lash of insult, or suffer injuries that a wise man should not bear. As if a good and brave and high-minded man could find a more honorable reason for entering public life than the desire to avoid the rule of scoundrels or to prevent them from rending the commonwealth, while he himself, though eager to aid, looks impotently on!
    Cicero, *De re publica* 1.5 (tr. Sabine and Smith)

20   **ad**: *for*, i.e., to fulfill the bodily nature, i.e. bodily needs.

        pauca: accusative plural neuter, subject of accusative and infinitive construction governed by **vidēmus**.

21   **opus esse**, idiom, *to be needed/requisite.*

        quae . . . cumque: = **quaecumque**, by tmesis; the antecedent is **pauca** (20); nominative plural as subject of relative clause of characteristic.

        dēmō, dēmere, dēmpsī, dēmptus, *to take away, remove.*

22   **dēliciās**: the emphatic position indicates that the fact that there are few necessities does not necessarily imply that life cannot be pleasant.

        quoque: *also*, introducing a purpose clause, governed by **utī** (= **ut**) . . . **possint**.

        substernō, substernere, substrāvī, substrātus, *to set out, provide.* The image of the verb, which literally means *to strew, spread*, brings to mind a picnic in which good things are spread upon a cloth. This image anticipates the picture of a pleasant picnic, which Lucretius creates in lines 29–33.

        possint: the subject is **pauca** (20).

23   **grātius**: accusative singular neuter acting as substantive, *anything more pleasant.*

        grātius interdum: enjambement, as an emphatic afterthought.

        nātūra: again, human nature.

        requīrit, here, *lack, feel a lack.*

24   **nōn**: emphatic position.

        simulācrum, -ī, n., *image, statue.*

        aurea . . . iuvenum simulācra: the elaborate description in lines 24–26 recalls the banquet at King Alcinous' palace in Homer's *Odyssey* 7.100–02.: "boys of gold on pedestals / holding aloft bright torches of pitch pine / to light the great rooms" (tr. Fitzgerald). Of course, Lucretius is also probably referring to the excesses of his own day. There are candelabra from Pompeii (a century later) which depict just such torch-bearing youths.

        aedēs, aedis, f., *room*, pl., *house.*

25   **lampas, lampadis**, f., *torch.*

        lampadas: the **-as** ending with the short vowel is a Greek accusative plural.

        ignifer, ignifera, igniferum, *fire-bearing, fiery.*

26   **lūmina**: nominative plural, subject of **ut suppeditentur**.

        suppeditō, -āre, -āvī, -ātus, *to provide, supply.*

27   **nec**: = **sī nōn**, continuing the description begun in line 24.

        argentum, -ī, n., *silver.*

        fulgeō, fulgēre, fulsī, *to gleam.*

        fulgēt: lengthening of a normally short vowel (diastole), preserving an archaic pronunciation.

        aurum, -ī, n., *gold.*

        renīdeō, renīdēre, *to glitter, be bright.*

28   **citharae**: dative singular with **reboant**, *to the lyre.*

        reboō, -āre + dat., *to echo, resound.*

        laqueātus, -a, -um, *with panelled ceiling.*

        aurātus, -a, -um, *golden, gilded.*

        laqueāta aurātaque: hendiadys, *with gilded panels.*

        templa: here, *rafters, cross-beams*, in a very unusual sense which possibly implies that the gilded ceilings of the rich are a profanation of the **templa** of the gods.

29   **cum tamen**: introducing a scene contrasting in its natural simplicity with the rich excesses depicted above.

        inter sē: *in groups.* Epicurean philosophy valued the company of friends very highly.

        prosternō, prosternere, prostrāvī, prostrātus, *to lay on the ground.*

        prostrātī: nominative plural masculine, modifying an understood noun such as "friends." The participle, followed by **in grāmine mollī**, lends an air of informality to the picture. Romans normally dined reclining on couches.

        grāmen, grāminis, n., *grass.*

20	Ergō corpoream ad nātūram pauca vidēmus
21	esse opus omnīnō, quae dēmant cumque dolōrem,
22	dēliciās quoque utī multās substernere possint;
23	grātius interdum neque nātūra ipsa requīrit,
24	sī nōn aurea sunt iuvenum simulācra per aedēs
25	lampadas igniferās manibus retinentia dextrīs,
26	lūmina nocturnīs epulīs ut suppeditentur,
27	nec domus argentō fulgēt aurōque renīdet
28	nec citharae reboant laqueāta aurātaque templa,
29	cum tamen inter sē prostrātī in grāmine mollī
30	propter aquae rīvum sub rāmīs arboris altae
31	nōn magnīs opibus iūcundē corpora cūrant,
32	praesertim cum tempestās arrīdet et annī
33	tempora cōnspergunt viridantīs flōribus herbās.

ᑺ Discussion Questions

1. Is a life that satisfies only the essential bodily needs necessarily unpleasant?

2. How can the few things necessary for satisfying bodily needs also provide **dēliciās multās**?

3. What adornments grace the picnic described in lines 29–33, and how do they contrast with those described in lines 24–28?

---

30 **propter aquae . . . arboris altae**: the tranquil picture of the tree-shaded picnic by the river-side is enhanced by assonance, particularly of the vowel *a*.

31 **ops, opis**, f., *power; wealth.*
    nōn magnīs opibus: ablative of price, *not at great cost.*
  corpora cūrant: i.e., refresh themselves with food and drink.

32 **praesertim**, adv., *especially.*
  tempestās, here, *weather.*
  arrīdeō, arrīdere, arrīsī, arrīsus, *to smile, be favorable.*
    tempestās arrīdet: the lovely personification is borrowed from the Roman poet Ennius' *Annales* 457: **tempestātēsque serēnae / rīsērunt**. The picture of the tranquil beauty of nature which Lucretius paints in lines 32–33 is reminiscent of the scene of springtime in the first proem.
  annī: genitive singular with **tempora** (33).

33 **tempora**, here, *season.*
  cōnspergō, cōnspergere, cōnspersī, cōnspersus, *to sprinkle, strew.*
  viridāns, viridantis, *green, verdant.*
  herba, -ae, f., *grass.*

37 **quāpropter**, adv., *because of which, therefore.*
    nīl: adverbial accusative of respect, *not at all.*
    nostrō in corpore: i.e., our physical well-being.
    gāza, -ae, f., *treasure, riches.*

38 **prōficiō, proficere, prōfēcī, prōfectūrus**, *to be of benefit, to help.*

39 **quod superest**: *for the rest; to continue the argument*, that is to apply the argument to the mind as
    well as to the body. For this formulaic phrase see 1.50 and 1.921.
    animō: dative with **prōdesse**.
    nīl: again adverbial accusative.
    prōsum, prōdesse, prōfuī + dat., *to be helpful, good* (for).
        prōdesse: as subject of the infinitive understand **haec** (acc. pl. n.), referring to **gāzae** (37),
            nōbilitās and **glōria rēgnī** (38).
    putandum: supply **est** with the impersonal gerund governing an indirect statement, *one must
    think.*

40 **sī nōn forte**: = **nisi forte**, *unless by chance*; introducing an ironical suggestion of a possible
    exception—that our fears might be put to rout if we command large armies.
    campī: probably referring to the Campus Martius in Rome where military exercises were held.

41 **fervō, fervere, fervī**, *to move quickly; to seethe.*
    simulācra: *imitation, mimicry*; accusative plural with **cientīs**.
    cieō, ciēre, cīvī, citus, *to move, stir, rouse.*
        cientīs: accusative plural modifying **legiōnēs** (40).

42 **subsidium, -ī**, n., *reserve troops, auxiliaries.*
        subsidiīs: ablative of means with **cōnstabilītās**.
    ecum: = **equum**, archaic genitive = **equōrum**; however, the reading **et ecum vī** is a conjecture
    by Munro, since the manuscript is corrupt here.
    cōnstabiliō, -īre, -īvī, -ītus, *to strengthen.*
        cōnstabilītās: accusative plural modifying **legiōnēs** (40).

44 **hīs . . . rēbus**: i.e., by the sight of armies in mock combat.
    tibi: dative of reference with **animō** (45), but here in an emphatic position, stressing the exclu-
    sive power "you" have as hypothetical commander.
    tum: introducing the conclusion of the conditional clause begun with **sī nōn** (40).
        tibi tum . . . timefactae: alliteration with *t*, perhaps imitating the clanging sound of the
            weapons.
    timefactus, -a, -um, *made afraid, intimidated.*
    rēligiōnēs: *superstitious fears.*

45 **animō**: ablative of separation.
    pavidus, -a, -um, *trembling, terrified.*
    timōrēs: poetic plural.

46 **vacuum**: *free*; predicative adjective.

47 **Quod sī**: *but if.*
    rīdiculus, -a, -um, *absurd, ridiculous.*
    haec: i.e., all the bravado of military display.
    lūdibrium, -ī, n., *mockery.*

48 **rē vērāque**: *and in truth, and in fact.*
    metūs: nominative plural.
    sequāx, sequācis, *pursuing, dogging.*

49 **metuō, metuere, metuī**, *to fear.*
        metūs (48) **. . . metuunt**: an interesting thought—that fear itself can fear!
    ferus, -a, -um, *fierce.*
    tēlum, -ī, n., *spear, shaft, missile; weapon.*

18. Only Philosophy Frees the Mind from Fear

As riches and power cannot help the body, neither can they free the mind from its cares and fears. Only reason can dispel the fears that assail us. The passage concludes with the vividly contrasting imagery of light versus darkness.

37   Quāpropter quoniam nīl nostrō in corpore gāzae
38   prōficiunt neque nōbilitās nec glōria rēgnī,
39   quod superest, animō quoque nīl prōdesse putandum;
40   sī nōn forte tuās legiōnēs per loca campī
41   fervere cum videās bellī simulācra cientīs,
42   subsidiīs magnīs et ecum vī cōnstabilītās,

. . .

44   hīs tibi tum rēbus timefactae rēligiōnēs
45   effugiunt animō pavidae, mortisque timōrēs
46   tum vacuum pectus linquunt cūrāque solūtum.
47   Quod sī rīdicula haec lūdibriaque esse vidēmus,
48   rē vērāque metūs hominum cūraeque sequācēs
49   nec metuunt sonitūs armōrum nec fera tēla

☙ Discussion Questions

1.   Why does Lucretius here describe military exercises (41) rather than an actual military engagement (as in did in lines 5–6)?

2.   What image does the phrase **cūrae sequācēs** (48) convey?

50   **audācter**, adv., *boldly.*

     potēns, potentis + gen., *powerful* (in), *master* (of).

       rērumque potentīs: applying to political power, *potentates.*

51   **versor, -ārī, -ātus sum**, here, *to walk, strut.* Note the postponement by enjambement, adding emphasis.

     fulgor, fulgōris, m., *glitter, brightness, gleam.*

     revereor, reverērī, reveritus sum, *to feel awe for, fear.*

52   **splendor, splendōris**, m., *brilliance, luster.*

     purpureus, -a, -um, *purple, crimson.*

       vestis . . . purpureāī: purple or crimson clothing was a mark of wealth and distinction, since purple dye was made from the rare and expensive murex shell. Purple is still the color associated with royalty.

         clārum vestis splendōrem purpureāī: chiasmus. Also note the unusual pentasyllabic line-end.

53   **quid**: *why?*

     quīn, conj.+ subjunctive, with **dubitās**, *that.*

     omni': nominative singular modifying **potestās**; the final *s* has been suppressed.

       omni' . . . haec potestās: i.e., the ability to free the mind from fear and care.

     ratiōni': genitive singular, also with the final *s* suppressed. It is most unusual to find two such suppressions in the same line; a predicate genitive of possession.

54   **Omnis**: emphatically displaced from its noun **vīta**.

     tenebrae, -ārum, f. pl., *darkness.*

       in tenebrīs vīta: recalling the phrase **in tenebrīs vītae** (15) with which Lucretius summarized the foolish and misguided behavior of many men. The repeated image acts as a transition to the vivid simile of lines 55–58.

     vīta labōret: personification of **vīta**.

55   **velutī**: = **velut**.

     puerī: *children*; cf. 1.939.

     trepidō, -āre, -āvī, -ātus, *to be alarmed; to tremble.*

     omnia: accusative plural neuter, *everything*; direct object of **metuunt** (56).

     caecīs: *impenetrable, black*, modifying **tenebrīs** (54).

56   **nōs**: adults, who should know better, especially since they are tormented by their fears even **in lūce**, whereas the children are literally **in tenebrīs** and thus have some reason for their fears.

57   **interdum**: enjambement.

     nīlō: adverbial use of ablative, *not at all.*

     quae: i.e., **ea quae** (**ea**, the direct object of **timēmus**, 56, having been ellipsed); nominative plural neuter, subject of **sunt metuenda**.

     sunt metuenda: passive periphrastic.

58   **quae**: again the antecedent **ea** has been omitted.

     in tenebrīs: the third occurrence of this phrase within five lines!

     pavitō, -āre, *to tremble at.*

       pavitant: repeating the root **pavi-** from **pavidae** (45). The entire passage is full of images of trembling (cf. **trepidant**, 55) and fear (**timōres**, 45; **metūs**, 48; **metuunt**, 49; **reverentur**, 51; **metuunt**, 56; **timēmus**, 56; and **metuenda**, 57).

     fingō, fingere, fīxī, fīctus, *to imagine.*

     futūra: supply **esse**, future active infinitive agreeing with **quae**, *will be, will happen.*

59   **Hunc igitur terrōrem. . . speciēs ratiōque** (61): these lines are repeated verbatim from Book 1.146–48. Consult the notes there. The context in the two locations is similar; in both Lucretius laments that man is controlled by his fears, from which he can be freed only by the power of philosophy.

50   audācterque inter rēgēs rērumque potentīs

51   versantur neque fulgōrem reverentur ab aurō

52   nec clārum vestis splendōrem purpureāī,

53   quid dubitās quīn omni' sit haec ratiōni' potestās?

54   Omnis cum in tenebrīs praesertim vīta labōret.

55   Nam velutī puerī trepidant atque omnia caecīs

56   in tenebrīs metuunt, sīc nōs in lūce timēmus

57   interdum, nīlō quae sunt metuenda magis quam

58   quae puerī in tenebrīs pavitant finguntque futūra.

59   Hunc igitur terrōrem animī tenebrāsque necessest

60   nōn radiī sōlis neque lūcida tēla diēī

61   discutiant, sed nātūrae speciēs ratiōque.

○3 Discussion Questions

1.   What connotation would the phrase **rēgēs rērumque potentīs** have for the Romans? (50)

2.   Among the Romans, who wore purple garments? (52)

3.   What is it that men foolishly fear? (56–58)

The mind possesses the full and complete benefit of its human existence only when it spurns all evil, seeks the lofty and the deep, and enters the innermost secrets of nature. Then as the mind wanders among the very stars it delights in laughing at the mosaic floors of the rich and at the whole earth with all its gold. . . . The mind cannot despise colonnades, panelled ceilings gleaming with ivory, trimmed shrubbery, and streams made to approach mansions, until it goes around the entire universe and [looks] down upon the earth from above.
        Seneca, *Natural Questions* 1, Preface 7–8 (tr. Corcoran)

Men fear death as children fear to go into the dark: and as that natural fear in children is increased with tales, so is the other.
        Sir Francis Bacon, "Of Death" (1625)

Let me show in a figure how far our nature is enlightened or unenlightened:—Behold! human beings living in an underground den, which has a mouth open towards the light and reaching all along the den; here they have been from their childhood, and have their legs and necks chained so that they cannot move, and can only see before them, being prevented by the chains from turning round their heads. Above and behind them a fire is blazing at a distance. . . .
        You have shown me a strange image, and they are strange prisoners.
        Like ourselves, I replied; and they see only their own shadows, or the shadows of one another, which the fire throws on the opposite wall of the cave?
        True, he said; how could they see anything but the shadows if they were never allowed to move their heads?
        Plato, *Republic* Book 7.514a–b (tr. Bakewell)

95 **nīmīrum**, adv., *without doubt, certainly.*

  est: with **reddita** (96). Interesting line-end with this monosyllable, which is usually weak.

96 **reddita**: *is granted, is given*; enjambement with **est**.

  ināne: here referring to all space.

  profundus, -a, -um, *deep, profound.*

   prīmīs per . . . profundum: alliteration.

97 **sed magis**: *but rather.*

  assiduus, -a, -um, *incessant, constant.*

  exercita: *driven on*; modifying the understood subject **prīma corpora** = **prīmōrdia**.

98 **partim**, adv., *partly.*

  intervāllīs magnīs: ablative of description or circumstance with **resultant**.

  cōnfultus, -a, -um, *having clashed together.* The word occurs only here in Latin!

  resultō, -āre, *to rebound.*

99 **pars**: anaphora with **partim** (98). Even though **pars** is the nominative subject, note that the verb **vexantur** is plural, since Lucretius is describing the behavior of many atoms.

  brevibus spatiīs: in contrast with **intervāllīs magnīs** above (98).

  vexantur: *are driven.*

  ab ictū: *from the blow.*

114 **contemplō, -āre, -āvī, -ātus**, *to consider.*

  Contemplātor: second person singular future imperative, *Consider.* The future imperative was often used in legal contracts and conveys a sense of solemnity.

  lūmina: direct object of **fundunt** (115).

  cum . . . cumque: tmesis of an adverb equivalent to **quandōcumque**, *whenever.* **Cumcumque** is a word unique to Lucretius, who seems fond of the ending -**cumque**.

115 **īnserō, īnserere, īnseruī, īnsertus**, *to insert, let in.*

  īnsertī . . . radiī: light is considered to be an emission from the sun's rays.

  fundō, fundere, fūdī, fūsus, *to pour out, pour forth.*

  opācus, -a, -um, *darkened, dim.*

   per opāca domōrum: another periphrasis, equivalent to **per opācās domōs**.

116 **minūtus, -a, -um**, *small, minute.*

  minūta: modifying **corpora** (117).

   multa minūta modīs multīs: a favorite alliteration with *m*; cf. 1.341 and 1.1024, also in the context of motion.

  ināne: strictly referring to the apparently empty air, not to the void.

117 **corpora**: *motes.*

  miscērī: *to be mixed in confusion.*

118 **velut**: almost as if apologizing for the personified language he applies to the motes, which here wage war with one another.

  proelia pugnās: alliteration and asyndeton create a lively effect.

119 **ēdō, ēdere, ēdidī, ēditus**, *to give rise to, cause, produce.*

  ēdere: infinitive in accusative and infinitive construction with **vidēbis** (116); the subject is still **corpora** (117).

  turmātim, adv., *in troops, troop by troop*; with **certantia**, creating the picture of battle-formations.

  certantia: nominative plural neuter with **corpora** (117). Note how the participle holds the same metrical position as **certāmine** in 118.

  pausa, -ae, f., *pause, respite.*

120 **concilium, -ī**, n., *meeting, union.*

  conciliīs et discidiīs: Lucretius' terms for the processes first of the union of atoms to form compounds and then of the opposing dissolution.

  exercita, again, *driven on* (cf. 97).

121 **cōnicere**: *to guess.*

  ex hōc: i.e., from the action of motes in a sunbeam.

  prīmōrdia rērum: with **iactārī** (122), infinitive subject of **sit**.

19. The Perpetual Motion and Speed of the Atoms

Lucretius illustrates the perpetual motion of the atoms by describing the movements of motes in a sunbeam. Motion proceeds up the scale from the atoms to molecules and finally to the visible motes. Lucretius then similarly uses the speed of sunlight as an indication of the speed of atomic movement.

95	Nīmīrum nūlla quiēs est
96	reddita corporibus prīmīs per ināne profundum,
97	sed magis assiduō variōque exercita mōtū
98	partim intervāllīs magnīs cōnfulta resultant,
99	pars etiam brevibus spatiīs vexantur ab ictū.

. . .

114	Contemplātor enim, cum sōlis lūmina cumque
115	īnsertī fundunt radiī per opāca domōrum:
116	multa minūta modīs multīs per ināne vidēbis
117	corpora miscērī radiōrum lūmine in ipsō
118	et velut aeternō certāmine proelia pugnās
119	ēdere turmātim certantia nec dare pausam,
120	conciliīs et discidiīs exercita crēbrīs;
121	cōnicere ut possīs ex hōc, prīmōrdia rērum
122	quāle sit in magnō iactārī semper inānī.

. . .

142	Nunc quae mōbilitās sit reddita māteriāī
143	corporibus, paucīs licet hinc cognōscere, Memmī.

Brownian Motion (postulated by Robert Brown in 1826; confirmed by Einstein in 1905):
> The irregular motion of a body arising from the thermal motion of the molecules of the material in which the body is immersed. Such a body will of course suffer many collisions with the molecules, which will impart energy and momentum to it. Because, however, there will be fluctuation in the magnitude and direction of the average momentum transferred, the motion of the body will appear irregular and erratic.
>
> *McGraw Hill Encyclopedia of Science and Technology* (1992), 73

---

122   **quāle sit**: indirect question introduced by **conicere** (121), *what sort of thing it is.*
     iactārī: *to be tossed about*, as the result of collisions.
     in magnō . . . inānī: i.e., the real void of space, rather than the insignificant space of a room. The atoms are subject to much more violent collisions in the immensity of space than are the motes in a protected room.

142   **mōbilitās, mōbilitātis**, f., *speed.*
     sit reddita: *is granted, given* (cf. 96); subjunctive in indirect question with **cognōscere** (143).

143   **paucīs**: supply **verbīs.**
     hinc: i.e., from the example that follows

144   **Prīmum**: take closely with **cum**, *When first, As soon as.*
       aurōra, -ae, f., *dawn.*
       spargō, spargere, sparsī, sparsus, *to strew, sprinkle.*
         Prīmum aurōra . . . spargit . . . terrās: in lines 144–46 Lucretius paints a picture of natural
          beauty that rivals that of the first proem. The beauty of the scene is enhanced by assonance
          and the alliteration of *v* in line 145 and by liquid sounds, imitating the birds described, in
          line 146.

145   **nemus, nemoris**, n., *grove, forest.*
       nemora āvia: direct object of **pervolitantēs**.
       pervolitō, -āre, -āvī, -ātus, *to flit through.*

146   **āer, āeris**, m., *air* (technically the lower atmosphere).
       tener, tenera, tenerum, *delicate, soft.*
       liquidus, -a, -um, *clear; clear-sounding, bright.*
       oppleō, opplēre, opplēvī, opplētus, *to fill, fill up.*

147   **quam**: *how*, introducing an indirect question.
       soleat: subjunctive in the indirect question that is the subject of the accusative and infinitive
         construction that is dependent on **vidēmus**: *we see that how suddenly the sun . . . is obvious to*
         all.
       subitō soleat sōl: the alliteration sizzles like the sun.
       ortus: perfect passive participle from **orior, orīrī**.
       tempore tālī: i.e., at the moment of sunrise.

148   **convestiō, -īre, -īvī, -ītus**, *to clothe, cover, cloak.*
       perfundō, perfundere, perfūdī, perfūsus, *to pour over, dye, steep.*
       omnia: accusative plural neuter, direct object of **convestīre**, *everything, all nature.*

149   **omnibus**: i.e., to all people.
       in prōmptū, idiomatic phrase, *in evidence*; with **esse**, *to be clear.*
       manifestus, -a, -um, *plain, evident, obvious.*
         in prōmptū manifestumque: neuter accusative predicate adjective agreeing with the **quam**
          subitō soleat indirect question.

150   **At**: now Lucretius draws a crucial distinction between the speed of the sun's rays and of the
         atoms, since the rays pass through atmosphere, whereas the atoms pass through void.
       is quem sōl mittit: a parenthetical expression further defining **vapor**.
       lūmenque serēnum: together with **vapor** by hendiadys forming a single subject for **meat** (151).

151   **nōn**: emphatic position
       meō, -āre, -āvī, -ātūrus, *to pass, travel.*
       quō: *because of which*; i.e., because the rays are not passing through void.

152   **cōgitur**: the subject is the hendiadys of line 150: **vapor . . . lūmenque serēnum**.
       āeriās . . . undās: an unusual image, as if light were crossing a sea.
       quasi: with **dīverberat**, softening the unusual metaphor.
       dum, conj. + indic, *while.*
       dīverberō, -āre, -āvī, -ātus, *to cut, cleave, divide.*

157   **solidā . . . simplicitāte**: ablative of description.
         sunt solidā . . . simplicitāte: alliteration.
       prīmōrdia: the antecedent is embedded within the relative clause which describes it.

158   **per ināne meant vacuum**: note the phrasing almost identical to line 151.
       rēs . . . ūlla (159): i.e., any obstacle.
       remoror, -ārī, -ātus sum, *to delay, check.*

159   **forīs**, adv., *from without, from outside.*

161   **praecellō, praecellere**, *to excel, surpass.*
       mōbilitāte: ablative of specification.

162   **multō**: modifying **citius**.
       citus, -a, -um, *quick, speedy, rapid.*

144 Prīmum aurōra novō cum spargit lūmine terrās

145 et variae volucrēs nemora āvia pervolitantēs

146 āera per tenerum liquidīs loca vōcibus opplent,

147 quam subitō soleat sōl ortus tempore tālī

148 convestīre suā perfundēns omnia lūce,

149 omnibus in prōmptū manifestumque esse vidēmus.

150 At vapor is quem sōl mittit lūmenque serēnum

151 non per ināne meat vacuum; quō tardius īre

152 cōgitur, āeriās quasi dum dīverberat undās.

157 At quae sunt solidā prīmōrdia simplicitāte,

158 cum per ināne meant vacuum nec rēs remorātur

159 ūlla forīs . . .

161 dēbent nīmīrum praecellere mōbilitāte

162 et multō citius ferrī quam lūmina sōlis

163 multiplexque locī spatium trānscurrere eōdem

164 tempore quō sōlis pervulgant fulgura caelum.

ℂℬ Discussion Questions

1. Lines 145–46 are strictly unnecessary for Lucretius to make his point. What do they describe and why does he include them?

2. Explain the metaphor created by **convestīre** (148).

3. Can you think of a modern example of the speed of atomic motion analogous to the rapidity of the sun's light? (144–48)

4. What would Lucretius think of the Bose-Einstein condensate actually produced at the University of Colorado at Boulder in June 1995? (for details see *Discover*, January 1996, 58–59).

   [A] Bose-Einstein condensate . . . consists of a gas so dense and cold that individual atoms lose nearly all their motion and condense into a 'superatom' with the characteristics of a single atom. . . . Somewhere near absolute zero . . . atoms . . . begin to be governed by the laws of quantum mechanics, which hold that such particles can be thought of as waves. . . . At a low enough temperature, Einstein and Bose theorized, the wavelengths of each of the atoms in a group would begin to overlap, and the atoms would enter a single quantum state that would make them indistinguishable from one another.

   Kim A. McDonald, "New State of Matter," *The Chronicle of Higher Education* (7/21/95), A6

---

163 **multiplex, multiplicis**, *many times as large*.
   multiplex: neuter agreeing with **spatium**.
   locī spatium, *area of void*, i.e., the atoms cover a much greater distance.
   trānscurrō, trānscurrere, trāns(cu)currī, trānscursus, *to move rapidly across, race across*.
164 **quō**: *in which, as*.
   pervulgō, -āre, -āvī, -ātus, *to spread over, fill*.
   fulgur, fulguris, n., *a flash of light*.

216 **Illud**: summarizing Lucretius' statement in lines 217–20.

in hīs . . . rēbus: i.e., in his discussion of the structure of the universe.

aveō, avēre, *to be eager; to desire, wish.*

217 **corpora**: = **prīmōrdia**.

deorsum, adv., *downwards*. The letters *eo* scan as one long syllable by synizesis, here and in line 221.

> **deorsum feruntur**: describing what we term gravity. Epicurus believed that matter universally tended downwards, whereas we know that gravity is actually a pull that any mass exerts on another. On earth gravity therefore appears to be a downward motion, as matter is attracted to the center. Since, in establishing his philosophy, Epicurus relied on the evidence of the senses, he could not know that in the vast reaches of space, when an atom is very far from any other matter and thus is subject to no gravitational attraction, it is essentially weightless and can move freely in any direction. Moreover, in anything other than a local area, and particularly in an infinite universe, such as Epicurus has described, there really is no "downwards" direction.

rēctum: *straight*. Transferred epithet; though modifying **ināne**, it has the force of an adverb and should be taken closely with **deorsum**; *straight (downwards) through the void.*

218 **pondus, ponderis**, n., *weight.*

proprius, -a, -um, *one's own, its own, their own.*

> **ponderibus propriīs**: to be taken closely with **feruntur** (217) in enjambement; also note the alliteration.

fermē, adv., *quite, entirely*; as its position indicates, take with both **incertō** and the following **incertīsque locīs** (219).

219 **spatiō**: *course*; ablative of separation with **dēpellere**.

dēpellō, dēpellere, dēpulī, dēpulsus, here intransitive, *to deviate, swerve.*

> **dēpellere**: infinitive in indirect statement governed by **cognōscere** (216).
>> **spatiō dēpellere**: a metaphor from a race-course.

paulum: here adverbial accusative, *a little.*

220 **tantum**: adverbial accusative with **quod**, *only so much that.*

mōmen, mōminis, n., *movement, direction.*

> **tantum quod mōmen mūtātum**: in other words, the atom does not veer wildly from its downward course, but only so much that you could say its direction has shifted.

possīs: potential subjunctive.

221 **Quod**: *But.*

nisi: introducing one of Lucretius' favorite forms of argumentation, a contrary-to-fact condition.

dēclīnō, -āre, -āvī, -ātus, *to change direction, deviate, swerve.*

omnia: supply **corpora**.

222 **utī**: = **ut**, introducing a short simile.

gutta, -ae, f., *drop.*

per ināne profundum: phrase repeated from 96.

223 **foret**: = **esset**, with **nātus** and **creāta**; now pluperfect subjunctive in a past contrary-to-fact condition, *would not have been born nor . . . created.*

offēnsus, -ūs, m., *collision.*

nāta: perfect passive participle from **nāscor**.

plāga: the *blow* is important, since it causes both motion, as one atom hits another, and destruction, when a blow is strong enough to break up an aggregate of matter.

224 **prīncipiīs**: enjambement; equivalent to **prīmordiīs**, as often; dative of reference.

creāsset: syncopated pluperfect = **creāvisset**.

251 **cōnectō, cōnectere, cōnexuī, cōnectus**, *to tie, link together; to connect, join.*

20. The Swerve of the Atoms: Free Will

As they move downwards, atoms deviate ever so slightly from the vertical. As one atom swerves, it collides with another, which in turn hits a third, and so on. In this way the swerve (**clīnāmen**) causes the collisions which are responsible for all creation. Moreover, because it occurs randomly, the swerve breaks what would otherwise be an endless succession of pre-determined motions. Thus the swerve explains the existence of human free will.

216	Illud in hīs quoque tē rēbus cognōscere avēmus,
217	corpora cum deorsum rēctum per ināne feruntur
218	ponderibus propriīs, incertō tempore fermē
219	incertīsque locīs spatiō dēpellere paulum,
220	tantum quod mōmen mūtātum dīcere possīs.
221	Quod nisi dēclīnāre solērent, omnia deorsum,
222	imbris utī guttae, caderent per ināne profundum,
223	nec foret offēnsus nātus nec plāga creāta
224	prīncipiīs: ita nīl umquam nātūra creāsset.

. . .

251	Dēnique sī semper mōtus cōnectitur omnis
252	et vetere exoritur semper novus ōrdine certō
253	nec dēclīnandō faciunt prīmōrdia mōtūs
254	prīncipium quoddam quod fātī foedera rumpat,

ᘓ Discussion Questions

1. How does Lucretius emphasize that the swerve happens randomly without predetermination? (217–20)

2. In an omitted section Lucretius argues that collisions could not be caused by a heavier object falling on a lighter one. All objects fall at the same rate. What famous experiment does this belief anticipate?

252	**vetere**: ablative with **exoritur** modifying an understood **mōtū**.
	novus: modifying an understood **mōtus**.
	ōrdine certō: the important point here — the chain of causation could not be broken.
253	**dēclīnandō**: gerund in ablative of means.
	prīmōrdia: nominative plural.
	mōtūs: genitive singular with **prīncipium quoddam** (254).
254	**quod**: introducing a relative clause of characteristic.
	foedus, foederis, n., *treaty, compact, law.*
	fātī foedera: unusual alliteration with *f.*

255   **ex īnfīnītō**: supply **tempore**.

     nē: the linking conjunction has, as often, been delayed.

     causam causā: emphatic anaphora, which by the word order literally demonstrates Lucretius' point —and in the correct order! Here cause does follow cause.

256   **līber, lībera, līberum**, *free*.

       lībera: strongly emphatic in its severe displacement from its noun **voluntās**, which closes the next line.

     unde: introducing the main clause, which follows the conditional idea begun in line 251.

     haec: another dangling adjective, leaving the reader in suspense about the subject, **voluntās** (257).

     exstō, exstāre, exstitī, *to exist, be found*.

257   **inquam**, irreg., *I say*.

     inquam: an unusually emphatic intrusion of the poet.

     fatīs: ablative of separation with **āvulsa**.

     āvellō, āvellere, āvellī, āvulsus, *to tear away, wrest*.

     voluntās, voluntātis, f., *will*.

     fatīs āvulsa voluntās: a very forceful image; note the ironic alliteration **āvulsa voluntās**.

258   **quō**: *where*.

     voluptās: the subject is placed in the emphatic line-end position. **Voluptās** is the goal of Epicurean philosophy. Lucretius seems to be punning on the relationship between **voluntās**, which ends line 257, and **voluptās**: your will is your pleasure.

259   **dēclīnāmus . . . regiōne locī certā** (260): by using the same phrasing with which he described the free swerve of the atoms (218–19, 221), Lucretius demonstrates that the same principles apply across the entire scale of the universe—from the atoms to man. Thus he also intimately connects the operation of human free will to the actions of the atoms.

260   **ubi**, referring to both **tempore** (259) and **regiōne**, thus both *when* and *where*.

     mēns: in emphatic line-end position, as was **voluptās** (258); the monosyllabic ending also adds stress.

261   **dubiō procul**, idiom, *doubtless, undoubtedly*.

     hīs rēbus: dative, referring to voluntary actions such as motion. Take with **prīncipium dat** (262).

     sua cuique voluntās: *his own free will for each man*; an emphatic statement.

262   **prīncipium**: supply the genitive **mōtūs**, as in line 253.

     hinc: i.e., from the will (**sua cuique voluntās**).

     membrum, -ī, n., *limb*.

     rigō, -āre, -āvī, -ātus, *to lead/conduct water*; in middle sense, *to flow, diffuse*.

       rigantur: the verb, which describes flowing water, nicely indicates the ease with which the motions pass from the mind to the limbs.

For, indeed, it were better to follow the myths about the gods than to become a slave to the destiny of the natural philosophers: for the former suggests the hope of placating the gods by worship, whereas the latter involves a necessity which knows no placation.

     Epicurus, *Epistle to Menoeceus* 134

The physical movement of the atoms is now recognized as something very like Lucretius' 'swerve.' Sir James Jeans . . . says in describing Bohr's theory: "The electron did not move continuously through space and time but jumped, and its jumps were not governed by the laws of mechanics, but . . . by the laws of probability. . . . Before the jumps occurred, there was nothing to show which atoms were going to jump."

     Cyril Bailey, *Titi Lucreti Cari De Rerum Natura Libri Sex* (1947), vol 2, 842 regarding Niels Bohr's theory of electron jumps

255   ex īnfīnītō nē causam causa sequātur,

256   lībera per terrās unde haec animantibus exstat,

257   unde est haec, inquam, fātīs āvulsa voluntās

258   per quam prōgredimur quō dūcit quemque voluptās,

259   dēclīnāmus item mōtūs nec tempore certō

260   nec regiōne locī certā, sed ubi ipsa tulit mēns?

261   Nam dubiō procul hīs rēbus sua cuique voluntās

262   prīncipium dat et hinc mōtūs per membra rigantur.

⟨⟩ Discussion Questions

1.   If everything is thought to be pre-determined, is there any point in developing an ethical system?

2.   What would Lucretus think of the determinism of the Newtonian system as described below?

     "The French scientist the Marquis de Laplace [1749–1827] . . . suggested that there should be a set of scientific laws that would allow us to predict everything that would happen in the universe, if only we knew the complete state of the universe at one time. For example, if we knew the positions and speeds of the sun and the planets at one time, then we could use Newton's laws to calculate the state of the solar system at any other time. Determinism seems fairly obvious in this case, but Laplace went further to assume that there were similar laws governing everything else, including human behavior.

     Stephen Hawking, *A Brief History of Time* (1988), 53

3.   How does the Lucretian swerve compare with quantum theory, as described below?

The greatest single discovery of twentieth-century physics is that this principle [of absolute determinism] is false. This discovery has two different facets, the first of which is the uncertainty principle of quantum mechanics. According to quantum theory, things that happen in the world do so quite without cause, . . . as to when a particular nucleus of uranium will decay, quantum theory is silent. . . . Similarly, an exact accounting of the position and velocity of every particle in the universe cannot be drawn up . . . because there is no such thing. . . . Laws of cause and effect are replaced by laws of chance.

     George Greenstein, *Frozen Star* (1983), 255

One could not predict the specific result of an individual measurement. Quantum mechanics therefore introduces an unavoidable element of unpredictability or randomness into science.

     Stephen Hawking, *A Brief History of Time* (1988), 56

I find the idea quite intolerable that an electron exposed to radiation should choose *of its own free will*, not only its moment to jump off, but also its direction. In that case, I would rather be a cobbler, or even an employee in a gaming house, than a physicist.

     Albert Einstein, *The Born-Einstein Letters* (1971), 82, objecting to the results of his own discoveries in quantum physics

263   **Nōnne vidēs**: introducing an explanatory example, which would be familiar to all Romans from the frequent races held as part of festivals.

     patefaciō, patefacere, patefēcī, patefactus, *to open, throw open*.

       patefactīs . . . carceribus (264): ablative absolute.

     tempore pūnctō, idiom, *in a moment, an instant*; **pūnctus** means *pricked*, as with a pin, so in a "pin-prick" of time.

264   **carcer, carceris**, m., *prison*; here, *stall, starting-gate*.

     posse: main infinitive in an accusative and infinitive construction despendent on **vidēs** (263).

     tamen, i.e., despite the fact that the gates have opened.

265   **vim**: accusative subject of the infinitive **posse**.

     cupidus, -a, -um, *eager, keen*.

       cupidam: transferred epithet; it is really the horses that are eager.

     dē subitō: archaic adverbial expression, *suddenly*; with **tam**, *as suddenly*.

     quam: comparative, *as*.

266   **Omnis**: nominative singular, severely displaced from its noun, **cōpia** (267), for emphasis (cf. **lībera**, 256; **haec**, 257).

267   **conciō, concīre, concīvī, concītus**, *to stir up, rouse*.

     concīta, *once stirred up*; agreeing with **copia māteriāī**, the understood subject of the purpose clause **ut . . . sequatur** (268).

       copia concīrī . . . concīta: strong alliteration, preceded by **corpus** (266). Also note the repetition of the verb **concīre**, reinforcing the idea of motion.

     artus, -ūs, m., *limb*.

268   **omnīs**: accusative plural modifying **artūs** (267), in enjambement.

     ut: the conjunction , which introduces the clause **concīta . . . sequātur** (268) has been delayed.

     cōnītor, cōnītī, cōnixus sum, *to strive, make an effort*.

       cōnixa: modifying the understood subject **cōpia māteriāī**.

289   **nē**: introducing a substantive clause, which is then summarized by **id** in line 292.

     necessum: old form of **necesse**; here a true substantive, *necessity*; accusative singular neuter.

290   **intestīnus, -a, -um**, *internal*.

       necessum intestīnum habeat cūnctīs in rēbus agendīs: i.e., absolute predetermination.

291   **dēvincō, dēvincere, dēvīcī, dēvictus**, *to conquer thoroughly, subjugate, subdue*.

     quasī: softening the metaphor of **dēvicta**. The *i* has been lengthened by diastole.

292   **id**: accusative singular, direct object of **facit**; summarizing the **nē** clause above (289).

     facit: the subject remains **mēns ipsa** (265).

     exiguus, -a, -um, *small, slight*.

     clīnāmen, clīnāminis, n., *swerve*.

       clīnāmen: the only instance of the famous word after which the theory is named The root is, of course, the same as in the descriptive verb forms **dēclīnāre** (221), **dēclīnandō** (253), and **dēclīnāmus** (259). Unfortunately we do not know the corresponding Greek term used by Epicurus.

293   **nec regiōne . . . certō**: the line is repetitive (cf. 218–19 and 259–60) and therefore accentuates the point that the **clīnāmen** is absolutely unpredictable.

263   Nōnne vidēs etiam patefactīs tempore pūnctō
264   carceribus nōn posse tamen prōrumpere equōrum
265   vim cupidam tam dē subitō quam mēns avet ipsa?
266   Omnis enim tōtum per corpus māteriāī
267   cōpia concīrī dēbet concīta per artūs
268   omnīs ut studium mentis cōnixa sequātur.

. . .

289   Sed nē mēns ipsa necessum
290   intestīnum habeat cūnctīs in rēbus agendīs
291   et dēvicta quasī cōgātur ferre patīque,
292   id facit exiguum clīnāmen prīncipiōrum
293   nec regiōne locī certā nec tempore certō.

ℭ Discussion Questions

1.   How does the Lucretian belief in the swerve, a limited randomness, compare with the modern theory of chaos (see description below)?

2.   How does Lucretius' picture of horses at a starting gate illustrate his point about the operation of free will?

Exploring the question of how one can reconcile the operation of chance with belief in divinity:

Chance is perhaps the pseudonym of God when He did not wish to sign.
   Anatole France, *The Garden of Epicurus* (1894)

I shall never believe that God plays dice with the world.
   Albert Einstein, quoted by Philipp Frank, *Einstein, His Life and Times* (1947), 208

God not only plays dice but also sometimes throws them where they cannot be seen.
   Stephen Hawking, quoted by Michael Harwood, "The Universe and Doctor Hawking," *New York Times Magazine*, January 23, 1983, 56

The Theory of Chaos (randomness within limits):

   Chaos cuts away at the tenets of Newton's physics. . . . Chaos eliminates the Laplacian fantasy of deterministic predictability. The simplest systems are now seen to create extraordinarily difficult problems of predictability. Yet order arises spontaneously in these systems—chaos and order together. (7–8)
   [On Lorenz's computer weather program]: He saw a fine geometrical structure, order masquerading as randomness. . . . The map displayed a kind of infinite complexity. It always stayed within certain bounds . . . The shape signaled pure disorder, since no point or pattern of points ever recurred. Yet it also signaled a new kind of order. (30)
   [On strange attractors]: Nature was *constrained*. Disorder was channeled, it seemed, into patterns with some common underlying theme. (152)
   James Gleick, *Chaos: Making a New Science* (1987)

308   **Illud**: to be explained by the clauses beginning **quāre, omnia cum.** . . .

      Illud . . . mīrābile: as in Book 1 regarding the existence of invisible particles, Lucretius is careful to anticipate the objections of his reader when faced with phenomena he cannot physically sense.

      quāre: here interrogative adv., *why*.

309   **cum**: here *although*, the usual meaning when **tamen** (310) follows.

      sint in mōtū: unusual slow spondaic ending for the line, which at first seems especially odd since the line is describing perpetual motion; yet Lucretius' point is to illustrate that moving objects may appear stationary, as this line almost comes to a halt.

310   **summa**:*the whole*.

      summa . . . summā: one of the word-plays Lucretius so loves; here he uses the same root, once as a substantive, once as an adjective, in different senses—*the whole* and *complete*. In his translation Bailey maintains the word-play "yet the whole seems to stand wholly at rest."

312   **Omnis**: typical Lucretian separation of an adjective from its noun for emphasis; modifying **nātūra** (313).

      īnfrā, adv., *below, beneath*.

      longē nostrīs ab sēnsibus īnfrā: *far beneath our senses*.

313   **prīmōrum**: here = **prīncipiōrum** or **prīmōrdiōrum** (which would not scan).

      quāpropter, adv., *therefore*.

      ubi: here = **cum**, *since*, with subjunctive.

      ipsa: accusative plural neuter, modifying the understood noun **prīmōrdia**.

314   **surpere**: contracted form of **surripere**, *to steal, take away*.

      dēbent: the subject is understood to be the **prīmōrdia**, which are thus personified.

315   **praesertim**, adv., *especially*.

      quae: accusative plural neuter; understand **ea** as antecedent.

      possīmus: subjunctive by attraction.

      cēlent: the subject is the understood antecedent of the preceding relative clause.

316   **tamen**: i.e., although we can see the objects, nevertheless we cannot see that they are moving.

      spatiō . . . locōrum: i.e., by the distance or interval between the two places—your location and that of the object.

      dīdūco, dīdūcere, dīdūxī, dīductus, *to separate, divide*.

317   **Nam**: introducing the first example showing that the movements of something visible, here a flock of sheep, can be hidden by distance.

      collī: archaic ablative ending, similarly in line 322.

      tondeō, tondēre, totondī, tōnsus, *to browse on, crop*.

      tondentēs: nominative plural modifying **pecudēs** (318).

      pābula laeta: the formulaic phrase seen in the opening proem, again with **pecudēs** (1.14) and similarly in 1.257.

318   **lāniger, lānigera, lānigerum**, *wool-bearing, wooly, fleecy*.

      reptō, -āre, -āvī, -ātūrus, *to move slowly, creep*.

      reptant: the verb nicely depicts the slow movement of a flock across a hillside, as does the slow spondaic movement of line 317.

      quamque: feminine, referring to each sheep (**ovis, ovis**, f.).

      vocantēs: nominative plural feminine modifying **herbae** (319) in a very vivid personification. The lush grass seems actually to call and beckon (**invītant**) the sheep, as each successive blade seems juicier and more enticing.

319   **gemmō, -āre, -āvī, -āturus**, *to glitter, sparkle* (like a gem).

      rōs, rōris, m., *dew*.

      recēns, recentis, *new, fresh*.

      gemmantēs rōre recentī: a beautiful picture of a meadow sparkling in the early morning.

21. The Invisibility of Atomic Motion

Although the atoms of an object are constantly in motion, at its surface it may seem to be completely at rest. To show how distance can render motion invisible, Lucretius describes two lively but contrasting scenes: of sheep and of armies. When observed from a distance, the participants in each scene seem stationary.

308   Illud in hīs rēbus nōn est mīrābile, quārē,

309   omnia cum rērum prīmōrdia sint in mōtū,

310   summa tamen summā videātur stāre quiēte.

. . .

312   Omnis enim longē nostrīs ab sēnsibus īnfrā

313   prīmōrum nātūra iacet; quāpropter, ubi ipsa

314   cernere iam nequeās, mōtūs quoque surpere dēbent;

315   praesertim cum, quae possīmus cernere, cēlent

316   saepe tamen mōtūs spatiō dīducta locōrum.

317   Nam saepe in collī tondentēs pābula laeta

318   lānigerae reptant pecudēs quō quamque vocantēs

319   invītant herbae gemmantēs rōre recentī,

320   et satiātī agnī lūdunt blandēque coruscant;

321   omnia quae nōbīs longē cōnfūsa videntur

322   et velut in viridī candor cōnsistere collī.

---

320   **satiō, -āre, -āvī, -ātus**, *to satisfy, fill.*

    agnus, -ī, m., *lamb.*

      satiātī agnī lūdunt: Lucretius turns from the slow grazing of the adult sheep to the frolicking of the young lambs. Their lively movements accentuate his point, since even these are invisible at a distance. Again, the season depicted is springtime. For a similarly charming scene, see 1.257–61. There the sated adults lie **per pābula laeta**, but their offspring, almost drunk with fresh milk, cavort through the grass on wobbly limbs.

    coruscō, -āre, -āvī, *to thrust/push with the horns; here, to butt.*

321   **omnia**: with **quae**, nominative plural, referring to the activities of the previous scene.

    nōbīs: with **videntur**; remember we are to imagine ourselves watching the scene from afar (**longē**).

    cōnfundō, cōnfundere, cōnfūsī, cōnfūsus, *to confuse, blur.*

    cōnfūsa: predicative adjective, *blurred.*

322   **viridis, -is, -e**, *green.*

    candor, candōris, m., *whiteness, gleam.*

    cōnsistere: *to stand still*; as a contrast to the actual movement of the animals.

      candor cōnsistere collī: the alliteration acts as a transition into the next description, in which the movements of armies are described with frequent *c* and *s* sounds to replicate the clang of armor.

323   **loca**: accusative plural as direct object of **complent**, and in periphrasis with **campōrum** (324).
        cum: the conjunction is delayed.
        cursus, -ūs, m., *running, rapid motion;* here, *charging.*

324   **simulācrum, -ī**, n., *image.*
        cieō, ciēre, cīvī, citus, *to move, stir, rouse.*
          bellī simulācra cientēs: the phrase is repeated from 2.41, where Lucretius also described the exercises of an army over a field, probably the Campus Martius.

325   **fulgor, fulgōris**, m., *gleam.*
        tōta: nominative singular feminine, emphatically displaced from its noun **tellūs** (326).
        circum: adverbial, *around, roundabout.*
          fulgor ibi . . . clāmōreque montēs (327): the description alludes to a description in Homer, *Iliad* 19.362–64: "The shining swept to the sky and all earth was laughing about them / under the glitter of bronze and beneath their feet stirred the thunder / of men, within whose midst brilliant Achilleus helmed him" (tr. Lattimore).

326   **aes, aeris**, n., *bronze* (of the weapons).
        renīdēscō, renīdēscere, *to gleam, shine.*
        subter: here adverbial, *beneath, down below;* take closely with **excītur** (327).
        virum: = **virōrum**.
          virum vī: alliteration and monosyllabic line-ending.

327   **exciō, excīre, excīvī, excītus**, *to rouse, produce.*
        pedibus: ablative of means, clarifying the meaning of **virum vī** (326).
        clāmōreque: ablative of means effecting the transition to the next description.
        montēs: nominative plural.

328   **īciō, īcere, īcī, ictus**, *to strike.*
        rēiectō, -āre, -āvī, -ātus, *to throw back.*
        sīdus, sīderis, n., *star.*
          ad sīdera mundī: i.e., to the heavens.

329   **circumvolitō, -āre, -āvī**, *to fly round about, dash about.*
        eques, equitis, m., *horseman.*
          equitēs: nominative plural.
        mediōs: another adjective severely displaced from its noun, **campōs** (330).

330   **trānsmittō, trānsmittere, trānsmīsī, trānsmissus**, *to go across.*
        quatiō, quatere, quassus, *to shake.*
        impete: old ablative formation = **impetū**, which would not scan.
        campōs: direct object of both **trānsmittunt** and **quatientēs**.

331   **tamen**: i.e., despite all the movement, as so vividly described especially in lines 329–30.

332   **stāre**: *to be stationary, motionless.*
        videntur: the subject is **equitēs** (329), as well as all the activities of the **magnae legiōnēs** (323).
        in campīs cōnsistere fulgor: Lucretius intentionally echoes the phraseology of the conclusion of his first description in line 322.

323   Praetereā magnae legiōnēs cum loca cursū

324   campōrum complent bellī simulācra cientēs,

325   fulgor ibi ad caelum sē tollit tōtaque circum

326   aere renīdēscit tellūs, subterque virum vī

327   excītur pedibus sonitus clāmōreque montēs

328   ictī rēiectant vōcēs ad sīdera mundī

329   et circumvolitant equitēs mediōsque repente

330   trānsmittunt validō quatientēs impete campōs.

331   Et tamen est quīdam locus altīs montibus unde

332   stāre videntur et in campīs cōnsistere fulgor.

✑ Discussion Questions

1.   From Lucretius' description do you think that he actually witnessed or participated in military maneuvers? How vivid is his description?

2.   Does the description of a distant vantage point in lines 331–32 remind you of an earlier passage? What associations do the lines evoke?

3.   Can you think of other examples to illustrate the invisibility of motion?

4.   What poetic devices do you find in lines 324–25?

333   **Nunc age**: a formulaic phrase repeated from 1.265 and 1.921.

      iam, i.e., now that we have reached this point in the argumentation.

      deinceps, adv., *in turn, next.* The vowels *ei* scan as one long syllable by synizesis.

      exōrdia: a substitute for **prīmōrdia**, in the usual phrase **prīmōrdia rērum**. Nominative plural as subject of an indirect question governed by **percipe** (335).

334   **quam**: *how.*

      distō, distāre, *to differ, be different.*

        sint distantia: = **distent**, *they differ.*

      fōrmīs: ablative of specification, *in shapes.*

335   **percipiō, percipere, percēpī, perceptus**, *to learn.*

      multigenus, -a, -um, *of many kinds, manifold.* This compound adjective is found only here in Latin and seems to have been coined by Lucretius. It follows his usual dactylic pattern.

      quam: again, *how,* introducing a third indirect question.

      variātus, -a, -um, *varied, diversified.*

        multigenīs . . . figūrīs: ablative of specification.

338   **sit**: in emphatic position.

      eōrum: = **prīncipiōrum**.

339   **fīnis**: *limit*; i.e., there is an infinite number of atoms.

      utī: = **ut**.

        utī docuī: in 1.1035–37, passage 16. The phrase is an aside which briefly interrupts the grammatical flow of the line, but which serves to remind the reader of an important point.

      summa: *definite sum, definite quantity.*

340   **dēbent**: emphatic position for the verb, further strengthened by **nīmīrum**; the subject is an understood **prīmōrdia** modified by **omnia**.

      omnibus: dative dependent on **parī** and **similī** (341).

        omnibus omnia: anaphora, which by the juxtaposition illustrates Lucretius' point—one can theoretically set the atoms side by side and compare them closely.

      prōrsum, adv., *altogether, absolutely.*

        omnia prōrsum, *absolutely all.*

341   **fīlō**, here, *size* (as in the thickness of a thread), in ablative of description.

        esse parī fīlō, *to be of equal size.*

      adfectus, -a, -um + abl., *endowed with, possessed of.*

342   **Praetereā**: introducing a section in which Lucretius charmingly describes how each living creature is unique. In its enthusiastic celebration of the delights and bounties of nature, this passage is reminiscent of the first proem and of Book 2.317–20 just preceding.

      mutaeque natantēs: modifying **pecudēs** (343).

343   **squāmigerum**: genitive plural, *scale-bearing,* i.e., *fish.*

      armenta, -ōrum, n. pl., *herds, cattle.*

344   **et variae volucrēs**: the phrasing here is interesting, since it together with the end of line 346 replicates 2.145: **et variae volucrēs nemora āvia pervolitantēs**.

      laetāns, laetantis, *delightful, cheerful, agreeable.*

      quae: nominative plural; its antecedent is **volucrēs**.

      loca aquārum: periphrasis, *watering-places,* i.e., streams, pools, etc., as will be detailed in line 345.

345   **concelebrō, -āre, -āvī, -ātus**, *to throng, crowd.*

      lācus, -ūs, m., *lake.*

346   **pervulgō, -āre, -āvī, -ātus**, here, *to frequent, haunt.*

22. The Variety of Atomic Shapes

Atoms exhibit a great variety of different shapes. Lucretius points out that the infinite variety among created things would not be possible if there were a severely limited number of atomic shapes. Each individual is unique, as Lucretius poignantly illustrates by the picture of a cow seeking her lost calf.

333	Nunc age iam deinceps cūnctārum exōrdia rērum
334	quālia sint et quam longē distantia fōrmīs
335	percipe, multigenīs quam sint variāta figūrīs.
	. . .
338	Nam cum sit eōrum cōpia tanta
339	ut neque fīnis, utī docuī, neque summa sit ūlla,
340	dēbent nīmīrum nōn omnibus omnia prōrsum
341	esse parī fīlō similīque adfecta figūrā.
342	Praetereā genus hūmānum mūtaeque natantēs
343	squāmigerum pecudēs et laeta armenta feraeque
344	et variae volucrēs, laetantia quae loca aquārum
345	concelebrant circum rīpās fontīsque lacūsque,
346	et quae pervulgant nemora āvia pervolitantēs;
347	quōrum ūnum quidvīs generātim sūmere perge,
348	inveniēs tamen inter sē differre figūrīs.

CS **Discussion Question**

1. Compare lines 342–46 with the proem to Book 1. What similarities of phrasing do you find?

---

347 **quōrum**: the antecedent is the entire series of living things described above.
  ūnum quidvīs: *any one you want.*
  generātim, adv., *species by species.*
  sūmere perge, *continue to take, keep on taking;* i.e., examine each species of animal one after the other.

348 **differre**: as subject of accusative and infinitive construction understand "the individual members of each species."
  figūrīs: ablative of specification.

349 **Nec**: note the emphatic effect of the anaphora of **nec** here and beginning lines 350 and 351.

ratiōne: here, *way.*

prōlēs, prōlis, f., *offspring.*

cognōscere: dependent on **posset** (350).

350 **posset**: imperfect subjunctive in understood contrary-to-fact condition with **nec ratiōne aliā** (349).

quod: *whereas, but.*

posse: understand **animālia** as subject of the accusative and infinitive construction, *whereas we see they can,* i.e., recognize one another.

351 **atque**: here comparative, *than.*

nōta: predicative adjective; neuter plural referring generally to the plural implied in **ūnum quidvīs** (347).

clueō, cluēre, *to be called, named;* here simply, *to show (oneself) to be, to appear.*

nōta cluēre, *show that they are known.*

352 **Nam**: an example of how animals recognize one another, in a beautifully descriptive passage, Lucretius shows how a cow misses and searches vainly for her calf who has been slaughtered. She cannot be comforted by another calf.

ante: governing **dēlūbra decōra**.

deum: = **deōrum**.

vitulus, -ī, m., *calf.*

dēlūbrum, -ī, n., *temple, shrine.*

decōrus, -a, -um, *graceful, beautiful.*

ante deum vitulus dēlūbra decōra: the interlocking word order traps the calf in front of the temple; the harsh alliteration of *d* echoes the similar alliteration of the phrase **ductōrēs Danaum dēlectī** (1.86) in the sacrifice of Iphigenia.

353 **tūricremus, -a, -um**, *incense-burning;* probably a Lucretian coinage.

propter: anastrophe; the preposition governs **tūricremās . . . ārās**, which again surrounds the helpless calf who falls slaughtered in the middle of the line.

mactō, -āre, -āvī, -ātus, *to slaughter, sacrifice.*

354 **sanguinis**: emphatic placement at line-beginning, severely separated from **flūmen**.

sanguinis exspīrāns: alliteration, which gives the sighing effect of breath and heat escaping.

exspīrō, -āre, -āvī, -ātus, *to breathe out, exhale, spurt.*

flūmen: metaphorical exaggeration; the calf's blood seems to flow like a river.

355 **At māter**: an abrupt shift of focus from the terrors of the slaughtered calf to the grief of its mother.

saltus, -ūs, m., *woodland, glade.*

viridīs saltūs: governed by **per** of **peragrāns**.

orbō, -āre, -āvī, -ātus, *to deprive by death, bereave.*

orbāta: *bereft.*

peragrō, -āre, -āvī, -ātus, *to traverse.*

356 **quaerit**: a textual emendation by Bailey. Others scholars have suggested **nōvit** and **nōscit**.

pedibus: the feet are those of the calf, as made clear by **vēstīgia pressa**.

pressa: perfect passive participle from **premō, premere**.

bisulcus, -a, -um, *cloven* (as are hooves).

357 **convīsō, convīsere, convīsī, convīsus**, *to look at attentively, examine, search.*

sī: *to see whether.*

358 **āmittō, āmittere, āmīsī, āmissus**, *to lose.*

fētum: *offspring, calf.*

querēla, -ae, f., *complaint, lament.*

349 Nec ratiōne aliā prōlēs cognōscere mātrem

350 nec māter posset prōlem; quod posse vidēmus

351 nec minus atque hominēs inter sē nōta cluēre.

352 Nam saepe ante deum vitulus dēlūbra decōra

353 tūricremās propter mactātus concidit ārās

354 sanguinis exspīrāns calidum dē pectore flūmen.

355 At māter viridīs saltūs orbāta peragrāns

356 quaerit humī pedibus vēstīgia pressa bisulcīs,

357 omnia convīsēns oculīs loca sī queat usquam

358 cōnspicere āmissum fētum, completque querēlīs

359 frondiferum nemus adsistēns et crēbra revīsit

360 ad stabulum dēsīderiō perfīxa iuvencī,

361 nec tenerae salicēs atque herbae rōre vigentēs

362 flūminaque illa queunt summīs lābentia rīpīs

363 oblectāre animum subitamque āvertere cūram,

⊂℥ Discussion Question

1.   What sound effects does Lucretius create in lines 352–53?

---

359 **adsistēns**: *stopping*. Take closely with **complet** (358); *stopping she fills* . . . .
   crēber, crēbra, crēbrum, here, *frequent, repeated*.
      crēbra: nominative singular feminine, modifying **māter** (355), but here used adverbially, *frequently, repeatedly*.
   revīso, revīsere, *to return*.
360 **stabulum, -ī**, n., *stable*.
   dēsīderium, -ī, n., *desire for, grief for*.
   perfīgō, perfīgere, perfīxi, perfīxus, *to pierce through*. This verb is found only in Lucretius.
   iuvencus, -ī, m., *young bullock, calf*.
      iuvencī: objective genitive with **dēsīderiō**.
361 **nec**: negating the entire series of three nouns **salicēs** . . . **herbae** . . . **flūmina**; *neither* . . . *nor* . . . *nor*.
   salix, salicis, f., *willow*.
   vigeō, -ēre, -uī, here, *to flourish, thrive*.
      herbae rōre vigentēs: cf. **herbae gemmantēs rōre recentī** (2.319).
362 **illa**, i.e., those familiar to her.
   summīs . . . rīpīs: ablative of place, *by*.
      summīs lābentia rīpīs: i.e., the streams are full.
363 **oblectō, -āre, -āvī, -ātus**, *to delight, amuse, divert*.
      oblectāre: dependent upon **queunt** (362).

364   **aliae**: transferred epithet; in sense modifying **vitulōrum**.

      speciēs: *shapes, forms.*

        nec vitulōrum aliae speciēs: the point of the passage—the cow is not deceived by the appearance of other calves, even though they look very similar.

      pābula laeta: formulaic phrase indicating plenty; cf. 1.14 and 1.257; 2.317.

365   **dērīvō, -āre, -āvī, -ātus**, *to divert, distract.*

      levō, -āre, -āvī, -ātus, *to relieve, lighten; to release from* + abl.

366   **usque adeō**, idiom, *to such an extent.*

      proprius, -a, -um, here, *of her own.*

      requīrit: the subject is **māter** (355).

367   **Praetereā**: introducing a second, but much shorter example drawn from animals.

      tremulus, -a, -um, *trembling, unsteady.*

      haedus, -ī, m., *kid, young goat.*

368   **corniger, cornigera, cornigerum**, *having horns, horned.*

      nōrunt: syncopated perfect = **nōvērunt**; as usual with this verb, perfect in present sense, *they know, recognize.*

      agnus, -ī, m., *lamb.*

      petulcus, -a, -um, *butting.*

        agnīque petulcī: for this behavior see 2.320.

369   **bālō, -āre, -āvī, -ātūrus**, *to bleat.*

        bālantum: genitive plural participle modifying an understood noun **ovum**, *sheep.* The participle is wonderfully onomatopoeic.

      quod: here causal, *because.*

      nātūra: *their nature.*

      reposcō, reposcere, *to demand.*

370   **sua**: agreeing with but displaced from **ūbera**.

      quisque: i.e., each young animal; singular, but governing the plural **dēcurrunt**.

      ferē, adv., *generally, usually.*

      dēcurrō, dēcurrere, dē(cu)currī, dēcursus, *to run directly (to).*

      ūber, ūberis, n., *udder.*

364   nec vitulōrum aliae speciēs per pābula laeta

365   dērīvāre queunt animum cūrāque levāre:

366   usque adeō quiddam proprium nōtumque requīrit.

367   Praetereā tenerī tremulīs cum vōcibus haedī

368   cornigerās nōrunt mātrēs agnīque petulcī

369   bālantum pecudēs: ita, quod nātūra reposcit,

370   ad sua quisque ferē dēcurrunt ūbera lactis.

ℭ **Discussion Questions**

1.   After reading lines 352–65 what do you imagine Lucretius thought about animal sacrifice? Also, compare this sacrifice with the sacrifice of Iphigenia at the beginning of Book 1.

2.   The phrase **per pābula laeta** usually occurs in a context of joyful plenty. What is its context and effect here? (364)

523   **prīmōrdia rērum . . . cluēre** (525): an indirect statement which here can be translated as a direct statement, or preface with "I say that."

524   **similī**: agreeing with **figūrā**, ablative with **perfecta**.
     quae: the relative has been delayed.
     sunt perfecta: *have been made, are endowed* (with) + abl.

525   **cluēre**: *to be reckoned as existing/being.*
     etenim, conj., *for indeed.*
     distantia, -ae, f., *diversity.*
     sit: with **fīnīta** (526); here in emphatic line-end position as monosyllable.

526   **fōrmārum**: genitive with **distantia** (525).
     necesse est: with accusative and infinitive construction as its subject.
     quae: the antecedent **eās (fōrmās)** has been suppressed.
     sint: subjunctive in subordinate clause within accusative and infinitive construction.

527   **īnfīnītās**: i.e., in number.

532   **quod**: here, *whereas.*
     rārus, -a, -um, *rare, infrequent.*
     vidēs: by using the second person Lucretius again relies on the reader's own observations.
     magis: take closely with **rāra**, *rather rare.*
     animal, animālis, n., *living thing, animal.*

533   **fēcundus, -a, -um**, *fertile, rich, prolific.*
     minus: adverb; take closely with **fēcundam**.
     nātūram: subject of accusative and infinitive construction with **cernis**; understand **esse**.

534   **aliō**: modifying both **regiōne** and **locō**.
     remōtus, -a, -um, *distant, far off, remote.*
       regiōne . . . remōtīs: the whole line is an ablative of place, with the key word in the emphatic final position!

535   **multa**: modifying **animālia** understood.
     licet: its subjects are the two accusative and infinitive constructions **multa genere esse** and **numerumque replērī**.
     genere: dependent on **in** and modified by **eō**.
     numerum: i.e., the total, the right number required by the law of *isonomiā*.
     repleō, replēre, replēvī, replētus, *to fill up, fill.*

536   **sīcut**, adv., *just as.*
     quadrupēs, quadrupedis, m., *four-footed animal, quadruped.*
       quadrupedum: genitive plural with **genere** (537), displaced here following **sīcut** to show immediately the type he will be discussing; *just as of quadrupeds.*
     cum prīmīs, idiom, *especially, in particular.*

537   **anguimanus, -ūs**, *snake-handed*, (referring to the snaky appearance of elephants' trunks, which they use like hands). The adjective is a charming Lucretian invention in the typical dactylic form, but unusual as a fourth declension adjective, here in accusative plural.
     elephantus, -ī, m., *elephant.*
     India, -ae, f., *India.*

538   **mīlibus ē multīs**: *(made) from many thousands* (of elephants), referring to the wall's structure.
     vāllum, -ī, n., *defense wall, palisade* (made from stakes).
     mūniō, -īre, -īvī, -ītus, *to fortify.*
     eburnus, -a, -um, *made of ivory, ivory.*
       vāllō mūnītur eburnō: there is no other reference in antiquity to this extraordinary and rather fanciful legend. Some scholars believe it may refer to the defensive use of elephants against Alexander; however, the Romans were familiar with the military use of elephants in Italy by Hannibal's Carthaginians.

539   **penitus**, adv., *inside, deeply.*
     nequeat: the subject is **India** (537).

540   **perpaucī, -ae, -a**, pl., *very few, extremely few.*
     exemplum, -ī, n., *example, specimen.*

23. Infinite Examples of Each Atomic Shape

Lucretius has proved that, though there are many different types of atoms, the number of types is nevertheless finite. Thus, to create the proven infinity of matter, there must be infinite examples of each type. Lucretius now introduces the principle of *isonomiā* or equal distribution. Although some types of things may seem rare here, they are common elsewhere. As a delightful example Lucretius offers the relative concentration of elephants in Italy and in India.

523   . . . prīmōrdia rērum,
524   inter sē similī quae sunt perfecta figūrā,
525   īnfīnīta cluēre. Etenim distantia cum sit
526   fōrmārum fīnīta, necesse est quae similēs sint
527   esse īnfīnītās.

                    . . .

532   Nam quod rāra vidēs magis esse animālia quaedam
533   fēcundamque minus nātūram cernis in illīs,
534   at regiōne locōque aliō terrīsque remōtīs
535   multa licet genere esse in eō numerumque replērī;
536   sīcut quadrupedum cum prīmīs esse vidēmus
537   in genere anguimanūs elephantōs, India quōrum
538   mīlibus ē multīs vāllō mūnītur eburnō,
539   ut penitus nequeat penetrārī: tanta ferārum
540   vis est, quārum nōs perpauca exempla vidēmus.

∞ Discussion Questions

1.   By the law of *isonomiā* what do you imagine Lucretius believed about the question of the uniqueness of our planet and the possibility of life elsewhere in the universe?

2.   What other animals might Lucretius have used as examples of creatures rare in Italy but common elsewhere?

3.   How might one interpret the impenetrability of India in the context of Roman history and conquests? How much did the Romans know about India? Did they have any contacts with it?

The universe does seem to be roughly the same in every direction, provided one views it on a scale large compared to the distance between galaxies and ignores the differences on small scales.
   Stephen Hawking, *A Brief History of Time* (1988), 40

Newton argued that [a collapse of the universe] would indeed happen if there were only a finite number of stars distributed in a finite region of space. But he reasoned that if . . . there were an infinite number of stars, distributed more or less uniformly over infinite space, this would not happen, because there would not be any central point for them to fall to.
   Stephen Hawking, *A Brief History of Time* (1988), 5

646 **Omnis**: as often, separated from its noun, **nātūra**.

dīvum: = **dīvōrum**.

necessest: the subject is a subjunctive clause with **omnis . . . dīvum nātūra** as its own subject.

647 **aevum, -ī**, n., *life*.

immortālī aevō: ablative with **fruātur**.

fruor, fruī, fructus sum + abl., *to enjoy*.

fruātur. . . . prīvāta perīclīs (649): the description of the life of the gods shares much vocabulary (e.g., **fruor, dolor, sēmōtus, sēiunctus**) with lines 2.17–19, which describe how simply human needs can be satisfied. Thus, by implication, men are to emulate the tranquil life of the gods.

648 **sēmoveō, sēmovēre, sēmōvī, sēmōtus**, *to remove, separate*.

rēbus: *affairs*.

ab nostrīs rēbus: the phrase, sandwiched between the two participles, applies to both. Lucretius believes the gods live in the **intermundia**, the spaces between worlds.

sēiungō, sēiungere, sēiūnxī, sēiūnctus, *to separate*.

longē: emphatic in line-end position and separated from the rest of the clause.

immortālī aevō . . . longē (648): lines 647–48, excepting the fifth-foot dactyls, are completely spondaic, which adds weight to the description. Additionally, the surrounding lines 646 and 649 are also heavily spondaic.

649 **prīvō, -āre, -āvī, -ātus** + abl., *to release* (from), *relieve* (of); here as an adjective, *free from*.

prīvāta: modifying **dīvum nātūra (646)**.

perīclīs: = **perīculīs**, by syncope.

650 **pollēns, pollentis**, *powerful, strong*.

opibus: *resources*; ablative of specification; the gods are self-sufficient.

nīl: adverbial accusative, *not at all*.

indigus, -a, -um + gen., *having need* (of), *needing*.

nostrī: substantive, *us*.

nīl indiga nostrī: i.e., the gods do not need our worship or sacrifices.

651 **bene prōmeritum, -ī**, n., *a good turn, good deed*.

capitur: here, *is won over*.

prōmeritīs capitur neque tangitur īrā: note the chiastic order as well as the completely dactylic line (excepting, of course, the sixth foot). The gods are completely uninterested in our behavior, whether good or bad.

652 **Terra**: Lucretius returns to the misinterpretation of the earth, which has been worshiped as the Magna Mater. He now offers the truth about the earth as an insensate agglomeration of atoms.

vērō: modifying **sēnsū**; embedded order with the adjective-noun pair enclosing **omnī tempore**.

653 **potitur**: here governing the accusative and conjugating in the third rather than fourth conjugation; *contains, possesses*.

654 **multa**: substantive, *many things*; in the context of the formula **in lūmina sōlis**, which generally refers to birth (cf. 1.5, 2.162; see also the very similar formulaic phrase **in lūminis orās**, 1. 22 and 170), probably *many creatures*.

multa modīs multīs: alliterative formula; cf. 1.341, 2.116.

24. Divine Tranquillity

In a passage not included here Lucretius has just described the elaborate worship of Magna Māter, the earth mother. Now, in contrast, he offers an account of the true nature of the gods, who live in perfect tranquillity. They are remote from us and have no interest in nor effect on human events. He concedes that one may use a god's name in metonymy to represent a substance such as the earth, provided that one is careful to remember that the god has no power to affect us.

646   Omnis enim per sē dīvum nātūra necessest
647   immortālī aevō summā cum pāce fruātur
648   sēmōta ab nostrīs rēbus sēiūnctaque longē.
649   Nam prīvāta dolōre omnī, prīvāta perīclīs,
650   ipsa suīs pollēns opibus, nīl indiga nostrī,
651   nec bene prōmeritīs capitur neque tangitur īrā.
652   Terra quidem vērō caret omnī tempore sēnsū,
653   et quia multārum potitur prīmōrdia rērum,
654   multa modīs multīs effert in lūmina sōlis.

C8 Discussion Questions

1. What is the main characteristic of the gods' existence? (646–47)

2. If the gods did need something from us, what would this imply about their condition? (650–51)

3. If, as Lucretius says, the gods are neither impressed by our good deeds nor angered by our evils (651), how might their passivity affect human behavior and society?

4. If the Epicurean gods are incapable of affecting humans, do they fit your definition of divinity?

The blessed and immortal nature knows no trouble itself nor causes trouble to any other, so that it is never constrained by anger or favour. For all such things exist only in the weak.
     Epicurus, *Principal Doctrines* 1 (tr. Bailey)

First of all, believe that god is a being immortal and blessed . . . and do not assign to him anything alien to his immortality or ill-suited to his blessedness. . . . The statements of the many about the gods are not conceptions derived from sensation, but false suppositions, according to which the greatest misfortunes befall the wicked and the greatest blessings the good by the gift of the gods.
     Epicurus, *Epistle to Menoeceus* 123–24 (tr. Bailey)

655   **Hīc**: *Here, In this situation.*

      sīquis: = **sī quis**, equivalent to **sī aliquis**. It has been suggested that here Lucretius has in mind the Stoics, who interpreted the names of the gods as personifications of natural forces.

      Neptūnus, -ī, m., *Neptune* (god of the sea).

        Neptūnum: predicative with **māre . . . vocāre**.

      Cerēs, Cereris, f., *Ceres* (goddess of agriculture).

        Cereremque: predicative with **vocāre . . . frūgēs** (656).

656   **cōnstituet**: future indicative in a mixed future condition.

      Bacchus, -ī, m., *Bacchus* (god of the vine and wine).

      abūtor, abūtī, abūsus sum + abl., *to misuse.*

657   **māvult**: third person singular present indicative from **mālō, mālle**.

      quam: comparative after **māvult**, *rather than.*

      laticis: *grape-juice, wine.*

      proprium: *true, right, correct.*

      prōferre: *to mention, use.*

      vocāmen, vocāminis, n., *name, term.* A probable coinage of Lucretius to replace the unscannable **vocābulum**.

658   **concēdō, concēdere, concessī, concessūrus** (+ **ut** + subj.), *to allow.*

      concēdāmus: hortatory subjunctive.

      hīc: nominative singular, referring to **quis** above in line 655.

      terrārum . . . orbem, idiom, *the whole earth.*

      dictitō, -āre, -āvī, -ātus [frequentative], *to keep saying, to say often.*

659   **dum**, conj. + subj., here, *provided that.*

      vērā rē: *in truth, in fact;* here referring to the person's own understanding.

660   **rēligiōne**: ablative with **contingere**.

      animum: imprisoned in the word order by **rēligiōne . . . turpī**.

      turpis, -is, -e, *foul, base.*

      contingō, contingere, contigī, contactus, here, *to defile, pollute, taint.*

      parcat: *avoids, refrains* (from); here with infinitive.

655   Hīc sīquis mare Neptūnum Cereremque vocāre

656   cōnstituet frūgēs et Bacchī nōmine abūtī

657   māvult quam laticis proprium prōferre vocāmen,

658   concēdāmus ut hīc terrārum dictitet orbem

659   esse deum mātrem, dum vērā rē tamen ipse

660   rēligiōne animum turpī contingere parcat.

○8 Discussion Questions

1.   Lucretius allows the poetic use of metonymy in calling the earth mother. What other examples of such metonymy have already occurred in the text? What other Roman gods represent specific natural substances or conditions?

2.   The Epicureans have often been accused of being atheists. In the context of this passage, how do you interpret that charge?

It is obviously true . . . that Epicurus did not believe the gods existed at all and that what he said about them was said merely to avoid the odium of atheism. . . . he merely paid lip-service to gods whom he had in fact destroyed. And finally, if this is all that a god is, a being untouched by care or love of human kind, then I wave him good-bye. Why should I ask his favor? He cannot do a favor to anybody.

Cotta the Academician in Cicero, *De natura deorum* 1.123–24 (tr. McGregor)

991   **caelestis, -is, -e**, *coming from heaven, celestial.*

     oriundus, -a, -um + abl., *descended, sprung* (from).

       oriundī: here trisyllabic with the first *i* suppressed to fit the meter.

         caelestī sumus omnēs sēmine oriundī: not in the sense of a divine origin, but "heavenly" because the elements, such as heat, wind, and air, which make up our **animus** and **anima** (cf. Book 3) come from the sky.

992   **omnibus**: emphatic position.

     omnibus ille īdem pater est: Lucretius returns to the allegorical imagery of 1.250–64, in which he described the sky-father's fertilization of mother earth.

     unde: = **ā quō**.

     almus, -a, -um, *kindly, gracious, nurturing.*

       alma: modifying **māter** (993) in the phrase, which, strangely, in our era has become synonymous with our place of education.

     liquēns, liquentis, *liquid, flowing.*

       liquentīs: probably accusative modifying **guttās**, with a long final syllable.

993   **gutta, -ae**, f., *drop.*

     ūmōris guttās . . . recēpit: a very spondaic line perhaps simulating the effect of a steadily falling rain.

     māter . . . terra: a word play on the syllable **ter**.

994   **fētus, -a, -um**, *pregnant, fruitful.*

     pariō, parere, peperī, partus, *to give birth to, produce, create.*

     nitidus, -a, -um, *bright, shining, gleaming.*

     arbusta, -ōrum, n. pl., *trees, woods, orchards.*

     laetus, -a, -um, here, *fertile, productive.*

       nitidās frūgēs arbustaque laeta: note the chiastic order and the echo of **nitidae frūgēs** (1.252).

995   **et genus hūmānum**: enjambement, perhaps significant in leaving mankind almost as an afterthought.

     saecla: = **saecula**, by syncope.

996   **praebet**: **māter . . . terra** (993) continues as the subject.

     quibus: ablative of means; the antecedent is **pābula**.

     omnēs: supply **animantēs**, i.e., **genus hūmānum et saecla ferārum**.

997   **prōlēs, prōlis**, f., *offspring.*

     propāgō, -āre, -āvī, -ātus, *to produce, propagate.*

998   **quāpropter**, adv., *because of which, therefore.*

     adipīscor, adipīscī, adeptus sum, *to obtain.*

       adepta est: the subject is **terra** (993).

999   **Cēdit**: the subject is the following clause **dē terrā quod fuit ante**.

     item: *in turn*; Lucretius now turns from the process of union to the opposite process of dissolution.

     retrō: take closely with **in terrās** (1000).

1000   **terrās**: plural for the expected singular, apparently for metrical reasons.

     aether, aetheris, m., *ether, sky.*

     quod missumst ex aetheris ōrīs: referring to the second source of matter, the sky.

1001   **id**: the antecedent is the preceding **quod** clause.

     rūrsum, here, *back again.*

     caelī: genitive singular with **templa**.

     rellātum: formed as if from the archaic **redferō**, thus the doubled *l* in the participial form.

     templa: *quarters, regions*, as in 2.8.

     receptō, -āre, *to take back, recover, receive.*

25. Father Rain and Mother Earth Recycle Their Elements

The earth, fertilized by rain, produces all life. Both the celestial and terrestrial elements are later recycled into new creatures. The variety of creation results from shifts in the types, positionings, and motions of the atoms, just as the letters of the alphabet create all words.

991   Dēnique caelestī sumus omnēs sēmine oriundī;
992   omnibus ille īdem pater est, unde alma liquentīs
993   ūmōris guttās māter cum terra recēpit,
994   fēta parit nitidās frūgēs arbustaque laeta
995   et genus hūmānum, parit omnia saecla ferārum,
996   pābula cum praebet quibus omnēs corpora pāscunt
997   et dulcem dūcunt vītam prōlemque propāgant;
998   quāpropter meritō māternum nōmen adepta est.
999   Cēdit item retrō, dē terrā quod fuit ante,
1000 in terrās et quod missumst ex aetheris ōrīs,
1001 id rūrsum caelī rellātum templa receptant.

☙ **Discussion Questions**

1.   What poetic device do you find in the word order of line 991?

2.   Compare the role of **māter terra** here with that of Venus in the first proem.

Greatest Earth and Zeus' Ether,
he is father of men and gods,
she, having received the moistening drops of showers,
bears mortals,
bears plants and the races of wild beasts,
whence not unjustly
she is deemed mother of all.
But backwards go
things borne of earth into earth,
those come forth from an airy birth
into the heavenly sphere return again.
Nothing of those things born dies,
but one thing separated from another
reveals a different shape.
    Euripides, *Chrysippus*, Fragment 839

We are all star stuff.
    Carl Sagan, *Cosmos* (TV Series)

1002   **interimō, interimere, interēmī, interēmptus**, *to destroy.*
     rēs: accusative plural, again used for neuter, *things.*
     materiāī corpora: here referring to the atoms, which by definition cannot be destroyed or altered.

1003   **cōnficiat**: *destroys.*
     coetus, -ūs, m., *union.*
     dissipō, -āre, -āvī, -ātus, *to scatter, disperse, demolish.*
     ollīs: archaic form = **īllīs**; archaic dative of possession.

1004   **Inde**: *then* (after the dissolution of an object into its constituent atoms).
     coniungit et efficit: the subject is still, surprisingly, **mors** (1002), here, *destruction*, which in this context has a creative side; only by the dissolution of one thing can the atoms recombine to form something new.
       efficit: governing the following subjunctive clause (with **ut** suppressed).

1005   **convertant**: *alter.*

1006   **pūnctus, -a, -um**, *pricked in.*
     pūnctō tempore, *in a moment of time*; cf. 2.263.
       capiant sēnsūs et pūnctō tempore reddant: indicating how fleeting a phenomenon the possession of sensation can be. Lucretius will further explore this topic in Book 3 in his discussion of the soul's mortality.

1007   **nōscō, nōscere, nōvī, nōtus**, *to get to know, learn.*
     rēferre: from impersonal **rēfert**, (it)*matters*; the following indirect questions (1007–09) are its subject.
     eadem prīmōrdia: nominative plural subject of the following indirect questions.

1008   **quibus**: modifying an understood **aliīs (prīmōrdiīs)**, *with what other (atoms).*
     positūra, -ae, f., *position, arrangement.*

1009   **quōs inter sē dent mōtūs accipiantque**: the internal motions of what we call molecules. The motions are caused by the blows (**plāgae**). The line is heavily spondaic.

1013   **quīn**, adv., *but.*
     rēfert: again the impersonal verb, (it) *matters.*

1014   **cum quibus et quālī . . . ōrdine**: intentionally echoing the language of line 1008 to create a close analogy.
     sint . . . locāta: take together.
     quaeque: nominative plural neuter, here modifying an understood **elementa**, a word that Lucretius uses for both the atoms, **prīmōrdia**, and **litterae**, the letters of the alphabet. Lucretius is drawing an analogy between atoms and letters to show how great a variety can be produced by simple alterations.

1015   **eadem**: nominative plural neuter, modifying **elementa** understood.
     caelum mare terrās flūmina sōlem: the rapid effect which the asyndeton (omission of conjunctions) of these accusative nouns produces effectively shows the great potential variety.

1016   **significant**: *signify, denote.* The enjambement of the verb then leads into the next series in asyndeton.
     eadem: the repetition is emphatic.

1017   **omnia**: i.e., *elements* (of words); modifying an understood **cōnsimilia**, *alike.*
     multō: adverbial modifying **maxima**, *by far the greatest.*
     est: emphatic line-end position for this monosyllable.

1018   **cōnsimilis, -is, -e**, *similar, like, alike.*
     vērum, adv., *but.*
     positūrā: ablative of means; *because of a change in position* (of the letters).
     discrepitō, -āre, *to be different, differ.*
     rēs: another monosyllabic line-ending; it is most unusual to have two such lines in a row.

1019   **Sīc**: concluding the comparison, Lucretius returns to the atoms.
     rēbus: i.e., in physical objects from molecules to larger units.
     materiāī: genitive with all the nominative nouns in the following line.

1002 Nec sīc interimit mors rēs ut māteriāī
1003 corpora cōnficiat, sed coetum dissipat ollīs.
1004 Inde aliīs aliud coniungit et efficit omnēs
1005 rēs ita convertant fōrmās mūtentque colōrēs
1006 et capiant sēnsūs et pūnctō tempore reddant,
1007 ut nōscās rēferre eadem prīmōrdia rērum
1008 cum quibus et quālī positūrā contineantur
1009 et quōs inter sē dent mōtūs accipiantque.

. . .

1013 Quīn etiam rēfert nostrīs in versibus ipsīs
1014 cum quibus et quālī sint ōrdine quaeque locāta;
1015 namque eadem caelum mare terrās flūmina sōlem
1016 significant, eadem frūgēs arbusta animantīs;
1017 sī nōn omnia sunt, at multō maxima pars est
1018 cōnsimilis; vērum positūrā discrepitant rēs.
1019 Sīc ipsīs in rēbus item iam māteriāī
1021 concursūs mōtūs ōrdō positūra figūrae
1022 cum permūtantur, mūtārī rēs quoque dēbent.

ℭ Discussion Questions

1. Lucretius draws an analogy between the variety created by the alphabet and by the atoms. Is the analogy a complete one? Is the comparison between the two valid point by point?

2. What principle of organization does Lucretius follow in his two lists of things created by varying atomic combinations? (1015–16)

Nature contrives enormous complexity of structure and dynamics from the six leptons and six quarks now thought to be the fundamental constituents of matter.
  Chris Quigg, "Elementary Particles and Forces," *Scientific American*, April 1985, 89

Every atom acts for all the world as if it were festooned with a variety of grappling devices — hooks, clamps, pincers, bits of Velcro, spots of tar: a different set for each element, each device operating differently, and each specifically tailored to grapple in differing ways with differing mates. . . . Life depends for its workings on the infinitely varied possibilities provided by this richness.
  George Greenstein, *The Symbiotic Universe* (1988), 35

1021 **concursus, -ūs**, m., *meeting* (by collision).
     concursūs mōtūs ōrdō positūra figūrae: another major instance of asyndeton.
1022 **permūtō, -āre, -āvī, -ātus**, *to change completely*.
     rēs: i.e., the physical objects that are composed of the rearranged atoms.

1023   **nōbīs**: poetic plural, dative of interest, almost as an appeal, *for my sake.*
    adhibeō, -ēre, -uī, -itus, *to apply, direct to.*
      adhibē vēram ad ratiōnem, a formulaic phrased repeated from 1.51; of course, the "true philosophy" is Epicureanism.

1024   **vēmenter**: a metrically required contraction of **vehementer**.
    mōlior, mōlīrī, mōlītus sum, *to strive, struggle, try.*
      vēmenter . . . mōlītur: a strong personification of **nova rēs**.
    auris, auris, f., *ear.*

1025   **accidō, accidere, accidī**, *to fall on, to strike;* here with **ad** (1024).
    nova . . . speciēs . . . rērum: a new understanding of the universe; the repetition of **nova** from line 1024 is significant, since it is the fear of new ideas that Lucretius initially tries to dispel.
    ostendere: dependent on **mōlītur** (1024) in a continuation of the strong personification of newness, as if ideas could parade themselves before us.

1026   **facilis**: i.e., easy to understand and accept.
    rēs: here almost, *concept.*
    quīn: here, *but that.*
    prīmum, adv., *at first.*

1027   **magis**: take closely with **difficilis**, *rather difficult*, in opposition to **facilis** (1026).
    ad crēdendum: gerund with **ad** to express purpose.
    cōnstet: *is.*

1028   **nīl**: Lucretius switches from the use of **rēs** for *thing* to the neuter.
    magnum . . . mīrābile: supply **est**.

1029   **quod**: introducing a relative clause of result, anticipated by **adeō** and **tam** (1028).
    minuant: here, *gradually cease* (to).
    mīrārier: -ier is an archaic ending that Lucretius often uses for the passive infinitive.
    omnēs: supply **hominēs**.

1030   **Prīncipiō**: *First*, to introduce an example. Interestingly, there is no second example!
    clārum pūrumque colōrem: introducing a series of examples in the accusative. There is an anacoluthon (break in grammatical continuity) between lines 1030–32 and the following passage. To solve this break, understand these accusatives as the object of an imperative such as **cape**, *take* (as an example).

1031   **quaeque**: **quae**, the accusative plural neuter relative pronoun (antecedent suppressed), plus the enclitic **-que**; introducing a series of appositive examples: **pālantia sīdera**, etc.
    cohibeō, -ēre, -uī, -itus, *to contain.*
      cohibet: the subject is **caelum**.
    pālor, -ārī, -ātus sum, *to wander, stray.*
    sīdus, sīderis, n., *star; constellation.*
      pālantia sīdera: i.e., the planets (the word means "the wanderers"), considered mysterious because in their retrograde motion they do not follow the progression of the other stars.

1032   **praeclārā**: *very bright, brilliant.*
    nitor, nitōris, m., *brilliance, brightness, splendor.*

1033   **omnia**: nominative plural neuter, summarizing the preceding series of accusatives.
    essent: imperfect subjunctive in present contrary-to-fact condition, *were to come into existence.*

1034   **imprōvīsus, -a, -um**, *unexpected, unforeseen.*
    ex imprōvīsō, idiom, *unexpectedly, suddenly.*
    obiciō, obicere, obiēcī, obiectus, *to put before, present to* (one's eye's).
      sint obiecta: subject remains **omnia quae** (1033); Lucretius has switched into a future less vivid condition, *if they should be presented (to us)*; supply **nōbīs** as indirect object.
    repente: the inclusion of this adverb, synonymous with **ex imprōvīsō**, stresses the surprise that the sudden appearance would create. Also, the heavily spondaic pattern of this line and line 1033 makes us pause to ponder the stunning effect.

26. Fear of Newness

New ideas are hard to accept, just as celestial phenomena would be considered incredible if seen for the first time. Lucretius asks his reader not to reject his reasoning out of fear, but to examine his argumentation and then pass judgment. Lucretius wonders what exists beyond our world.

1023	Nunc animum nōbīs adhibē vēram ad ratiōnem.
1024	Nam tibi vēmenter nova rēs mōlītur ad aurīs
1025	accidere et nova sē speciēs ostendere rērum.
1026	Sed neque tam facilis rēs ūlla est quīn ea prīmum
1027	difficilis magis ad crēdendum cōnstet, itemque
1028	nīl adeō magnum neque tam mīrābile quicquam
1029	quod nōn paulātim minuant mīrārier omnēs.
1030	Principiō caelī clārum pūrumque colōrem,
1031	quaeque in sē cohibet, pālantia sīdera passim,
1032	lūnamque et sōlis praeclārā lūce nitōrem;
1033	omnia quae nunc sī prīmum mortālibus essent,
1034	ex imprōvīsō sī sint obiecta repente,
1035	quid magis hīs rēbus poterat mīrābile dīcī
1036	aut minus ante quod audērent fore crēdere gentēs?

If you put new ideas before the eyes of fools
They'll think you fooish and worthless into the bargain;
And if you are thought superior to those who have
Some reputation for learning, you will become hated.
    Medea in Euripides' *Medea* 298–301 (tr. Warner)

Look up in time to see clouds turn pink, red, orange, purple. A cliché. Ah, but imagine if sunsets happened only once every fifty years. People would build their lives around them.
    John P. Wiley, "New Phenomena," *Smithsonian*, October 1995, 28

1035 **magis**: going closely with **mīrābile** and governing **hīs rēbus** in ablative of comparison.
    poterat: the indicative, rather than the subjunctive, to express potentiality: i.e., what could possibly be . . .?
1036 **quod**: here an interrogative adjective modifying an implied accusative noun such as **mīrāculum**, *marvel, wonder,* or **dictum**, *report, story.*
    minus: modifying **audērent**. Reorder the clause: **quod gentēs ante minus audērent crēdere fore**.
    gentēs: i.e., **hūmānae gentēs**.
    fore: alternative form of future infinitive = **futūrum esse**.

1037   **opīnor, -ārī, -ātus sum**, *to think, believe.*
     speciēs: *spectacle*, i.e., the first appearance of the celestial bodies detailed in lines 1030–32.
     mīrandus, -a, -um, *wonderful, amazing.*
     fuisset: Lucretius concludes with a pluperfect subjunctive in past contrary-to-fact, since he is indeed describing what would have happened in the past (cf. **ante**, 1036).

1038   **Quam**: here exclamatory, *How.*
     tibi: dative of interest, almost, *let me tell you.*
     fessus, -a, -um, *tired, weary.*
     satiās, satiātis, f., *satiety, surfeit.*

1039   **suspiciō, suspicere, suspexī, suspectus**, *to look upwards.*
     dignor, -ārī, -ātus sum + infin., *to consider worthy, to deign* (to).
     templa: *quarters, regions*; cf. 2.8 and 1001.

1040   **Dēsine**: Lucretius gives a direct command to the reader, in the most emphatic position.
     novitās, novitātis, f., *newness, strangeness.*
     exterreō, -ēre, -uī, -itus, *to scare, terrify.*
     novitāte exterritus: stressing the innate fear of newness, as with **nova** (1024 and 1025).

1041   **exspuō, exspuere, exspuī, exspūtus**, *to spit out*; a wonderfully onomatopoeic word!
     magis: *rather, on the contrary.*

1042   **iūdicium, -ī**, n., *judgment.*
     perpendō, perpendere, perpendī, perpēnsus, *to weigh carefully, examine closely.*
     perpende: supply *things* or **argūmenta**, *reasonings, conclusions*, as direct object.
     videntur: the subject is the understood direct object of **perpende**.

1043   **dēdō, dēdere, dēdidī, dēditus**, *to give up, surrender.*
     dēde manūs: the universal gesture of surrender.
     falsum: Lucretius has switched to the neuter singular, with a subject such as **argūmentum** or **dictum**.
     accingō, accingere, accīnxī, accīnctus, *to arm.*
     accingere: second person singular passive imperative in middle sense, *arm yourself.*

1044   **Quaerit enim ratiōnem animus**: Lucretius finally reaches the new idea that he feared his reader would reject simply because of its newness.
     ratiōnem: *explanation.*
     summa locī: *the totality of space.*
     sit: again an emphatic line-end position for this monosyllable, *it is.*

1045   **īnfīnīta**: emphatic enjambement.
     forīs, adv., *outside* (explained by the phrase **haec extrā moenia mundī**).
     mundus, -ī, m., *world, earth.*

1046   **quid sit**: indirect question depending upon **ratiōnem** (1044), i.e., *the mind seeks to understand . . . what is there beyond.*
     ibī: final syllable long by diastole; referring to the immensity of space beyond our world.
     porrō, adv., *further, beyond.*
     quō, adv. with **usque**, *as far as.*
     prōspiciō, prōspicere, prōspexī, prōspectus, *to look forward, look out.*
     velit: present subjunctive of **volo, velle**; subjunctive by attraction.
     mēns: monosyllable in emphatic line-end position. The reader, in his examination of the universe, will act as Epicurus, who traversed the universe **mente animōque** (1.72–74).

1047   **iactus, -ūs**, m., *the action of throwing*; here, *the projection* (of the mind).
     animī iactus: a translation of the Epicurean phrase ἐπιβολὴ τῆς διανοίας. The mind, relying on the basis of sense perception, can extrapolate from that evidence to consider matters beyond our immediate sense perception, such as what is going on beyond our world.
     quō: the adverb is displaced from the front of the clause **animī iactus**.
     pervolō, -āre, -āvī, -ātus, *to fly through.*
     pervolet: subjunctive by attraction.
     ipse: reinforcing the adjective **līber**; the mind has freedom to explore wherever it wishes.

1037   Nīl, ut opīnor: ita haec speciēs mīranda fuisset.
1038   Quam tibi iam nēmō, fessus satiāte videndī,
1039   suspicere in caelī dignātur lūcida templa!
1040   Dēsine quāpropter novitāte exterritus ipsā
1041   exspuere ex animō ratiōnem, sed magis ācrī
1042   iūdiciō perpende et, sī tibi vēra videntur,
1043   dēde manūs, aut, sī falsum est, accingere contrā.
1044   Quaerit enim ratiōnem animus, cum summa locī sit
1045   īnfīnīta forīs haec extrā moenia mundī,
1046   quid sit ibī porrō quō prōspicere usque velit mēns
1047   atque animī iactus līber quō pervolet ipse.

⚬ **Discussion Questions**

1.   Can you think of scientific revolutions or breakthroughs which at first were met with skepticism, hostility and fear? Are there currently any such controversial ideas?

2.   Why are people reluctant to accept or even to listen to new ideas?

3.   Lucretius invites the reader to explore the universe with his mind. Whom has he shown accomplishing this feat?

Shallow ideas can be assimilated; ideas that require people to reorganize their picture of the world provoke hostility.

    James Gleick, *Chaos: Making a New Science* (1987), 38

1052   **iam**: here inferential, *now* (considering all the evidence).

       pactum, -ī, n., *way*.

       vērī simile est, idiom, *it is likely, probable*.

         vērī simile esse: the indirect statement itself introduces other indirect statements, beginning in line 1056, which are first preceded by circumstantial clauses reminding the reader of the physical constitution of the universe.

       putandumst: = **putandum est**; impersonal use of gerund with the indirect statement as its subject; literally, *that is likely must be thought, it must be thought that*.

1053   **versum**: going closely with **undique**, *turned on all sides*, i.e., *in all directions*.

       vacō, -āre, -āvī, -ātūrus, *to be vacant, empty*.

         undique cum versum spatium vacet īnfīnītum: i.e., there is an infinite amount of void in which the atoms can move, combine, and recombine. See the description of void, 1.421.

       īnfīnītum: spondaic and pentasyllabic line-ending, which slows the line and stresses the infinity of space.

1054   **sēmina**: = **prīmōrdia**.

       innumerō numerō: a clever word-play; ablative of description.

       profundus, -a, um, here, *vast, boundless*.

         summā profundā: there is dispute over the interpretation of the phrase. Merrill, taking **profunda** as nominative, reads *"vast in their sum,"* referring to the atoms, whereas Bailey, referring to the void, translates *"in the sum total of the void."* I interpret **profundā** as ablative and see a typical Lucretian emphatic exaggeration or pleonasm after **innumerō numerō**; *in boundless sum*.

1055   **multimodīs**, adv., *in many ways*.

       volitō, -āre, -āvī, -ātūrus, *to fly, fly about*.

       percieō, perciēre, perciī, percitus, *to propel*.

1056   **terrārum orbis**, idiom, *the whole earth, the world*.

         hunc ūnum terrārum orbem caelumque: accusative subject of the indirect statement; a hendiadys, thus to be construed as a singular entity; note that the modifying participle **creātum** is singular.

       creātum: understand **esse**; perfect passive infinitive in the indirect statement.

1057   **nīl agere . . .**: asyndeton (omission of conjunction) between line 1056 and this line, the second indirect statement, which contrasts with the first.

       forīs: i.e., outside our world, in outer space.

1058   **cum praesertim**: offering another reason why it is most unlikely that our world is unique.

       hīc: modifying **orbis terrārum** understood.

       nātūrā: ablative of means; i.e., *not by the gods*.

       ut: *when*.

       ipsa: modifying **sēmina rērum** (1059), reinforcing the idea that the atoms acted independently, without divine intervention.

1059   **sponte suā**: *by their own will*.

       offēnsō, -āre, -āvī, -ātus [frequentative], *to collide*.

         offēnsandō: gerund in ablative of means.

1060   **temere**, adv., *at random, by chance, accidentally*.

       incassum, adv., *without aim/purpose, fortuitously*.

         temere incassum frūstrā: a remarkable series of synonyms, which with **sponte suā** and **forte** in line 1059 enforce the idea of the total spontaneity and randomness of the movements of the atoms, which ultimately resulted in our world.

       coācta: perfect passive participle from **cōgō, cōgere**; *driven*.

1061   **coalēscō, coalēscere, coaluī, coalitus**, *to combine, unite*.

         cōluerunt: an archaic contraction of **coāluērunt** with a short *e*, *they came together*.

       ea: nominative plural neuter, modifying **sēmina** (1059).

       quae: introducing a relative clause of characteristic with the indefinite antecedent **ea**.

       coniecta: here, *once thrown together*.

27. Other Worlds Exist

Since the same physical laws operate throughout the universe and both space and matter exist in infinite supply, one must conclude that there is life elsewhere in other worlds.

1052   Nūllō iam pactō vērī simile esse putandumst,
1053   undique cum versum spatium vacet īnfīnītum
1054   sēminaque innumerō numerō summāque profundā
1055   multimodīs volitent aeternō percita mōtū,
1056   hunc ūnum terrārum orbem caelumque creātum,
1057   nīl agere illa forīs tot corpora māteriāī;
1058   cum praesertim hīc sit nātūrā factus, ut ipsa
1059   sponte suā forte offēnsandō sēmina rērum
1060   multimodīs temere incassum frūstrāque coācta
1061   tandem cōluerunt ea quae coniecta repente
1062   magnārum rērum fierent exōrdia semper,
1063   terrāī maris et caelī generisque animantum.

ℂଃ   Discussion Questions

1.   How does Lucretius enhance our comprehension of the infinity of void? (1053)

2.   Why is it important to Lucretius' argumentation about other worlds that our world was made by nature? (1058)

3.   What is the main force responsible for the creation of our world and thus of other worlds? (1058–62)

1062   **magnārum rērum**: will be specified in line 1063 as the constituent elements of an earth such as ours.
        exōrdium, -ī, n., *starting point, beginning*.
        semper: i.e., when the right atoms have come together, they *always* create worlds; another reminder that our world is not unique.
1063   **terrāī maris . . . animantum**: the string of genitives is in apposition to **magnārum rērum** (1062).

1064 **quāre etiam atque etiam**: the formulaic phrase of conclusion; cf. 1.295.
tālīs: accusative plural masculine modifying **congressūs** (1065).
fateor, fatērī, fassus sum, *to concede, admit*.
   fateāre: second person singular passive (alternative ending); subjunctive subject of **necesse est**.

1065 **alibī**, adv., *elsewhere*. The term should be familiar to all, since it has been taken unchanged into English legal terminology as the plea that a suspect was "elsewhere" at the time of a crime.

1074 **cōnfiteor, cōnfitērī, cōnfessus sum**, *to confess, admit*.
   necesse est cōnfiteāre: repeating the construction from above (1064) in summarizing his conclusion.

1075 **aliōs aliīs terrārum in partibus orbīs**: a very interwoven phrase; unravel to **aliōs terrārum orbīs in aliīs partibus**.

1076 **variās hominum gentīs**: this is the point that always intrigues us! Are there extra-terrestrials? Lucretius firmly believes the answer is yes!

1064   quāre etiam atque etiam tālīs fateāre necesse est
1065   esse aliōs alibī congressūs māteriāī.

                                . . .

1074   Necesse est cōnfiteāre
1075   esse aliōs aliīs terrārum in partibus orbīs
1076   et variās hominum gentīs et saecla ferārum.

CB Discussion Question

1.   Lucretius clearly believes in the existence of extraterrestrial life. Do you think that he imagines
      these extraterrestrial creatures would look the same as or similar to those here? Why or why not?

We must believe that in all worlds there are living creatures and planets and other things we see in this
world.
      Epicurus, *Epistle to Herodotus* 74

That organic life is diffused through all parts of the Universe can hardly be doubted . . . . It is . . . natural
to suppose that life has developed [elsewhere] . . . under conditions analogous in the main to those in
which it manifests itself with us—under animal and vegetable forms . . . . We are bound to suppose that
the same causes that have produced life from the nebulous nucleus we call the Earth engender it in all
others.
      Anatole France, *The Garden of Epicurus* (1894), 13–14

[Mandelbrot's] studies of irregular patterns in natural processes and his exploration of infinitely complex shapes had an intellectual intersection: a quality of *self-similarity*. . . . Self-similarity is similarity
across scale. It implies recursion, pattern inside of pattern.
      James Gleick, *Chaos: Making a New Science* (1987), 103

Ever since astronomers realized that stars were like the sun . . . they have wondered whether these
other suns might have their own planets—perhaps inhabited ones. So when astronomers Michel Mayor
and Didier Queloz of the University of Geneva quietly reported in October that they had detected a
Jupiter-size planet circling a fairly mediocre star 57 light-years away, the news did not stay quiet long.
. . . Astronomer Geoff Marcy [comments]: "This is a discovery that any human being who is curious
about the universe should rejoice in. Everyone can now look up in the night sky and look at the stars
and say 'There are planets out there.'"
      Jeffrey Winters, "Finding a new planet outside our solar system," *Discover*, January 1996, 86–87

1090   **Quae**: neuter plural accusative with no expressed antecedent; referring to Lucretius' atomic theories and, in particular, to the independent actions of the atoms.

      cognita: predicative adjective with **quae** and modified by **bene**, *well-understood, well-learned*.

      teneās: understand **memoriā**, *if you should keep in mind*; present subjunctive in a mixed condition.

      vidētur: here in true passive sense, *is seen*.

1091   **continuō**, adv., *immediately, at once*; take closely with **lībera**.

      prīvō, -āre, -āvī, -ātus + abl., *to free from*.

1092   **suā**: modifying **sponte**, *by her own will*.

        ipsa suā per sē sponte: an extraordinary accumulation of words indicating nature's free will; also highly alliterative.

      omnia: accusative plural neuter, direct object of **agere**.

      dīs: = **deīs**.

      agere: infinitive with **vidētur** (1090).

      expers, expertis + abl., *free from, unaffected by*.

1093   **prō**, interjection + acc., *by*; introducing an extended exclamation (1093–94).

        prō sāncta deum . . . pectora: it may seem strange to appeal to the gods while denying their influence. The point is that humans generally misunderstand the true nature of the gods, as described in 2.646–51. We should emulate their tranquil lives rather than tainting them with emotions alien to them, such as anger and vengefulness.

          sāncta . . . tranquillā pectora pāce: interlocking word order.

1094   **quae**: synecdoche (use of part for the whole), technically referring in gender to **pectora**, but by transference to the gods themselves.

      dēgō, dēgere, *to spend, pass* (one's life).

      aevum -ī, n., here, *time*.

1095   **quis**: after the prolonged exclamation, Lucretius reaches his main point.

      regere: dependent on **potis est** (1096).

      immēnsī: here a substantive, *of the immense, of the universe*.

      quis: emphatic anaphora as well as asyndeton.

      habēre: another infinitive dependent on **potis est** (1096) in a clause parallel to the preceding one.

      profundī: like **immēnsī**, a substantive, *of the deep*; genitive with **validās . . . habēnās** (1096).

1096   **indu**: archaic form of the preposition **in**, adding a solemn effect.

      validus, -a, -um, here, *mighty*.

      potis est, idiom with indecl. adj. + infin., *has the power, is able* (to).

      moderanter, adv., *with controlling force*; i.e., in control. The word occurs only here in Latin.

1097   **pariter**, adv., *equally, at the same time*; take closely with **convertere**.

      caelōs: a most unusual form, accusative plural *masculine*, an archaism; plural to indicate the many skies of many worlds.

      omnīs: the second instance agrees with **terrās** (1098).

1098   **aetherius, -a, -um**, *heavenly, ethereal*.

      suffiō, -īre, -iī or **īvī, -ītus**, *to warm*.

      ferāx, ferācis, *fruitful, fertile*; here probably predicative with **suffīre**: the warming results in fertility.

1099   **inve**: the preposition **in** with the enclitic **-ve**, connecting this clause to the preceding.

      esse: infinitive still dependent on **potis est** (1096).

      omnī tempore: ablative of time when.

      praestō, adv., *present*; take closely with **esse**.

28. Nātūra Lībera

The force of nature alone, free from divine intervention, controls the universe. Indeed, Lucretius asks, what god could be omnipresent or omnipotent? Lucretius concludes with a series of sarcastic questions about the divine use of the thunderbolt.

1090 Quae bene cognita sī teneās, nātūra vidētur
1091 lībera continuō dominīs prīvāta superbīs
1092 ipsa suā per sē sponte omnia dīs agere expers.
1093 Nam prō sāncta deum tranquillā pectora pāce
1094 quae placidum dēgunt aevum vītamque serēnam,
1095 quis regere immēnsī summam, quis habēre profundī
1096 indu manū validās potis est moderanter habēnās,
1097 quis pariter caelōs omnīs convertere et omnīs
1098 ignibus aetheriīs terrās suffīre ferācēs,
1099 omnibus inve locīs esse omnī tempore praestō,

ℭ Discussion Questions

1. How does Lucretius emphasize that the gods lead a completely calm existence? (1093–94)

2. What metaphorical image does Lucretius create with the clause **quis habēre profundī . . . habēnās** (1095–96)? What picture does this create in your mind?

Strepsiades:
But the lightning—tell me whence come its blazing flashes
Which char or singe us. Surely Zeus firing at perjurers?

Socrates:
Fool, you reek of antediluvian ignorance. If perjurers
Are the target why has Simon never been struck, or Cleonymus,
Or Theorus, perjurers all? But Zeus' own temple he strikes
And Sunium, Athens' headland, and the mighty oaks. Why?
Oaks are no perjurers.
    Aristophanes, *Clouds* 394–402 (tr. Hadas)

1100   **nūbibus**: ablative of means.
   tenebrae, -ārum, f. pl., *darkness, shadows.*
   serēna: modifying **loca** understood. A typically Lucretian periphrasis with a neuter plural
    plus genitive.
1101   **concutiō, concutere, concussī, concussus**, *to shake violently, agitate.*
   fulmen, fulminis, n., *thunderbolt.*
   aedēs, aedis, f., *room*, pl., *house.*
    aedēs . . . suās: i.e., *his own temples.*
1102   **disturbō, -āre, -āvī, -ātus**, *to destroy, demolish, ruin.*
    aedēs saepe suās disturbet: striking alliteration with *s*. The Capitoline hill, sacred to
     Jupiter, was apparently frequently struck by lightning as were other temples, since they
     are built on high ground; cf. Cicero, *De divinatione*, 2.20.45 and Livy 28.11. The point is, of
     course, that it makes no sense for Jupiter to strike his own temple.
   dēserta: modifying **loca** understood.
   recēdō, recēdere, recessī, recessūrus, *to withdraw.*
1103   **saeviō, -īre, -iī, -itūrus**, *to rage, be furious.*
   tēlum, -ī, n., *weapon;* here, *thunderbolt.*
    in dēserta recēdēns saeviat exercēns tēlum: again, this behavior would be illogical. As
     Lucretius facetiously asks at 6.397, are we to assume Jupiter is practicing when he throws
     thunderbolts in the desert?
   nocentīs: the participle here has a substantive force, *the guilty.*
1104   **exanimō, -āre, -āvī, -ātus**, *to kill* (literally to take the **anima** out of someone).
   indignus, -a, -um, *unworthy, not deserving.*
    indignōs: *those who don't deserve to die;* in opposition to **nocentīs** (1103).
   immerēns, immerentis, *undeserving, blameless.*
    inque merentīs: tmesis of preposition from the adjective, for metrical reasons.

1100 nūbibus ut tenebrās faciat caelīque serēna
1101 concutiat sonitū, tum fulmina mittat et aedēs
1102 saepe suās disturbet et in dēserta recēdēns
1103 saeviat exercēns tēlum quod saepe nocentīs
1104 praeterit exanimatque indignōs inque merentīs?

∽ Discussion Questions

1.   What aspects of the hypothetical omnipotent god are emphasized in lines 1100–04?

2.   What sound effects does Lucretius create in line 1101?

The crux and center of the argument is the question whether the gods do nothing, care for nothing, and take their ease detached from all concern with the care and government of the world: or whether on the contrary all things have been created and formed by them from the dawn of time, and will be ruled and governed by them to all eternity.

    Cicero, *De natura deorum* 1.1–2 (tr. McGregor)

During the Second Punic War in 206 B.C.:

    It was inevitable that in critical times like these men should attribute everything that happened, whether favorable or adverse, to divine agency. Many prodigies were reported: the temple of Jupiter at Tarracina and of Mater Matuta at Satricum were struck by lightning.

    Livy, *The War with Hannibal* 28.11 (tr. de Selincourt)

For the father, thundering from on high, standing on starry Olympus, himself once attacked his own hills and sanctuaries and hurled fire at the temples of the Capitoline.

    Cicero, *De divinatione* 2.20.45

1150   **Iamque adeō**: *Indeed even now.*

         aetās, aetātis, f., here, *prime of life;* in conjunction with the following clause, meaning the prime of the earth.

         effētus, -a, -um, *exhausted, worn out, feeble.*

1151   **animālia parva**: probably referring to worms, which were mentioned at 2.871. Lucretius erroneously believed that they were spontaneously generated by the earth, as indeed he believed the young earth had spontaneously created all animals from "wombs" within herself (cf. 5.805–12.). The **animālia parva** are contrasted with the **ferārum ingentia corpora** below (1152), which perhaps refers to animals such as elephants (cf. 2.537).

         creat quae cūncta creāvit saecla: strong alliteration.

1152   **partus, -ūs**, m., *birth.*

         dedit . . . partū: *brought to birth.*

1157   **Praetereā**: Lucretius continues to describe the original fertility of the earth, with which her current depletion contrasts.

         nitidās frūgēs: a formulaic phrase for the richness of produce, cf. 1.252, 2.994.

         vīnētum, -ī, n., *vineyard.*

         laetus, -a, -um, here, *fertile, productive.*

1158   **sponte suā**: a formulaic phrase for free will, cf. 2.1059 and 2.1092.

         mortālibus: dative of reference; an interesting addition here, since it has a teleological flavor (i.e., action with a design or purpose), which inference Lucretius has stridently denied elsewhere.

         ipsa: reinforcing the meaning of **sponte suā**, as also in 2.1058.

1159   **ipsa**: the anaphora increases the emphasis on the earth as the creator.

         pābula laeta: the formulaic phrase connoting richness and plenty; cf. 1.14 and 1.257, 2.317 and 2.364.

1160   **quae**: the antecedent is **pābula**. Lucretius now returns to the contrasting picture of the earth's increasing infertility.

         grandēscō, grandēscere, *to grow.*

         aucta: perfect passive participle from **augeō, augēre**; here, *assisted.*

         nostrō . . . aucta labōre: once the earth freely and without assistance provided sufficient food for man (cf. 5. 937–44); now even with agriculture men struggle to find enough to eat.

1161   **conterō, conterere, contrīvī, contrītus**, *to wear out, exhaust.*

         agricola, -ae, m., *farmer.*

1162   **cōnficimus**: *we wear down/out.*

         ferrum, -ī, n., here, *iron* (of the plow).

         vix: modifying **suppeditātī**; this third occurrence in seven lines is emphatic.

         arvum, -ī, n., *plowed field, field.*

         suppeditō, -āre, -āvī, -ātus, *to supply.*

            suppeditātī: modifying **nōs** understood, from the first person plural of the verb. The pentasyllabic ending both here and in line 1161 is preceded by a spondaic fourth foot.

1163   **parcunt**: understand **arva**, *fields*, as the subject; here the verb takes the accusative for the object.

1164   **Iamque**: to personalize his point about the continuing degeneration of the earth, Lucretius now paints a very effective picture of a discouraged farmer who yearns for the "good old days."

         quassō, -āre, -āvī, -ātus, *to shake repeatedly, keep on shaking.*

         grandis, -is, -e, *aged, old.*

         suspīrō, -āre, -āvī, -ātūrus, *to sigh.*

         arātor, arātōris, m., *plowman.*

29. The Decrepit Earth

Like all created things, the earth is subject to old age and decay. The diminishing fertility of the earth causes disgruntled farmers to complain about the ever-increasing labor. The decay here described contrasts with and balances the fertility of the first proem and the Epicurean calm of the second proem.

1150 Iamque adeō frācta est aetās effētaque tellūs
1151 vix animālia parva creat quae cūncta creāvit
1152 saecla deditque ferārum ingentia corpora partū.

. . .

1157 Praetereā nitidās frūgēs vīnētaque laeta
1158 sponte suā prīmum mortālibus ipsa creāvit,
1159 ipsa dedit dulcīs fētūs et pābula laeta;
1160 quae nunc vix nostrō grandēscunt aucta labōre,
1161 conterimusque bovēs et vīrīs agricolārum,
1162 cōnficimus ferrum vix arvīs suppeditātī:
1163 usque adeō parcunt fētūs augentque labōrem.
1164 Iamque caput quassāns grandis suspīrat arātor

∞ Discussion Questions

1. In the context of lines 1150–52 what would Lucretius think about dinosaurs and their extinction?

2. Does Lucretius' description of the early earth's fertility in lines 1157–59 resemble a Golden Age? To what else might you compare it?

3. Lucretius laments the decreasing fertility of the earth. Could agricultural practices have contributed to this decay? Consider crop rotation, type of crop, deforestation, and the resulting loss of topsoil, etc.

4. Can you think of any social and political reforms during the second and first centuries B.C. that resulted from agricultural crises?

5. In the face of agricultural decline, how did the Romans continue to feed their expanding population?

1165 **crēber, crēbra, crēbrum**, *frequent.*
    crēbrius: comparative adverb, *rather frequently/often;* the enjambement stresses the frequency of the sighs.
  incassum, adv., *without aim/purpose, in vain.*
  magnōs cecidisse labōrēs: indirect statement dependent on **suspīrat** (1164), which implies mental activity.

1166 **temporibus**: dative with **cōnfert**.
  praesēns, praesentis, *present.*
  cōnfert: *compares.*

1167 **praeteritīs**: modifying **temporibus** (1166) in another effective instance of enjambement.

1168 **Trīstis item**: now Lucretius provides a parallel example of a disgruntled vintner who voices similar complaints.
  vetulus, -a, -um [diminutive], *little old.*
  vītis, vītis, f., *vine.*
  sator, satōris, m., *planter.*
  viētus, -a, -um, *shriveled, withered.* (The adjective is a textual suggestion.)
    Trīstis . . . viētae: embedded and interlocking word order. Moreover the alliteration of **vetulae vītis . . . viētae** adds a pathetic note, as if mimicking the wails of the vintner.

1169 **incūsō, -āre, -āvī, -ātus**, *to accuse, blame, find fault with.*
  mōmen, mōminis, n., *movement, motion;* here, *trend.*
  saeclum: = **saeculum**, by syncope.
  fatīgō, -āre, -āvī, -ātus, *to criticize, assail.*

1170 **crepō, crepāre, crepuī**, *to rattle on, clatter, crackle.*
  ut: the linking conjunction is typically delayed; introducing a substantive clause acting as the object of **crepat**; *that.*
  pietās, pietātis, f., *dutifulness, devotion, piety.*
  repleō, replēre, replēvī, replētus, *to fill up, fill.*
    pietāte replētum: implying that the current problems result from a lack of moral standards and proper religious observance, a common complaint of elders in every age!

1171 **perfacile**, adv., *very easily.*
  angustus, -a, -um, *limited, confined.*
  tolerō, -āre, -āvī, -atūs, *to support, maintain.*
    tolerārit: syncopated perfect subjunctive = **tolerāverit**; subjunctive with **ut** (1170).
  fīnibus: *plots* (of land).

1172 **agrī**: partitive genitive with **minor . . . modus**.
  multō: adverbial with **minus**, *by far less.*
  modus: *measure, allotment.*
    minor . . . agrī multō modus: note the alliteration.
  virītim, adv., *man by man, per man.*

1173 **tenet**: here, *grasps, understands,* introducing an indirect statement. The subject is still the vintner.
  tābēscō, tābēscere, tābuī, *to waste away.*

1174 **capulus, -ī**, m., *coffin, grave.* The manuscript reading is in dispute; an alternate reading is **scopulum**, *rock, cliff,* with the sense *go on the rocks.*
  spatiō: *extent, span, duration.*
  dēfessa: modifying **omnia** (1173).
  vetustus, -a, -um, *old, long-continued.*

1165 crēbrius, incassum magnōs cecidisse labōrēs,
1166 et cum tempora temporibus praesentia cōnfert
1167 praeteritīs, laudat fortūnās saepe parentis.
1168 Trīstis item vetulae vītis sator atque viētae
1169 temporis incūsat mōmen saeclumque fatīgat,
1170 et crepat, antīquum genus ut pietāte replētum
1171 perfacile angustīs tolerārit fīnibus aevum,
1172 cum minor esset agrī multō modus ante virītim.
1173 Nec tenet omnia paulātim tābēscere et īre
1174 ad capulum spatiō aetātis dēfessa vetustō.

∞ Discussion Questions

1.   Are the plowman and vintner justified in their envy of earlier generations?

2.   Do you think that understanding the general principle of decay (1173–74) provides much comfort?

3.   Which reading, *capulum* or *scopulum*, do you prefer in line 1174?

I have seen seeds, though picked long and tested with much pains, yet degenerate, if human toil, year after year, culled not the largest by hand. Thus by law of fate all things speed towards the worst, and slipping away fall back.
      Vergil, *Georgics* 1.197–200 (tr. Fairclough)

In old times it was thought that to observe moderation in the size of a farm was of primary importance, inasmuch as the view was held that it was more satisfactory to sow less land and plow it better; and I observe that Virgil was of this opinion [*Georgics* 2.412]. And if the truth be confessed, large estates [**lātifundia**] have been the ruin of Italy, and are now proving the ruin of the provinces too.
      Seneca, *Natural History* 18.7.35 (tr. Rackham)

There is a famous utterance of Manius Curius, who after celebrating triumphs and making a vast addition of territory to the empire, said that a man not satisfied with seven acres must be deemed a dangerous citizen; for that was the acreage assigned for commoners after the expulsion of the kings. What therefore was the cause of such great fertility?
      Seneca, *Natural History* 18.18 (tr. Rackham)

1   **tenebrae, -ārum**, f. pl., *darkness*.

     Ē tenebrīs tantīs: echoing many earlier uses of **tenebrae** representing ignorance and confusion; cf. 1.146 and 2.59: **hunc igitur terrōrem animī tenebrāsque**, also 2.15: **in tenebrīs vītae**, 2.54: **in tenebrīs . . . vīta labōret**, 2.56: **in tenebrīs metuunt**, and 2.58: **in tenebrīs pavitant**. The strong alliteration of *t*, which is continued by **tam** and **extollere**, almost sounds like a trumpet call to attention.

   extollō, extollere, *to lift up, raise*.

     extollere: dependent upon **potuistī** (2). The infinitive also echoes Lucretius' assertion of Epicurus' original daring in 1.66–67: **prīmum Grāius homō mortālīs tollere contrā / est oculōs ausus**. Here he creates a metaphorical image of Epicurus raising a torch to illuminate the darkness.

   tam clārum . . . lūmen: echoing the earlier contrasting light-dark imagery, particularly of 1.146–48: **tenebrāsque necessest / nōn radiī sōlis neque lūcida tēla diēī / discutiant**, and 2.56: **in tenebrīs metuunt, sīc nōs in lūce timēmus**.

2   **quī**: the subject is left in suspense until line 3.

   prīmus: quite a bold claim, since philosophers such as Socrates, Plato, Aristotle, and many others lived before Epicurus. In particular Lucretius here ignores the atomic predecessors Democritus and Leucippus.

   inlūstrō, -āre, -āvī, -ātus, *to throw light on, make clear, illuminate*.

     inlūstrāns: continuing the light imagery of **tam clārum extollere lūmen** (1).

   commoda: accusative plural neuter substantive, here, *pleasant things, joys, blessings*.

3   **tē**: emphatic position.

   decus, decoris, n., *pride, glory*.

     ō Grāiae gentis decus: apostrophe referring to Epicurus, who earlier has been called simply **Grāius homō** (1.66).

   inque: = **in** + **-que**.

   tuīs: modifying **signīs** (4).

4   **fīgo, fīgere, fīxī, fīctus** (or **fīxus**), *to make firm, fix firmly*.

   pedum: understand **meōrum**.

     fīcta pedum: with **vēstīgia**, *my firm footsteps*.

   premō, premere, pressī, pressus, *to press*.

   signīs: *tracks, traces*; with **pressīs**, *tracks which you impressed*.

     inque tuīs . . . vēstīgia signīs: embedded and interwoven word order, as Lucretius hopes to keep closely on Epicurus' trail; reorder for translation: **nunc in tuīs pressīs signīs pōnō fīcta pedum vēstīgia**.

5   **nōn**: emphatic position.

     nōn ita . . . quam, *not so much . . . as*.

   certō, -āre, -āvī, -ātus, *to strive, compete, rival*.

     certandī: genitive gerund with **cupidus**; contrasting with **quod tē imitārī aveō** (6).

   propter amōrem: balancing **certandī cupidus** and explaining the following clause, i.e., love is his motivation for desiring to imitate Epicurus.

6   **imitor, -ārī, -ātus sum**, *to imitate, copy, follow*.

   aveō, avēre, *to be eager; to desire, wish*.

   quid: here adverbial, *how?*

   contendō, contendere, contendī, contentus + dat., *to compete, contend* (with).

     contendat: potential subjunctive; also **possint** (8).

   hirundō, hirundinis, m., *swallow*.

7   **cycnus, -ī**, m., *swan*.

     contendat hirundō / cycnīs: swallows make a twittering sound, which is not terribly melodious, whereas swans, despite the fact that they only honk, were reputed to sing most beautifully, perhaps to match the beauty of their appearance. The contrast between the birds is accentuated by their juxtaposition and the enjambement of **cycnīs**.

⊂3 BOOK 3 ℰ

30. Praise of Epicurus

In a passage filled with the imagery of light and dark, Lucretius praises his master Epicurus and attempts to follow in his footsteps. Epicurus freed man from his fears and allowed him to see beyond the confines of this world. The peaceful abodes of the gods appear but, significantly, no underworld of torment is seen. In this third Book, Lucretius is concerned to prove that the soul is mortal and therefore cannot suffer after death.

1	Ē tenebrīs tantīs tam clārum extollere lūmen
2	quī prīmus potuistī inlūstrāns commoda vītae,
3	tē sequor, ō Grāiae gentis decus, inque tuīs nunc
4	fīcta pedum pōnō pressīs vēstīgia signīs,
5	nōn ita certandī cupidus quam propter amōrem
6	quod tē imitārī aveō; quid enim contendat hirundō
7	cycnīs, aut quidnam tremulīs facere artubus haedī
8	cōnsimile in cursū possint et fortis equī vīs?

⊂3 Discussion Questions

1. How does Lucretius depict himself in comparison to Epicurus? What words might you use to describe the relationship? (1–8)

2. What typical Lucretian device do you find in the phrase **fortis equī vīs**? (8)

Imitation is the sincerest of flattery.
   Charles Caleb Colton, *Lacon* (1820–22), vol. I, no. 217

---

7   **quisnam, quidnam**, *who indeed, what indeed?*
    facere: dependent on **possint** (8).
    artus, -ūs, m., *limb.*
       artubus: archaic ablative.
    haedus, -ī, m., *kid, young goat.*
8   **cōnsimilis, -is, -e**, *similar, like, alike.*
       cōnsimile: modifying **quidnam** (7).
    cursus, -ūs, m., *running;* here, *race.*
    et: here comparative with **cōnsimile**, *as, to.*
    fortis: the case is ambiguous; either genitive with **equī** or nominative with **vīs**, but probably really applying to both.
    vīs: another monosyllabic line-ending stressing the word.

9   **Tū . . . tū**: emphatic anaphora.

pater: a particularly Roman idea. The gods are often referred to as **patrēs**, and this usage is transferred to philosophers and others who deeply affect mankind.

inventor, inventōris, m., *discoverer*.

   rērum inventor: predicate with understood **es**; for Epicurus' role as explorer and discoverer see lines 1.72–79.

patria: adjective modifying **praecepta** (10); the repetition of the root **patr-** reinforces the sense that Epicurus acted like a kindly father in providing for and instructing his children.

10   **suppeditō, -āre, -āvī, -ātus**, *to provide, supply*.

praeceptum, -ī, n., *teaching, precept*.

inclutus, -a, -um, *celebrated, famous, renowned*.

charta, -ae, f., *page, writing*.

   tuīsque ex, inclute, chartīs: unusual word order with both anastrophe of the preposition and interruption of the prepositional phrase by the vocative.

11   **flōrifer, flōrifera, flōriferum**, *flower-bearing, flowery*; a Lucretian coinage in the typical dactylic form.

ut: the linking conjunction has been delayed; here, *as, like*, introducing a simile comparing poets to bees, a commonplace in antiquity.

apis, apis, f., *bee*.

saltus, -ūs, m., *woodland, glade*.

lībō, -āre, -āvī, -ātus, *to sip, taste*.

12   **omnia**: modifying **aurea dicta**; placed at line-beginning for emphasis.

nōs: making the comparison clear.

itidem, adv., *in like manner, likewise*.

dēpāscor, dēpāscī, dēpāstus sum, *to feed on*.

aureus, -a, -um, *golden*.

13   **aurea**: anaphora, especially emphatic in this position.

dignus, -a, -um + abl., *worthy* (of), *deserving*.

   aurea, perpetuā semper dignissima vītā: interlocking word order.

14   **Nam**: giving the reason for the immortality of Epicurus' writings.

ratiō: *philosophy*.

coepit: *begins*.

vōciferor, -ārī, -ātus sum, *to cry aloud, proclaim*.

15   **nātūram rērum**: the enjambement is most effective in accentuating the topic of Epicurus' investigations, Περὶ φύσεως.

dīvīnā: by using this adjective, Lucretius implies that one who has performed such services for mankind and whose writings will be immortal (cf. 13 above) is godlike; the adjective anticipates the elevation of Epicurus to divine stature in the proem to Book 5.

   dīvīnā mente: ablative of source with **coorta**.

coorta: modifying **ratiō** (14).

16   **diffugiō, diffugere, diffūgī**, *to scatter, disperse*.

animī terrōrēs: the two great fears of mankind: of the gods and of punishment after death.

mundus, -ī, m., *world, earth*.

   diffugiunt . . . discēdunt . . . videō: the asyndeton between the clauses conveys the rapidity with which the philosophy of Epicurus illuminated the darkness of ignorance; the enjambement of **diffugiunt** and **discēdunt** further emphasizes the verbs.

17   **discēdō, discēdere, discessī, discessūrus**, *to come apart, divide, open*.

moenia mundī discēdunt: echoing 1.73, where Epicurus himself proceeded far beyond the **moenia mundī** and wandered through the universe with his mind.

tōtum: modifying **ināne** and displaced here for emphasis.

ināne: *space*.

gerī rēs: *that things are done, that action takes place, action taking place*. The significant point is that he can see action taking place throughout the infinity of space and he sees nothing for mankind to fear.

9   Tū pater es, rērum inventor, tū patria nōbīs

10   suppeditās praecepta, tuīsque ex, inclute, chartīs,

11   flōriferīs ut apēs in saltibus omnia lībant,

12   omnia nōs itidem dēpāscimur aurea dicta,

13   aurea, perpetuā semper dignissima vītā.

14   Nam simul ac ratiō tua coepit vōciferārī

15   nātūram rērum, dīvīnā mente coorta,

16   diffugiunt animī terrōrēs, moenia mundī

17   discēdunt, tōtum videō per ināne gerī rēs.

∽ **Discussion Questions**

1.   To what are Epicurus' writings compared? (10–13)

2.   Why are Epicurus' writings worthy of immortality?

3.   From the brief quotes from Epicurus that you have read, how does Lucretius' writing compare
     with that of Epicurus in style and content? What significant differences do you find?

18   **Appāret**: placed first to indicate wonder at the sudden and surprising view.

     nūmen, nūminis, n., here, *majesty*.

19   **concutiō, concutere, concussī, concussus**, *to shake violently, agitate, assail*.

     nūbila, -ōrum, n. pl., *clouds*.

     nimbus, -ī, m., *rainstorm*.

20   **nix, nivis**, f., *snow*.

     ācrī: *biting*.

     concrētus, -a, -um, *hard, frozen*.

     pruīna, -ae, f., *frost, rime*.

       nix ācrī concrēta pruīnā: nicely interlocking word order replicating the frozen solidity of deep winter.

21   **cānus, -a, -um**, *white*.

       cāna: going almost adverbially with **cadēns**, *falling white*.

     violat: *mar, disturb* (the tranquillity of the gods).

     innūbilus, -a, -um, *cloudless, clear*; another fine Lucretian coinage.

     aether, aetheris, m., *ether, sky*.

22   **integō, integere, intēxī, intēctus**, *to cover, cover over*.

     largē, adv., *bounteously, plentifully*.

     diffundō, diffundere, diffūdī, diffūsus, *to spread widely, diffuse*.

       aether (21) / **... rīdet**: a lovely image, reminiscent of 1.8–9: **rīdent aequora pontī / plācātumque nitet diffūsō lūmine caelum**.

23   **Omnia**: emphatic position for the direct object.

     porrō, adv., *moreover*.

     nātūra: by supplying the gods' wants, nature is shown to be in control, whereas in the usual mythological interpretation the gods themselves represent the forces of nature.

24   **animī pācem**: i.e., the *ataraxiā* that is the Epicurean goal.

     dēlībō, -āre, -āvī, -ātus, *to mar, diminish, infringe*.

     sēdēsque quiētae (18) ... tempore in ūllō: the passage is closely modelled on Homer's description of the life of the gods on Olympus (*Odyssey* 6.42–46). Also see Lucretius' earlier description of the gods at 2.646–51.

25   **At contrā**: signalling the realm normally contrasting with heaven—hell.

     Acherūsius, -a, -um, *Acherusian, of the underworld* (the Acheron was a river in the underworld).

     templa: here again, *quarters, realms*.

26   **obstō, obstāre, obstitī, obstātus** + **quin** + subj., *to be an impediment to; to prevent*.

     omnia: nominative plural neuter, to be specified by the **quaecumque** clause (27).

     dispiciō, dispicere, dispexī, dispectus, *to see clearly*.

       obstat quīn omnia dispiciantur: *prevent everything from being seen clearly*.

27   **quīcumque, quaecumque, quodcumque**, *whoever, whatever, whichever*.

     īnfrā, adv., *below, beneath*.

28   **Hīs ... rēbus**: i.e., *Because of these visions and thoughts*; ablative of cause.

     dīvīna voluptās: a pleasure such as the gods enjoy. **Voluptās** is the Epicurean ideal.

29   **percipit**: *seizes*.

     horror: initially seemingly incompatible with **voluptās** (28), but here referring to a thrill of awe and wonderment, such as makes one's hair stand on end (the literal meaning of the word). This type of **horror** can indeed be pleasurable.

     tuā vī: emphatic position and ending with two monosyllables stressing the fact that Epicurus alone is responsible for this enlightenment.

30   **manifestus, -a, -um**, *clear, visible*.

     patēns: *open to view*.

     retegō, retegere, retēxī, retēctus, *to lay bare, uncover, reveal*.

       manifesta patēns ... retēcta est: a metaphorical image of an unveiling.

18   Appāret dīvum nūmen sēdēsque quiētae
19   quās neque concutiunt ventī nec nūbila nimbīs
20   aspergunt neque nix ācrī concrēta pruīnā
21   cāna cadēns violat semperque innūbilus aether
22   integit et largē diffūsō lūmine rīdet.
23   Omnia suppeditat porrō nātūra neque ūlla
24   rēs animī pācem dēlībat tempore in ūllō.
25   At contrā nusquam appārent Acherūsia templa
26   nec tellūs obstat quīn omnia dispiciantur,
27   sub pedibus quaecumque īnfrā per ināne geruntur.
28   Hīs ibi mē rēbus quaedam dīvīna voluptās
29   percipit atque horror, quod sīc nātūra tuā vī
30   tam manifesta patēns ex omnī parte retēcta est.

☙ Discussion Questions

1.   What name or names might we apply to the place described in lines 19–22?

2.   Why does Lucretius emphasize that despite his clearer vision he cannot see **Acherūsia templa** (25)? Where are they imagined to be?

3.   Is the phrase **quod sīc nātūra . . . retēcta est** (29–30) an exaggeration?

These gods of Epicurus have often been ridiculed, these gods who, like human beings, dwell in the intermundia of the real world, have no body but a quasi-body, no blood but quasi-blood, and, content to abide in blissful peace, lend no ear to any supplication, are unconcerned with us and the world, are honored because of their beauty, that majesty and their superior nature, and not for any gain.

And yet these gods are no fiction of Epicurus. They did exist. They are the plastic gods of Greek art.

Karl Marx, doctoral dissertation, *The Difference between Democritus' and Epicurus' Philosophy of Nature* (1841), Ch. I

Olympus, where the abode of the gods stands firm and unmoving
forever, they say, and is not shaken with winds nor spattered
with rains, nor does snow pile ever there, but the shining bright air
stretches cloudless away, and the white light glances upon it.
And there, and all their days, the blessed gods take their pleasure.

Homer, *Odyssey* 6.42–46 (tr. Lattimore)

37   **metus ille**: that great terror of death; further explained by **Acheruntis**.

    praeceps, praecipitis, *headlong, headfirst*.

    Acherūns, Acheruntis, m. / f., *Acheron* (a river in the underworld, thus the underworld*)*.

        metus ille forās praeceps Acheruntis agendus: the imagery personifies fear as a creature that could be hurled from a precipice, like a criminal, to its death.

38   **funditus**, adv., *from the bottom, utterly, completely*.

    quī: the relative has been delayed; its antecedent is **metus**.

    turbō, -āre, -āvī, -ātus, *to confuse, disturb*.

    īmus, -a, -um, *lowest*.

        īmō: here a substantive, *from the bottom*, with **funditus . . . turbat** a vivid image which suggests stirring up noxious sediments as from the bottom of a well.

39   **suffundō, suffundere, suffūsī, suffūsus**, *to stain, cloud*.

    nigror, nigrōris, m., *blackness*.

40   **liquidam pūramque**: predicative adjectives; **liquidam** nicely continues the metaphor of life as a well that should be clear but is fouled by fear.

    relinquit: *allows*; taking an accusative and infinitive construction.

41   **quod**: here, *whereas, although*.

    morbōs magis esse timendōs: indirect statement with **ferunt** (42).

42   **īnfāmis, -is, -e**, *disreputable, infamous*.

        īnfāmem . . . vītam: a second subject of the indirect statement with **esse timendōs**.

    ferunt: here, *say*.

    quam: comparative with **magis** (41).

    Tartara, -ōrum, n. pl., *Tartarus* (the infernal regions, the underworld).

    lētum, -ī, n., *death*.

        lētī: possessive genitive with **Tartara**, *Tartarus, which belongs to death*.

43   **sē scīre**: a second indirect statement dependent upon **ferunt** and governing its own indirect statement.

    sanguinis: genitive of material.

44   **ventī**: also genitive of material. Lucretius is referring to popular conceptions in which the physical components, blood and breath, most associated with life are assumed to constitute the soul.

    fert, here, *leads* (to that conclusion).

    voluntās, voluntātis, f., *will, whim*.

        sī fert ita forte voluntās: implying that ordinary men's beliefs about the nature of the soul are the result of chance whims rather than true contemplation and investigation.

45   **prōrsum**, adv., *at all*.

    quicquam, here adverbial, *in any way*.

    nostrae ratiōnis: Epicureanism.

    egeō, egēre, eguī + gen., *to need*.

        egēre: infinitive in the last indirect statement dependent upon **ferunt** (42); supply **sē** as its subject.

46   **hinc**, adv., *from here*; from the behaviors described in lines 48–54.

    licet: the subjunctive **advertās**, with **ut** understood, is the subject of this impersonal verb.

    advertō, advertere, advertī, adversus, *to turn towards, direct*.

        animum advertere, idiom, *to notice, perceive*.

    omnia: supply **dicta**; accusative subject of accusative and infinitive construction governed by **advertās animum**.

    laudis: genitive with **causā** (47); *for the sake of praise*, i.e., to show off, brag. The line-end position and separation from **causā** emphasize the word.

47   **iactārī**: *are tossed, bandied about*.

    quam: comparative with **magis** (46).

    rēs ipsa: *the claim itself* (that the soul is material and that death is preferable to disease and ignominy).

    probō, -āre, -āvī, -ātus, *to prove, demonstrate*; here, *is believed*.

31. The Fear of Death

The fear of death pollutes man's existence. Though men sometimes profess to fear disease and infamy more than death, this is mere boasting. In their fear of death they cling to life at all costs and commit the most heinous crimes.

37   Et metus ille forās praeceps Acheruntis agendus,
38   funditus hūmānam quī vītam turbat ab īmō
39   omnia suffundēns mortis nigrōre neque ūllam
40   esse voluptātem liquidam pūramque relinquit.
41   Nam quod saepe hominēs morbōs magis esse timendōs
42   īnfāmemque ferunt vītam quam Tartara lētī
43   et sē scīre animī nātūram sanguinis esse
44   aut etiam ventī, sī fert ita forte voluntās,
45   nec prōrsum quicquam nostrae ratiōnis egēre,
46   hinc licet advertās animum magis omnia laudis
47   iactārī causā quam quod rēs ipsa probētur.
48   Extorrēs īdem patriā longēque fugātī
49   cōnspectū ex hominum, foedātī crīmine turpī,
50   omnibus aerumnīs adfectī dēnique vīvunt,

CB Discussion Questions

1. What picture does the phrase **omnia suffundēns mortis nigrōre** (39) convey? What metaphor does it contain?

2. With what region of the underworld is Tartarus specifically associated? (42)

---

48   **extorris, -is, -e**, *exiled*.
     īdem: nominative plural, referring to the boasters above.
     patriā: ablative of separation with **extorrēs**.
     fugō, -āre, -āvī, -ātus, *to drive into exile, banish*.
       longēque fugātī: possibly referring to one type of exile, **relēgātiō**, in which the disgraced person was exiled to some specific distance from Rome. Cicero, exiled in 58 B.C., was not allowed to come within 400 miles of Rome. Sometimes the unfortunate exile was sent to a specific location; this was Ovid's fate, who in A.D. 8 was exiled to Tomis on the Black Sea.
49   **cōnspectus, -ūs**, m., *sight*.
     cōnspectū ex: typically Lucretian anastrophe of the preposition and its noun.
     foedō, -āre, -āvī, -ātus, *to defile, dishonor, disgrace*.
     crīmen, crīminis, n., *charge, accusation; crime*.
     turpis, -is, -e, *foul, base*.
50   **aerumna, -ae**, f., *trouble, hardship*.
     adfectus, -a, -um, *affected, afflicted, impaired*.
     dēnique: here, *still*; take with **vīvunt**.
     vīvunt: the punch is delivered at the very end of the line. Those who professed disdain for death still cling to life even when in deepest disgrace. Lines 48–50 nicely describe the **īnfāmem vītam** (42) to which these men claimed death was preferable.

51 **quōcumque**, adv., *wherever.*
> **vēnēre**: alternative third plural perfect = **vēnērunt**; translate as present in present general structure.
> **parentō, -āre, -āvī, -ātus**, *to make offerings to the dead of the family.*

52 **mactō, -āre, -āvī, -ātus**, *to slaughter, sacrifice.*
> **nigrās mactant pecudēs**: animals sacrificed to the gods of the underworld were black; cf. Homer's *Odyssey* 10.524–27: "dedicate an all-black / ram, the one conspicuous in all your sheepflocks. / But when with prayers you have entreated the glorious hordes / of the dead, then sacrifice one black ram and one black female." (tr. Lattimore).
> **mānibu' dīvīs**: metrical variation of the phrase **dīs mānibus**, found often in inscriptions on tombs, *to the spirits of the dead* (considered to be minor supernatural powers).

53 **multōque**: adverbial, modifying **ācrius** (54), *much more keenly, fiercely.*
> **acerbus, -a, -um**, *bitter, painful, severe, harsh.*

54 **advertunt animōs**: *they turn their minds.*
> **acerbīs / ācrius advertunt animōs**: startling assonance, perhaps imitating the woeful sighs of the men being described.

55 **Quō**, adv., *Therefore.*
> **dubiīs**: here, *critical*, i.e., when the outcome is in doubt; modifying **perīclīs**.
> **spectāre**: infinitive subject of the impersonal **convenit** (56) and taking **hominem** as its direct object.

56 **convenit**: here impersonal, *(it) is fitting.*
> **adversīsque in rēbus**: essentially equivalent to **in dubiīs . . . perīclīs** (55).
> **nōscō, nōscere, nōvī, nōtus**, *to get to know, learn.*
> **quī**: here interrogative in indirect question, equivalent to **quālis**, *what sort of man.*
> > **quī sit**: unusual line-ending with two monosyllables; **sit** is placed in a very emphatic position to stress the final revelation of the true character of the man.

57 **dēmum**, adv., *at last, finally.*
> **īmus, -a, um**, *lowest, deepest (part of).*

58 **ēliciō, ēlicere, ēlicuī, ēlicitus**, *to draw out, extract.*
> **persōna, -ae**, f., *mask (as worn by actors).*
> **rēs**: here the emphatic monosyllable, closing the line, represents *the truth*, which then stands exposed.

59 **Dēnique**, adv., *furthermore*; introducing a final example of the evils caused by man's fear of death.
> **avāritiēs, -ēī**, f., *greed, avarice.*
> **honōrum**, here, *political offices.*
> **caecus, -a, -um**, *blind.*
> **cupīdō, cupīdinis**, f., *longing*; + gen., *desire* (for).

60 **trānscendō, trānscendere, trānscendī, trānscēnsus**, *to overstep, transgress.*

61 **iūs, iūris**, n., *right, law, justice.*
> > **trānscendere fīnīs iūris**: a vivid metaphor, which imagines legality as a defined space within which one can safely step, but whose borders it is dangerous to overstep.
> **socius, -ī**, m., here, *partner.*
> **minister, ministrī**, m., here, *accomplice.*
> > **sociōs . . . ministrōs**: predicative with **miserōs hominēs** (60), *as partners and accomplices.*

62 **noctēs atque diēs**: accusatives of duration of time.
> **nītor, nītī, nīxus sum** + infin., *to strive, strain, exert oneself* (to).
> **praestāns, praestantis**, *exceptional, extraordinary.*

51   et quōcumque tamen miserī vēnēre parentant

52   et nigrās mactant pecudēs et mānibu' dīvīs

53   īnferiās mittunt multōque in rēbus acerbīs

54   ācrius advertunt animōs ad religiōnem.

55   Quō magis in dubiīs hominem spectāre perīclīs

56   convenit adversīsque in rēbus nōscere quī sit;

57   nam vērae vōcēs tum dēmum pectore ab īmō

58   ēliciuntur et ēripitur persōna, manet rēs.

59   Dēnique avāritiēs et honōrum caeca cupīdō

60   quae miserōs hominēs cōgunt trānscendere fīnīs

61   iūris et interdum sociōs scelerum atque ministrōs

62   noctēs atque diēs nītī praestante labōre

63   ad summās ēmergere opēs, haec vulnera vītae

64   nōn minimam partem mortis formīdine aluntur.

ↄ Discussion Questions

1. What is Lucretius implying is the reason why exiles continually make sacrifice to the gods of the underworld? What do they hope to gain? (51–54)

2. With what earlier scene does the phrase **vērae vōcēs . . . ab īmō / ēliciuntur** (57–58) contrast?

3. Why does Lucretius describe the wrongdoers as **miserōs**? (60)

4. What does Lucretius think of politics and politicians? How do politicians behave?

People are fools who hate life and yet wish to live through fear of Hades.
    Democritus, *Fragment* 199 (tr. Freeman)

Life's but a walking shadow, a poor player
That struts and frets his hour upon the stage
    Shakespeare, *Macbeth* V.5.24–25

---

63   **ēmergō, ēmergere, ēmersī, ēmersūrus,** *to come forth, arise, emerge.*
     ēmergere: a vivid image, which suggests rising out of water, as if from a murky swamp.
   ops, opis, f., *power;* pl., *wealth.*
     noctēs atque diēs . . . ēmergere opēs (63): repeated verbatim from the proem of Book 2 (12–13), where Lucretius described the wanderings of those who do not know the proper way of life.
   vulnera: a forceful metaphor; these harmful activities are like physical wounds.
     vulnera . . . aluntur (64): a strange, oxymoronic image, that wounds can be fed.
64   **nōn minimam partem:** adverbial accusative, *not in the least part, in no small way;* i.e., primarily.
   formīdō, formīdinis, f., *fear.*
     mortis formīdine: the fear of death motivates men to attain wealth and high position because they feel they will then be protected (perhaps physically by bodyguards) from the assaults of other men.

94   **Prīmum**: adverbial, *First of all.*

       quam: assimilated in gender to the predicate noun **mentem**, but the antecedent is **animum**.

95   **in quō**: returning to the masculine gender of **animus**.

       cōnsilium: *reasoning, deliberation.*

       regimen, regiminis, n., *control, guidance.*

96   **esse hominis partem**: predicate to **animum** in indirect statement governed by **dīcō** (94).

       nīlō, adv., *by nothing, not at all.*

       ac: here comparative with **minus**, *than.*

       et pēs: unusual final foot with two monosyllables, here without any apparent special emphasis, unlike in 3.56.

97   **partēs**: predicative with **exstant**, *as parts.*

       exstō, exstāre, exstitī, *to exist, be found.*

136   **coniūncta**: predicative with **tenērī**, *are held joined together;* neuter to modify nouns of two different genders.

137   **cōnficere**: *to form, compose.*

138   **quasi**: apologizing for the metaphorical use of **caput**, *(is)*, *as it were/so to speak, the head.*

       dominor, -ārī, -ātus sum, *to be master;* here, *is the master.*

         esse . . . et dominārī: the subject of these infinitives is **cōnsilium** (139).

139   **cōnsilium**: again, *reason.*

       quod nōs animum . . . vocāmus: an expansion of the relative clause in line 94. Lucretius is careful to make clear exactly what he means.

140   **Id**: = **cōnsilium**.

       mediā regiōne in: anastrophe of the preposition following the ablatives; technically the preposition is unnecessary, but is here for metrical reasons.

       pectoris: a defining genitive, *the middle region, that is, the region of the chest.*

         situm mediā regiōne in pectoris: in antiquity there was much debate over where the "mind" was placed—in the head or in the chest. To the ancients emotions and intellect were not considered to be separate, as we generally consider them to be. Therefore the Epicureans believed the **animus**, as both intellect and emotion, was situated in the chest, since it is there that we feel emotion.

       haeret: reinforcing the idea of the fixed position of the **animus**.

141   **Hīc**, adv., *Here.*

       exsultō, -āre, -āvī, *to leap up, throb* (referring to the physical throbbing of the heart).

       pavor, pavōris, m., *sudden fear, terror, fright.*

       haec loca: governed by **circum** in anastrophe.

142   **laetitia, -ae**, f., *joy, delight.*

       mulceō, mulcēre, mulsī, mulsus, *to soothe.*

       hīc: anaphora with **Hīc . . . haec** (141), connecting the various emotions and their placement in the chest.

       ergō, conj., *therefore.*

143   **cēterus, -a, -um**, *the other.*

       animae: here referring to the whole soul, comprised of both the mind and the spirit. The language is somewhat confusing, since **anima** has two meanings: (1) the entire soul, and (2) more commonly, the atoms of the vital principle spread throughout the body, as here.

       disserō, disserere, disseruī, dissitus, *to scatter, spread.*

144   **pāret**: understand **mentī animōque** (142); contrasting with the role of the **animus** (138).

       ad: here, *in accordance with, at.*

       nūmen, nūminis, n., here, *nod ; command.*

       mōmen, mōminis, n., here, *inclination, impulse.*

         nūmen mentis mōmenque movētur: the alliteration of *m* and *n* is exceptional, and the phrase is heavily spondaic; additionally, there is a fine **figūra etymologica** in **mōmenque movētur**.

32. The Mind/Soul Is Physical and Therefore Mortal

The mind (**animus**) and spirit (**anima**) are both corporeal and are inextricably united. The **animus**, located in the chest, controls the **anima**, whose atoms are spread throughout the body. When the mind is sufficiently affected, the body, stirred by **anima** atoms, necessarily reacts.

94   Prīmum animum dīcō, mentem quam saepe vocāmus,
95   in quō cōnsilium vītae regimenque locātum est,
96   esse hominis partem nīlō minus ac manus et pēs
97   atque oculī partēs animantis tōtius exstant.

. . .

136   Nunc animum atque animam dīcō coniūncta tenērī
137   inter sē atque ūnam nātūram cōnficere ex sē,
138   sed caput esse quasi et dominārī in corpore tōtō
139   cōnsilium quod nōs animum mentemque vocāmus.
140   Idque situm mediā regiōne in pectoris haeret.
141   Hīc exsultat enim pavor ac metus, haec loca circum
142   laetitiae mulcent; hīc ergō mēns animusquest.
143   Cētera pars animae per tōtum dissita corpus
144   pāret et ad nūmen mentis mōmenque movētur.

⋈ **Discussion Questions**

1.   What are the synonyms that Lucretius uses for the **animus**?

2.   To what does Lucretius compare the **animus**? (138)

3.   Why does Lucretius locate the **animus** in the chest rather than the head?

4.   Why does Lucretius believe that the mind is corporeal? What evidence does he provide? (141–42)

152   **vēmentī**: a contracted form of **vehementī**.

      magis: take closely with **vēmentī**.

         vēmentī magis est commōta metū mēns: interlocking word order and a continuation of the alliteration of *m* from line 144.

153   **cōnsentiō, cōnsentīre, cōnsēnsī, cōnsēnsūrus**, *to join/share in sensation.*

         cōnsentīre animam: accusative and infinitive construction dependent upon **vidēmus**.

      membrum, -ī, n., *limb.*

154   **sūdor, sūdōris**, m., *sweat.*

      ita: *therefore, then*, i.e., since the **anima** joins in the sensations of the **animus**.

      pallor, pallōris, m., *paleness, pallor.*

      exsistō, exsistere, exstitī, *to arise.*

      tōtō corpore: governed by the **ex-** of **exsistere**.

155   **īnfringō, īnfringere, īnfrēgī, īnfractus**, *to weaken, impair.*

      linguam: the *u* is consonantal and so does not scan.

         īnfringī linguam: the tongue is weakened, i.e., it stutters or stumbles.

      aborior, aborīrī, abortus sum, *to disappear, fail.*

156   **cālīgō, -āre**, *to see dimly.*

      sonō, sonāre, sonuī, sonitus, *to ring, buzz.*

         sonere: conjugated as if in the third conjugation, indicating the fluidity of the language.

      auris, auris, f., *ear.*

      succidō, succidere, succidī, *to give way under one, collapse.*

      artus, -ūs, m., *limb.*

         sūdōrēsque (154) . . . succidere artūs: the description of fear seems closely modelled on Sappho's description of love in *Fragment* 31. Moreover, Lucretius' contemporary Catullus imitated the Sapphic lines in his famous poem 51.

157   **concidere**: the subject of the infinitive, **hominēs** (158), has been considerably delayed in enjambement for emphasis. Note the repetition of the root **cidere** from line 156 **succidere**.

      ex: the preposition is unnecessary grammatically, but assists metrically.

158   **facile**: displaced to the front of the clause for emphasis.

      quīvīs, quaevīs, quodvīs, *any (one, thing) you like.*

      hinc, i.e., from the physical reactions described above.

159   **esse**: infinitive with **coniūnctam** forming a perfect passive infinitive.

      cum animō . . . cum animī: the triple elision here quickens the line and shows the absolute interconnection between the **animus** and the **anima**.

160   **percussast**: enjambement for emphasis.

      exim, adv., *then.*

      corpus: accusative, direct object.

      prōpellō, prōpellere, prōpulī, prōpulsus, *to push, propel.*

      īciō, īcere, īcī, ictus, *to strike.*

         quae cum animī vī (159) . . . īcit: the sequence of the action moves from the self-generated impulse of the **animus**, to the dependent **anima**, to the body.

            prōpellit et īcit: an instance of *hysteron proteron* (reversal of order): first the **anima** strikes the body, then it drives it onward; but the verbs are reversed in the Latin.

152   Ubi vēmentī magis est commōta metū mēns

153   cōnsentīre animam tōtam per membra vidēmus

154   sūdōrēsque ita pallōremque exsistere tōtō

155   corpore et īnfringī linguam vōcemque aborīrī,

156   cālīgāre oculōs, sonere aurīs, succidere artūs,

157   dēnique concidere ex animī terrōre vidēmus

158   saepe hominēs; facile ut quīvīs hinc nōscere possit

159   esse animam cum animō coniūnctam, quae cum animī vī

160   percussast, exim corpus prōpellit et īcit.

☙ Discussion Question

1.   Examine the symptoms described in lines 154–56. What medical event is Lucretius depicting?

A similar symptomology describing the effects of love:

Like the very gods in my sight is he who
sits where he can look in your eyes, who listens
close to you, to hear the soft voice, its sweetness
          murmur in love and
laughter, all for him. But it breaks my spirit;
underneath my breast all the heart is shaken.
Let me only glance where you are, the voice dies,
          I can say nothing,
but my lips are stricken to silence, underneath my skin the tenuous flame suffuses;
nothing shows in front of my eyes, my ears are
          muted in thunder.
And the sweat breaks running upon me, fever
shakes my body, paler I turn than grass is;
I can feel that I have been changed, I feel that
          death has come near me.
                    Sappho, *Fragment* (tr. Lattimore)

He seems to me the equal of a god,
he seems, if that may be, the gods' superior,
who sits face to face with you and again and again
          watches and hears you
sweetly laughing, an experience which robs me,
poor wretch, of all my senses; for the moment I set
eyes on you, Lesbia, there remains not a whisper
          <of voice on my lips,>
but my tongue is paralyzed, a subtle flame
courses through my limbs, with sound self-caused
my two ears ring, and my eyes are
          covered in darkness.
                    Catullus 51.1–12 (tr. Goold)

323 **Haec . . . nātūra**: of the **animus** and **anima**.

    tenētur: *is held together, enclosed, protected.*

    ab: the preposition is here used with the ablative of means, probably for metrical reasons.

324 **salūs, salūtis**, f., *safety; health*; here, *life*, since, as Lucretius will show, the body cannot survive
    without the soul.

325 **rādīx, rādīcis**, f., *root.*

    commūnibus inter sē rādīcibus: the enclosing word order mimics Lucretius' point about
      how the soul is held enclosed by the body.

    haerent: the subject is the body and the soul.

326 **perniciēs, -ēī**, f., *destruction, disaster, ruin.*

    perniciē: of both the body and the soul.

    dīvellō, dīvellere, dīvellī, dīvulsus, *to tear apart, separate.*

    videntur: here, *are seen* (to); with **nec . . . posse**, *clearly cannot be.*

327 **quod genus**, idiom, *just as, for example.*

    thūs, thūris, n., *incense.*

    glaeba, -ae, f., *lump, clod.*

    ēvellō, ēvellere, ēvellī, ēvulsus, *to tear out, remove.*

    ēvellere: subject of **est** (328).

328 **haud facile est**: an instance of litotes (understatement), since the task described is virtually
    impossible.

    quīn, conj. + subj., *without it happening that, but that.*

    intereō, interīre, interiī, interitūrus, *to perish, be destroyed.*

    eius: of the incense.

329 **Sīc**: having concluded his example, Lucretius returns to his statement of the inseparability of
    body and soul.

    animī atque animae: the elisions reinforce the sense of the essential union of the two parts of
    the soul.

      animī atque animae nātūram: a typical Lucretian periphrasis meaning no more than
        animum atque animam.

    corpore tōtō: ablative governed by the **ex-** of **extrahere** (330).

330 **haud facile est quīn**: repeating the words from line 328, thus strengthening the connection
    between the two examples.

    omnia: i.e., **animus**, **anima**, and **corpus** will all three be destroyed.

    dissoluō, dissoluere, dissoluī, dissolūtus, *to break up, disintegrate.*

    dissoluantur: Lucretius uses the vocalic rather than consonantal *u* for metrical reasons.

331 **implectō, implectere, implexī, implexus**, *to interlace, intertwine.*

    prīncipiīs: of the body and the soul.

    implexīs ita prīncipiīs: ablative of description, *with their atoms thus interwoven.*

    orīgō, orīginis, f., *birth, origin.*

    ab orīgine prīmā: from the moment of conception, as will be seen below (344–46).

332 **inter sē**: going closely with **implexīs . . . prīncipiīs** (331).

    cōnsors, cōnsortis, *shared, common.*

    praeditus, -a, -um + abl., *endowed with, possessing.*

    praedita: predicative with **fīunt**.

333 **sibi**: dative of reference, here, *for itself*, i.e., independently.

    quisque, quaeque, quidque, *each, each one.*

    quaeque: technically modifying **potestās** (334), from which it is very separated, but can be
      understood here by itself. Reorder the entire two lines for translation: **nec sibi quaeque
      potestās corporis atque animī sine vī alterius vidētur posse sentīre sōrsum**.

    vidētur: in the typical Lucretian sense, *is seen*; with **nec . . . posse**, *clearly cannot*; cf. 326.

334 **corporis atque animī**: possessive genitives defining **quaeque . . . potestās**.

    s(e)ōrsum, adv., *apart, separately*; take closely with **sentīre**.

    sentīre: dependent on **posse** (333).

33. The Union of Soul and Body

The soul and body are interdependent. Bound together, they cannot be separated without the destruction of each. The soul and body developed together and will also perish together.

323   Haec igitur nātūra tenētur corpore ab omnī
324   ipsaque corporis est custōs et causa salūtis;
325   nam commūnibus inter sē rādīcibus haerent
326   nec sine perniciē dīvellī posse videntur.
327   Quod genus ē thūris glaebīs ēvellere odōrem
328   haud facile est quīn intereat nātūra quoque eius.
329   Sīc animī atque animae nātūram corpore tōtō
330   extrahere haud facile est quīn omnia dissoluantur.
331   Implexīs ita prīncipiīs ab orīgine prīmā
332   inter sē fīunt cōnsortī praedita vītā
333   nec sibi quaeque sine alterius vī posse vidētur
334   corporis atque animī sōrsum sentīre potestās,
335   sed commūnibus inter eās cōnflātur utrimque
336   mōtibus accēnsus nōbīs per vīscera sēnsus.

ℨ Discussion Questions

1.   The soul is held almost imprisoned by the body in line 323, but Lucretius then describes the soul as **custōs** in line 324. What paradoxical image is created here?

2.   What defines life and when does Lucretius believe that life begins?

3.   What metaphor does Lucretius create in lines 335–36?

---

335   **commūnibus**: modifying **mōtibus** (336) and echoing **commūnibus . . . rādīcibus** (325).
       eās: referring to the two **potestātēs**, of body and soul.
       cōnflō, -āre, -āvī, -ātus, *to blow into flame, ignite.*
         cōnflātur: the subject is **sēnsus** (336).
336   **accēnsus**, *kindled*, reinforcing the image of **cōnflātur**.
       nōbīs: dative of reference, *for us.*
       vīscera: here, *flesh.*
       sēnsus: the postponement of the subject perhaps conveys a sense of wonder at the existence of sensation. As Lucretius will go on to show, sensation is produced only by a delicate balance of the atoms and can easily be disrupted.

337 **Praetereā**: introducing a second argument that the soul and body are inextricably united.
    gignō, gignere, genuī, genitus, *to create*; here in passive, *to be born.*
    umquam: emphatic position.

338 **crēscō, crēscere, crēvī, crētus**, *to grow.*
    dūrō, -āre, -āvī, -ātus, *to endure, survive.*
    vidētur: again, *is seen.*

339 **Nōn**: very emphatic position for the negative, which in fact negates lines 341–42.
    ut: introducing a contrasting simile—the soul/body union does *not* behave like this.
    ūmor, ūmōris, m., *moisture, liquid.*
        ūmor aquae: a typical Lucretian periphrasis, simply meaning **aqua**.

340 **quī datus est**: i.e., the heat that has made the water hot has been supplied by some exterior
        source, such as a fire.
    eā causā: i.e., by the loss of heat.
    convellō, convellere, convellī, convulsus, *to tear apart, destroy.*

341 **incolumis**: predicative adjective.
    nōn: repeating the negative from line 339.
    inquam, irreg., *I say*; the personal intrusion is emphatic.

342 **discidium, -ī**, n., *separation, sundering, dissolution.*
    (animāī) discidium: direct object of **perferre**.
    artus, -ūs, m., *limb.*
        artūs: nominative plural as subject.
    perferre: here, *to endure, survive.*
    relictī: i.e., left behind after the dissolution of the soul.

343 **sed**: turning to what actually happens to the body at the dissolution of the soul.
    penitus, adv., *from within, inside, deeply.*
    convulsī: from **convellō** (cf. 340); modifying **artūs**, *torn apart.*
    conque: = **con-** + enclitic **-que**; the prepositional prefix **con-** is separated from its verb
        putrēscunt by tmesis.
    conputrēscō, conputrēscere, conputrēscuī, *to decay, rot, putrefy.*
        penitus pereunt convulsī conque putrēscunt: strong alliteration of *p, c,* and *q.*

344 **aevum -ī**, n., *life.*
        ex ineunte aevō: *from birth.*
    corporis atque animāī: possessive genitives with **mūtua . . . contāgia** (345).

345 **vītālīs . . . mōtūs**: accusative plural, referring to the motions that cause life.
    contāgium, -ī, n., *touch, contact.*
        mūtua vītālīs discunt contāgia mōtūs: a "golden" line, with two adjective-noun pairs
            framing the verb; the two adjectives precede, the nouns follow. The interweaving again
            echoes the relationship between the soul and the body.

346 **alvus, -ī**, f., *womb.*
    māternīs . . . membrīs alvōque: ablatives of place.
    repōnō, repōnere, reposuī, repositus, here, *to lay in store, hide.*
        reposta: = **reposita**, by syncope; agreeing with **contāgia** (345), but really meaning the atoms
            themselves of body and soul.

347 **discidium**: dissolution of the connection between body and soul.
    nequeō, nequīre, nequīvī, *to be unable* (to).
    pestis, pestis, f., *destruction, death.*
    malō: here a substantive, *ruin.*
        sine peste malōque: of both the body and the soul.

348 **salūtis**, again, *life.*
        causa salūtis: the cause of life lies in the fact that the soul and body are **coniūncta**.

349 **coniūnctam**, here predicative; the repetition of the word from 348 reinforces the argument.
    cōnsistō, cōnsistere, cōnstitī, here, *to be, exist.*
    eōrum: of body and soul.

337   Praetereā corpus per sē nec gignitur umquam

338   nec crēscit neque post mortem dūrāre vidētur.

339   Nōn enim, ut ūmor aquae dīmittit saepe vapōrem

340   quī datus est, neque eā causā convellitur ipse,

341   sed manet incolumis, nōn, inquam, sīc animāī

342   discidium possunt artūs perferre relictī,

343   sed penitus pereunt convulsī conque putrēscunt.

344   Ex ineunte aevō sīc corporis atque animāī

345   mūtua vītālīs discunt contāgia mōtūs

346   māternīs etiam membrīs alvōque reposta,

347   discidium ut nequeat fierī sine peste malōque;

348   ut videās, quoniam coniūnctast causa salūtis,

349   coniūnctam quoque nātūram cōnsistere eōrum.

∽ Discussion Question

1.   What is the essential difference in the contrasting comparisons of the soul to the fragrance of a lump of incense (327–28) and to the warmth of heated water (339–40)?

Contrasting views of the constitution of the soul:

First, know, a soul within sustains the heaven
and earth, the plains of water, and the gleaming
globe of the moon, the Titan sun, the stars;
and mind that pours through every member, mingles
with that great body. Born of these: the race
of men and cattle, flying things, and all
the monsters that the sea has bred beneath
its glassy surface. Fiery energy
is in these seeds, their source is heavenly;
but they are dulled by harmful bodies, blunted
by their own earthly limbs, their mortal members.
. . . And when the final day of life deserts them,
then, even then, not every ill, not all
the plagues of body quit them utterly; . . .
Therefore they are schooled by punishment.
    Vergil, *Aeneid* 6.724–40 (tr. Mandelbaum)

Men have been created under this condition, that they should keep that globe called earth. . . . And a soul has been supplied to them from those eternal fires which you call constellations and stars, and which, being globular and round, are animated with divine spirit, and complete their cycles with amazing rapidity. Therefore you . . . and all good men, must preserve your souls in the keeping of your bodies. . . . Cherish justice and duty, a great obligation to parents and kin but greatest to your country. Such a life is the way to heaven and to this assembly of those who have already lived, and, released from the body, inhabit the place which . . . you have learned from the Greeks to call the Milky Way.
    Cicero, *Somnium Scipionis* 15–16 (tr. Edmonds and Hadas)

830   **Nīl**: emphatic position for the negative.

      mors: not the process of dying but the condition of being dead.

        Nīl igitur mors est ad nōs: a direct translation of the Epicurean phrase from *Principle doctrines* ii: ὁ θάνατος οὐδὲν πρὸς ἡμᾶς. The four monosyllables of **mors est ad nōs** act as staccato drum-beats stressing the point.

      pertineō, -ēre, -uī, *to be a concern, to matter.*

      hīlum, -ī, n., *the least bit, a trifle.*

        hīlum; adverbial accusative, *the least bit.*

831   **habētur**: here, *is considered, is regarded as, is held to be.*

832   **velut**: introducing, for purposes of argument by comparison, a most significant episode from Roman history.

      anteāctus, -a, -um, *past, gone before.*

        anteāctō: the vowels *ea* scan as one long syllable by synizesis; cf. 1.233 and 1.234.

          anteāctō . . . tempore: i.e., in the time before we were born.

      aegrī: substantive use; partitive genitive wtih **nīl**, *nothing ill, nothing bad.*

833   **cōnflīgō, cōnflīgere, cōnflīxī, cōnflīctūrus**, *to clash, do battle, fight.*

        ad cōnflīgendum: **ad** + gerund expressing purpose.

      Poenī, -ōrum, m. pl., *the Carthaginians.* The Romans fought three wars against the Carthaginians before they finally eliminated them as rivals for power in the Western Mediterranean. These wars, called Punic from their Roman name, were always considered the greatest challenge that Rome ever faced, and consequently the greatest victory that she ever achieved.

        venientibus undique Poenīs: ablative absolute; **undique** probably refers with Roman pride to her victory in the second Punic war (218–201 B.C.), in which the famous Carthaginian general Hannibal attacked Rome from the north after crossing the Alps; there were also Carthaginian attacks on Roman possessions in Spain to the west, in Sicily and Sardinia to the south, and by the Carthaginians' ally Philip V of Macedon from the east.

834   **omnia**: all things, meaning *all the world;* to the Romans the Punic Wars were equivalent to world wars; thus note the phrase **sub altīs aetheris ōrīs** (835).

      trepidus, -a, -um, *fearful, perilous.*

      concutiō, concutere, concussī, concussus, *to shake violently, agitate.*

        omnia . . . bellī trepidō concussa tumultū: heavily interlocking word order perhaps conveying the confusion.

835   **horridus, -a, -um**, *shaking with fear, quaking, trembling.*

        horrida: modifying **omnia** (834).

      contremēscō, contremēscere, contremuī, *to tremble with fear, shake, quake.*

836   **in dubiōque**: the linking conjunction **-que** has been delayed.

      fuēre: alternative third plural perfect ending = **fuērunt**; the subject is still **omnia** (834).

      utrōrum: genitive with **ad rēgna**, *to whose power.*

      rēgna: plural perhaps indicating the large spheres of control and influence of each power.

      cadendum: gerundive with **esset** in impersonal passive periphrastic; imperfect subjunctive in indirect question introduced by **in dubiō fuēre**.

837   **omnibus hūmānīs**: dative of reference; **hūmānīs**, here meaning *human matters.*

        utrōrum ad regna cadendum omnibus hūmānīs esset, literally, *to whose power there must be a falling with respect to all human matters;* thus, *to whose power all human matters must fall.*

      terrāque marīque: the phrase reinforces the claim of the world-wide importance of the war.

34. The Folly of the Fear of Death

In a long series of proofs based upon physical evidence, Lucretius has shown that the soul is physical and therefore mortal. For instance, the fact that the mind (one part of the soul) both experiences and can be cured of disease shows that it is mortal, for anything that is subject to change indicates its own mortality. Since the soul cannot endure separation from the enclosing and protecting body, it cannot have an independent existence after death. Death, therefore, is irrelevant to us who can have no perception of anything once we are dead. As we felt nothing before our birth, so we will feel nothing after our death.

830   Nīl igitur mors est ad nōs neque pertinet hīlum,
831   quandoquidem nātūra animī mortālis habētur.
832   Et velut anteāctō nīl tempore sēnsimus aegrī,
833   ad cōnflīgendum venientibus undique Poenīs,
834   omnia cum bellī trepidō concussa tumultū
835   horrida contremuēre sub altīs aetheris ōrīs,
836   in dubiōque fuēre utrōrum ad rēgna cadendum
837   omnibus hūmānīs esset terrāque marīque,

Death is nothing to us: for that which is dissolved is without sensation; and that which lacks sensation is nothing to us.

Epicurus, *Principal Doctrines* 2 (tr. Bailey)

Death is nothing to us. For all good and evil consists in sensation, but death is deprivation of sensation. And therefore a right understanding that death is nothing to us makes the mortality of life enjoyable, not because it adds to it an infinite span of time, but because it takes away the craving for immortality. For there is nothing terrible in life for the man who has truly comprehended that there is nothing terrible in not living. . . . So death, the most terrifying of ills, is nothing to us, since so long as we exist, death is not with us; but when death comes, then we do not exist. It does not then concern either the living or the dead, since for the former it is not, and the latter are no more.

Epicurus, *Epistle to Menoeceus* 124–25 (tr. Bailey)

838   **sīc**: reaching the conclusion of the comparison.

        ubi nōn erimus: i.e., when we are dead.

839   **discidium, -ī**, n., *separation, sundering, dissolution.*

        fuerit: future perfect.

        quibus ē: anastrophe of pronoun and preposition.

        ūniter, adv., *into one.*

        aptus, -a, -um [the perfect passive participle of an obsolete verb **apiō, apere**, *to tie, fasten, bind*], *tied, fastened, bound*; here with **sumus**.

840   **scīlicet**, adv., *certainly, undoubtedly.*

        haud . . . quicquam: = **nihil**.

        nōbīs: dative with **accidere** (841).

        quī nōn erimus tum: further defining the condition of **nōbīs**, but interrupting the flow of the main clause; note the emphatic line-end position of the monosyllable **tum**.

841   **omnīnō**, adv., *at all, altogether.*

        sēnsum movēre: a key phrase; if nothing can move our senses, then we can have no perception of anything, whether pleasurable or painful. Anything that happens will be irrelevant to us, even the greatest catastrophe, such as is summarized in the next line.

842   **nōn sī terra marī . . .** : a proverbial expression; with the two ablatives understand **cum**; also note the alliteration of *m*.

Sī quicquam mūtis grātum acceptumve sepulcrīs
   accidere ā nostrō, Calve, dolōre potest,
quō dēsīderiō veterēs renovāmus amōrēs
   atque ōlim missās flēmus amīcitiās,
certē nōn tantō mors immātūra dolōri est
   Quīntiliae, quantum gaudet amōre tuō.

If the silent grave can receive any pleasure, or sweetness at all from our grief, Calvus, the grief and regret with which we make our old loves live again, and weep for long-lost friendships, surely Quintilia feels less sorrow for her too early death, than pleasure from your love.

   Catullus 96 (tr. Mackail)

The Ciceronian view of death:

A certain place in heaven is assigned to all who have preserved, or assisted, or improved their country, where they are to enjoy an endless duration of happiness. For there is nothing which takes place on earth more acceptable to that Supreme Deity who governs all this world, than those councils and assemblies of men bound together by law, which are termed states; the governors and preservers of these go from hence, and hither do they return. . . They have escaped from the fetters of body as from a prison; that which is called life is really death.

   Cicero, *Somnium Scipionis* 13–14 (tr. Edmonds and Hadas)

838   sīc, ubi nōn erimus, cum corporis atque animāi

839   discidium fuerit quibus ē sumus ūniter aptī,

840   scīlicet haud nōbīs quicquam, quī nōn erimus tum,

841   accidere omnīnō poterit sēnsumque movēre,

842   nōn sī terra marī miscēbitur et mare caelō.

✑ Discussion Question

1.   Are you convinced by Lucretius' argumentation that the time before our birth provides a mirror image of the time after our death?

A dialogue on the condition of the dead between two unknown speakers:

M.   For whosoever is miserable, must *be*. But just now you said the dead *are not*; if then, they *are not*, nothing can they *be*—not even miserable.

A.   Perhaps I do not express quite clearly what I have in my head: for it is that very fact of *not being*, after you *have been*, that I consider so miserable.

M.   What! More so than never to have been at all? Then the yet unborn are miserable already, because they *are not* (if *not being* is miserable). . . .

A.   Very well, then; I will grant that the dead are not miserable, since you have forced me to confess that they who *are* not cannot *be miserable*. But how then? Are not we who live, miserable, seeing that we must die? For what pleasure can there be in life when, night and day, the thought cannot fail to haunt us, that at any moment we must die?
        Cicero, *Tusculan Disputations* 1.6 –7 (tr. Black)

M.   For simultaneously with life consciousness is lost; and nothing can make any difference to the unconscious.
        Cicero, *Tusculan Disputations* 1.11 (tr. Black)

M.   As birth introduces us to the beginning of things, so does death to the end, it follows that, as before birth there was nothing which concerned us, so there will be nothing that concerns us after death. What bane, then, can there be in this, inasmuch as death concerns neither the living nor dead? The latter *are not*; the former it appertains not to.
        Cicero, *Tusculan Disputations* 1.38 (tr. Black)

The chorus of Trojan Women:

There is nothing after death, and death itself is nothing, the final goal of a course full swiftly run. Let the eager give up their hopes; their fears, the anxious; greedy time and chaos engulf us altogether. . . . Death is something that admits no cleavage, destructive to the body and unsparing of the soul. Taenarus and the cruel tyrant's kingdom and Cerberus, guarding the portal of no easy passage—all are but idle rumors, empty words, a tale light as a troubled dream. Do you ask where you will lie when death has claimed thee? Where they lie who were never born.
        Seneca, *The Trojan Women* 397–408 (adapted from the translation of Miller)

894   **Iam iam**: the repetition is effective in establishing a tone of pathos.
     Iam iam nōn, *Now never again*.
   tē: the hypothetical mourners are speaking to the dead person.
   laeta: delayed from its noun, **domus**, for emphasis.

895   **optima**: the enjambement emphasizes the feelings the deceased man might have for his wife, if
     he had any awareness. The whole imagined scene paints an idealized picture of domestic
     bliss. Note also how the assonance of *o* and *a* in the line adds a softness to the scene.
   dulcis, -is, -e, *sweet*.
   occurrent: here, *they run or hurry* (to) + infin.
   ōscula: accusative, direct object of **praeripere** (896).
   nātī: *children*.

896   **praeripiō, praeripere, praeripuī, praereptus**, *to seize, snatch first*.
     praeripere: infinitive expressing purpose with **occurrent** (895); *they will run to be first to
       snatch kisses*.
   tacitus, -a, -um, *silent*.
   dulcēdō, dulcēdinis, f., *sweetness, pleasure*.

897   **poteris**: again addressing the deceased.
   factīs: *affairs* (of business and politics).
   flōreō, -ēre, -uī, *to flourish*.
     factīs flōrentibus: dative of respect with **praesidium** (899).
   tuīsque: dative, here a substantive, *and your family*.

898   **praesidium, -ī**, n., *means of security, defense, protection*.
   Miserō: dative of separation, agreeing with postponed **tibī** (898).
     Miserō miserē: repetition again establishing a mood of pathos, or perhaps of irony.
   aiunt: the subject is the relatives and friends of the dead who make this sort of typical lament;
     the inclusion of the verb reminds us that this is a hypothetical situation.
   omnia: modifying **praemia** (899); displaced here for pathetic emphasis.
   adēmit: from **adimō, adimere**.

899   **īnfestus, -a, -um**, *hostile*.
   tibī: the final *i* has been lengthened by diastole to fit the meter.
   praemium, -ī, n., *reward, prize*.
     omnia . . . tot praemia vītae: all the pleasures that life has to offer.

900   **Illud**: described by the following quote.
     Illud in hīs rēbus: a Lucretian formula usually used to introduce a rebuttal; cf. 1.80, 2.308.
   addunt: subject is the hypothetical speakers of the quote above.
   tibi: again, the deceased.
   eārum: modifying **rērum** (901), displaced here for emphasis.

901   **dēsīderium, -ī**, n., *desire/longing for*.
   super: here adverbial, *any more*, i.e., after death.
   īnsideō, īnsidēre, īnsēdī, īnsessūrus + dat., *to lie heavy on, beset, trouble*.
   ūnā: adverbial, *together with you*, i.e., in the grave, *at the same time, still*.

902   **Quod**: neuter relative pronoun, accusative singular. The antecedent is the previous idea: that
     the dead will not miss these pleasures.
   videant animō: = **intellegant**.
     videant animō dictīsque sequantur: i.e., their beliefs and words should agree.

903   **dissoluō, dissoluere, dissoluī, dissolūtus**, here, *to release, free*.
   animī: genitive singular with **angōre metūque**.
   angor, angōris, m., *anguish, anxiety*.
     angōre metūque: ablatives of separation with **dissoluant**.

912   **Hōc**: explained by **ex animō ut dīcant** (914).
   faciunt: the subject is **hominēs** (913).

35. Mistaken Regrets

The mistaken assumption of the survival of consciousness after death leads men to make maudlin lamentations over lost pleasures, especially domestic happiness. Here Lucretius quotes some hypothetical mourners and makes a reply. He then introduces a second scenario in which men complain about the ephemeralness of human existence and bewail the pleasures they will soon miss. Lucretius comments that those who make such laments forget that the dead will be incapable of feeling such longings. Instead, the insensibility of death is even more profound than the deepest sleep, in which there is no consciousness of self.

894   "Iam iam nōn domus accipiet tē laeta, neque uxor
895   optima, nec dulcēs occurrent ōscula nātī
896   praeripere et tacitā pectus dulcēdine tangent.
897   Nōn poteris factīs flōrentibus esse tuīsque
898   praesidium. Miserō miserē," aiunt, "omnia adēmit
899   ūna diēs īnfesta tibī tot praemia vītae."
900   Illud in hīs rēbus nōn addunt, "Nec tibi eārum
901   iam dēsīderium rērum super īnsidet ūnā."
902   Quod bene sī videant animō dictīsque sequantur,
903   dissoluant animī māgnō sē angōre metūque.

. . .

912   Hōc etiam faciunt ubi discubuēre tenentque

○ Discussion Questions

1. How is the home personified in line 894?

2. What facet of Epicurean philosophy does line 903 express? How does the line relate to Lucretius' epic as a whole?

But even if it be granted that men are deprived by death of good fortune, does it follow that the dead *lack* the blessings of life, and that this is misery? Yet such must be the argument. But *can* he who *is not*, "lack" anything at all? For a pathetic term is this same "lack," because there is at the bottom of it an idea of "having not, after having had," of "missing," of "wanting back again," of "needing" . . . but of the dead none "lacks," not only the advantages of life, but even life itself.
    Cicero, *Tusculan Disputations* 1.36 (tr. Black)

---

912   **discumbō, discumbere, discubuī, discubitūrus,** *to lie down (at table);* the Romans dined in a reclining position on couches.
    discubuēre: alternate third plural perfect = **discubuērunt**; present perfect, *have lain down.*

913   **saepe**: though placed here in the **ubi** clause, its force really applies to **faciunt** (912), since it immediately precedes the subject, **hominēs**.

     inumbrō, -āre, -āvī, -ātus, *to shade, cover.*

     ōra: from **ōs, ōris**, n., *face;* here *brows, temples.*

914   **ex animō**, *from the heart, sincerely.*

     ut dīcant: substantive noun clause in apposition to **hōc** (912).

     frūctus: here, *enjoyment.*

     homullus, -ī, m. [diminutive of **homō**], *little man, poor little man.*

915   **iam**: here, *soon.*

     fuerit: future perfect; the subject is **frūctus** (914).

     post: here adverbial, *afterwards.*

     revocāre: understand **eum** (i.e., **frūctum**) as the direct object.

916   **mālī**: substantive, partitive genitive with **hōc**.

     cum prīmīs: idiom, *especially, in particular;* here, *the greatest, the worst;* predicate to **hōc**.

     sit: subjunctive with **tamquam** as a type of future-less-vivid condition.

     eōrum: of the feasters.

917   **quod**: here, *that,* defining **hōc** (916); the clause governs the subjunctive, since Lucretius is presenting not facts but the beliefs of the maudlin banqueters.

     sitis, sitis, f., *thirst.*

     exūrō, exūere, exussī, exustus, *to parch.*

     miserōs: modifying **eōs** understood.

     atque: connecting the two verbs.

     āridus, -a, -um, *dry.*

       ārida: predicative, *that dries* (their throats).

     torreō, torrēre, torruī, tostus, *to scorch, burn.*

       torrāt: probably a contracted form of **torreat**; the reading is much disputed here.

918   **aliae**: unusual feminine genitive singular; regularly **alīus** in all three genders.

     cuius: equivalent to **alicuius**, since **tamquam** (916) has acted as a conditional, which causes the **ali-** to drop from the form.

     īnsideat: see above, line 901.

     reī: here scanning as a long monosyllable by synizesis.

919   **Nec sibi enim. . . .**: introducing the comparison between a deep sleep and death.

       sibi: dative of interest, *for himself,* here somewhat redundant with **sē** and **vītamque**.

     quisquam, quicquam, *anyone, anything.*

     tum: defined by the **cum** clause in the following line.

     requīrit: here, *does . . . miss.*

920   **pariter**, adv., *equally, at the same time.*

     sōpītus, -a, -um, *lulled to sleep, asleep.*

       sōpīta: neuter plural to agree with subjects of different genders.

921   **licet**: here with accusative and infinitive as subject.

     per nōs: *by us;* with **licet**, *is permitted by us,* i.e., *for all we care.*

     sīc: equivalent to **hunc**, referring to the line above, *this sleep.*

     sopor, sopōris, m., *deep sleep.*

922   **dēsīderium, -ī**, n., *desire /longing* (for) + gen.

     nostrī: objective genitive with **dēsīderium**, *of ourselves* (i.e., our waking selves).

     adficit: = **afficit**.

     ūllum: separated from its noun **dēsīderium**, with the effect here of *not any at all.*

913   pōcula saepe hominēs et inumbrant ōra corōnīs,

914   ex animō ut dīcant, "Brevis hīc est frūctus homullīs;

915   iam fuerit neque post umquam revocāre licēbit."

916   Tamquam in morte malī cum prīmīs hōc sit eōrum,

917   quod sitis exūrat miserōs atque ārida torrāt,

918   aut aliae cuius dēsīderium īnsideat reī.

919   Nec sibi enim quisquam tum sē vītamque requīrit,

920   cum pariter mēns et corpus sōpīta quiēscunt.

921   Nam licet aeternum per nōs sīc esse sopōrem,

922   nec dēsīderium nostrī nōs adficit ūllum.

CO   Discussion Questions

1.   Are the characters of line 912–15 enjoying the present pleasures? What does Lucretius think of their attitude?

2.   What mythological underworld inhabitant is alluded to by the torments described in lines 916–17?

3.   What is the essential difficulty implicit in worrying that the dead suffer physical torments?

Another trick of [nature] . . . is to prevent our imagination from representing ourselves as genuinely dead. When I think of myself defunct, the self that is thinking merges subtly with the cadaver and animates it. The cheating cadaver stealthily raises itself on its elbow to look around.
  Oscar Mendel, "Who's Diphilus?," *The Phi Beta Kappa Key Reporter* 48.2 (1982–83), 2

Death as sleep:

Sleep, the brother of death. (Homer, *Iliad* 14.231)
Sleep and Death, who are twin brothers (*Iliad* 16.672)

Death is one of two things. Either it is annihilation, and the dead have no consciousness of anything; or, as we are told, it is really a change: a migration from this place to another. Now, if there is no consciousness but only a dreamless sleep, death must be a marvellous gain. I suppose that if someone were told to pick out the night on which he slept so soundly as not even to dream, and then to compare it with all the other nights and days of his life, and then were told to say, after due consideration, how many better and happier days and nights than this he had spent in the course of his life—well, I think that the Great King himself, to say nothing of any private person, would find these days and nights easy to count in comparison with the rest. If death is like this, then, I call it gain.
  Socrates in Plato, *The Apology* 40c5–40e2 (tr. Tredennick)

Now in sleep we have a semblance of death, and this semblance we daily assume. Have you, then, any doubt that there is no consciousness in death, when you see that in its semblance there is no consciousness?
  Cicero, *Tusculan Disputations* 1.38 (tr. Black)

923 **tamen**: despite the apparently complete lack of sensation in sleep, the senses can be quickly roused again.

haudquāquam, adv., *by no means, not at all.*

tunc: = **tum**: i.e., in sleep.

illa: modifying **prīmōrdia** (924).

artus, -ūs, m., *limb.*

924 **sēnsifer, sēnsifera, sēnsiferum**, *sense-bearing, that cause sensation.*

longē ab sēnsiferīs prīmōrdia mōtibus errant: the Epicureans believed that in sleep some atoms of the soul left the body and the remaining atoms, being thus more widely distributed, left their usual positions. Reawakening was like kindling a fire in those remaining atoms, which would return to their sense-bearing positions, and other soul atoms would make up the whole. Of course, if the soul-atoms were too disturbed, the man would not awake, and death would result.

925 **correptus**: from **corripiō, corripere**; here middle in force; he snatches himself from sleep.

colligō, colligere, collēgī, collectus, *to gather together, collect.*

ipse: stressing that this is an independent action.

cum correptus . . . colligit ipse: showing the speed with which the atoms can be properly rearranged upon waking.

926 **Multō**: adverbial with **minus**.

mortem . . . esse: indirect statement governed by **putandumst**.

mortem ad nōs esse: recalling Lucretius' introduction to the folly of the fear of death, **nīl igitur mors est ad nōs** (3.830).

minus: less of an existence, or a thing of less importance.

multō igitur mortem minus: note the memorable alliteration.

putandumst: impersonal passive periphrastic, as is usual with intransitive verbs; the subject is the accusative and infinitive construction; literally, *must be thought*, i.e., *one must think, consider.*

927 **minus**: here substantive, *a less.*

quod: understand **id** as antecedent, referring to the state of deep sleep.

928 **maior**: *greater* (at death than in sleep).

turba: *disturbance.*

disiectus, -ūs, m., *scattering, dispersal.*

929 **cōnsequitur**: *ensues, follows.*

lētum, -ī, n., *death.*

lētō: ablative; *in death.*

expergō, expergere, expergī, expergitus, *to rouse, awaken.*

exstat: *exist, is*, but probably also with a play on the idea of "standing up" or "rising" from the dead.

nec quisquam expergitus exstat. . . .: Lucretius clearly placed no credence in mythical stories of successful returns from death (the underworld) by heroes such as Hercules, Odysseus, Orpheus, or even the Roman Aeneas.

930 **frīgida**: displaced from its noun, **pausa**, for emphasis.

semel, adv., *once.*

est: with **secūta**, forming a perfect passive indicative; here, *has overtaken*; the verb perhaps was chosen to balance **cōnsequitur** (929).

pausa: here, *cessation, break.*

[Oliver recognized] that death had been hovering there, for many days and nights, and might yet fill [the room] with the gloom and dread of his awful presence. . . . Gradually, he fell into that deep tranquil sleep which ease from recent suffering imparts; that calm and peaceful rest which it is pain to wake from. Who, if this were death, would be roused again to all the struggles and turmoils of life; to all its cares for the present; its anxieties for the future; more than all, its weary recollections of the past!

Charles Dickens, *Oliver Twist* (1837–39), Ch. 12

923   Et tamen haudquāquam nostrōs tunc illa per artūs

924   longē ab sēnsiferīs prīmōrdia mōtibus errant,

925   cum correptus homō ex somnō sē colligit ipse.

926   Multō igitur mortem minus ad nōs esse putandumst,

927   sī minus esse potest quam quod nīl esse vidēmus;

928   maior enim turba et disiectus māteriāī

929   cōnsequitur lētō nec quisquam expergitus exstat,

930   frīgida quem semel est vitāī pausa secūta.

      To die, to sleep—
No more—and by a sleep to say we end
The heartache, and the thousand natural shocks
That flesh is heir to. 'Tis a consummation
Devoutly to be wished. To die, to sleep—
To sleep—perchance to dream: ay, there's the rub,
For in that sleep of death what dreams may come
When we have shuffled off this mortal coil,
Must give us pause. There's the respect
That makes calamity of so long life.
For who would bear the whips and scorns of time
Th' oppressor's wrong, the proud man's contumely,
The pangs of despised love, the law's delay,
The insolence of office, and the spurns
That patient merit of th' unworthy takes,
When he himself might his quietus make
With a bare bodkin? Who would fardels bear,
To grunt and sweat under a weary life,
But that the dread of something after death
The undiscovered country, from whose bourn
No traveller returns, puzzles the will
And makes us rather bear those ills we have
Than fly to others that we know not of?
     Hamlet's soliloquy, Shakespeare, *Hamlet* III.1.60–82

Methought I heard a voice cry "Sleep no more!
Macbeth does murder sleep"—the innocent sleep,
Sleep that knits up the ravelled sleave of care,
The death of each day's life, sore labor's bath,
Balm of hurt minds, great nature's second course,
Chief nourisher in life's feast.
     Macbeth, Shakespeare, *Macbeth* II.ii.34–39

931 **dēnique**, adv., *in short, indeed, finally; furthermore.*
 vōcem . . . mittat (932): equivalent to **dīcat**.
 rērum nātūra: a grand personification of all of nature. To address an audience by means of the personification of an abstraction is an ancient rhetorical device which allows the author greater freedom to criticize his audience.
 repente, adv., *suddenly, unexpectedly.*

932 **hōc**: archaic lengthening of accusative singular object, referring to the following quote.
 nostrum: partitive genitive with **alicui**.
 increpō, increpāre, increpuī, increpitus, *to blame/reproach loudly; to chide, rebuke.*
 ipsa: emphasizing the personification, *in person.*

933 **tantō opere**, adv., *to such a great degree, so greatly, so much;* here the adverbial expression approximates a noun phrase: *so great a thing,* with the sense of trouble or concern.
   Quid tibi tantō operest: *What is so troubling to you?*
 mortālis: vocative, stressing his insignificant position in relation to all of nature.
 quod: here, *that;* with the indicative, whereas in prose it would govern the subjunctive.
 nimis: take closely with **indulgēs** (934).

934 **indulgeō, indulgēre, indulsī, indultūrus** + dat., *to indulge* (in).
 Quid, here, *Why?*
 congemō, congemere, congemuī, congemitus, *to bewail, lament.*

935 **anteāctus, -a, -um**, *past, gone before.* As usual, the vowels *ea* scan as one long syllable by synizesis.
   anteācta priorque: a nice redundancy, *past and gone.*

936 **omnia**: nominative plural neuter, modifying **commoda** (937); placed here for emphasis.
 pertundō, pertundere, pertudī, pertūsus, *to bore through, perforate, puncture.*
   pertūsum: modifying **vās**.
 congerō, congerere, congessī, congestus, *to heap up, pile up.*
   congesta: nominative plural neuter, also modifying **commoda** (937).
 vās, vāsis, n., *vessel, vase.*
   omnia pertūsum congesta quasi in vās: interlocking word order concluding with a surprising monosyllable, which completes the unexpected image.

937 **commoda**: here a substantive, nominative plural; *pleasures.*
 perfluō, perfluere, perflūxī, *to flow/run through.*
   perflūxēre: alternate third plural perfect = **perflūxērunt**.
 ingrātus, -a, -um, *unpleasant, unpleasing;* here, *unenjoyed, unappreciated.*
   ingrāta: here predicative.
 intereō, interīre, interiī, interitūrus, *to perish, be destroyed.*
   interiēre: = **interiērunt**.
     perflūxēre atque ingrāta interiēre: the triple elision replicates the speed with which the pleasures flowed metaphorically through the leaky vase. The simile in lines 936–37 refers to the myth of the Danaids, who as their punishment in the underworld were compelled to fill leaky vases. Lucretius will elucidate the metaphorical significance of this myth at some length at 3.1003–1010.

938 **cūr nōn. . . .**: having concluded the condition introduced by **sī** in line 935, Lucretius phrases his main point as a question.
 ut: introducing a simile, *as, like.*
 plēnus: governing the genitive.
 convīva: the noun is masculine.
 recēdō, recēdere, recessī, recessūrus, *to withdraw.*
   cūr nōn . . . recēdis: the slow metrical progression of the line is noteworthy and perhaps mimics the difficulty in forcing oneself to leave a magnificent banquet.

939 **aequō animō**: a formulaic phrase representing the Epicurean goal of tranquillity (ἀταραξία); cf. 1.42.; *with a tranquil mind.*
 sēcūram . . . quiētem: the rest of death, which is completely untroubled.
 stulte: the vocative insult again puts the man in his place.

36. Nātūra Rērum Personified

Nature herself rebukes mankind for clinging excessively to life rather than leaving gracefully like a satisfied dinner guest. There are no new pleasures that she can devise for us. Finally, Nature berates an old man, who, having squandered life's pleasures, refuses to die.

931   Dēnique sī vōcem rērum nātūra repente
932   mittat et hōc alicui nostrum sīc increpet ipsa,
933   "Quid tibi tantō operest, mortālis, quod nimis aegrīs
934   lūctibus indulgēs? Quid mortem congemis ac flēs?
935   Nam sī grāta fuit tibi vīta anteacta priorque
936   et nōn omnia pertūsum congesta quasi in vās
937   commoda perflūxēre atque ingrāta interiēre,
938   cūr nōn ut plēnus vītae convīva recēdis
939   aequō animōque capis sēcūram, stulte, quiētem?
940   Sīn ea quae frūctus cumque es periēre profūsa

⌘ Discussion Questions

1. What sound device do you find in line 933?

2. Where have you already seen the living compared to banqueters? How similar are the two comparisons?

The right-minded man is he who is not grieved by what he has not, but enjoys what he has.
     Democritus, *Fragment* 231 (tr. Freeman)

---

940   **sīn**, conj., *but if, if however;* paired in contrast to **sī** (935).
     ea: nominative plural neuter, referring to **commoda** (937) and further defined by the
       quaecumque clause.
     quīcumque, quaecumque, quodcumque, *whoever, whatever, whichever.*
       quae . . . cumque: tmesis.
     fruor, fruī, frūctus sum, *to enjoy;* usually with ablative, but here with accusative.
       frūctus: with **es**.
         quae frūctus cumque es: quite exceptional interlocking word order for this relative clause.
     periēre: = **periērunt**.
     profundō, profundere, profūdī, profūsus, *to pour out, spill.*
       profūsa: continuing the metaphor of the leaky vase.

941   **offēnsa, -ae**, f., *displeasure, disfavor.*

       in offēnsāst: = **in offēnsā est**, *is hateful, offensive.*

    amplius, indecl. neuter noun, *a greater amount, more.*

942   **rūrsum**: = **rūrsus**; note the emphatic position.

    pereat: subjunctive in a relative clause of characteristic; also **occidat**.

       pereat male, *come to a bad end.*

    occidō, occidere, occidī, occāsūrus, *to fall down, perish, be ruined.*

       pereat male et ingrātum occidat: chiasmus.

943   **nōn potius**: still governed by the force of **cūr** (941), *why not rather.*

       vītae fīnem: Lucretius is not actively advocating suicide, but expounding Natura's argument that you should be ready to die when it is your natural time and you have experienced and appreciated all the pleasures life has to offer.

944   **tibi**: emphatic position; can be understood as dative of interest with **māchiner inveniamque** or dative with **placeat** (945).

    praetereā: here, *in addition* (to the pleasures which Nature has already provided).

    quod: the antecedent *follows* in line 945, **nīl**.

    māchinor, -ārī, -ātus sum, *to invent, devise.*

       māchiner inveniamque: subjunctives in a relative clause of characteristic.

945   **quod placeat**: relative clause of characteristic.

    nīl est: the statement is forceful because of its brevity.

    eadem sunt omnia semper: Epicurus believed that there were a limited number of types of pleasure; if one lived indefinitely one would not find any new ones. Therefore it is important to appreciate the pleasures one has and not yearn for more.

946   **annīs**: ablative of means.

    marceō, marcēre, *to be enfeebled, weak; to waste away, wither.*

    artus, -ūs, m., *limb.*

947   **cōnfectī**: *weakened, worn out, exhausted.*

    languent: *are weak, feeble.*

       sī tibi nōn (946) **. . . languent**: i.e., if you are in the prime of life.

    eadem: predicative.

       eadem . . . omnia: echoing line 945.

    restant: *remain.*

948   **omnia**: accusative plural neuter, modifying **saecla**; placed here as usual for emphasis.

    sī: here equivalent to **etsī**, *even if.*

    pergō, pergere, perrēxī, perrēctus, *to proceed, continue.*

    vīvendō: gerund in ablative of means.

    saecla: = **saecula**, as usual by syncope.

       omnia sī . . . saecla: to live longer than any known individual; perhaps referring to someone such as Nestor, who lived an exceptionally long life.

949   **potius**: *more* (than if you outlived all).

    sīs moritūrus: periphrastic future subjunctive, *if you should never die.*

950   **quid respondēmus**: Nature's harangue now complete, Lucretius finally reaches the main clause of the sentence that began in line 931!

941   vītaque in offēnsāst, cūr amplius addere quaeris,

942   rūrsum quod pereat male et ingrātum occidat omne,

943   nōn potius vītae fīnem facis atque labōris?

944   Nam tibi praetereā quod māchiner inveniamque,

945   quod placeat, nīl est: eadem sunt omnia semper.

946   Sī tibi nōn annīs corpus iam marcet et artūs

947   cōnfectī languent, eadem tamen omnia restant,

948   omnia sī pergās vīvendō vincere saecla,

949   atque etiam potius, sī numquam sīs moritūrus,"

950   quid respondēmus, nisi iūstam intendere lītem

951   nātūram et vēram verbīs expōnere causam?

952   Grandior hīc vērō sī iam seniorque querātur

ᘓ Discussion Questions

1. What does Lucretius equate with life in line 943? Do you agree with his assessment?

2. Do you know of a mythological character who was granted immortality but who, without the gift of eternal youth, withered away, as Lucretius describes in lines 946–47?

3. Does immortality seem attractive if the future contains no new pleasures? (947–49)

4. What setting does Lucretius evoke in the language of lines 950–51? What sort of terminology does he employ?

---

950   **nisi**: understand **respondēmus**, introducing two indirect statements.
  iūstus, -a, -um, *legitimate, just, reasonable, valid.*
  intendō, intendere, intendī, intentus, *to bring/enter* (a charge).
  līs, lītis, f., *plea.*
    iūstam . . . lītem: direct object of **intendere** in indirect statement with **nātūram** (951) as
      subject.

951   **expōnō, expōnere, exposuī, expositus**, *to set forth, expound.*
  causam: *case.*
    iūstam intendere . . . causam: phrased in technical legal terminology.

952   **Grandior hīc**: Lucretius now begins a second personification of **nātūra**, in which she bitterly
    reproaches an old man who woefully laments his impending death. The character is reminis-
    cent of the complaining farmer and vintner who closed Book 2.
      grandis, -is, -e, *aged, old.*
  hīc: acting as a true demonstrative, i.e. pointing to the man as if we could see him.
  sī iam: the linking conjunction has typically been delayed to emphasize **grandior hīc**.
  senior: comparative of **senex**; virtually synonymous with **grandior**, but such elaboration is
      characteristic of the Lucretian style.
  queror, querī, questus sum, *to complain, grumble, protest.*

953   **obitus, -ūs**, m., *death.*

       lāmentor, -ārī, -ātus sum, *to bewail, lament excessively.*

       amplius, comparative adv., *more.*

       aequō: substantive in ablative of comparison, *fitting, just, right.*

954   **meritō**, adv., *deservedly, with reason.*

       inclāmō, -āre, -āvī, -ātus, *to shout at, abuse, revile.*

          inclāmet: the subject is **Nātūra rērum**.

       magis: more than she would revile a younger man.

       increpet: repeating the unusual word from line 932, thus unifying the two personifications.

955   **abhinc**, adv., *from this place, from here.*

       baratre: vocative of a very rare noun, **baratrus, -ī**, m., which means something like *one who should be thrown into the pit where the bodies of executed criminals are exposed.* Obviously a colloquial term of abuse. Translate as *crook, villain, scoundrel, dead man,* etc.

       compēscō, compēscere, compēscuī, *to stop.*

       querēla, -ae, f., *complaint, lament.*

          Aufer . . . querēlās: read the line aloud to get the full effect of Nature's bitter reproach.

956   **perfungor, perfungī, perfūnctus sum**, *to go through, experience, enjoy;* here with the accusative.

       praemium, -ī, n., *reward, prize.*

       marcēs: repeating the unusual word from line 946, again linking this personification to the first; very sarcastic line-ending.

957   **quia**, conj., *because.*

       aveō, avēre, *to desire, wish for.*

       quod: i.e., **id quod**.

       praesentia: modifying an understood **commoda** or **praemia**.

       temnō, temnere, *to scorn, despise.*

          avēs . . . temnis: asyndeton between the two verbs; understand **et**.

958   **imperfectus, -a, -um**, *incomplete* (because the man has not yet begun truly to live).

          imperfecta: modifying **vīta**.

       tibi: dative of separation.

       ēlabor, ēlabī , ēlapsus sum, *to slip by, pass away.*

       ingrāta: with the same meaning as in line 937, providing another link between the two personifications; predicative use.

959   **nec**: negating only **opīnantī**.

       opīnor, -arī, -ātus sum, *to think, believe.*

          opīnantī: modifying **tibi** (958).

       mors ad caput adstitit: death stands at the man's head as he lies on his bier; here in the imagery the funeral bier and banquet couch become one, just as in Latin the noun **lectus** is used for both.

       ante/quam: tmesis of the conjunction allows enjambement over the line.

960   **satur, satura, saturum**, *well-fed, sated.*

       rērum: governed by **plēnus**.

       ante/quam satur . . . discēdere: returning to the image of life as a banquet (938).

961   **aliēna**: here with ablative, *inappropriate, unsuitable* (to).

       aetās, aetātis, f., *time, age.*

       aliēna tuā . . . aetāte omnia: embedded word order.

962   **aequō animōque**: the formulaic phrase for tranquillity and acceptance; cf. 939 above.

       agedum: a strengthened form of the imperative, *come on!*

       gnātīs: archaic spelling for **nātīs**, here, *children;* a suggested reading where the manuscript is corrupt. The image implies the recycling of atoms from one generation to the next.

       concēde: with dative, *yield* (to).

963   **iūs, iūris**, n., *right, law, justice.*

       iūre: adverbial ablative, *with right, rightly.*

953   atque obitum lāmentētur miser amplius aequō,

954   nōn meritō inclāmet magis et vōce increpet ācrī?

955   "Aufer abhinc lacrimās, baratre, et compēsce querēlās.

956   Omnia perfūnctus vītāī praemia marcēs.

957   Sed quia semper avēs quod abest, praesentia temnis,

958   imperfecta tibi ēlapsast ingrātaque vīta

959   et nec opīnantī mors ad caput adstitit ante

960   quam satur ac plēnus possīs discēdere rērum.

961   Nunc aliēna tuā tamen aetāte omnia mitte

962   aequō animōque agedum gnātīs concēde! Necessest."

963   Iūre, ut opīnor, agat, iūre increpet incīletque.

964   Cēdit enim rērum novitāte extrūsa vetustās

965   semper, et ex aliīs aliud reparāre necessest.

ℭ Discussion Questions

1.   What does Nature specifically criticize in the old man's behavior? What is wrong with the
     way he has conducted his life? (956–60)

2.   At the close of the passage how does Lucretius place Nature's diatribe in a larger context?

It is not the young man who should be thought happy, but an old man who has lived a good life. . . . The
old man has come to anchor in old age as though in port, and the good things for which before he
hardly hoped he has brought into safe harbourage in his grateful recollections.
   Epicurus, *Vatican Sayings* 17 (tr. Bailey)

---

963   **agat:** here, *would plead* (her case); the subject is **nātūra**.
      iūre: emphatic anaphora.
      increpet: Lucretius summarizes the quoted words/speech with the same verb with which he
         introduced it (954), again connecting this personification to the first (cf. 932).
      incīlō, -āre, -āvī, -ātus, *to revile, abuse.*
         incīletque: unusual spondaic fifth foot accentuating the conclusion.
964   **Cēdit:** a most unusual position for the verb—at the beginning of the line; the subject **vetustās** is
         delayed to the end.
      novitās, novitātis, f., *newness.*
      extrūdō, extrūdere, extrūsī, extrūsus, *to eject, expel, force out.*
      vetustās, vetustātis, f., *old age.*
         novitāte . . . vetustās: forceful opposition, enhanced by the unceremonious effect of **extrūsa.**
965   **semper:** the postponement of the adverb in enjambement adds great emphasis.
      reparō, -āre, -āvī, -ātus, *to replace, restore;* here, *to construct.*
         ex aliīs aliud reparāre necessest: for the idea of recycling of matter to create new genera-
            tions, see 1.263–64.

978 **ea**: defined by the **quaecumque** clause, referring to the torments of the underworld.
　　nīmīrum, adv., *without doubt, certainly.*
　　quīcumque, quaecumque, quodcumque, *whoever, whatever, whichever.*
　　Acherūns, Acheruntis, m./f., *Acheron* (a river in the underworld, thus the underworld itself).
　　　Acherunte profundō: ablative of place.
979 **prōdō, prōdere, prōdidī, prōditus**, *to report.*
　　in vītā: in opposition to **Acherunte** = in death.
　　nōbīs: emphatic position.
980 **miser**: modifying **Tantalus** (981).
　　impendeō, impendēre, impēnsus, *to hang over, overhang.*
　　　impendēns: accusative neuter modifying **saxum**.
　　āēr, āeris, m., *air.*
　　　āere: ablative of place; take closely with **impendēns**; the rock, as if ever about to fall from a
　　　　protruding ledge, overhangs Tantalus' head.
　　saxum, -ī, n., *rock.*
981 **Tantalus, -ī**, m., *Tantalus.* There are two stories of his punishment, the less familiar of which
　　　Lucretius uses here. In this version, in punishment for his theft of the nectar and ambrosia of
　　　the gods, a rock was suspended above him. In his fear of immediate destruction, he could
　　　not eat or drink and thus was also tortured by hunger and thirst. (The more familiar version
　　　depicts Tantalus standing in a pool of water, which recedes whenever he tries to drink, and
　　　surrounded by fruit-trees, whose boughs the wind blows away whenever he tries to eat.)
　　ut fāmast: a parenthetical statement reinforcing the point that these are only stories.
　　cassus, -a, -um, *unfounded, baseless, empty.*
　　formīdō, formīdinis, f., *fear.*
　　　cassā formīdine: the fear is unfounded because Tantalus, already dead, has no body and
　　　　thus cannot be physically harmed.
　　torpeō, -ēre, *to be struck motionless, be paralyzed.*
　　　torpēns: modifying **Tantalus**.
982 **sed magis in vītā**: Lucretius now turns to the allegorical interpretation of Tantalus' story: that
　　　pointless fear of the gods oppresses men. The imagery is reminiscent of Book 1.62–65, where
　　　religion loomed menacingly over men.
　　dīvum: = **dīvōrum**.
　　inānis, -is, -e, *empty, groundless, foolish.*
983 **mortālīs**: accusative plural.
　　cāsus, -ūs, m., *fall, destruction, downfall.*
　　　cāsum: cleverly alluding to the fall of Tantalus' rock as well as any individual's future
　　　　misfortune.
　　timent: **mortālēs** have now become the subject.
　　quisque, quaeque, quidque, *each, each one.*
　　ferat: subjunctive in relative clause of characteristic.
　　fors, fortis, f., *chance, luck.*
　　　fors: the monosyllabic line-ending emphasizes that disasters can be attributed to simple
　　　　chance rather than to the vengefulness of the gods.

37. Living Hell

The underworld with its tormented sinners does not exist; rather, famous sufferers such as Tantalus, Tityos, Sisyphus, and the Danaids are really allegorical representations of self-imposed sufferings in life. Fear of future punishment at death tortures those who do not understand that death frees us from all fear and passion, and their fear makes their lives a living hell here on earth.

978	Atque ea nīmīrum quaecumque Acherunte profundō
979	prōdita sunt esse, in vītā sunt omnia nōbīs.
980	Nec miser impendēns magnum timet āere saxum
981	Tantalus, ut fāmast, cassā formīdine torpēns;
982	sed magis in vītā dīvum metus urget inānis
983	mortālīs cāsumque timent quem cuique ferat fors.

∞ Discussion Question

1. What earlier passage does the phrase **dīvum metus urget inānis / mortālīs** (982–83) evoke?

If they who watch on Olympos have honored
any man, that man was Tantalos; but he was not
able to swallow his great fortune, and for his high stomach
drew a surpassing doom when our father
hung the weight of the stone above him.
He waits ever the stroke at his head and is divided from joy.
That life is too much for his strength; he is buckled fast in torment,
agony fourth among three others, because he stole
and gave to his own fellowship
that ambrosia and nectar
wherewith the gods made him immortal.
    Pindar, *Olympian Ode* 1.54–61 (tr. Lattimore)

And I saw Tantalus also, suffering hard pains, standing
in lake water that came up to his chin, and thirsty
as he was, he tried to drink, but could capture nothing;
for every time the old man, trying to drink, stooped over,
the water would drain away and disappear, and the black earth
showed at his feet, and the divinity dried it away. Over
his head trees with lofty branches had fruit like a shower descending,
pear trees and pomegranate trees and apple trees with fruit shining,
and figs that were sweet and olives ripened well, but each time
the old man would straighten up and reach with his hands for them,
the wind would toss them away toward the clouds overhanging.
    Odysseus in Homer, *Odyssey* 11.582–92 (tr. Lattimore)

984   **Tityos, -ī**, acc., **Tityon**, m., *Tityos* (a giant, son of Jupiter; having attempted to rape Latona, he was punished by being stretched over nine acres with two vultures perpetually eating his liver, which was supposed to be the seat of the passions).

        volucris, volucris, f., *bird.*

        ineunt: here, *enter, pry into.*

985   **quod**: direct object of **scrūtentur** and introducing a relative clause of characteristic with the antecedent **quicquam**.

        sub magnō . . . pectore: though he is a giant, his body is still insufficient to feed vultures forever.

        scrūtor, -ārī, -ātus sum, *to thrust at, probe for.*

        quisquam, quicquam, *anyone, anything.*

936   **aetās, aetātis**, f., *time, age.*

        perpetuam aetātem: accusative of duration of time.

        reperiō, reperīre, repperī, repertus, *to find.*

        profectō, adv., *indeed, certainly;* the line-end position emphasizes the adverb.

987   **quamlibet**, adv., *however;* qualifying **immānī**.

        prōiectus, -ūs, m., *extent, expanse, spread.*

        exstō, exstāre, exstitī, *to exist, be found.*

        exstet: concessive, *although he be.*

988   **quī**: introducing a relative clause of characteristic.

        nōn sōla novem: agreeing with **iūgera** and giving the traditional number of acres as found in Homer's account in *Odyssey* 11.576–81.

        dispandō, dispandere, dispessus, *to spread out.*

        iūgerum, -ī, n., *acre* (actually a Roman acre is about 2/3 of a modern acre).

        membrum, -ī, n., *limb.*

        novem dispessīs iūgera membrīs: interlocking word order.

989   **obtineat**: here, *cover.*

        quī: introducing a second relative clause of characteristic governed by the same verb **obtineat**.

        terrāī . . . orbem: a variant of the phrase **orbis terrārum**, *the earth.*

990   **nōn tamen**: signalling the end of the concessive statements.

        perferō, perferre, pertulī, perlātus, irreg., *to endure.*

        dolor, dolōris, m., *pain.*

991   **proprius, -a, um**, *his own.*

        semper: again an emphatic position for an adverb, as with **profectō** in line 986.

992   **Sed Tityos nōbīs hīc est**: turning to the allegorical interpretation of the myth.

        nōbīs: *for us,* i.e., *in our world.*

        hīc: probably the adverb, *here,* i.e., on earth, but it could be the demonstrative, *this man.*

        iacentem: modifying the delayed relative pronoun **quem** (993) and echoing the close of line 984, **Acherunte iacentem**. Here, instead of lying shackled in death, the allegorical Tityos is shackled by the bonds of love.

993   **volucrēs**: referring sarcastically to the birds of love, Erotes, or Cupids, winged creatures who are often depicted tormenting a lover. See especially Book 4.1089–1101 for a fuller description of the torments lovers experience.

        lacerō, -āre, -āvī, -ātus, *to mangle, tear.*

        atque: here explanatory, *and so, that is.*

        exēdō, exesse, exēdī, exēsus, irreg., *to eat up, devour, consume.*

        ānxius, -a, -um, *worried, disturbed, uneasy.*

        angor, angōris, m., *anguish, anxiety.*

994   **quīvīs, quaevīs, quodvīs**, *any (one, thing) you like.*

        cuppēdine: = **cupīdine**, *longing, desire.*

        aut aliā . . . curae: broadening the scope of the comparison from love to include all other passions and desires. Also note the alliteration of *c* and *s*, which mimics the cutting action of the verb **scindunt**.

984   Nec Tityon volucrēs ineunt Acherunte iacentem

985   nec quod sub magnō scrūtentur pectore quicquam

986   perpetuam aetātem possunt reperīre profectō.

987   Quamlibet immānī prōiectū corporis exstet,

988   quī nōn sōla novem dispessīs iūgera membrīs

989   obtineat, sed quī terrāī tōtius orbem,

990   nōn tamen aeternum poterit perferre dolōrem

991   nec praebēre cibum propriō dē corpore semper.

992   Sed Tityos nōbīs hīc est, in amōre iacentem

993   quem volucrēs lacerant atque exēst ānxius angor

994   aut aliā quāvīs scindunt cuppēdine cūrae.

C3   Discussion Question

1.   Can rational argumentation overcome irrational fears, as Lucretius attempts to do in lines 987–91?

And I saw Tityos, earth's glorious son, lying
in the plain, and sprawled over nine acres. Two vultures,
sitting one on either side, were tearing his liver,
plunging inside the caul. With his hands he could not beat them
away. He had manhandled Leto, the honored consort
of Zeus, as she went through spacious Panopeus, toward Pytho.
    Odysseus in Homer, *Odyssey* 11.576–81 (tr. Lattimore)

And I saw Tityos, the foster child
of Earth, mother of all, his body stretched
on nine whole acres; and a crooked-beaked
huge vulture feeds upon his deathless liver
and guts that only grow the fruits of grief.
The vulture has his home deep in the breast
of Tityos, and there he tears his banquets
and gives no rest even to new-grown flesh.
    The Sibyl in Vergil, *Aeneid* 6.594–600

995   **Sīsyphus, -ī,** m., *Sisyphus* (an arch trickster, who was punished by having to push a large stone up a hill. The stone, when nearly to the top, always tumbled back down, and Sisyphus would have to start again. The exact crime for which he was punished by this futile labor is unclear).

        ante oculōs est: i.e., *is visible.* Note the emphatic position of the monosyllable **est.**

996   **petere:** dependent on **imbibit** (997).

        secūris, secūris, f., *axe.*

            petere a populō fascīs saevāsque secūrīs: to seek election to a magistracy **cum imperiō,** i.e., with the power of life and death; this **imperium** was symbolized by an axe surrounded by rods (**fascēs**) carried by an official attendant called a lictor. The word **fascis** as a symbol of power is the root of the term fascism.

997   **imbibō, imbibere, imbibī, imbibitus,** here + infin., *to resolve* (to); *to thirst* (to).

        recēdō, recēdere, recessī, recessūrus, *to withdraw.* The candidate is defeated.

            quī . . . imbibit et . . . recēdit: the indicatives show that this is a factual relative clause; it describes the Sisyphus who is actually among us.

998   **petere . . . sufferre** (999): infinitives summarized by **hōc** (1000) and serving as the subject of **est** (1000).

        inānis, -is, -e, *empty, meaningless.*

            quod inānest: in the Epicurean view one should avoid involvement in politics. Political offices are to be avoided since they particularly disrupt tranquillity and produce a mere illusion of security in comparison with the true peace of philosophy.

        nec datur umquam: an exaggeration, but perhaps reflecting the great political instability of Lucretius' lifetime. For instance, Cicero was exiled only five years after his consulship of 63.

999   **in eō:** in running for office and, in general, in political life.

        dūrus, -a, -um, *hard, harsh.*

        sufferō, sufferre, sustulī, sublātus, *to endure, suffer.*

1000   **hōc:** summarizing the statements made by the infinitive phrases in the previous two lines.

        adversō . . . monte: ablative absolute, literally, *with the hill opposed,* thus, *up a hill.*

        nixor, -ārī [frequentative], *to struggle, strain continually.*

            nixantem: accusative modifying understood subject of infinitive.

        trūdō, trūdere, trūsī, trūsus, *to push.*

            hōc est . . . monte: the slow spondaic movement of the line creates the effect of labor.

1001   **saxum:** the enjambement lends force to the word; also, postponed until the beginning of the line, the word **saxum** seems to teeter before falling rapidly downhill in the quick flow of the line.

        iam: here, *immediately.*

        vertex, verticis, m., *summit, peak.*

        rūrsum: = **rūrsus.**

1002   **volvō, volvere, volvī, volūtus,** *to roll.*

            volvitur: here middle in force, *rolls (itself).*

        plānus, -a, -um, *level, flat.*

            plānī: modifying **campī.**

        raptim, adv., *hastily, suddenly, in a rush.*

        aequora: *level places.*

            plānī . . . petit aequora campī: a play on words, since Romans went down to the Campus Martius to run for election. The candidate's hopes are dashed just as the rock crashes back down to the plain.

995   Sīsyphus in vītā quoque nōbīs ante oculōs est
996   quī petere ā populō fascīs saevāsque secūrīs
997   imbibit et semper victus trīstisque recēdit.
998   Nam petere imperium quod inānest nec datur umquam,
999   atque in eō semper dūrum sufferre labōrem,
1000 hōc est adversō nixantem trūdere monte
1001 saxum quod tamen ē summō iam vertice rūrsum
1002 volvitur et plānī raptim petit aequora campī.
1003 Deinde animī ingrātam nātūram pāscere semper
1004 atque explēre bonīs rēbus satiāreque numquam,

❁ Discussion Question

1.   Do you think political life is as futile as Lucretius depicts? What would happen if everyone in a society took Lucretius' advice and avoided public office?

Also I saw Sisyphos. He was suffering strong pains,
and with both arms embracing the monstrous stone, struggling
with hands and feet alike, he would try to push the stone upward
to the crest of the hill, but when it was on the point of going
over the top, the force of gravity turned it backward,
and the pitiless stone rolled back down to the level.
He then tried once more to push it up, straining hard, and sweat ran
all down his body, and over his head a cloud of dust rose.
   Odysseus in Homer, *Odyssey* 11.593–600 (tr. Lattimore)

1003 **Deinde**: the *e* and *i* scan as one long syllable by synizesis; the adverb introduces the next
         example, that of the Danaids. Forced to marry their cousins, all but one of them murdered
         their husbands on their wedding night. For their crime they were condemned forever to
         attempt to fill up a large urn that was punctured by holes. With this example Lucretius
         reverses his order of presentation, giving the allegorical interpretation before the descrip-
         tion of the underworld inhabitants.
      ingrātus, -ā, -um: here, *unappreciative, ungrateful.*
         animī ingrātam nātūram: a typical Lucretian periphrasis = **animum ingrātum**.
      pāscere: introducing a series of three infinitives which are then summarized by **hōc** (1008)
         and serve as the subject of **est** (1008). The construction parallels lines 998–1000.
1004 **expleō, explēre, explēvī, explētus**, *to fill.*
      satiō, -āre, -āvī, -ātus, *to satisfy, satiate, make content.*
         satiāreque: the force of **-que** is adversative, *and yet.*
      numquam: postponed to the emphatic line-end position, just as the contrasting **semper**
         above.

1005 **quod**: here, *as*.

nōbīs: *for us, for our benefit*.

annōrum tempora: *the seasons of the year*.

  quod faciunt nōbis annōrum tempora: explaining the clause **explēre bonīs rēbus** (1004).

circum: adverbial with **redeunt**; here, *in their cycle*.

1006 **redeunt**: the subject is **annōrum tempora**.

  circum cum redeunt: indicating the cyclical passage of the seasons and here, particularly, of the fruitful seasons.

fētus, -ūs, m., *fruit, produce*.

  fētūs: accusative plural.

lepos, lepōris, m., *charm, grace, pleasure*.

1007 **explēmur**: an interesting use of the first person plural to involve and thereby criticize his readers.

frūctus, -ūs, m., *fruit*.

umquam: again, as in 1003 and 1004, the adverb is positioned at the line-end.

1008 **hōc**: the behavior explained in lines 1003–06.

  id: predicate or complement to **hōc**; the accusative and infinitive clause **puellās . . . congerere** (1009) is in apposition to **id**.

aevum -ī, n., *life*.

flōreō, -ēre, -uī, *to flourish*.

  aevō flōrente: i.e., *in the prime of life*.

puellās: accusative subject of **congerere** (1009); though Lucretius doesn't name the girls, they are clearly the famous Danaids.

1009 **memorō, -āre, -āvī, -ātus**, *to relate, tell*.

  memorant: the subject is understood, probably *poets*, but possibly just *people*.

  quod memorant: the antecedent of this clause is **id . . . congerere** (1008–09).

latex, laticis, m., *liquid, water*.

pertundō, pertundere, pertudī, pertūsus, *to bore through, perforate, puncture*.

  pertūsum: modifying **vās**.

congerō, congerere, congessī, congestus, *to heap up, pile up*.

  laticem pertūsum congerere in vās: strongly echoing Lucretius' description of the man who was rebuked by **Nātūra rērum** for wasting all of life's pleasures: **omnia pertūsum congesta quasi in vās / commoda perflūxēre atque ingrāta interiēre** (936–37).

1010 **ratiōne**: here, *way*.

potestur: an archaic passive form, third person singular present, attracted into the passive by the passive complementary infinitive **explērī**; translate simply *is able*.

1011 **Cerberus, -ī**, m., *Cerberus* (the three-headed dog who guarded the entrance to the underworld).

Furiae, -ārum, f., *Furies* (the three dreadful goddesses of vengeance; they were portrayed as winged, having snakes for hair and carrying whips).

iam vērō, here, *moreover*.

egestās, egestātis, f., *lack, absence (of)*.

1012 **egestās, / Tartarus**: asyndeton; the connection between lines 1011 and 1012 has been much disputed, as well as that between 1012 and 1013. There may be a lacuna at either place; if so, it probably included a description of the punishment of Ixion, as alluded to by Servius, the commentator on Vergil (on *Aeneid* 6.596).

Tartarus, -ī, m., *Tartarus* (the region of the underworld reserved for the punishment of particularly heinous crimes). The darkness of the underworld and especially of Tartarus was considered terrifying. The phrase **lūcis egestās** may act here as a synonymn for Tartarus, or it may serve as an adjective, thus removing the asyndeton; perhaps translate *dark Tartarus*.

horrifer, horrifera, horriferum, *frightening, dreadful*.

1005	quod faciunt nōbīs annōrum tempora, circum
1006	cum redeunt fētūsque ferunt variōsque lepōrēs,
1007	nec tamen explēmur vītāī frūctibus umquam,
1008	hōc, ut opīnor, id est, aevō flōrente puellās
1009	quod memorant laticem pertūsum congerere in vās,
1010	quod tamen explērī nūllā ratiōne potestur.
1011	Cerberus et Furiae iam vērō et lūcis egestās,
1012	Tartarus horriferōs ēructāns faucibus aestūs
1013	quī neque sunt usquam nec possunt esse profectō.
1014	Sed metus in vītā poenārum prō male factīs
1015	est īnsignibus īnsignis, scelerisque luella,

ℭ Discussion Question

1.   How does the plenty described in lines 1005–06 compare with the plowman's opinion of the earth's fertility at the close of Book 2?

Some men, not knowing about the dissolution of mortal nature, but acting on knowledge of the suffering in life, afflict the period of life with anxieties and fears, inventing false tales about the period after the end of life.
>   Democritus, *Fragment* 297 (tr. Freeman)

1012   **ēructō, -āre, -āvī, -ātus**, *to belch forth, throw up.*
      faucēs, faucium, f. pl., *throat, jaws.*
         horriferōs ēructāns faucibus aestūs: the imagery personifies Tartarus, who was often portrayed as an underworld monster. Also, entrances to the underworld were regularly identified as places where sulphurous and other noxious fumes escaped, such as the Phlegraean Fields near Pompeii.

1013   **quī**: perhaps another indication of a lacuna. In normal Lucretian practice the relative would be **quae**, referring to antecedents of differing genders; here translate *these.*
      usquam, adv., *anywhere.*
      nec possunt esse profectō: emphatically stating the absolute physical impossiblity of such creatures who violate the laws of nature. At 5.878–924 Lucretius strongly denies that such hybrid creatures could be formed.

1014   **in vītā**: the repetition of the phrase from lines 982 and 995 returns us to the allegorical interpretation of the punishments of the underworld. Moreover, the fear of future punishment exists here **in vītā**. The mind sees the punishments exacted in life and transfers these with amplification to the underworld. The constant fear of future punishment thus makes life itself hellish.
      prō: here, *in return for.*
      male factum, -ī, n., *misdeed, wrong, crime.*

1015   **īnsignis, -is, -e**, here, *remarkable, extraordinary, notable.*
      īnsignibus īnsignis: a typical Lucretian juxtaposition for dramatic effect.
      luella, -ae, f., *expiation, punishment.* The word is apparently a Lucretian invention from the verb **luō, luere**, *to suffer a punishment, to atone,* and occurs only here. The following lines detail some of the punishments used by the Romans.

1016 **carcer, carceris**, m., *prison*.

dē saxō: the Tarpeian rock in Rome from which criminals were thrown to their deaths.

iactus, -ūs, m., here, *throwing, hurling*. The final *s* has been suppressed.

deorsum, adv., *downwards*; not necessary for sense but added for dramatic effect.

1017 **verbera, verberum**, n. pl., *lashings, whippings*.

carnifex, carnificis, m., *executioner, hangman*.

rōbur, rōboris, n., *stock, rack* (indicating something made of oak, the root meaning of the word; the exact instrument referred to is uncertain).

pix, picis, f., *pitch* (smeared on criminals who were then set on fire).

lammina, -ae, f., *metal plate* (heated and used for torture).

taedae: a third instance of torture by fire.

> **verbera . . . taedae**: the gruesome catalogue of tortures would make anyone shudder; its terror is further enhanced by the asyndeton, so that one punishment after another flies into the mind of the man conscious of his own guilt.

1018 **quae**: nominative plural neuter, referring to all the punishments catalogued above.

etsī, conj., *even if, although*.

mēns, mentis, f., *mind*.

sibi: the dative can be taken with **cōnscia** as well as **praemetuēns** and **adhibet** (1019).

cōnscius, -a, -um, here + dative, *inwardly aware/conscious* (of).

factīs: here, *crimes*; the dative can also go with **cōnscia** and with **praemetuēns**.

1019 **praemetuō, praemetuere** + dat., *to be apprehensive/fear* (for).

adhibeō, -ēre, -uī, -itus + dat., *to apply, direct* (to).

stimulus, -ī, m., *goad, prick* (used in the discipline of slaves).

torreō, torrēre, torruī, tostus, *to scorch, burn*.

> **torret**: supply **sē** as the direct object. The verb is used to convey the heat felt when the blood rushes to the skin during a beating.

flagellum, -ī, n., *whip*.

> **adhibet stimulōs torretque flagellīs**: a very vivid physical description of a mental process, making a closer analogy between the mythical punishments of the underworld and our own self-created hells.

1020 **quī**: interrogative adjective introducing an indirect question.

terminus, -ī, m., here, *limit*.

> **terminus . . . malōrum**: the limit is, of course, death.

1021 **quae**: a second interrogative adjective, introducing a second indirect question.

dēnique, adv., here, *at last*.

fīnis: here feminine.

1022 **atque**: here, *and so*.

eadem: nominative plural feminine, referring to **poenae** and displaced from **haec**, with which it agrees.

magis: *rather* (than seeing the limit of his troubles).

> **eadem metuit magis . . . nē in morte**: note the alliteration.

gravēscō, gravēscere, *to become/grow worse*.

1023 **Hīc**: adverbial, *Here*, i.e., *In this life*.

Acherūsius, -a, -um, *Acherusian, hellish*.

> **Acherūsia**: predicative.

stultōrum: i.e., those who do not understand philosophy, particularly Epicurean philosophy.

dēnique: *in short, indeed*.

> **Acherūsia . . . vīta**: an oxymoron which returns to the beginning of the passage: **quaecumque Acherunte profundō / prōdita sunt esse, in vītā sunt** (978–79).

1016	carcer et horribilis dē saxō iactu' deorsum,
1017	verbera carnificēs rōbur pix lammina taedae;
1018	quae tamen etsī absunt, at mēns sibi cōnscia factīs
1019	praemetuēns adhibet stimulōs torretque flagellīs
1020	nec videt intereā quī terminus esse malōrum
1021	possit nec quae sit poenārum dēnique fīnis
1022	atque eadem metuit magis haec nē in morte gravēscant.
1023	Hīc Acherūsia fit stultōrum dēnique vīta.

○♂ Discussion Questions

1.   In line 1019 whose goads and whips does the guilty man fear?

2.   What is the end or limit of punishment to which Lucretius refers? (1021) How does this view compare with ancient as well as modern beliefs?

M.   Tell me, now, is there for you anything terrible in the legendary three-headed Cerberus of the Lower World? In the roar of Cocytus? In the transportation over Acheron? In the picture of Tantalus who dies o' thirst, with water reaching to his chin? Or in that of Sisyphus who rolls—rolls the stone and sweats and struggles, ever rolling it in vain? . . .

A.   Do you really believe me dotard enough to suppose that such things are?

M.   Do you not?

A.   Of course not.

M.   That is most unfortunate.

A.   How so?

M.   Because I would have waxed quite eloquent in refutation of them.

A.   As who could not? Or what possible difficulty is there in refuting such monstrosities of painters and poets? . . . for who could be stupid enough to be impressed by such nonsense?
     Cicero, *Tusculan Disputations* 1.5–6 (tr. Black)

Reflect that there are no ills to be suffered after death, that the reports that make the Lower World terrible to us are mere tales. . . . All these things are the fancies of the poets who have harrowed us with groundless terrors. Death is a release from all suffering, a boundary beyond which our ills cannot pass—it restores us to that peaceful state in which we lay before we were born. . . . Death is neither a good nor an evil; for that only which is something is able to be a good or an evil. But that which itself is nothing and reduces all things to nothingness consigns us to neither sphere of fortune: for evils and goods must operate upon something material.
    Seneca, *ad Marciam* 19.4–5 (tr. Basore)

Later in the same work Seneca takes the diametrically opposite view when consoling Marcia on the loss of her son:

What lies [in the tomb] is his basest part and a part that in life was the source of much trouble—bones and ashes are no more parts of him than were his clothes and the other protections of the body. He is complete—leaving nothing of himself behind, he has fled away and wholly departed from earth; for a little while he tarried above us while he was being purified and was ridding himself of all the blemishes and stain that still clung to him from his mortal existence, then soared aloft and sped away to join the souls of the blessed. A saintly band gave him welcome.
    Seneca, *ad Marciam* 25 (tr. Basore)

1058   **Haec**: referring to the noun **cupīdō**, denoting sexual desire, from the previous line.
    Haec Venus est nōbīs: Venus is thus used in metonymy for physical lust.
  hinc, adv., *from here*, i.e., from desire.
    Haec . . . hinc . . . hinc (1059): the anaphora is particularly emphatic in the context of a
      tricolon crescens (a series of three examples, each of which is more extensive than the last).
  autem: *moreover*.
  nōmen amōris: i.e., the name of the god, **Cupīdō**, the personification of sexual desire.

1059   **illaec**: archaic demonstrative form of **illa**, nominative singular feminine, probably used for
    metrical reasons; modifying **gutta** (1060); here with a pejorative flavor.
  prīmum: adverbial, *first*.
  Veneris: possessive genitive with **dulcēdinis**.
  dulcēdō, dulcēdinis, f., *sweetness*.
    dulcēdinis: genitive dependent on **gutta** (1060).
  in cor: unusual and thus emphatic line-ending with two monosyllables.

1060   **stīllō, -āre, -āvī, -ātūrus**, *to drip*.
  gutta, -ae, f., *drop*.
  succēdō, succēdere, successī, successūrus, *to follow*.
  cūra: as often in Latin, used of the pains of love; see above **scindunt . . . curae** (3.994) in the
    description of Tityos, the allegorical representation of love.
    dulcēdinis in cor / stīllāvit gutta et successit frīgida cūra: the drop of sweetness, rather
      than bringing pleasure, as one would expect, acts rather as a poison. The slow spondaic
      progression of the meter suggests the slow drip of the poison.

1061   **si**: the normally long vowel has been shortened by the hiatus (lack of elision).
  quod amēs: a relative clause of characteristic; the antecedent **id** has been suppressed.
  praestō, adv., *present*; here predicative with **sunt**.
  simulācrum, -ī, n., *image*. This is a technical term in Lucretius, which he has treated in great
    detail earlier in Book 4, particularly in his theory of vision. To summarize: Each thing
    constantly sheds incredibly thin films or shells (**simulācra**) of itself. When one of these
    images strikes our eyeballs, we see the object. The **simulācra** also affect our thoughts, since
    when they strike our minds we generally think of the object of which they are the image.
  sunt: emphatic position; though the woman is not present, her images *are* present.

1062   **illius**: of the woman.
  dulcis, -is, -e, *sweet*.
  obversor, -ārī, -ātus sum, *to come frequently, present (itself)*.
  auris, auris, f., *ear*.
    nōmen dulce obversātur ad aurīs: the **simulācra** bring to mind the sound of the woman's
    name, which the lover then seems to hear.

1063   **fugitō, -āre, -āvī**, *to run away from, flee from, avoid*.
  simulācra: of the beloved.
    fugitāre . . . simulācra: the further one gets from an object, the fewer of its **simulācra** will be
    floating around; thus Lucretius advises the lover to keep his distance. Also, one can
    diminish the effect of the **simulācra** by not focusing on them. We are constantly assaulted
    by many **simulācra**, but notice only those that interest us.
  pābulum, -ī, n., *food*.
    pābula amōris: = the **simulācra**; **pābula** is accusative plural, direct object of **absterrēre**
    (1064).

1064   **absterreō, -ēre, -uī, -itus**, *to drive off* (i.e., not pay attention to).
  sibi: dative of separation.
  aliō, adv., *to another place, elsewhere*.

1089   **haec**: i.e., passionate love.
  quam plūrima: here, *however much*.

1090   **tam magis**: correlative with **quam plūrima**, *so much the more*.

☞ BOOK 4 ☜

38. The Folly of Love

Lucretius begins a diatribe against the passion of love, which disturbs and destroys our tranquillity. Love seems to promise pleasure, but results in pain.

1058   Haec Venus est nōbīs; hinc autemst nōmen amōris,
1059   hinc illaec prīmum Veneris dulcēdinis in cor
1060   stīllāvit gutta et successit frīgida cūra.
1061   Nam si abest quod amēs, praestō simulācra tamen sunt
1062   illius et nōmen dulce obversātur ad aurīs.
1063   Sed fugitāre decet simulācra et pābula amōris
1064   absterrēre sibi atque aliō convertere mentem.

. . .

1089   Ūnaque rēs haec est, cuius quam plūrima habēmus,
1090   tam magis ārdēscit dīrā cuppēdine pectus.

☞ Discussion Questions

1.   How does this picture of Venus compare to that in the first proem?

2.   What metaphorical image is used to describe love in line 1090? How does this image compare to the depiction of love today?

Love distills desire upon the eyes,
love brings bewitching grace into the heart
of those he would destroy.
    Euripides, *Hippolytus* 525–27 (tr. Grene)

While you still have a chance, and your heart is moved, but not deeply,
    If you're uncertain at all, never step over the sill.
Crush, before they are grown, the swelling seeds of your passion, . . .
Fight the disease at the start, for once the symptoms develop
    Medicine comes too late, losing effect from delay. . . .
I have seen a wound that might have been healed when inflicted
    Fester with long delay, aggravated by time. . . .
Meanwhile the devious flame creeps subtly into our vitals,
    Meanwhile the evil tree thrives with roots going deep.
    Ovid, *Remedia amoris* 77–102 (tr. Humphries)

1090   **ārdēscō, ārdēscere**, *to catch fire, become ignited/inflamed.*
        dīrus, -a, -um, *awful, dreadful, cruel.*
        cuppēdine: = **cupīdine.**

1091   **Nam**: introducing an explanation of how, in contrast to love, which is an unnecessary desire, natural and necessary wants are easily satisfied.

     ūmor, ūmōris, m., *moisture, liquid*; here, *drink*.

     membrum, -ī, n., *limb*.

     assūmō, assūmere, assūmpsī, assūmptus, *to take in*.

     intus, adv., *within, inside*.

       membrīs . . . intus: the adverb acts as a preposition with a locative ablative, *within the limbs*.

1092   **quae**: unusual use of neuter relative, since the antecedents are both masculine.

     obsīdō, obsīdere, *to occupy, fill*.

1093   **hōc**: supply **modō**, ablative of means, *in this way*.

     expleō, explēre, explēvī, explētus, *to fill*.

     latex, laticis, m., *liquid, water*.

     frūgēs, frūgum, f. pl., *produce, crops, fruit*; here, *food*.

       laticum frūgumque: more poetic version of **cibus atque ūmor** above (1091).

1094   **hominis**: particularly here, *a human being*.

     vērō: here with adversative force, *but, however*; introducing the contrasting experience of love, which cannot be sufficiently nourished.

     faciēs, -ēī, f., *face*.

1095   **fruor, fruī, frūctus sum**, *to enjoy*.

     fruendum: gerundive modifying **nīl**, *to be enjoyed, enjoyable*.

1096   **tenvis, -is, -e**, *thin, insubstantial*.

     tenvia: modifying **simulācra** and emphasized by the enjambement.

     quae: accusative plural neuter; its antecedent is **simulācra . . . tenvia**.

     ventō: ablative, *in/on the wind*.

     spēs, speī, f., *hope*; i.e., of the lover.

     raptō, -āre, -āvī, -ātus, *to carry away forcibly, drag off violently*.

       quae ventō spēs raptat saepe misella: the phrase has been much disputed. Some consider **ventō** to be suspect, others **raptat**.

     misellus, -a, -um, *wretched little, miserable, pathetic* (a diminutive with pejorative tone).

       quae . . . misella: the lover's hope is described as **misella** because it cannot be fulfilled (compare the simile below) and so makes the lover wretched. The lover's hope of fulfillment nevertheless impels him to drag off violently the **simulācra** of his beloved that are carried about on the wind.

1097   **Ut**: with **cum**, *as when*, introducing a comparison between the lover and a thirsty man who is asleep but dreaming.

     bibere: dependent on **quaerit**.

     in somnīs: a formulaic early Latin phrase for *in a dream*.

     sitiō, sitīre, *to be thirsty*.

     sitiēns: acting as subject, *a thirsty man*.

1098   **ārdor, ārdōris**, m., *burning, heat*.

     quī: introducing relative clause of characteristic.

     membrīs: archaic dative with **ardōrem**, equivalent to genitive of possession.

     stinguō, singuere, stīnxī, stīnctus, *to extinguish, annihilate, destroy*

1099   **sed . . . petit**: in his dream-state.

1100   **torrēns, torrentis**, *flowing headlong, rushing*.

     flūmen, flūminis, n., *river, stream, flow*.

       in mediōque sitit torrentī flūmine: the word order mirrors the image described.

     pōtō, -āre, -āvī, -ātus, *to drink*.

       pōtāns: paradoxically the dreamer, though drinking, is still thirsty; just as the lover, violently seizing the **simulācra** of his beloved, can never satisfy his longings.

1101   **sīc**: concluding the comparison with the situation of the lover.

     lūdit: *tricks, cheats, mocks*.

     amāns, amantis, m./f., *lover*.

1091   Nam cibus atque ūmor membrīs assūmitur intus;

1092   quae quoniam certās possunt obsīdere partīs,

1093   hōc facile explētur laticum frūgumque cupīdō.

1094   Ex hominis vērō faciē pulchrōque colōre

1095   nīl datur in corpus praeter simulācra fruendum

1096   tenvia; quae ventō spēs raptat saepe misella.

1097   Ut bibere in somnīs sitiēns cum quaerit et ūmor

1098   nōn datur, ārdōrem quī membrīs stinguere possit,

1099   sed laticum simulācra petit frūstrāque labōrat

1100   in mediōque sitit torrentī flūmine pōtāns,

1101   sīc in amōre Venus simulācrīs lūdit amantīs.

ᘒ Discussion Question

1.   Compare the images of wind in line 1096 and in Catullus poem 70 (below).

Nullī sē dīcit mulier mea nūbere mālle
    quam mihi, nōn sī sē Iuppiter ipse petat.
Dīcit: sed mulier cupidō quod dīcit amantī
    in ventō et rapidā scrībere oportet aquā.

My woman says she prefers to marry no one
    rather than me, not if Jupiter himself should seek her.
She says: but what a woman says to her desirous lover
    should be written in wind and rushing water.

He seems to me the equal of a god,
he seems, if that may be, the gods' superior,
who sits face to face with you and again and again
        watches and hears you
sweetly laughing, an experience which robs me,
poor wretch, of all my senses; for the moment I set
eyes on you, Lesbia, there remains not a whisper
        <of voice on my lips,>
but my tongue is paralyzed, a subtle flame
courses through my limbs, with sound self-caused
my two ears ring, and my eyes are
        covered in darkness.
Idleness, Catullus, is your trouble;
idleness is what delights you and moves you to passion;
idleness has proved ere now the ruin of kings and
        prosperous cities.
                Catullus 51 (tr. Goold)

1120   **Usque adeō,** *To such an extent, So greatly.*
    incertus, -a, -um, *uncertain* (how to fulfill their longing).
    tābēscō, tābēscere, tābuī, *to waste away.*
      tābēscunt: the subject is **amantēs** understood.
    caecus, -a, -um, *unseen, invisible, hidden.*
      tābēscunt vulnere caecō: combining two images of love, as a disease and a wound.

1121   **Adde:** in addition to the physical symptoms described above.
    quod: here, *that.*
    absūmō, absūmere, absūmpsī, absūmptus, *to wear out, exhaust, consume, waste.*

1122   **adde quod:** emphatic anaphora.
    alterius: of the woman.
    nūtus, -ūs, m., *nod, command.*
    dēgō, dēgere, *to live, spend* (one's time).
    aetās, aetātis, f., *time.*
      alterius sub nūtū dēgitur aetas: the ultimate humiliation for a man was considered to be
        subservience to a woman. In elegiac poetry this became the pose of **servitium amōris.**

1129   **pariō, parere, peperī, partus,** *to give birth to; to produce, create.*
      parta: the neuter plural passive participle used substantively for *earnings, savings.*
      bene parta patrum, *the well-earned savings of their fathers;* i.e., *their patrimony.*
    anadēma, anadēmatis, n., *ornamental headband.*
    mitra, -ae, f., *an oriental headress fastened with ribbons under the chin.*
      anadēmata, mitrae: The transliteration of the Greek terms suggests decadence to the
        Romans, who considered the Greeks their moral inferiors. Both adornments were associ-
        ated with prostitutes. The asyndeton also conveys a sarcastic effect, contrasting with **bene
        parta patrum.**

1130   **palla, -ae,** f., *palla* (a woman's full-length outer garment).
    Alidēnsius, -a, -um, *from Elis, Elean.*
    Cīus, -a, -um, *from Cos, Cian* (an island celebrated for its diaphanous silk).
      Alidēnsia Cīaque: accusative plural neuters; though the exact references are uncertain,
        Lucretius is clearly referring to exotic, expensive, and probably risqué clothing. The
        names are probably the ancient equivalent of designer labels and *haute couture.*
    vertunt: here intransitive with **in:** the hard-earned patrimony turns into fancy clothing.

1131   **veste:** here referring to the draperies and coverings used to decorate the banquet hall.
    vīctus, -ūs, m., *food.*
      Eximiā veste et vīctū: ablatives of quality with **convīvia; eximiā** applies also to **vīctū.**
    lūdī: games such as dice, which were popular as after-dinner entertainment.

1132   **crēber, crēbra, crēbrum,** *frequent, repeated.*
    unguenta: the *u* is consonantal with *g*, and so does not scan (cf. **sanguen**).
    serta, -ōrum, n. pl., *chains of flowers, garlands, festoons.*
      convīvia, lūdī . . . corōnae serta: the rapid asyndeton conveys the reckless extravagance of
        the lover.

1133   **nēquīquam:** the telling climax, strengthened by enjambement. The lover has spent a fortune
    on all the material pleasures of life, but can find no enjoyment in them.
    fōns, fontis, m., *spring, fountain.*
    lepos, lepōris, m., *charm, grace, pleasure.*
      mediō dē fonte lepōrum: a wonderful metaphorical phrase.

1134   **surgit:** emphatic position.
    amārus, -a, -um, *bitter.*
      amārī: partitive genitive with **aliquid,** *something bitter.* There may be a pun here, contrast-
        ing **amārī** with **amōris.**
        surgit amārī aliquid: the lover is compared to someone drinking from a beautiful
          spring and suddenly choking on an unexpectedly foul taste.

39. The Deluded Lover

The lover wastes all his possessions on his darling, but still suffers anguish in the midst of pleasure. It is best to avoid love, or to escape as soon as possible. Men, blinded by love, do not see their beloveds' faults.

1120	Usque adeō incertī tābēscunt vulnere caecō.
1121	Adde quod absūmunt vīrīs pereuntque labōre,
1122	adde quod alterius sub nūtū dēgitur aetās.

. . .

1129	Et bene parta patrum fīunt anadēmata, mitrae,
1130	interdum in pallam atque Alidēnsia Cīaque vertunt.
1131	Eximiā veste et vīctū convīvia, lūdī,
1132	pōcula crēbra, unguenta corōnae serta parantur,
1133	nēquīquam, quoniam mediō dē fonte lepōrum
1134	surgit amārī aliquid quod in ipsīs flōribus angat,
1135	aut cum cōnscius ipse animus sē forte remordet
1136	dēsidiōsē agere aetātem lustrīsque perīre,

೮ଃ Discussion Questions

1. Do we still use the imagery of love as a disease and / or a wound? (1120)

2. How is the lover trying to gain the favor of his darling? How does this behavior compare to modern romance?

To be ruled by a woman is the ultimate outrage for a man.
    Democritus, *Fragment* 111 (tr. Freeman)

1134   **in ipsīs flōribus**: continuing the metaphor of the spring, which, by the convention of the **locus amoenus**, was surrounded by flowers; also referring to the **coronae** and **serta** (1132).
     angō, angere, ānxī, ānctus, *to choke.*

1135   **aut**: introducing the first of three reasons why the lover can not enjoy himself; the passage is carefully composed with each reason comprising two lines introduced by **aut**.
     cōnscius, -a, -um, *inwardly aware, conscious of guilt.*
     sē: accusative subject of the indirect statement that follows in line 1137; technically as reflexive referring to **animus**, but transferred to the lover himself in indirect statement.
     remordeō, remordēre, remordī, remorsus, *to vex, torment, nag.*

1136   **dēsidiōsē**, adv., *idly, slothfully.*
     agere aetātem: *to spend his life.*
     lustrum, -ī, n., *place of debauchery, den of vice.*
       lustrīs: ablative of place.

1137   **quod**: *because.*

        in ambiguō: *in doubt;* the phrase acts adjectively with **verbum**.

        iaculor, -ārī, -ātus sum, *to utter rapidly, toss out.*

           iaculāta: modifying **domina**, *mistress*, understood

               in ambiguō verbum iaculāta: the lover fears every word which could possibly be construed as a sign of infidelity.

        relīquit: having said something that is ambiguous, she does not bother to correct it.

1138   **quod**: here relative; the antecedent is **verbum**.

        adfīgō, adfīgere, adfīxī, adfīxus + dat., *to fix to, fasten to.*

        cupīdō . . . cordī: of the lover.

           quod cupīdō adfīxum cordī: interlocking word order.

        vīvēscō, vīvēscere, *to grow strong, thrive.*

           quod cupīdō . . . ut ignis: combining the imagery of the wound of love (cf. 1120) with the fire of its passion.

1139   **nimium**, adv., *too much.*

        tueor, tuērī, tuitus sum, here, *to look at.*

           iactāre oculōs aliumve tuērī: indirect statements dependent on **quod putat** (1140); the subject of the indirect statement, **eam**, the beloved, has been omitted. Both statements refer to the lover's insecurity and fear of his mistress' unfaithfulness.

1140   **quod**: *because.*

        in vultū: on her face.

        vēstīgia: *traces.*

           vultūque videt vēstīgia rīsūs: note the alliteration. This is the climax of a three-part series. The lover fears (1) that his beloved is looking around for other lovers, (2) that she is now actually looking at someone else, and (3) that her smile indicates that she is enjoying looking at that other man.

1144   **Ut melius vigilāre**: having catalogued the sufferings and folly of the lover, Lucretius now offers advice in the form of a result clause.

        vigilāre: here, *to be wary, be on the alert;* subject of **sit** and modified by the predicative adjective **melius**.

1145   **ratiōne**: here, *way.*

           quā docuī ratiōne: in lines 1063–64.

        cavēreque: another infinitive subject of **sit** (1144).

        inliciō, inlicere, inlexī, inlectus, *to lure, entice.*

           nē inliciāris: substantive clause of purpose; *(to be wary) lest you be enticed.*

1146   **vitāre**: infinitive as subject of **est** (1147); *to avoid.*

        plaga, -ae, f., *net, snare.*

           plagās in amōris nē iaciāmur: introducing an extended image of hunting with nets, here applied metaphorically to love. Order for translation: **nē iaciāmur in plagās amōris**.

1147   **nōn**: emphatic position.

        quam: comparative, *as.*

        captum: accusative modifying an understood word for lover; *once captured;* subject of the infinitives **exīre** and **perrumpere** (1148).

        rēte, rētis, n., *net* (larger than the **plaga**).

           rētibus ipsīs: ablative of separation with **exīre** (1148).

1148   **perrumpō, perrumpere, perrūpī, perruptus**, *to burst through, break through.*

        nōdus, -ī, m., *knot* (at the corner of each diamond shape in the mesh of a net).

1149   **Et tamen**: even if ensnared by love, the situation is not hopeless.

        implicitus, -a, -um, *entangled.*

        quoque: here, *even*, with **implicitus** and **in- . . . pedītus**.

        possīs: present subjunctive in future less vivid condition, *you would be able.*

           implicitus . . . inque pedītus: acting as the protasis of a future less vivid condition; *if you should be entangled and hobbled . . . .*

1137   aut quod in ambiguō verbum iaculāta relīquit

1138   quod cupīdō adfīxum cordī vīvēscit ut ignis,

1139   aut nimium iactāre oculōs aliumve tuērī

1140   quod putat in vultūque videt vēstīgia rīsūs.

. . .

1144   Ut melius vigilāre sit ante,

1145   quā docuī ratiōne, cavēreque nē inliciāris.

1146   Nam vītāre, plagās in amōris nē iaciāmur,

1147   nōn ita difficile est quam captum rētibus ipsīs

1148   exīre et validōs Veneris perrumpere nōdōs.

1149   Et tamen implicitus quoque possīs inque pedītus

1150   effugere īnfestum, nisi tūte tibi obvius obstēs

1151   et praetermittās animī vitia omnia prīmum

1152   et quae corporī' sunt eius, quam praepetis ac vīs.

○ℨ Discussion Questions

1.   What type of love is being described? What would you call it? (1133–40)

2.   In lines 1135–40 compare the themes and phraseology to those found in Catullus' Poem 51 (given above with passage 38).

Remove sight, association, and contact, and the passion of love is at an end.
     Epicurus, *Vatican Sayings* 18 (tr. Bailey)

1149   **inque pedītus**, tmesis of **impedītus**, adding to the sense of entanglement, *hindered, hobbled* (the verb retains the sense of **pēs**).

1150   **īnfestus, -a, -um**, *hostile*; here substantival, *the enemy, the foe*.
     nisi: introducing an important qualification—not all lovers want to escape their misery.
     tūte, emphatic form of **tū**, *you yourself*.
       tūte tibi: alliterative emphasis with play on pronoun repeated in diferent cases..
     obvius, -a, -um, *in the way*.
     obstō, obstāre, obstitī, obstātūrus + dat., *to stand in the way, obstruct, block*.
       obvius obstēs: a second alliterative repetition increasing the emphasis.

1151   **praetermittō, praetermittere, praetermīsī, praetermissus**, *to disregard, overlook*.
     animī: of the woman.
     vitium, -ī, n., *fault, defect*.
       praetermittās animī vitia omnia: it is interesting that Lucretius considers the qualities of the woman's mind before those of her body.
     prīmum: i.e., at the beginning of the love affair.

1152   **quae**: the antecedent is **vitia** (1151).
     corporī': the final *s* has been suppressed for metrical convenience.
     eius: of the woman.
     praepetō, praepetere, *to seek / desire particularly*.
     vīs: second person singular present from **volō, velle, voluī**, *to wish*.

1153   **faciunt**: supply **sīc**, referring to the lover's blatant disregard of the woman's faults, as described in lines 1151–52.

        plērumque, adv., *generally, often.*

        cupīdine caecī: echoing the conventional image of the blindness associated with love, as in **vulnere caecō** (1120).

1154   **tribuō, tribuere, tribuī, tribūtus**, *to grant, attribute* (to).

        hīs: dative both with **tribuunt** and as dative of possession in the relative clause.

        commoda: substantive, *charms, graces.*

          quae nōn sunt hīs . . . vērē: *which they do not truly have.*

1155   **multimodīs**, adv., *in many ways;* modifying **prāvās turpīsque**.

        prāvus, -a, -um, *misshapen, deformed.*

        turpis, -is, -e, *foul, base;* here, *ugly.*

          prāvās turpīsque: modifying **fēminās** understood.

1156   **esse in dēliciīs**, *are in especial favor, are treated as darlings.* **Dēliciae** was the term Catullus chose to describe Lesbia's pampered pet sparrow (**dēliciae meae puellae**, 2.1 and 3.4) whom he envied.

        summōque in honōre: a sardonic expression, since **honor** was usually reserved only for men. The phrase is thus similar in effect to the humiliation of **alterius sub nūtū dēgitur aetās** (1122).

        vigeō, vigēre, viguī, *to flourish, prosper, thrive.*

1157   **irrideō, irridēre, irrīsī, irrīsus**, *to laugh at, mock.*

    Venerem: direct object of **ut plācent** (1158).

        suādeō, suādēre, suāsī, suāsus, *to urge.*

          suādent: unusual scansion with the *u* acting as a vowel, thus the word scans ᴗᴗ –.

1158   **plācent**: here, *propitiate, appeal to.* The subject is the persons included in **aliōs** (1157).

    foedus, -a, -um, *foul.*

    adflictō, -āre, -āvī, -ātus, *to oppress, burden, vex, afflict.*

        adflictentur: subjunctive giving the opinion of **aliī** (1157).

          foedō adflictentur amōre: the imagery again compares love to a disease.

1159   **nec sua respiciunt . . . mala maxima**: a proverbial idea, as expressed in Aesop's fable in which a man carries on his back a sack full of his own faults. See also Catullus 22.21: **sed non vidēmus manticae quod in tergō est.**

        miserī mala maxima: the alliteration conveys a sarcastic tone.

1177   **exclūdō, exclūdere, exclūsī, exclūsus**, *to shut out, exclude.*

    amātor, amātōris, m., *lover.*

        lacrimāns exclūsus amātor: Lucretius here begins a sardonic caricature of a conventional scene, termed *paraclausithyon* (Greek for "beside the shut door"), that is particularly prevalent in Latin elegiac poetry, but which is found earlier in New Comedy and Hellenistic epigram. The lover abases himself at his mistress' door and showers it with the flowers and kisses intended for her. Catullus in poem 67 humorously rebukes a door which has been too open to lovers. Examples of the **exclūsus amātor** figure have also survived from Propertius, Tibullus, and Ovid.

1178   **serta, -ōrum**, n. pl., *chains of flowers, garlands, festoons.*

    postīsque superbōs: even the doorposts have assumed the haughty character of the mistress, whereas the lover is **miser** (1179).

1179   **amāracinum, -ī**, n., *exotic, marjoram-scented perfume.*

    foris, foris, f., *door.*

    fīgō, fīgere, fīxī, fīxus, *to fix on, plant, impress.*

One thing did me some good, a most repetitious insistence
    on every one of her faults; that brought effective relief.
      Ovid, *Remedia amoris* 315–16 (tr. Humphries)

1153   Nam faciunt hominēs plērumque cupīdine caecī

1154   et tribuunt ea quae nōn sunt hīs commoda vērē.

1155   Multimodīs igitur prāvās turpīsque vidēmus

1156   esse in dēliciīs summōque in honōre vigēre.

1157   Atque aliōs aliī irrīdent Veneremque suādent

1158   ut plācent, quoniam foedō adflictentur amōre,

1159   nec sua respiciunt miserī mala maxima saepe.

. . .

1177   At lacrimāns exclūsus amātor līmina saepe

1178   flōribus et sertīs operit postīsque superbōs

1179   unguit amāracinō et foribus miser ōscula fīgit.

ᴄꙅ Discussion Questions

1.   What explanation does Lucretius give for the fact that lovers overlook their mistresses' faults? (1150–54)

2.   Lucretius was a contemporary of Catullus. What would he have thought of Catullus' obsession with Lesbia? What advice might he have given him?

Snow, hail, make darkness, lighten, thunder, shake out upon the earth all thy black clouds! If thou slayest me, then I shall cease, but if thou lettest me live, though I pass through worse than this, I will go with music to her doors; for the god compels me who is thy master too, Zeus, he at whose bidding thou, turned to gold, didst pierce the brazen chamber.

Night, for I call thee alone to witness, look how shamefully Nico's Pythias, ever loving to deceive, treats me. I came at her call and not uninvited. May she one day stand at my door and complain to thee that she suffered the like at my hands.

    Asclepiades, *The Greek Anthology* 5. 64 and 5.164 (tr. Paton)

Phaedromus addresses his beloved's door in the company of his servant Palinurus:

Ph: Oh, 'tis the most delectable door, the discreetest door I ever saw! It never breathes a single word! When it opens—silent! When *she* steals out to me at night—silent still! . . . (*pouring wine on the sill*)

Drink, ye portals of pleasure, drink! Quaff deep, and deign to be propitious unto me!

Pal: (*mimicking his master*) Will ye have some olives, portals,—a croquette—a pickled caper? . . .

Ph: See you how it opens—the bower of bliss beyond compare? Hear you a creak from the hinge?

    Oh, lovely hinge!

Pal.: Why don't you kiss it?

    Plautus, *Curculio* 20–22, 88–94 (tr. Nixon)

Janus, crueler than my mistress
    why are you silent,
        the folding doors closed tight?
Why no admittance, love undisclosed,
    why no thought of giving in
        to the transit of my secret prayers? . . .
I have spun out tunes
    with new verses in your service;
        I have planted kisses on your steps,
and I have often turned
    before your dingy columns
        and brought due offering with secret hands.
    Propertius 1.16.17–19, 41–44 (See also Tibullus 1.2, Horace, *Odes* 3.10, Ovid, *Amores* 1.6.)

1278   **dīvīnitus**, adv., *by divine agency, power; divinely.*

      sagitta, -ae, f., *arrow.*

        Veneris sagittīs: a sarcastic touch.

1279   **dēterior, dēterior, dēterius**, gen. **dēteriōris**, *worse, inferior, less desirable.*

        dēteriōre: modifying **formā**, but put at the line-beginning for emphasis.

        ut . . . amētur: substantive clause serving as subject of **fit**.

        muliercula, -ae, f. [diminutive with negative connotations], *little woman.*

1280   **facit**: here, *brings it about, sees to it* (that); governing the **ut** plus subjunctive clause in line 1282.

        suīs . . . factīs: significantly her actions are mentioned first, since by them one can judge her character.

1281   **mōriger, mōrigera, mōrigerum**, *compliant, agreeable.*

      mundus, -a, -um, *clean, neat.*

        mundē: modifying **cultō**.

      cultus, -a, -um, *cultivated, groomed, adorned.*

        mōrigerīsque . . . corpore cultō: a highly alliterative line.

1282   **īnsuēscō, īnsuēscere, īnsuēvī, īnsuētus**, *to accustom.*

      dēgō, dēgere, *to live, spend* (one's time).

        tē sēcum dēgere vītam: an intriguing phrase, since it might refer to marriage, which was generally avoided by Epicureans.

1283   **Quod superest**: the formulaic phrase found at 1.50 and 921, 2.39; literally *as to what remains,* simply meaning *next, moreover*; the idea that by her good qualities a woman can habituate a man to love her leads to the idea that habit itself can produce love.

      cōnsuētūdō, cōnsuētūdinis, f., *habit, familiarity.*

      concinnō, -āre, -āvī, -ātus, *to bring about, cause, produce.*

        cōnsuētūdō concinnat: an alliterative phrase containing a word play with **īnsuēscat** (1282).

1284   **nam leviter**: introducing two comparisons showing how our behavior is similar to other natural phenomena. Habituation is compared to frequent small blows and to the incessant dripping of water.

      leviter, adv., *lightly.*

      quamvīs, adv., *no matter how, however*; take closely with **leviter**.

      quod: i.e., **id quod**.

      crēber, crēbra, crēbrum, *frequent, repeated.*

      tundō, tundere, tutudī, tūnsus, *to strike, beat.*

      ictus, -ūs, m., *blow.*

        cōnsuētūdō concinnat . . . ictū: the hard alliteration of *c, q,* and *t* sounds replicates the sound of the blows (cf. 2.323–25 with *c* imitating the clang of armor).

1285   **labāscō, labāscere**, *to break up, dissolve.*

1286   **gutta, -ae**, f., *drop.*

      saxum, -ī, n., *rock.*

1287   **ūmor, ūmōris**, m., *moisture, liquid.*

        ūmōris: here, *water*; genitive singular with **guttās** (1286).

      longō in spatiō: repeating, with metrical variation, the key phrase from line 1285; habituation is gradual.

      pertundō, pertundere, pertudī, pertūsus, *to bore through, perforate, puncture.*

        guttās in saxa . . . pertundere saxa: for other examples of gradual effects, see Lucretius' proofs of the existence of invisible particles in 1.311–18, especially **stīlicidī cāsus lapidem cavat** (1.313). The image of falling water also recalls Lucretius' description of love at 4.1059–60: **illaec prīmum Veneris dulcēdinis in cor / stillāvit gutta et successit frīgida cūra**.

40. Non-Passionate Love is Possible and Desirable

After his severe diatribe against the passion of romantic love or infatuation, Lucretius closes Book 4 with a contrasting view. One can gradually come to love a woman who is not beautiful but who has a pleasant character. Here love is depicted more as a long-standing friendship, a relationship that was most highly valued by the Epicureans.

1278	Nec dīvīnitus interdum Venerisque sagittīs
1279	dēteriōre fit ut formā muliercula amētur.
1280	Nam facit ipsa suīs interdum fēmina factīs
1281	mōrigerīsque modīs et mundē corpore cultō,
1282	ut facilē īnsuēscat tē sēcum dēgere vītam.
1283	Quod superest, cōnsuētūdō concinnat amōrem;
1284	nam leviter quamvīs quod crebrō tunditur ictū,
1285	vincitur in longō spatiō tamen atque labāscit.
1286	Nōnne vidēs etiam guttās in saxa cadentīs
1287	ūmōris longō in spatiō pertundere saxa?

CB **Discussion Questions**

1. Why does Lucretius include the phrase **dīvīnitus interdum Venerisque sagittīs** (1278)? What explanation might these words provide?

2. How quickly does a non-passionate love develop? How does this pace compare with the typical view of the onset of love?

All friendship is desirable in itself, though it starts from the need of help.
> Epicurus, *Vatican Sayings* 23 (tr. Bailey)

Friendship goes dancing round the world proclaiming to us all to awake to the praises of a happy life.
> Epicurus, *Vatican Sayings* 52 (tr. Bailey)

Of all the things which wisdom acquires to produce the blessedness of the complete life, far the greatest is the possession of friendship.
> Epicurus, *Principal Doctrines* 27 (tr. Bailey)

1   **potis**, indecl. adj. + infin., *able (to), capable (of)*.

    potis est: governing the infinitive **condere** (2).

    dignus, -a, -um, *worthy*; here with **prō** + abl. (2).

    pollēns, pollentis, *powerful, strong*.

      pollentī pectore: ablative of means; referring to the hypothetical poet's **animus**, located in the chest.

    carmen, carminis, n., *song; poetry*.

2   **condere**: here, *to compose, write*.

    prō: *in proportion to, to match*; here with **dignum**, *of*.

    rērum: referring to nature or the universe.

    maiestās, maiestātis, f., *greatness, grandeur, majesty*.

    repertum, -ī, n., *discovery*.

      hīs . . . repertīs: those of Epicurus.

6   **Nēmō**: Lucretius boldly answers his own question.

    opīnor, -ārī, -ātus sum, *to think, believe*.

    erit: with **crētus**, perfect passive participle of **crēscō, crēscere**, *to be born*; here future perfect, *will ever be born*.

    mortālī corpore: ablative of source, *from/of mortal body*.

      Nēmō . . . crētus: to complete the meaning, supply "who will be able to compose such a poem."

7   **si**: the vowel is shortened by hiatus (lack of elision).

    petit: here, *demands*.

    cognita: *made known, revealed to us* (by Epicurus).

8   **dīcendum est**: impersonal passive periphrastic, *(it) must be said*, here with a direct statement as its subject.

    deus . . . deus: emphatic repetition in a startling statement, the apotheosis of Epicurus, who has already been highly praised in the proems to Books 1 (62–79) and 3 (1–30). In interpreting this passage, however, one must remember the Epicurean definition of a god as a being who lives in perfect tranquillity. As Epicurus himself said, the man who devotes his life to philosophy will "live like a god among men" (*Ep. ad Men.* 135). Secondly, Lucretius claims that Epicurus' benefits to mankind are far more praiseworthy than those of the traditional gods.

    inclutus, -a, -um, *celebrated, famous, renowned, illustrious*.

    Memmī: Gaius Memmius, the dedicatee of the poem.

9   **prīnceps, prīncipis**, *first*.

    vītae ratiōnem: *principle/doctrine/plan of life*, i.e., Epicurean philosophy.

10   **sapientia, -ae**, f., *wisdom, philosophy*.

    per artem: *by his skill*; we might say *by his scientific method*.

11   **flūctus, -ūs**, m., *wave; turbulence, trouble*.

    tenebrae, -ārum, f. pl., *darkness*.

      flūctibus . . . tenebrīs: combining two image systems from earlier proems: (1) shipwreck (2.1–2), and (2) the light of Epicurean philosophy illuminating the darkness of ignorance (3.1–2, where we find the same phrase **ē tantīs tenebrīs**). For the darkness of ignorance see also 2.14–15 and 2.54–56 and the recurring formulaic passage **Hunc igitur terrōrem animī tenebrāsque necessest . . .** (1.146–48, 2.59–61, 3.91–93), which explicitly points out that light cannot allay our fears, but only philosophy. In this passage note also the strong alliteration of *t* and how the chiastic **flūctibus ē tantīs . . . tantīsque tenebrīs** imprisons **vitam**.

12   **tranquillō**: here substantive, *tranquillity, calm*.

      in tam . . . locāvit: the line is devoted to the contrasting imagery of light. Note how the sharp *t* sounds of the previous line gradually yield to the soft vowel sounds and liquids of **clārā lūce locāvit**.

❧ BOOK 5 ❧

41. Godlike Epicurus

Who can adequately praise the findings of Epicurus? If one compares his benefits to mankind with those of other gods, Epicurus must be considered far more worthy of our reverence.

1   Quis potis est dignum pollentī pectore carmen
2   condere prō rērum maiestāte hīsque repertīs?

. . .

6   Nēmō, ut opīnor, erit mortālī corpore crētus.
7   Nam si, ut ipsa petit maiestās cognita rērum,
8   dīcendum est, deus ille fuit, deus, inclute Memmī,
9   quī prīnceps vītae ratiōnem invēnit eam quae
10   nunc appellātur sapientia, quīque per artem
11   flūctibus ē tantīs vītam tantīsque tenebrīs
12   in tam tranquillō et tam clārā lūce locāvit.
13   Cōnfer enim dīvīna aliōrum antīqua reperta.

❧ Discussion Questions

1.   What two subjects does the hypothetical poet attempt to praise? How do these subjects compare with the content of *De Rerum Natura*?

2.   What personification occurs in line 7? What is its effect? Does it remind you of an earlier passage?

3.   By calling Epicurus **deus** (8) does Lucretius actually mean that Epicurus is immortal? If not, what exactly does he mean?

4.   Lucretius says that Epicurus placed human existence **in tam tranquillō et tam clārā lūce** (12). What earlier description does the passage echo? What comparison is Lucretius making with this imagery?

---

13   **Cōnfer**: here, *compare*.
        dīvīna: transferred epithet applied to **reperta** rather than more logically as a substantive with **aliōrum**; equivalent to **antīqua reperta aliōrum dīv(ōr)um**.
        reperta: as above (2), *discoveries*.

14 **Cerēs, Cereris**, f., *Ceres (goddess of agriculture)*.

fertur: *is said*; governing **īnstituisse** (15). Note that Lucretius does not actually credit the gods with these gifts; we will see later how man by trial and error developed agriculture.

frūgēs, frūgum, f. pl., *produce, crops, fruit*.

Līber, Līberī, m., *Liber (an Italian god of vegetation, later identified with Bacchus, god of wine)*.

Namque . . . liquōris: the line contains interesting alliterative pairs: (1) of *q* and *c*, (2) of *f*, and (3) of *l*.

15 **vītigenus, -a, -um**, *produced from the vine*.

liquōris vītigenī: *vine-produced liquid*, i.e., *wine*.

latex, laticis, m., *liquid*.

īnstituisse: here, *to have introduced*.

16 **cum tamen**: *although, nevertheless*.

hīs . . . sine rēbus: i.e., grain and wine, which could be considered unnecessary. Later in this book Lucretius will examine the diet of early men.

posset: imperfect subjunctive, attracted into secondary sequence by the past tense of **īnstituisse**.

cum tamen . . . vīta manēre: ancient man could still have survived without these alleged gifts of the gods.

17 **fāma**: here, *rumor, report*, introducing an indirect statement.

ut fāma est: for instance, Caesar reports (*Bellum Gallicum* 6.22.1) that the Germans survived on a diet of cheese, milk, and meat.

18 **bene**: modifying **vīvī**, but severely separated from it for emphasis.

nōn poterat: idiomatic use of the imperfect indicative, rather than subjunctive, to express potentiality, *would not have been possible*; the subject is the impersonal passive infinitive phrase **bene . . . vīvī**.

pūrō pectore: i.e., free from fear and worry.

poterat . . . pūrō pectore: alliteration.

19 **quō**, adv., *for which reason, therefore*.

meritō, adv., *deservedly, with reason*.

nōbīs: *by us, in our eyes*; i.e., the Epicureans.

vidētur: *is seen/considered*.

20 **nunc etiam**: despite the passage of time his teachings still benefit us. (Epicurus died two centuries before Lucretius composed this poem.)

per magnās . . . gentīs: i.e., throughout the Greco-Roman world.

dīdō, dīdere, dīdidī, dīditus, *to spread, diffuse*.

dīdita: modifying **sōlācia** (21).

21 **dulcis, -is, -e**, *sweet*.

permulceō, permulcēre, permulsī, permulsus, *to soothe, refresh, relieve*.

sōlācium, -ī, n., *comfort, solace*.

vītae: here including the idea of the hardships involved.

dulcia . . . sōlācia vītae, *sweet solaces for life's troubles*; the phrase could be taken as a motto for the entire poem, which aims to free man from his fears and worries. Also note the soothing softness of the line's assonance.

22 **Herculis**: the demi-god who was considered one of the greatest benefactors of man, since he slew many dreadful beasts, such as are mentioned in the following lines. Significantly, he was also the patron god of the Stoics, whose philosophy was the main rival to Epicureanism.

antistō, antistāre, antistitī, *to surpass, excel, be superior to*.

Herculis antistāre . . . facta: understand *those of Epicurus*.

autem, here, *moreover*.

23 **longius . . . multō**, *by far further* (than when you valued the gifts of the gods).

ferēre: future, alternate second person singular passive.

14   Namque Cerēs fertur frūgēs Līberque liquōris
15   vītigenī laticem mortālibus īnstituisse;
16   cum tamen hīs posset sine rēbus vīta manēre,
17   ut fāma est aliquās etiam nunc vīvere gentīs.
18   At bene nōn poterat sine pūrō pectore vīvī;
19   quō magis hīc meritō nōbīs deus esse vidētur,
20   ex quō nunc etiam per magnās dīdita gentīs
21   dulcia permulcent animōs sōlācia vītae.
22   Herculis antistāre autem sī facta putābis,
23   longius ā vērā multō ratiōne ferēre.
24   Quid Nemeaeus enim nōbīs nunc magnus hiātus
25   ille leōnis obesset et horrēns Arcadius sūs?

ᚼ Discussion Questions

1.   Can you think of other cultures which do not eat bread or drink wine? (14–17)

2.   What does the phrase **ā vērā ratiōne** (23) mean?

It is not possible to live pleasantly without living prudently and honorably and justly.
     Epicurus, *Principal Doctrines* 5 (tr. Bailey)

---

24   **Nemeaeus, -a, -um**, *of Nemea, Nemean* (Nemea was a valley in the Argolid, Greece, Hercules'
     homeland).
       Nemeaeus: the epithet has been transferred from **leōnis** (25) to his gaping jaws (**hiātus**)
       perhaps, in the context of the elevated language of the passage, to create a mock-heroic
       tone. The reference is to Hercules' first labor imposed by King Eurystheus—to bring him
       the skin of the Nemean lion.
     nōbīs: dative with **obesset** (25).
     nunc: the beast would be long since dead.
     hiātus, -ūs, m., *gape*.
25   **obsum, obesse, obfuī** + dat., *to be a hindrance* (to), *to harm*.
       obesset: imperfect subjunctive in an understood contrary-to-fact condition: *if the lion were*
       alive. . . .
     horrēns, horrentis, *bristling*.
     Arcadius, -a, -um, *Arcadian* (Arcadia was a mountainous region of the Greek Peloponnesus).
     sūs, suis, m./f., *boar*.
       Arcadius sūs: Hercules' fourth labor was to bring back the fierce boar from Mt. Erymanthus
       in Arcadia. The monosyllable **sūs** closing the line, creating a sing-song pattern with the **-us**
       ending of **Arcadius**, deflates the heroic tone of the passage.

26 **dēnique**, adv., *again, furthermore*.

    taurus, -ī, m., *bull*.

       Crētae taurus: Hercules' seventh labor was to bring the untameable bull back to Greece. Crete, particularly in the Minoan period, was associated with the image of a bull.

    Lernaeus, -a, -um, *of Lerna* (a marsh in the Argolid).

    pestis, pestis, f., *bane, curse, ruin, pest*.

27 **hydra, -ae**, f., *hydra* (a monster that Hercules had to kill as his second labor. It produced venomous breath from its many snake-heads. Each time Hercules cut off one of the heads, it grew back. He solved this problem by cauterizing the stumps).

    venēnātus, -a, -um, *poisonous*.

    vāllō, -āre, -āvī, -ātus, *to surround with palisades, fortify, defend*.

    colubra, -ae, f., *snake*.

       venēnātīs . . . vallāta colubrīs: a striking image reminiscent of the palisade of a Roman military camp.

37 **Cētera dē genere hōc**: in the omitted lines Lucretius mentions four more of Hercules' traditional twelve labors. Many other labors were also associated with the hero.

       Cētera: modifying **portenta**, the subject, which is placed in the relative clause, probably to create alliteration.

    portentum, -ī, n., *monster*.

    perimō, perimere, perēmī, perēmptus, *to destroy*.

38 **victa forent**: = **victa essent**, pluperfect passive subjunctive in a mixed contrary-to-fact condition.

    tandem, here with **quid**, *now*.

    vīva: with conditional force, *if they were alive*.

    nocērent: imperfect subjunctive in contrary-to-fact conclusion, referring to a present possibility.

39 **Nīl, ut opīnor**: Lucretius answers his rhetorical question, just as he did in line 6. The monosyllable beginning the line accents his answer.

    satiās, satiātis, f., *satiety, surfeit*.

    fera, -ae, f., *wild beast*.

       ferārum: genitive with **scatit** (40).

40 **scatō, scatere** + gen., *to swarm/teem/abound* (with).

    trepidus, -a, -um, *fearful, perilous, restless, anxious*.

       trepidō terrōre: alliteration producing almost a trembling effect.

    repleō, replēre, replēvī, replētus, *to fill up, fill*.

41 **nemus, nemoris**, n., *grove, forest*.

    profundus, -a, -um, *deep, profound; vast, boundless*.

       per nemora . . . profundās: a particularly sonorous line.

42 **quae loca**: accusative plural neuter, object of **vītandī**.

    vītandī: genitive gerund with **potestās**.

    plērumque, adv., *generally*.

       vītandī . . . est nostra potestās: equivalent to **possumus vītare**, *we can avoid*.

43 **pūrgātum**: *cleansed, free* (from fear).

    quae: interrogative adjective with **proelia**.

    nōbīs: dative of agent with **est . . . īnsinuandum** (44).

44 **tumst**: contraction of **tum est**, with **est** separated from **īnsinuandum**.

    ingrātīs, adv., *unwillingly, against our will*.

    īnsinuō, -āre, -āvī, -ātus, *to enter in*.

       īnsinuandum: here the impersonal gerund with accusatives of the places entered (**proelia . . . perīcula**).

          quae proelia . . . īnsinuandum, freely translated, *what battles and dangers then must we enter against our will*.

26 Dēnique quid Crētae taurus Lernaeaque pestis
27 hydra venēnātīs posset vāllāta colubrīs?

. . .

37 Cētera dē genere hōc quae sunt portenta perēmpta,
38 sī nōn victa forent, quid tandem vīva nocērent?
39 Nīl, ut opīnor: ita ad satiātem terra ferārum
40 nunc etiam scatit et trepidō terrōre replēta est
41 per nemora ac montīs magnōs silvāsque profundās;
42 quae loca vītandī plērumque est nostra potestās.
43 At nisi pūrgātumst pectus, quae proelia nōbīs
44 atque perīcula tumst ingrātīs īnsinuandum?

ᵍ **Discussion Question**

1. To what terrifying beasts might Lucretius be referring in lines 39–41? Was the Italian country-side so wild?

45 **Quantae**: modifying **cūrae**, postponed until line 46, with which **ācrēs** also agrees.
    cuppēdinis: = **cupīdinis**.
    ācer, ācris, ācre, *keen, fierce, bitter.*
        scindunt . . . cuppēdinis ācrēs . . . cūrae: echoing the description of Tityos in the underworld, who represented the man enthralled by passion: **quem . . . aliā quāvīs scindunt cuppēdine curae** (3.993–94).

46 **sollicitum**: separated from its noun **hominem**, just as his bitter cares tear the man apart.
    perinde, adv., *similarly, likewise.*

47 **Quidve**: *or what about?*
    superbia, -ae, f., *pride, arrogance.*
    spurcitia, -ae, f., *filth, dirt* (of a moral not a literal nature).
        superbia spurcitia: the *a* of **superbia** is not lengthened by the following *sp*; this metrical license, though rare, was allowed when a short vowel preceded *sc, st*, etc.
    petulantia, -ae, f., *insolence, impudence.*
        superbia spurcitia ac petulantia: subjects of the verb **efficiunt** (48), interrupted by a second interrogative, **Quantās**.

48 **efficiō, efficere, effēcī, effectus**, *to bring about, accomplish.*
    clādēs, clādis, f., *calamity, disaster, ruin.*
    lūxus, -ūs, m., *luxury, excess, extravagance.*
    dēsidia, -ae, f., *idleness, inactivity.*
        dēsidiae: plural to convey continual acts that create the habit of idleness; translate *sloth.*

49 **Haec**: accusative plural neuter, referring to all the fears and flaws catalogued above.
    quī: the relative precedes the antecedent **hunc hominem** (51).
    subigō, subigere, subēgī, subāctus, *to suppress, subdue.*
        subēgerit: perfect subjunctive in a relative clause of characteristic; similarly **expulerit** (50). Interestingly, Lucretius begins the sentence with the subjunctive indicating a man of such a sort or character but then concludes the sentence triumphantly in the indicative of factual statement by giving us *this man*, i.e., Epicurus.

50 **expulerit**: from **expellō, expellere**.
    dictīs, nōn armīs: an important distinction. Unlike the hero Hercules, Epicurus succeeded in conquering our fears without violence.
    decēbit: the subject of the impersonal verb is the accusative and infinitive construction, **hunc hominem . . . dignārier** (51).

51 **hominem**: unnecessary for meaning, but contrasting with **dīvum**; though a mere mortal, he should be considered a god.
    numerō: perhaps *in the place of* (the false gods of superstition, such as Ceres, Bacchus and Hercules).
    dīvum: = **divōrum**.
    dignor, -ārī, -ātus sum + infin., *to consider/count worthy* (to).
        dignārier: alternate form of the passive infinitive, *to be considered/deemed worthy.*

45   Quantae tum scindunt hominem cuppēdinis ācrēs

46   sollicitum cūrae quantīque perinde timōrēs?

47   Quidve superbia spurcitia ac petulantia? Quantās

48   efficiunt clādēs? Quid lūxus dēsidiaeque?

49   Haec igitur quī cūncta subēgerit ex animōque

50   expulerit dictīs, nōn armīs, nōnne decēbit

51   hunc hominem numerō dīvum dignārier esse?

⚄ Discussion Question

1.   If you were compiling a list of vices, would it be the same as Lucretius' list? What characterizes his list? (47–48)

Meditate therefore on these things and things akin to them night and day by yourself, and with a companion like to yourself, and never shall you be disturbed waking or asleep, but you shall live like a god among men. For a man who lives among immortal blessings is not like to a mortal being.
Epicurus, *Epistle to Menoeceus* 135 (tr. Bailey)

64   **Quod superest**: the formulaic phrase first found in 1.50, *For what remains, Next.*

       hūc: i.e., to this point in his argumentation.

         nunc hūc: a singularly ugly combination of sounds in one of Lucretius' more prosaic lines.

       dētulit: supply **mē**, *has brought me.*

       ōrdō, ōrdinis, m., *order.*

         ratiōnis . . . ōrdō: *the order of my plan.*

65   **mihi**: dative of agent with **reddunda sit** (66).

       mortālī: ablative with **corpore**, dependent on **cōnsistere**.

       cōnsistere: here, *to be composed* (of), *to consist* (of) + abl.; infinitive in indirect statement governed by **reddunda sit** (66).

       mundus, -ī, m., *world, earth.*

66   **nātīvus, -a, -um**, *having a birth/origin, created.*

         nātīvum: modifying **mundum** (65); predicative adjective with **esse** in indirect statement.

            mortālī cōnsistere corpore . . . nātīvum . . . esse: the earth, as a created object, had a birth and will have a death.

       simul: going closely with **nātīvum**, *as well, also.*

       reddunda: = **reddenda**.

         ratiō reddunda sit: idiom, *an explanation must be given.* The phrase governs the indirect statements in lines 65–66 and a series of five indirect questions (67–75).

67   **quibus**: interrogative, introducing an indirect question; ablative of means.

68   **fundō, -āre, -āvī, -ātus**, *to base, found, establish.*

       fundārit: syncopated form of the perfect subjunctive = **fundāverit**.

       sīdus, sīderis, n., *star; constellation.*

       terram caelum . . . sōlem: effective asyndeton indicating the immense scope of creation.

69   **globus, -ī**, m., *sphere.*

       quae: feminine with **animantēs**; feminine in Lucretius when referring to non-human animals, perhaps by analogy with **fera, -ae**, f.

       tellūs, tellūris, f., *earth.*

       tellūre: ablative of source, governed by *ex* of **exstiterint** (70).

70   **exsistō, exsistere, exstitī**, *to come into being, emerge, arise.*

         exstiterint: another perfect subjunctive in indirect question, governed by **ratiō reddunda sit** (66).

       quae: supply **animantēs**.

       sint . . . nātae: separation of verb **nāscor, nāscī, nātus sum** in interlocking word order.

         quae nūllō sint tempore nātae: mythical creatures such as centaurs, chimaeras, etc. (see 5.878–924), which could never exist because of the limits of atomic combination.

71   **quōve**: here the enclitic **-ve** has lost the alternative sense *or* and is equivalent to **-que**.

       loquēla, -ae, f., *speech.*

         variante loquēlā: ablative with **vēscī** (72).

72   **inter sē**: pointing out that language is social in nature; also, language was developed cooperatively by humans, not imposed upon them from outside, as Lucretius will discuss at 5.1028–90.

       vēscor, vēscī + abl., here, *to use.*

       per nōmina rērum: by giving names to things.

42. Summary of Book 5: Creation

Lucretius summarizes the topic of the fifth book—the creation of the earth and its inhabitants, including man.

64	Quod superest, nunc hūc ratiōnis dētulit ōrdō,
65	ut mihi mortālī cōnsistere corpore mundum
66	nātīvumque simul ratiō reddunda sit esse;
67	et quibus ille modīs congressus māteriāī
68	fundārit terram caelum mare sīdera sōlem
69	lūnāīque globum; tum quae tellūre animantēs
70	exstiterint, et quae nūllō sint tempore nātae;
71	quōve modō genus hūmānum variante loquēlā
72	coeperit inter sē vēscī per nōmina rērum;

∞ **Discussion Questions**

1. Do you think that Lucretius' belief in the mortality of the earth surprised his contemporary readers? What views existed about the stability of the earth?

2. Which of the four Empedoclean elements does Lucretius emphasize in lines 68–69? Why?

3. Who / what is responsible for the creation of living things? (69–70)

73 **dīvum**: = **dīvōrum**.

    ille . . . dīvum metus: it is Lucretius' stated goal to free men from this irrational fear.

  īnsinuō, -āre, -āvī, -ātus, *to enter by sinuous means, to work one's way into.*

    īnsinuārit: syncopated perfect subjunctive = **īnsinuāverit**; the verb gives the sense that the fear of the gods *wormed its way into* men's hearts.

74 **terrārum**: with **orbī**, *the earth.*

  quī: the antecedent is **metus** (73).

  sāncta: predicative, accusative plural neuter, modifying the series of nouns in line 75.

  tueor, tuērī, tuitus sum, here, *to keep.*

    sāncta tuētur: *keeps (them) holy, hallowed.*

75 **fānum, -ī**, n., *shrine, temple.*

  lacus, -ūs, m., *lake;* some lakes were considered sacred, such as Lake Nemi in Aricia, sacred to Diana, or Lake Henna in Sicily, sacred to Ceres.

  lūcus, -ī, m., *sacred grove.*

    fāna lacūs lūcos ārās: the rapid effect of the asyndeton perhaps lends a contemptuous and diminishing effect, giving the impression that these monuments are not really worth noticing closely.

76 **Praetereā**: Lucretius has concluded the series of indirect questions governed by **ratiō reddunda sit** (66), but then continues his catalogue of topics with yet another indirect question governed by **expediam** (77).

  cursus, -ūs, m., here, *course, motion.*

  meātus, -ūs, m., *course, path.*

    cursūs . . . meātūs: both accusative plural.

      sōlis cursūs lūnaeque meātūs: the scientific understanding of celestial movements is important, because their misunderstanding has led directly to fear of the gods.

77 **expediō, expedīre, expedīvī** or **expediī, expedītus**, *to explain.*

  flectō flectere, flexī, flexus, *to guide, steer, direct.*

  gubernō, -āre, -āvī, -ātus, *to pilot, direct, control, govern.*

    nātūra gubernāns: with **flectēns** creating a metaphorical image of nature as a charioteer; a very important phrase, since here Lucretius explicitly reverses the imagery of the proem to Book 1 (**quoniam rērum nātūram sōla gubernās**, 1.21) in which Venus was apparently dominant. Of course, he began to show his reader that Venus merely represented the creative aspect of nature as soon as Book 1, lines 56–57: **unde omnīs nātūra creet rēs auctet alatque / quōve eadem rūrsum nātūra perēmpta resolvat**.

73 et quibus ille modīs dīvum metus īnsinuārit
74 pectora, terrārum quī in orbī sāncta tuētur
75 fāna lacūs lūcōs ārās simulācraque dīvum.
76 Praetereā sōlis cursūs lūnaeque meātūs
77 expediam quā vī flectat nātūra gubernāns.

ᘓ Discussion Questions

1. What two attributes does Lucretius consider particularly to characterize humanity? (71–75)

2. What is the force of **nātūra gubernāns** (77) in the context of the preceding lines 73–76?

195   **Quod**: here, *But.*

ignōrem: idiomatic use of the present subjunctive rather than the imperfect subjunctive for contrary-to-fact, *if I were ignorant of.*

Quod sī . . . quae sint: the slow spondees of the line stress Lucretius' point.

196   **hōc**: summarizing lines 198–99.

ratiōnibus: here, *workings, behavior.*

   caelī ratiōnibus: specifically, climate and weather; see lines 204–05.

ausim: an archaic form of **audeō, audēre, ausus sum**, present subjunctive, analogous to **sim** of **esse**; *I would dare.*

197   **reddere**: supply **ratiōnem** in the idiom, *to give an explanation, explain, prove.*

multīs: the displacement of the modifier from **rēbus** emphasizes the number of possible examples.

198   **nēquāquam**, adv., *by no means, not at all.*

nōbīs: *for us humans.*

dīvīnitus, adv., *by divine agency/power; divinely.*

esse parātam: indirect statement governed by the infinitives **cōnfirmāre** and **reddere** (197).

199   **nātūram rērum**: effective enjambement.

tantā . . . culpā: ablative with **praedita**.

stat: here, *remains*; supply **nātūra rērum** as subject, with which **praedita** agrees.

praeditus, -a, -um + abl., *possessing, beset* (with).

culpā: here, *imperfection.*

   tantā stat praedita culpā: the succinct phrasing emphasizes the damning indictment. Lucretius will support his claim with three different proofs introduced by **prīncipiō** (200), **praetereā** (218), and **tum porrō** (222).

200   **Prīncipiō**: here adverbial, *First.*

quantum: substantive, *as much as*, i.e., *all that.*

impetus: here, *expanse, sweep.*

201   **avidam partem**: *the greedy part*, i.e., *the majority.*

silvae ferārum: the possessive implies that the forests, belonging to the wild beasts, are no place for men.

202   **possideō, possidēre, possēdī, possessus**, *to hold, occupy, control.*

   possēdēre: alternate third plural perfect = **possēdērunt**.

tenent: asyndeton with **possēdēre**; also taking **avidam partem** (203) as its object.

rūpēs, rūpis, f., *steep rocky cliff, crag.*

palūs, palūdis, f., *swamp, marsh, bog.*

203   **lātē**, adv., *widely.*

distineō, distinēre, distinuī, distentus, *to hold/keep apart, separate.*

204   **Inde**: anaphora with line 201.

duās . . . partīs: i.e., *two-thirds* (of the earth).

porrō, adv., *moreover.*

prope: adverb qualifying **duās**, *nearly.*

   porrō prope partīs: alliteration.

fervidus, -a, -um, *burning, searing.*

ārdor, ārdōris, m., *heat.*

205   **assiduus, -a, -um**, *incessant, constant, continual.*

gelum, -ī, n., *frost, cold.*

cāsus, -ūs, m., *fall.*

   assiduusque gelī cāsus: Lucretius believed that frost fell from the sky like snow.

mortālibus: dative of separation.

   Inde duās . . . mortālibus aufert: the Epicureans believed that there were three zones in the sky, which created, respectively, the arctic, temperate, and equatorial zones on earth. Only the temperate climate was hospitable to man.

43. Antiteleology: Argument against a Divine Creation of the Earth

The proof that the gods did not create the earth for men is that it is so full of defects, which Lucretius catalogues in detail. These flaws often make the earth inhospitable to us. On the other hand, nature seems to provide freely for other animals.

195   Quod sī iam rērum ignōrem prīmōrdia quae sint,
196   hōc tamen ex ipsīs caelī ratiōnibus ausim
197   cōnfirmāre aliīsque ex rēbus reddere multīs,
198   nēquāquam nōbīs dīvīnitus esse parātam
199   nātūram rērum: tantā stat praedita culpā.
200   Prīncipiō quantum caelī tegit impetus ingēns,
201   inde avidam partem montēs silvaeque ferārum
202   possēdēre, tenent rūpēs vāstaeque palūdēs
203   et mare quod lātē terrārum distinet ōrās.
204   Inde duās porrō prope partīs fervidus ārdor
205   assiduusque gelī cāsus mortālibus aufert.

CS Discussion Questions

1.   How does Lucretius use juxtaposition in line 198?

2.   Is Lucretius accurate in his assessment that the arctic and equatorial regions are uninhabitable? Or is he exaggerating?

The teleological view as expressed by the ever-optimistic Dr. Pangloss:
   Things cannot be other than they are . . . . Everything is made for the best purpose. Our noses were made to carry spectacles, so we have spectacles. Legs were clearly intended for breeches, and we wear them.
       Voltaire, *Candide* (1759), Ch. 1

"Life obeys the laws of physics . . . the laws of physics conform themselves to life." [Greenstein] approaches the anthropic principle with great humility. And rightly so, for—as he points out—most scientists feel profoundly uncomfortable with this concept, even ashamed to talk about it. Does the anthropic principle really mean that the whole universe has been designed solely so that we human beings can exist? Greenstein soothes these misgivings by pointing out the difference between the anthropic principle and anthropocentrism, which has been opposed by modern science ever since the Copernican revolution.
       Jeffrey A. Hoffman, review of George Greenstein, *The Symbiotic Universe, Amherst Magazine* (Fall 1988), 28–29.

206 **Quod superest**: here the phrase is not formulaic: *What is left, What remains.*

    arvum, -ī, n., *plowed field;* here, *arable land.*

        arvī: partitive genitive with **Quod**.

            Quod superest arvī: what is left within the temperate zone and is not occupied by forests, sea, cliffs, or swamps.

    vī: emphatic monosyllable as line-ending; similarly see **tuā vī** (1.13), referring to the power of Venus.

207 **sentis, sentis**, m., *briar, bramble.*

    obdūcō, obdūcere, obdūxī, obductus, *to cover, obstruct.*

    nī: = **nisi**.

    vīs hūmāna: the **vīs** of man is in direct opposition to the **vīs** of nature (206). Human power is obviously the weaker. The heavily spondaic line emphasizes the sense of a struggle.

208 **vītāī causā**: as usual in the construction, **causā** follows the noun it governs; the phrase makes clear that this is a life and death struggle.

    validus, -a, -um, *strong, powerful.*

    cōnsuēscō, cōnsuēscere, cōnsuēvī, cōnsuētus, *to be accustomed/used* (to).

        cōnsuēta: modifying **vīs hūmāna** (207), the subject; the *u* is consonantal, and so does not scan.

    bidēns, bidentis, m., *hoe* (with two teeth for breaking up clods of soil).

        validō . . . bidentī: dative or ablative with **ingemere** (209).

209 **ingemō, ingemere** + dat. or abl., *to groan over.*

    premō, premere, pressī, pressus, *to press.*

    proscindō, proscindere, proscidī, proscissus, *to cut the surface of, to break up.*

    arātrum, -ī, n., *plow.*

210 **fēcundus, -a, -um**, *fertile, rich.*

    vertentēs: nominative plural masculine modifying **nōs** understood.

    vōmer, vōmeris, m., *plowshare.*

    glēba, -ae, f., *lump of earth, clod.*

        fēcundās . . . glēbās: the adjective seems contradictory in the context of great effort; lines 210–11 are repeated almost verbatim from 1.211–12, which may account for the incongruity of **fēcundās**.

211 **solum, -ī**, n., *soil* (note that the short *o* differentiates this from **sōl**, *sun*, and **sōlus, -a, -um**, *only*).

    subigō, subigere, subēgī, subāctus, here, *to work, dig.*

    ciō, cīre, cīvī, citus, *to move, stir, rouse.*

        cīmus: as direct object understand a word for crops.

    ortus, -ūs, m., *birth;* here poetic plural.

212 **sponte**: ablative, *will.*

        sponte suā: a formulaic phrase indicating independent action (cf. 2.1059, 1092, and 1158); here, *on their own* (without our help).

    nequeō, nequīre, nequīvī, *to be unable* (to).

        nequeant: subjunctive in a mixed condition, *they would not be able;* the subject is *crops* understood.

    liquidus, -a, -um, *clear, bright.*

    exsistō, exsistere, exstitī, *to emerge, arise.*

    aura, -ae, f., *breeze.*

213 **tamen**: i.e., despite our labor.

    quaesīta: nominative plural neuter; substantive use of the participle, *things sought/obtained*, i.e., *crops.*

214 **frondeō, frondēre**, *to be in leaf, be green.*

    flōreō, -ēre, -uī, *to flourish.*

        per terrās frondent atque omnia flōrent: a picture of promising fertility precedes and contrasts with the destruction that is detailed below.

206   Quod superest arvī, tamen id nātūra suā vī
207   sentibus obdūcat, nī vīs hūmāna resistat
208   vītāī causā validō cōnsuēta bidentī
209   ingemere et terram pressīs proscindere arātrīs.
210   Sī nōn fēcundās vertentēs vōmere glēbās
211   terrāīque solum subigentēs cīmus ad ortūs,
212   sponte suā nequeant liquidās exsistere in aurās;
213   et tamen interdum magnō quaesīta labōre
214   cum iam per terrās frondent atque omnia flōrent,

❧ Discussion Questions

1.   In lines 206–07 nature displays a type of fertility, but is her abundance always beneficial to man?

2.   In scientific terms, what does Lucretius think the farmer is accomplishing when he plows the soil? Why is this labor beneficial? (210–12)

3.   What hazards does the farmer face? (215–17) Are his labors always rewarded?

You perceive that men dwell on but few and scanty portions of the earth, and that amid these spots, as it were, vast solitudes are interposed.... You observe that the same earth is encircled and encompassed as it were by certain zones, of which the two that are most distant from one another ... are rigid as you see with frost, while the middle and largest zone is burned up with the heat of the sun. Two of these [zones] are habitable.... [The one] lying toward the north, which you inhabit, observe what a small portion of it falls to your share.
      Cicero, *Somnium Scipionis* 19–20 (tr. Edmonds & Hadas)

I have seen seeds, though picked long and tested with much pains, yet degenerate, if human toil [**nī vīs hūmāna**], year after year, culled not the largest by hand. Thus by law of fate all things speed toward the worst, and slipping away fall back.
      Vergil, *Georgics* 1.197–200 (tr. Fairclough)

215   **nimius, -a, -um**, *excessive.*

     torreō, torrēre, torruī, tostus, *to scorch, burn.*

        torret: understand **quaesīta** (213), now accusative plural neuter, as the direct object of **torret**, **perimunt** (216), and **vexant** (217).

     fervor, fervōris, m., *fire, blaze, heat.*

     aetherius, -a, -um, *heavenly, ethereal, in the sky.*

     sōl: monosyllabic line-ending placing the blame squarely on the sun.

216   **aut**: emphatic anaphora, pointing to the multiple sources of potential disaster.

     perimō, perimere, perēmī, perēmptus, *to destroy.*

     gelidus, -a, -um, *cold, icy.*

     pruīna, -ae, f., *frost.*

217   **flābrum, -ī**, n., *gust, blast.*

     turbō, turbinis, m., *whirl, whirlwind, tornado.*

        ventōrum violentō . . . vexant: wonderfully onomatopoeic alliteration.

218   **horrifer, horrifera, horriferum**, *frightening, dreadful.*

        genus horriferum: accusative with genitive **ferārum**.

219   **īnfestus, -a, -um** + dat., *hostile* (to).

        īnfestum: modifying **genus** (218).

     terrāque marīque: ablatives of place; the all-encompassing phrase indicates that no place is safe.

220   **cūr alit atque auget?**: Lucretius makes his point in language that echoes the first proem: **nātūra creet rēs auctet alatque** (1.56).

     tempora: here, *seasons.*

221   **apportō, -āre, -āvī, -ātus**, *to bring.*

     quārē, *adv.*, here, *why.*

     immātūrus, -a, -um, *premature, untimely.*

     vagor, -ārī, -ātus sum, *to wander, roam, stalk about.*

        apportant . . . vagātur: the spondaic line suggests the heaviness of death.

222   **Tum porrō**: Lucretius turns from death as a source of sorrow to birth, which is usually associated with happiness but here produces wails.

     porrō, *adv.*, *moreover.*

     puer: here, *baby.*

     ut: introducing a most unusual simile.

     prōiciō, prōicere, prōiēcī, prōiectus, *to cast up on shore.*

223   **nāvita, -ae**, m., *sailor.* The enjambement adds to the surprising comparison.

     nūdus, -a, -um, *naked.*

     īnfāns, īnfantis, *unspeaking, speechless.*

     indigus, -a, -um + abl., *needing.*

     nāvita, nūdus . . . īnfāns, indigus: the alliterative pairs emphasize the meaning and create a tone of pathos.

224   **cum prīmum**: *as soon as.*

     in lūminis ōrās: repeating the formulaic phrase, borrowed from Ennius, first found in 1.22 in the description of creation; here the phrase nicely continues the marine imagery of the phrase **prōiectus nāvita**.

225   **nīxus, -ūs**, m., *birth pain, labor pain.*

     nīxibus: the initial position emphasizes the difficulty of childbirth.

     alvus, -ī, f., *womb.*

     profundō, profundere, profūdī, profūsus, *to bring forth, cast out.*

        profūdit: supply **eum**, i.e., the **puer** of line 222, as direct object.

215   aut nimiīs torret fervōribus aetherius sōl
216   aut subitī perimunt imbrēs gelidaeque pruīnae,
217   flābraque ventōrum violentō turbine vexant.
218   Praetereā genus horriferum nātūra ferārum
219   hūmānae gentī īnfestum terrāque marīque
220   cūr alit atque auget? Cūr annī tempora morbōs
221   apportant? Quārē mors immātūra vagātur?
222   Tum porrō puer, ut saevīs prōiectus ab undīs
223   nāvita, nūdus humī iacet, īnfāns, indigus omnī
224   vītālī auxiliō, cum prīmum in lūminis ōrās
225   nīxibus ex alvō mātris nātūra profūdit,
226   vāgītūque locum lūgubrī complet, ut aequumst

ℭ Discussion Questions

1.   What supposition is implicit in the framing of the questions in lines 218–21?

2.   The image of a shipwrecked sailor finally cast upon a shore usually brings a sense of relief and
      rescue. Is that true here? (222–23)

3.   What sound devices does Lucretius use in line 223?

Often, as the farmer was bringing the reaper into his yellow fields and was now stripping the brittle-stalked barley, my own eyes have seen all the winds clash in battle, tearing up the heavy crop far and wide from its deepest roots and tossing it on high; then with its black whirlwind the storm would sweep off the light stalk and flying stubble. Often, too, there appears in the sky a mighty column of waters, and clouds mustered from on high roll up a murky tempest of black showers: down falls the lofty heaven, and with its deluge of rain washes away the gladsome crops and the labors of men.
    Vergil, *Georgics* 1.316–26 (tr. Fairclough)

---

226   **vāgītus, -ūs**, m., *wail, howl.*
       lūgubris, -is, -e, *mournful, plaintive.*
           vāgītūque locum lūgubrī: the mournful effect of the onomatopoeic **vāgītū** is enhanced by
               the assonance, particularly of *u*, and the spondaic meter in this and the following line.
       complet: the subject is again **puer**.
       aequus, -a, -um, here, *fair, reasonable, right.*
           ut aequumst: commenting on the infant's reaction, *as is reasonable.*

227   **cui**: i.e., **eī cui**; the demonstrative antecedent has been omitted; introducing a relative clause of characteristic expressing cause, *since for him.*

     tantum: substantive, *so much*; direct object of **trānsīre**; governing the partitive genitive **malōrum**; Lucretius used the same phrase in his telling indictment of religion: **tantum rēligiō potuit suādēre malōrum** (1.101).

     restō, restāre, restitī, *to remain.*

       restet: subjunctive is probably causal, to explain **ut aequum** (226).

     trānsīre: infinitive subject of **restet**.

       cui tantum . . . malōrum: probably meant to describe the life of ordinary man rather than the Epicurean, who can achieve happiness.

228   **At**: introducing the contrasting situation of the animals; here Lucretius displays a particularly sanguine view of their existence. The relative ease of their existence is mirrored in the quicker movement of the dactyls.

     crēscō, crēscere, crēvī, crētūrus, *to grow.*

     pecus, pecudis, f., *herd, livestock, flock.*

     armenta, -ōrum, n. pl., *herds, cattle.*

       pecudēs armenta: asyndeton joining the two groups of tame animals, *flocks (and) herds.*

229   **crepitācillum, -ī**, n., *rattle* (for a baby), a wonderfully onomatopoeic word.

     opus est, idiom + abl., (it) *is essential, there is a need* (for).

     quisquam, quicquam, *anyone, anything.*

       cuiquam: *to any* (of the animals).

     adhibeō, adhibēre, adhibuī, adhibitus, *to apply.*

       adhibendast: the subject is **loquēla** (230).

230   **almus, -a, -um**, *kindly, gracious, nurturing.*

     nūtrīx, nūtrīcis, f., (child's) *nurse.*

     blandus, -a, -um, *charming, alluring, enticing.*

     īnfrāctus, -a, -um, *broken, disjointed.*

     loquēla, -ae, f., *speech.*

       blanda atque īnfrācta loquēla: i.e., baby-talk.

         nec crepitācillīs . . . loquēla: by implication the passage highlights the pathetic helplessness of a human infant.

231   **quaerunt**: supply **animālia** as subject.

     prō: here, *in response to, in accordance with.*

232   **dēnique**, adv., here, *last, finally.*

     opus est: repeating the idiom from line 229.

233   **quī**: archaic ablative form of the relative pronoun (used for both singular and plural) in ablative of means, *with which*; introducing a relative clause of purpose.

     sua: here as substantive, *their property, possessions* (of course, as animals they have none!).

     tūtor, tūtārī, tūtātus sum, *to protect, guard.*

     quandō: here, *since, because.*

     omnibus: supply **animālibus**.

       omnibus omnia: emphatically juxtaposed repetition of the same word in different cases.

     largē: here, *abundantly.*

234   **tellūs, tellūris**, f., *earth.*

     pariō, parere, peperī, partus, *to produce, create.*

     daedalus, -a, -um, *variegated, inventive.*

       nātūraque daedala rērum: echoing the fertility of the first proem: **daedala tellūs / summittit flōrēs** (1.7–8). The phrase ending the line seems almost an afterthought, but, with the singular verb, more likely shows that the earth is but one part of **nātūra creātrīx** (2.1117).

227   cui tantum in vītā restet trānsīre malōrum.
228   At variae crēscunt pecudēs armenta feraeque
229   nec crepitācillīs opus est nec cuiquam adhibendast
230   almae nūtrīcis blanda atque īnfrācta loquēla
231   nec variās quaerunt vestīs prō tempore caelī,
232   dēnique nōn armīs opus est, nōn moenibus altīs
233   quī sua tūtentur, quandō omnibus omnia largē
234   tellūs ipsa parit nātūraque daedala rērum.

ℭ Discussion Questions

1.   What is the effect of the positioning of **malōrum** in line 227?

2.   What are the things that Lucretius implies humans need in lines 229–33? Are all these things truly essential for human survival?

3.   Does Lucretius paint an overly-optimistic picture of the beneficence of nature towards living creatures other than humans? If so, why might he do this? (228–34)

235 **Prīncipiō**: adverbial, *First.*

terrāī corpus: a periphrasis for **terra**.

ūmor, ūmōris, m., *moisture, liquid, water.*

236 **aura, -ae**, f., *breeze.*

animae: here, *breath.*

aurārumque levēs animae: an elegant periphrasis for *air.*

terrāī . . . calidīque vapōrēs: the traditional four elements of the Empedoclean system: earth, water, air, and fire.

237 **summa, -ae**, f., *sum, whole; total.*

haec rērum . . . summa: i.e., our world; cf. the same phrase in 1.1028.

cōnsistere: here, *to exist.*

vidētur: here, *is seen.*

238 **omnia**: nominative plural neuter, modifying the four elements in lines 235–36.

nātīvus, -a, -um, *having a birth/origin, created.*

nātīvō ac mortālī corpore: ablative with **cōnstant**..

cōnstō, cōnstāre, cōnstitī + abl., *to be composed, consist* (of).

239 **dēbet**: emphatic position for the verb.

eōdem: supply **cōnstāre nātīvō et mortālī corpore**, i.e., to consist of a created and mortal body, be mortal.

omnis: ambiguous reference; probably nominative but possibly genitive.

omnis mundī nātūra: periphrasis.

mundus, -ī, m., *world, earth.*

240 **quippe**, adv., *surely, indeed.*

etenim, conj., *for.*

quōrum: neuter; supply **omnia**, *all things,* as the antecedent.

membrum, -ī, n., *limb.*

241 **figūra, -ae**, f., *shape.*

corpore nātīvō . . . mortālibus figūrīs: chiastic order; also the repetition of the phrase **corpore nātīvō** from line 238 is emphatic.

44. The Mortality of the World

Since the world is composed of mortal elements, it too must be mortal. Earth and sky were born and will also die.

235   Prīncipiō quoniam terrāī corpus et ūmor
236   aurārumque levēs animae calidīque vapōrēs,
237   ē quibus haec rērum cōnsistere summa vidētur,
238   omnia nātīvō ac mortālī corpore cōnstant,
239   dēbet eōdem omnis mundī nātūra putārī.
240   Quippe etenim quōrum partīs et membra vidēmus
241   corpore nātīvō ac mortālibus esse figūrīs,

ⅭꙄ **Discussion Question**

1.   How has Lucretius proved that the four elements (earth, water, air, and fire) are mortal? (238)

242   **fermē**, adv., *invariably, always*.

243   **nātīva**: it is curious that **nātīva** follows **mortālia** (242), where we would expect the reverse order; similarly see 5.65–66. The reversal is an instance of *hysteron proteron*, in which what occurs later is put before what occurs earlier.

       quāpropter, adv., *because of which, therefore*.

       maxima: accusative plural neuter, modifying **membra** (244).

244   **cum**: causal conjunction with the subjunctive; postponed and placed within its clause; translate before **maxima** (243).

       cōnsūmō, cōnsūmere, cōnsūmpsī, cōnsūmptus, *to destroy, consume*.

       cōnsūmpta: neuter plural to agree with nouns of different genders.

       regignō, regignere, *to bear or produce again*.

       regignī, *to be recreated*; the Latin word is apparently a Lucretian coinage.

245   **scīre**: introducing two indirect statements: **fuisse . . . tempus** and **clādemque futūram (esse)** (246).

       caelī . . . terraeque: genitives with **tempus** (246).

       item, adv., *likewise, similarly, in turn*.

246   **prīncipiālis, -is, -e**, *first, original*.

       prīncipiāle . . . tempus, *a time of beginning*.

       clādēs, clādis, f., *calamity, disaster, ruin*.

       futūram: supply **esse** for a future infinitive.

       clādem futūram: there will be a death balancing the birth.

Other views of the end of the world:

The philosophers of our [Stoic] school believe that in the end it will come about . . . that the whole universe will be consumed in flame: because when all the water is dried up, there will be no source from which air can be derived and nothing but fire will be left. From this divine fire a new universe will then be born and arise in splendor.

     Cicero, *De natura deorum* 2.118 (tr. McGregor)

A great part of the earth will be covered over by water when the fated day of the deluge comes.
. . . Will there be no single cause for such a catastrophe but rather all principles working together?

     Seneca, *Natural Questions* 3.27.1 (tr. Corcoran)

242	haec eadem fermē mortālia cernimus esse
243	et nātīva simul. Quāpropter maxima mundī
244	cum videam membra ac partīs cōnsūmpta regignī,
245	scīre licet caelī quoque item terraeque fuisse
246	prīncipiāle aliquod tempus clādemque futūram.

⋒ Discussion Questions

1. To what is Lucretius referring in the phrase **maxima mundī . . . membra ac partīs** (243–44)?

2. Lucretius writes of the idea of the coming destruction of the earth (246) and therefore, by implication, of humanity. Is this a distressing concept? Might anything happen following the destruction?

3. How would Lucretius interpret the scientific theory that 65 million years ago the impact of a large meteor perhaps caused mass extinctions, particularly of the dinosaurs? What word might he use to describe the impact?

4. Lucretius believed that the earth was born and is subject to destruction (246). What would he think of modern theories of cosmology, such as the Big Bang, in which matter and the universe blossomed from a singularity or from a vacuum? What would he think of the following two theories of the fate of the universe?
    1) that the universe, subject to gravitational attraction, will contract and implode in a Big Crunch, then burst out in another cycle of creation? In other words, will the universe oscillate cyclically?
    2) that the universe will continue its expansion and thus will cool to absolute zero and die. This is termed the Cosmic Whimper.

Worlds die,—for are they not born? Birth and death are unceasingly at work. Creation is never complete and perfect; it goes on for ever under incessant changes and modifications. . . . There is no more repose in the spaces of the sky than on earth, and the same law of strife and struggle governs the infinitude of the cosmic universe.
    Anatole France, *The Garden of Epicurus* (1894), Chapter 1

If entropy must constantly and continuously increase, then the universe is remorselessly running down, thus setting a limit (a long one, to be sure) on the existence of humanity.
    Isaac Asimov, *Asimov on Physics*, Chapter 13 "The Modern Demonology," 185

[Regarding time prior to the Big Bang]: To these scientists, the universe is a never-ending cycle of expansion and contraction, so the question of what was there before the universe is meaningless—there never was a "before."
    James Trefil, "'Nothing' may turn out to be the key to the universe," *Smithsonian* (December 1981),
      148

432 **Hīc**: *Here,* i.e. in these circumstances—in the chaos of atoms mixed together in complete confusion.

    rota: here, *orb, sphere.*

    cernō, cernere, crēvī, crētus, *to see, discern, perceive.*

        cernī: passive infinitive dependent on **poterat** (433).

    lūmen, lūminis, n., *light.*

        lūmine largō: alliterative ablative of description.

433 **altivolāns, altivolantis**, *flying high, soaring.*

    sīdus, sīderis, n., *star; constellation.*

    mundus, -ī, m., *world, earth.*

        magnī . . . mundī: encompassing the whole of our world, including its atmosphere and the celestial spheres, which were imagined to surround it.

434 **dēnique**: here, *indeed, even,* going closely with **terra**.

    āēr, āeris, m., *air.*

        nec mare . . . neque āēr: the four Empedoclean elements (cf. 235–36).

435 **nostrīs rēbus**: the things with which we are familiar.

    rēs: here, *substance, element.*

    vidērī: dependent on **poterat** (433); passive, *to be seen.*

436 **nova tempestās quaedam**: the initial confusion of atoms is compared to a storm; this phrase and those following are further subjects of **poterat . . . vidērī** (433–35).

    mōlēsque coorta: after endless random collisions and combinations, a mass of atoms suitable for the creation of earth arose.

437 **omnigenus, -a, -um**, *of every type.*

    prīncipium, -ī, n., *first-particle, first-beginning, atom.*

    discordia, -ae, f., *strife, discord.*

    quōrum: the relative has been slightly postponed.

438 **intervālla**: accusative plural, introducing a rapid series of accusative nouns in asyndeton.

    cōnexus, -ūs, m., *joining together, connection, union.*

    pondus, ponderis, n., *weight.*

    plāga, -ae, f., *blow* (the main causative force of Epicurean physics; cf. 2.223).

439 **concursus, -ūs**, m., *meeting* (by collision).

    mōtus, -ūs, m., *motion, movement.*

    turbō, -āre, -āvī, -ātus, *to confuse, disturb, confound.*

    proelium, -ī, n., *fight, battle.*

        proelia miscēns: the discordant atoms (**discordia quōrum**, 437) were metaphorically warring against one another.

440 **figūra, -ae**, f., *shape, size.*

441 **quod**: *because;* the conjunction linking to line 439 has been postponed to follow the **propter** phrase.

    omnia: supply **prīncipia**.

    sīc: in the warring confusion of atoms.

442 **mōtūs**: accusative plural.

    sēsē: intensive form of **sē**.

    convenientīs: here, *appropriate, suitable* (for union).

        quod nōn . . . dare convenientīs: certain atomic combinations, being inherently unstable, could not survive.

443 **diffugiō, diffugere, diffūgī**, *to scatter, disperse, separate.*

    Diffugere: i.e., to leave the undifferentiated mass of atoms. Note the emphatic position.

    inde locī, idiom, *then, next* (**locī** acts as a partitive genitive).

    partēs: referring to what *will* become the four elements.

    coepēre: alternate third person plural = **coepērunt**.

    pār, paris, *equal, matching, like.*

444 **rēs**: *substances, elements.*

    disclūdō, disclūdere, disclūsī, disclūsus, *to separate into parts.*

45. The Creation of the Earth

Out of a chaos of atoms, eventually like atoms attracted each other and the parts of the world—earth, sky, sea, and fire—became distinct from one another.

432   Hīc neque tum sōlis rota cernī lūmine largō
433   altivolāns poterat nec magnī sīdera mundī
434   nec mare nec caelum nec dēnique terra neque āer
435   nec similis nostrīs rēbus rēs ūlla vidērī,
436   sed nova tempestās quaedam mōlēsque coorta
437   omnigenīs dē prīncipiīs, discordia quōrum
438   intervālla viās cōnexūs pondera plāgās
439   concursūs mōtūs turbābat proelia miscēns,
440   propter dissimilīs fōrmās variāsque figūrās
441   quod nōn omnia sīc poterant coniūncta manēre
442   nec mōtūs inter sēsē dare convenientīs.
443   Diffugere inde locī partēs coepēre parēsque
444   cum paribus iungī rēs et disclūdere mundum

C3 Discussion Questions

1.   What is the effect of the rapid asyndeton of lines 438–39?

2.   To Lucretius the universe is eternal and has always operated under the same physical laws. Does Lucretius then believe in an initial creative moment?

4.   Of what process does creation essentially consist? What is the creative force? Is there any creator?

Another view of creation:

For God desired that, so far as possible, all things should be good and nothing evil; wherefore, when He took over all that was visible, seeing that it was not in a state of rest but in a state of discordant and disorderly motion, He brought it into order out of disorder, deeming that the former state is in all ways better than the latter.
     Plato, *Timaeus* 30a (tr. Bury)

445   **membrum, -ī**, n., *limb.*

    membra: here referring to the four elements.

  dispōnō, dispōnere, disposuī, dispositus, *to order, arrange.*

    disclūdere . . . dīvidere . . . dispōnere: the anaphora of the prefix *dis* stresses the concept of separation. Note also the chiastic construction of line 445. In essence the line repeats the concepts already described by **disclūdere mundum**; such repetition is characteristic of the Lucretian didactic style.

446   **hōc est**: in case there could be any possible doubt about his meaning, Lucretius provides a more specific picture in this and the following lines.

  altum . . . caelum: accusative.

  sēcernō, sēcernere, sēcrēvī, sēcrētus, *to separate, divide.*

    sēcernere: the grammar of the passage 446–48 is somewhat uncertain; the infinitive is dependent on **coepēre** (443) with the subject **parēs . . . rēs** (443–44).

447   **sōrsum**, adv., *apart.*

    sōrsum mare: dependent on **sēcernere**.

  utī: = **ut**.

  ūmor, ūmōris, m., *moisture, liquid.*

  sēcrētō: i.e., separated from the other three elements.

  patēret: the subject is **mare**.

448   **sōrsus**: = **sōrsum**; note the anaphora with line 447.

  item, adv., *likewise, similarly, in turn.*

  sēcrētī: *set apart* (from the rest), i.e., set in their own proper places; in the same metrical position as **sēcrētō** in line 447.

    pūrī sēcrētīque: grammatically problematic in an apparent anacoluthon (breakdown in grammatical construction); take as nominative plural with **ignēs**.

  aether, aetheris, m., *ether, sky.*

  ignēs: the editor takes this as nominative plural, attracted into the nominative by the proceeding **patēret** clause, which interrupted the grammatical flow of infinitives.

    aetheris ignēs: referring to the sun, moon, and stars.

445   membraque dīvidere et magnās dispōnere partīs,
446   hōc est, ā terrīs altum sēcernere caelum,
447   et sōrsum mare, utī sēcrētō ūmōre patēret,
448   sōrsus·item pūrī sēcrētīque aetheris ignēs.

✑ Discussion Question

1.   How does Lucretius' explanation of creation compare with the following Ovidian version?

Before the sea was, and the lands, and the sky that hangs over all, the face of Nature showed alike in her whole round, which state men have called chaos: a rough, unordered mass of things, nothing at all save lifeless bulk and warring seeds of ill-matched elements heaped in one. No sun as yet shone forth upon the world, nor did the waxing moon renew her slender horns; nor yet did the earth hang poised by her own weight in the circumambient air, nor had the ocean stretched her arms along the far reaches of the lands. And, though there was both land and sea and air, none could tread that land, or swim that sea; and the air was dark. No form of things remained the same; all objects were at odds, for within one body cold things strove with hot, and moist with dry, soft things with hard, things having weight with weightless things. God—or kindlier Nature—composed this strife; for he rent asunder land from sky, and sea from land, and separated the ethereal heavens from the dense atmosphere. When thus he had released these elements and freed them from the blind heap of things, he set them each in its own place and bound them fast in harmony.

    Ovid, *Metamorphoses* 1. 5–25 (tr. Miller)

[Orpheus] sang of that past age when earth and sky and sea were knit together in a single mold; how they were sundered after deadly strife; how the stars, the moon, and the travelling sun keep faithfully to their stations in the heavens; how mountains rose, and how, together with their Nymphs, the murmuring streams and all four-legged creatures came to be.

    Apollonius of Rhodes, *Argonautica* 1.496–502 (tr. Rieu)

925 **multō**: adverbial with **dūrius** (926), *by much, by far.*
    illud: *of that time,* i.e., the ancient race of man, in contrast with the modern.
    arvum, -ī, n., here, *land, country.*

926 **dūrus, -a, -um**, *hard, harsh.*
    dūrius: emphatic enjambement.
    tellūs, tellūris, f., *earth.*
    quod: introducing relative clause with causal force thus the subjunctive of **creāsset**, *since, because.*
    dūrius . . . dūra: emphatic repetition showing a similarity between the earth and her creation; note also the harsh alliteration of *d* and *t* reinforcing Lucretius' point.
    creāsset: syncopated pluperfect subjunctive = **creāvisset**.

927 **magis**: modifying **solidīs**, whose comparative form would not scan.
    maiōribus . . . ossibus: ablatives with **fundātum** (928).
    intus, adv., *within, inside.*

928 **fundō, -āre, -āvī, -ātus**, here + abl., *to base/build/construct* (on).
    fundātum: modifying **genus** (925).
    validus, -a, -um, *strong, powerful.*
    aptus, -a, -um, here + abl., *fitted/provided* (with).
    vīscera: here, *flesh.*
    nervus, -ī, m., *sinew, muscle.*

929 **frīgus, frīgoris**, n., *cold.*
    caperētur: here, *be affected by, be harmed*; subjunctive in a relative clause of result, i.e., *the human race was such as not to be affected. . . .*

930 **novitās, novitātis**, f., *newness, strangeness.*
    novitāte cibī: unaccustomed food that could cause indigestion. One wonders about their experience with mushrooms, which are often lethal to us.
    lābēs, lābis, f., *defect, ailment.*
    lābī: rare ablative form with *i* instead of *e*.

931 **volvō, volvere, volvī, volūtus**, *to roll.*
    volventia: transferred epithet; logically modifying **sōlis**; present participle of **volvō** used in middle or intransitive sense = *rolling.*
    lūstrum, -ī, n., *the period taken by a heavenly body to complete its rotation.*
    multaque . . . lūstra: accusative of duration of time; *through many rolling periods of the sun through the sky.*

932 **vulgivagus, -a, -um**, *widely-ranging, wandering*; another apparent Lucretian coinage.
    vulgivagō vītam: wonderful alliteration; the epithet **vulgivagō** is transferred to **mōre** from **ferārum**; by its placement it also affects **vītam**.
    tractō, -āre, -āvī, -ātus, here, *to drag out, prolong.*
    tractābant: supply **hominēs** as subject; the imperfect tense indicates the long duration of this way of life. Note that throughout this passage Lucretius continues to use the imperfect.
    fera, -ae, f., *wild beast.*

933 **rōbustus, -a, -um**, *sturdy, strong, robust.*
    moderātor, moderātōris, m., *one who directs, steers; steerer, guider.*
    arātrum, -ī, n., *plow.*
    rōbustus . . . curvī moderātor arātrī: interlocking word order.

934 **quisquam, quicquam**, here adjectival, *any.*
    quisquam: emphatic enjambement.
    scībat: contracted form of **sciēbat**; supply **quisquam** as the subject.
    ferrum, -ī, n., *iron* (of agricultural implements).
    mōlior, mōlīrī, mōlītus sum, here, *to work.*
    mōlīrier: archaic passive infinitive = **mōlīrī**.

46. The Life of Early Man

Early humans were larger and hardier than we are. Not knowing agriculture or fire, they ate what the earth provided. There were no communities, and each one had to fend for himself or herself.

925	At genus hūmānum multō fuit illud in arvīs
926	dūrius, ut decuit, tellūs quod dūra creāsset,
927	et maiōribus et solidīs magis ossibus intus
928	fundātum, validīs aptum per vīscera nervīs,
929	nec facile ex aestū nec frīgore quod caperētur
930	nec novitāte cibī nec lābī corporis ūllā.
931	Multaque per caelum sōlis volventia lūstra
932	vulgivagō vītam tractābant mōre ferārum.
933	Nec rōbustus erat curvī moderātor arātrī
934	quisquam, nec scībat ferrō mōlīrier arva.

CB Discussion Questions

1. How does Lucretius' belief that early humans were larger and hardier than modern humans compare to the current views of anthropology?

2. How did early people live? To what does Lucretius compare their existence? (931–32)

3. How does Lucretius' belief in the gradual development or softening of mankind compare to the views expressed in other ancient authors?

A different explanation for human hardiness: the story of Deucalion and Pyrrha's recreation of humanity after the great flood:

They go down, veil their heads, ungird their robes, and throw stones behind them just as the goddess had bidden. And the stones—who would believe it unless ancient tradition vouched for it?—began to lose their hardness and stiffness, to grow soft slowly, and softened to take on form. Then, when they had grown in size and become milder in their nature, a certain likeness to the human form, indeed, could be seen, still not very clear, but such as statues just begun out of marble have, not sharply defined, and very like roughly blocked-out images. That part of them, however, which was earthy and damp with slight moisture, was changed to flesh; but what was solid and incapable of bending became bone; that which was but now veins remained under the same name. And in a short time, through the operation of the divine will, the stones thrown by the man's hand took on the form of men, and women were made from the stones the woman threw. Hence comes the hardness of our race and our endurance of toil; and we give proof from what origin we are sprung.

Ovid, *Metamorphoses* 1.398–415 (tr. Miller)

937 **Quod**: accusative singular neuter, relative pronoun preceding its antecedent **id . . . dōnum** (938).

    creārat: syncopated pluperfect = **creāverat**.

938 **sponte**: ablative, *will*.

    sponte suā: the Lucretian formulaic phrase indicating independent activity; cf. 2.1059, 1092, 1158, 5.212. The example at 2.1158 is particularly relevant, since it describes the early fertility of the earth. Note also here the strong *s* alliteration with **satis**.

    plācō, -āre, -āvī, -ātus, *to appease, satisfy*.

939 **glandifer, glandifera, glandiferum**, *acorn-bearing*.

    inter: the preposition is postponed by anastrophe.

    cūrābant: again supply **hominēs** as subject; meaning *refresh* with food and rest (similarly at 2.31).

    quercus, -ūs, m., *oak*.

    glandiferās inter cūrābant corpora quercūs: a rather round-about way of saying that they ate acorns. Note the strong alliteration of *c* and *q*.

940 **plērumque**, adv., *generally, often*; note emphatic enjambement.

    quae: accusative plural neuter with antecedent **arbuta** (941), which has been drawn into the relative clause.

    hībernus, -a, -um, *of winter, wintry*.

    cernō, cernere, crēvī, crētus, *to see*.

941 **arbutum, -ī**, n., *wild-strawberry*.

    pūniceus, -a, -um, *brilliant red, scarlet, crimson*.

    mātūrus, -a, -um, *ripe*.

    arbuta pūniceō . . . mātūra colōre: interlocking order.

942 **plūrima**: agreeing with **arbuta** (941), which was attracted into the relative clause of 940–41.

    etiam maiōra: *and also larger*.

    plūrima . . . maiōra ferēbat: the passage seems to hint at a Golden Age view in which man's early life was blissful, since the earth then provided everything in great abundance. Lucretius' point, however, is that the young earth was itself stronger and capable of producing larger and more abundant fruits, but these were still **dūra**.

943 **Multaque**: accusative plural neuter with **pābula dūra** (944).

    praetereā, conj., *besides, too, moreover*.

    flōridus, -a, -um, *blooming, flourishing*.

    mundus, -ī, m., *world, earth*.

944 **pābulum, -ī**, n., *food*.

    pābula dūra: **dūra** as befits both a **dūra tellūs** (926) and a **genus hūmānum . . . dūrius** (925–26). Also the phrase is in stark contrast to Lucretius' usual formulaic phrase indicating richness, **pābula laeta** (cf. 1.14 and 257; 2.317, 364, and 1159).

    amplus, -a, -um + dat., *plenty/ample/sufficient* (for).

945 **sēdō, -āre, -āvī, -ātus**, *to allay, relieve*.

    sēdāre: poetic infinitive with **vocābant**.

    sitis, sitis, f., *thirst*.

    sitim: archaic accusative singular.

    fōns, fontis, m., *spring*.

    sēdāre sitim fluviī fontēsque: double alliterative pair; indeed the entire passage contains much alliteration, perhaps an indication that this is one of the passages that Lucretius composed most carefully.

946 **ut nunc**: introducing a comparison between the behavior of ancient man and that of wild animals, as was noted above in the phrase **vītam tractābant mōre ferārum** (932).

    dēcursus, -ūs, m., *descent, downward rush*.

937   Quod sōl atque imbrēs dederant, quod terra creārat

938   sponte suā, satis id plācābat pectora dōnum.

939   Glandiferās inter cūrābant corpora quercūs

940   plērumque; et quae nunc hībernō tempore cernis

941   arbuta pūniceō fierī mātūra colōre,

942   plūrima tum tellūs etiam maiōra ferēbat.

943   Multaque praetereā novitās tum flōrida mundī

944   pābula dūra tulit, miserīs mortālibus ampla.

945   At sēdāre sitim fluviī fontēsque vocābant,

946   ut nunc montibus ē magnīs dēcursus aquāī

∝ Discussion Questions

1.   What was early man's diet? (939–42)

2.   Compare Lucretius' depiction of early man's existence with the passage below from Hesiod.

In the beginning the immortals
    who have their homes on Olympos
created the golden generation of mortal people.
These lived in Kronos' time,
    when he was the king in heaven.
They lived as if they were gods,
    their hearts free from all sorrow,
by themselves, and without hard work or pain;
    no miserable
old age came their way; their hands, their feet,
    did not alter.
They took their pleasure in festivals,
    and lived without troubles.
When they died it was as if they fell asleep.
    All goods
were theirs. The fruitful grainland
    yielded its harvest to them
of its own accord; this was great and abundant,
    while they at their pleasure
quietly looked after their works,
    in the midst of good things.
        Hesiod, *Works and Days* 109–19 (tr. Lattimore)

947 **clārus**: here, *clear-sounding.*
    claru': suppression of the final *s* for metrical reasons.
    citō, -āre, -āvī, -ātus, *to summon, call.*
    lātē, adv., *widely, far and wide.*
    sitiō, sitīre, *to be thirsty.*
    saecla: = **saecula**, as always in Lucretius; here, *races, tribes.*
953 **necdum**, adv., *not yet.*
    rēs: accusative plural.
    scībant: contracted from of **sciēbant**; supply **hominēs** as subject.
    tractāre: here, *to treat.*
      rēs ignī . . . tractāre: i.e., in the most obvious sense to cook, but also to smelt metal.
954 **pellis, pellis**, f., *hide, skin.*
    et: explanatory, *that is.*
    spolium, -ī, n., *skin, hide stripped from an animal.*
    vestiō, -īre, -īvī, -ītus, *to clothe.*
955 **nemus, nemoris**, n., *grove, forest.*
    cavus, -a, -um, *hollow.*
      cavōs montīs: i.e., caves.
    colēbant: here, *they dwelled in, inhabited.*
956 **frutex, fruticis**, m., *shrub, bush.*
    inter: the preposition follows by anastrophe.
    condō, condere, condidī, conditus, here, *to hide.*
    squālidus, -a, -um, *rough, filthy, dirty, squalid.*
    membrum, -ī, n., *limb.*
957 **verber, verberis**, n., *blow, blast.*
    vītāre: dependent on **coāctī**.
      verbera ventōrum vītāre: onomatopoeic alliteration of *v*.
958 **bonum**: here a substantive, accusative.
    spectāre: here, *to pay regard to, consider.*
959 **ūllīs mōribus**: ablative with **ūtī**.
    lēx, lēgis, f., *law.*
      mōribus . . . lēgibus: unwritten customs and formally enacted laws.
960 **Quod**: supply **id** as antecedent; accusative singular neuter relative pronoun, governing the partitive genitive **praedae**.
    quisque, quaeque, quidque, *each, each one.*
    praeda, -ae, f., *booty, prey, prize.*
    ferēbat: supply **id** as direct object acting as antecedent of **quod**.
961 **sponte suā**: again the formulaic phrase of independence (cf. 938 above), which is further strengthened by the addition of **sibi**.
    doctus, -a, -um, *having learned, been trained.*
      doctus: the force of the adjective applies to the entire line, *having learned to thrive and live by his own will for himself.*

947   clāru' citat lātē sitientia saecla ferārum.

. . .

953   Necdum rēs ignī scībant tractāre neque ūtī

954   pellibus et spoliīs corpus vestīre ferārum,

955   sed nemora atque cavōs montīs silvāsque colēbant

956   et fruticēs inter condēbant squālida membra

957   verbera ventōrum vītāre imbrīsque coāctī.

958   Nec commūne bonum poterant spectāre neque ūllīs

959   mōribus inter sē scībant nec lēgibus ūtī.

960   Quod cuique obtulerat praedae fortūna, ferēbat

961   sponte suā sibi quisque valēre et vīvere doctus.

♋ Discussion Questions

1.   What is Lucretius' explanation for the reduced fertility of the earth? Compare his view with the accounts below from Hesiod and Vergil. (937–44)

2.   Could a group of early men be termed a society? (958–61) How did men interact with one another?

For the gods had hidden and keep hidden
  what could be men's livelihood.
It could have been that easily
  in one day you could work out
enough to keep you for a year,
  with no more working.
Soon you could have hung up your steering oar
  in the smoke of the fireplace,
and the work the oxen and patient mules do
  would be abolished,
but Zeus in the anger of his heart hid it away
because the devious-minded Prometheus had cheated him;
and therefore Zeus thought up dismal sorrows
  for mankind.
He hid fire; but Prometheus, the powerful son
  of Iapetos,
stole it again from Zeus of the counsels,
  to give it to mortals.
    Hesiod, *Works and Days* 42–51 (tr. Lattimore)

The great Father himself has willed that the path of husbandry should not be smooth, and he first made art awake the fields, sharpening men's wits by care, nor letting his realm slumber in heavy lethargy. Before Jove's day no tillers subdued the land. . . . Earth yielded all, of herself, more freely, when none begged for her gifts.
    Vergil, *Georgics* 1.121–25, 127–28 (tr. Fairclough)

966   **frētus, -a, -um** + abl., *relying on.*
     frētī: modifying **hominēs** understood.
  virtūs, virtūtis, f., *strength.*

967   **cōnsector, -ārī, -ātus sum**, *to seek, pursue, hunt down.*
     saecla ferārum: note the formulaic nature of the phrase, which occurred in the same position
         in line 947 (see also 2.995, 1076).

968   **missilis, -is, -e**, *that may be thrown/hurled.*
  saxum, -ī, n., *rock.*
     missilibus saxīs, *with rocks to hurl.*
  pondus, ponderis, n., *weight.*
  clāva, -ae, f., *club.*

969   **multaque**: modifying **animālia** understood.
     multaque vincēbant, vītābant pauca: a nice instance of chiasmus reinforced by alliteration
         of *v.*
  latebra, -ae, f., *hiding-place, lair.*

970   **saetiger, saetigera, saetigerum**, *covered with coarse hair, bristly.*
  pār, paris + dat., *equal to, like.*
  sūs, suis, m./f., *boar.*
     sūbus: dative plural of **sūs.**
  silvestria: here, *rough.*

971   **dabant terrae**: literally, *they gave to the ground,* i.e., they laid their bodies on the ground.
  captī: here, *overtaken by, surprised by;* with **nocturnō tempore.**

972   **circum**, here adverbial with **involventēs.**
  folium, -ī, n., *leaf.*
     foliīs ac frondibus: alliterative hendiadys, *leafy foliage.*
  involvō, involvere, involvī, involūtus, *to wrap up, cover.*
     involventēs: unusual line-ending with spondaic fifth foot.
       circum sē . . . involventēs, *wrapping themselves round.*

966   Et manuum mīrā frētī virtūte pedumque
967   cōnsectābantur silvestria saecla ferārum
968   missilibus saxīs et magnō pondere clāvae;
969   multaque vincēbant, vītābant pauca latebrīs;
970   saetigerīsque parēs sūbus silvestria membra
971   nūda dabant terrae nocturnō tempore captī,
972   circum sē foliīs ac frondibus involventēs.

❧ Discussion Question

1.   Compare Lucretius' description of early man's existence with Aeschylus' depiction as
      Prometheus relates it below.

For men at first had eyes but saw to no purpose; they had ears but did not hear. Like the shapes of dreams they dragged through their long lives and handled all things in bewilderment and confusion. They did not know of building houses with bricks to face the sun; they did not know how to work in wood. They lived like swarming ants in holes in the ground, in the sunless caves of the earth. For them there was no secure token by which to tell winter nor the flowering spring nor the summer with its crops; all their doings were indeed without intelligent calculation.

    Aeschylus, *Prometheus Bound* 447–57 (tr. Grene)

1011　**Inde**: here, *Next,* signaling a change in the human condition.
　　　pellis, pellis, f., *hide, skin.*
　　　parārunt: syncopated perfect = **parāvērunt**.
　　　　cāsās . . . pellīs ignemque: these inventions deliberately contrast with the description of
　　　　　primitive man's existence in lines 953–57.

1012　**coniūncta**: governing the dative **vīrō**.
　　　concēdō, concēdere, concessī, concessūrus + **in** + acc., *to yield/submit* (to).
　　　ūnum, here probably meaning *continuous, stable.*

1013　**cōnubium, -ī**, n., *marriage.* (A textual emendation where a line has probably been lost.)
　　　prōlēs, prōlis, f., *offspring.*
　　　vīdēre: alternate third plural perfect = **vīdērunt**; probably referring to fathers, who, within a
　　　　permanent family unit, could see that the children were their own.
　　　creātam: supply **esse** to form a perfect passive infinitive in an accusative and infinitive
　　　　construction with **vīdēre**.

1014　**mollēscō, mollēscere**, *to become soft, to soften.*
　　　　mollēscere: man begins to make the transition from a **dūrius genus** to modern man.

1015　**cūrāvit**: a verb of effort governing a substantive clause of result, *brought it about* (that).
　　　alsius, -a, -um, *chilly, cold.*
　　　　alsia corpora: nominative plural.
　　　frīgus, frīgoris, n., *cold.*

1016　**ita**: *so well* (as in their primitive state).
　　　tegmen, tegminis, n., *cover.*
　　　ferre: here, *to endure.*

1017　**imminuō, imminuere, imminuī, imminūtus**, *to diminish, lessen, weaken.*
　　　　Venus imminuit vīrīs: as at 4.1121 of lovers: **absūmunt vīrīs pereuntque labōre**.
　　　puerī: nominative plural as new subject.
　　　parentum: possessive genitive with **ingenium** (1018).

1018　**blanditia, -ae**, f., *flattery, charm, allure.*
　　　　blanditiīs: here, *winning/pleasing ways.*
　　　ingenium: here, *temperament, nature.*
　　　frēgēre: alternate perfect = **frēgērunt**, from **frangō**; *broke down*, i.e., *softened.*

1019　**Tunc**: emphatic form of **tum**, similar in formation to **nunc**.
　　　amīcitiēs, -ēī, f., *friendship.* (Normally first declension, only here in the fifth.)
　　　aveō, avēre, *to desire, wish.*
　　　　aventēs: governing the two infinitives in line 1020.

1020　**fīnimitī, -ōrum**, m. pl., *neighbors.*
　　　inter sē: take with **amīcitiem . . . iungere**.
　　　nec laedere nec violārī: a basic social contract—neither to harm nor be harmed.

From this Fundamental Law of Nature, by which men are commanded to endeavor Peace, is derived
this second Law; That a man be willing, when others are so too, as farre-forth, as for Peace, and
defence of himselfe he shall think it necessary, to lay down this right to all things, and be contented
with so much liberty against other men as he would allow other men against himself. For as long as
every man holdeth this Right, of doing anything he liketh; so long are all men in the condition of
Warre. But if other men will not lay down their Right, as well as he; then there is no reason for
anyone, to devest himselfe of his: For that were to expose himselfe to Prey, (which no man is bound
to) rather than to dispose himself to Peace.
　　Thomas Hobbes, *Leviathan* (1651), Part 1, Chapter 14.65

47. The Rise of Civilization

Humans gradually softened as they developed various skills by trial and error, discovered partnerships, and cared for children.

1011 Inde casās postquam ac pellīs ignemque parārunt,
1012 et mulier coniūncta virō concessit in ūnum
1013 cōnubium, prōlemque ex sē vīdēre creātam,
1014 tum genus hūmānum prīmum mollēscere coepit.
1015 Ignis enim cūrāvit ut alsia corpora frīgus
1016 nōn ita iam possent caelī sub tegmine ferre,
1017 et Venus imminuit vīrīs puerīque parentum
1018 blanditiīs facile ingenium frēgēre superbum.
1019 Tunc et amīcitiem coepērunt iungere aventēs
1020 fīnitimī inter sē nec laedere nec violārī,

ᘓ Discussion Questions

1. What were the first steps to civilization?

2. How and why did people begin to cooperate with one another?

The justice which arises from nature is a pledge of mutual advantage to restrain men from harming one another and save them from being harmed.
    Epicurus, *Principal Doctrines* 31 (tr. Bailey)

Justice . . . is a kind of compact not to harm or be harmed.
    Epicurus, *Principal Doctrines* 32 (tr. Bailey)

Glaucon expounds Thrasymachus' theory of an original social contract:
    By nature, they say, to commit injustice is good and to suffer it is an evil, but that the excess of evil in being wronged is greater than the excess of good in doing wrong. So that when men do wrong and are wronged by one another and taste of both, those who lack the power to avoid the one and take the other determine that it is for their profit to make a compact with one another neither to commit nor to suffer injustice; and that this is the beginning of legislation and covenants between men, and that they name the commandment of the law the lawful and the just, and that this is the genesis and essential nature of justice—a compromise between the best, which is to do wrong with impunity, and the worst, which is to be wronged and be impotent to get one's revenge.
    Plato, *Republic* 2.358e–359a (tr. Shorey)

1021   **puerōs**: here, *children*.

       commendō, -āre, -āvī, -ātus, *to commit or entrust for protection*.

         commendārunt: syncopated perfect = **commendāvērunt**; understand *to one another* as indirect object.

       saeclum: here, *kind, race*.

1022   **gestus, -ūs**, m., *gesture, sign*.

         vōcibus et gestū: ablatives of means.

       cum: the conjunction has been postponed to emphasize the people's means of communication.

       balbē, adv., *in broken words, inarticulately*. (Language developed gradually; see the next passage.)

       significārent: the subject is still **fīnitimī** (1020).

1023   **imbēcillus, -a, -um**, *weak, feeble*.

         imbēcillōrum: here substantive, genitive with **miserērier**.

       aequus, -a, -um, *fair, reasonable*.

       miserērier: archaic form of the passive infinitive = **miserērī**.

         miserērier omnīs: infinitive phrase as subject of **esse**, with **aequum** as a predicate adjective.

1021   et puerōs commendārunt muliēbreque saeclum,

1022   vōcibus et gestū cum balbē significārent

1023   imbēcillōrum esse aequum miserērier omnīs.

✺ Discussion Question

1.   How did people communicate at this early stage? How does this communication compare with your understanding of language development?

Now [the Epicureans] assert that the wise man is good, not because he is pleased with goodness and justice in and for themselves, but because the lives of good men are free from fear, worry, anxiety, and danger. Wicked men, on the other hand, always have a certain uneasiness at the bottom of their hearts, and always have before their eyes the penalities of the law. But according to [the Epicureans], there is no profit and no reward gained by injustice great enough to repay a man for being always in fear, or for believing that some punishment is always at hand and hanging over him.

    Cicero, *De re publica* 3.16.26 (tr. Sabine and Smith)

Hence Justice also cannot correctly be said to be desirable in and for itself; it is so because it is so highly productive of gratification. For esteem and affection are gratifying because they render life safe and fuller of pleasure.

    Cicero, *De finibus* 1.16.53 (tr. Rackham)

To Cicero the social contract protects and serves the community and the state:

    The surest means of strengthening the bonds of society is to bestow the greatest kindness on those who are nearest to us. Let us go to the root of the matter and seek in nature the first beginnings of society. The first is seen in the brotherhood of the entire human race. The bonds of connection are thought and speech, the instruments of teaching and learning, of communication, discussion, and reasoning, which unite man to man and bind them together by a kind of natural league. . . . Such is the universal brotherhood of mankind. Here the common right to all those things which nature has destined for the common use of man must be kept inviolate; and while property assigned by statute or by civil law must be held under the conditions established by these laws, we may learn from the Greek proverb, "Among friends all things in common," how to regard all other property. . . . While we enjoy these blessings we must always contribute to the common weal.

    Cicero, *De officiis* 1.16–17 (tr. Gardiner)

1028   **subigō, subigere, subēgī, subāctus** + infin., here, *to force, compel.*
     variōs linguae sonitūs: spontaneous and inarticulate sounds in reaction to sensation and representing emotion. These are similar to the cries of animals.

1029   **ūtilitās, ūtilitātis**, f., *usefulness, expediency.*
     expressit: here, *formed, molded.*
     ūtilitās expressit nōmina rērum: referring to a second stage in language development in which names were created and applied to objects. The names bore some natural relation to the objects described.

1041   **proinde**, adv., *then.* The *o* and *i* scan as one long syllable by synizesis.
     putāre: the infinitive is the subject of **est** (1043) and governs two indirect statements.
     aliquem: i.e., some one individual who acted as the name-giver.
     distribuō, distribuere, distribuī, distribūtus, *to allot.*

1042   **inde**: i.e., from the one man, *from him.*
     hominēs: accusative subject of the second indirect statement.
     didicisse: perfect infinitive of **discō**.
     vocābulum, -ī, n., *word used to designate a thing, term, name.*

1043   **dēsipiō, dēsipere**, *to be out of one's mind, be silly, be foolish.*
     dēsipere: predicative with **est** balancing **putāre**; the enjambement emphasizes the scornful comment.
     posset: imperfect subjunctive in past deliberative question, *why should this man have been able?*
     notō, -āre, -āvī, -ātus, *to identify, stamp, mark.*

1044   **variōs sonitūs . . . linguae**: a reordering of the phrase in line 1028.

1045   **tempore eōdem**: beginning a clause contrasting with **cūr hīc . . . ēmittere linguae** (1043–44); understand a linking *but.*
     facere: dependent on **quīsse**.
     id: i.e., to name things.
     queō, quīre, quīvī or **quiī, quitus**, *to be able*; **quīsse**: contracted form.
     putentur: continuing the deliberative mood, but here present subjunctive, *(why) should others be thought not to have been able. . . .*

1050   **Cōgere**: emphatic position for infinitive dependent on **poterat** (1051).
     item, adv., *likewise, similarly, in turn.*
     victōs: predicative participle, *vanquished, conquered.*
     domō, -āre, -āvī, -ātus, *to subdue, subjugate.*
     Cōgere . . . plūrīs . . . victōsque domāre: chiasmus.

1051   **ut . . . vellent**: dependent on **cōgere** (1050), *compel them to. . . .*
     perdiscō, perdiscere, perdidicī, *to learn thoroughly.*
     vellent: imperfect subjunctive of **volō, velle**.

1056   **postrēmō**, adv., *finally.*
     quid: introducing a question.
     tantopere, adv., *to such a great degree, so greatly, so much.*
     rē: the monosyllable, oddly separated from **hāc**, dangles awkwardly at the line-end.

1057   **cui**: dative of reference.
     vōx et lingua: taken as one concept (hendiadys), since the verb is singular. After all, the tongue forms intelligible words out of the exhalations that the voice emits.
     vigeō, -ēre, -uī, *to be active/lively/vigorous; to thrive, flourish.*
     vigēret: imperfect subjunctive in causal relative clause, *since the voice and tongue are strongly developed.* Perhaps Lucretius is referring to the much greater use of the tongue by man than by any other animal, since his main point here is that man, by producing sounds, acts in a manner similar to all other animals.

1058   **prō**: here, *in accordance with, in reaction to.*
     notāret: imperfect subjunctive, though the indicative would be more usual; probably attracted into the subjunctive to conform with **vigēret** (1057).

1059   **pecus, pecudis**, f., *herd.*

48. The Origin of Language

Language for humans developed from the natural need to express feelings, just as with other animals. There was no giver of language.

1028	At variōs linguae sonitūs nātūra subēgit
1029	mittere et ūtilitās expressit nōmina rērum.

. . .

1041	Proinde putāre aliquem tum nōmina distribuisse
1042	rēbus et inde hominēs didicisse vocābula prīma,
1043	dēsiperest. Nam cūr hīc posset cūncta notāre
1044	vōcibus et variōs sonitūs ēmittere linguae,
1045	tempore eōdem aliī facere id nōn quīsse putentur?

. . .

1050	Cōgere item plūrīs ūnus victōsque domāre
1051	nōn poterat, rērum ut perdiscere nōmina vellent.

. . .

1056	Postrēmō quid in hāc mīrābile tantōperest rē,
1057	sī genus hūmānum, cui vōx et lingua vigēret,
1058	prō variō sēnsū variā rēs vōce notāret?
1059	Cum pecudēs mūtae, cum dēnique saecla ferārum
1060	dissimilīs soleant vōcēs variāsque ciēre,
1061	cum metus aut dolor est et cum iam gaudia glīscunt?

ℭℬ   Discussion Questions
1. What main flaw does Lucretius find with the idea of one language-giver?
2. According to Epicurean theory words are naturally related to the objects described. Can you find any evidence for this theory in this passage?

The contrasting view of language development which Lucretius is disputing:
    Then it is not for every man, Hermogenes, to give names, but for him who may be called the name-maker; and he, it appears, is the law-giver, who is of all the artisans among men the rarest.
    Must not the lawgiver also know how to embody in the sounds and syllables that name which is fitted by nature for each object?
      Plato, *Cratylus* 388e–389a, 389d (tr. Fowler)
I cannot doubt that language owes its origin to the imitation and modification of various natural sounds, the voices of other animals, and man's own instinctive cries, aided by signs and gestures.
      Charles Darwin, *The Descent of Man* (1871), 87

1059	**dēnique**, adv., *in short, indeed; furthermore.*
	saecla ferārum: the formulaic phrase; cf. 967 above.
1060	**cieō** (or **ciō**), **ciēre** (or **cīre**), **cīvī**, **citus**, *to move, stir, rouse;* here, *to emit, utter.*
1061	**cum metus aut dolor est**: supply **eīs**, *for them,* as dative of possession; *when they feel fear or pain.*
	et cum: comparative use of **et**, *as when.*
	glīscō, glīscere, *to swell, increase, grow strong.*

1161 **deum**: = **deōrum**.

nūmen, nūminis, n., *divine power, will.*

per magnās . . . gentīs: i.e., worldwide.

1162 **pervulgō, -āre, -āvī, -ātus**, *to make publicly known, to spread abroad.*

pervulgārit: syncopated perfect subjunctive = **pervulgāverit** in an indirect question governed by **ratiōnem reddere** (1168); two more indirect questions follow.

arārum: genitive with **complēverit**, *made the cities full of altars.*

1163 **suscipiō, suscipere, suscēpī, susceptus**, *to take up, undertake.*

cūrārit: similar syncopation to **pervulgārit** above; here the verb governs a gerundive instead of the more usual **ut** + subjunctive, *brought it about that.*

sollemnis, -is, -e, *formal, ceremonial.*

1164 **in magnīs**: with both **rēbu'** and **lōcis**.

flōreō, -ēre, -uī, *to flourish.*

sācra /. . . săcra: the *a* of the base is short by nature; here we see the flexibility allowed by the Latin mute plus liquid rule; in line 1163 Lucretius counts *cr* as two consonants and thus scans the syllable *sac* long, whereas in 1164 it is short by the mute plus liquid rule.

rēbu': suppression of the final *s* for metrical convenience; the meaning is somewhat unclear, possibly *states, empires*, as a shortened form of **rēbus publicīs**.

1165 **unde**: i.e., from the sacred rites.

est: with **īnsitus**.

īnserō, īnserere, īnsēvī, īnsitus, *to implant, fix in.*

horror, horrōris, m., *dread, fear; awe.*

1166 **quī**: the **horror** is personified in the relative clause comprising lines 1166–67.

dēlūbrum, -ī, n., *temple, shrine.*

suscitō, -āre, -āvī, -ātus, *to raise, build.*

orbī: ablative with *-ī* instead of the usual *-e.*

1167 **terrārum**: enjambement.

celebrō, -āre, -āvī, -ātus, *to throng, fill, crowd.*

celebrāre: supply **hominēs** as subject of the infinitive, **dēlūbra** as direct object.

1168 **nōn ita difficilest**: after a series of indirect questions with dependent relative clauses, Lucretius finally reaches the main clause.

ratiōnem reddere, idiom, *to give an account/explanation.*

1183 **ratiōnēs**: accusative plural as subject of an accusative and infinitive construction governed by **cernēbant** (1184); here, *workings.*

ōrdō, ōrdinis, m., *order, position.*

1184 **cernō, cernere, crēvī, crētus**, *to see, discern, perceive.*

cernēbant: supply **hominēs** as subject.

tempora: here, *seasons.*

vertī: middle in force, *turn themselves, revolve, return.*

1185 **quibus**: introducing an indirect question dependent on **cognōscere**; ablative of means.

id: i.e., the orderly progression of the heavens and the seasons.

1186 **ergō**, conj., *therefore.*

perfugium, -ī, n., *refuge, way of escape* (from their ignorance).

perfugium sibi habēbant: the noun acts in apposition to the object of **habēbant**, which is the two infinitive clauses; *they considered it as a refuge for themselves to. . . .*

omnia: accusative plural neuter.

dīvus, -ī, m., *god.*

1187 **nūtus, -ūs**, m., *nod, command, will.*

illōrum nūtū: by the will of the gods.

facere: parallel with **trādere**, here, *to decide/suppose that*; governing an indirect statement.

flectō, flectere, flexī, flexus, *to guide, steer, direct.*

49. The Origin of Religion

Religion resulted from man's inability to understand the workings of the heavens. As Lucretius describes in the intervening passage (1169–82), men saw marvelous images (**simulācra**) of the gods who exist beyond our world (for an earlier description see 3.18–24), and to them they then attributed marvelous powers. In particular they ascribed the celestial phenomena to the gods, whose homes they believed were in the heavens. Lucretius then bewails the woes that the erroneous belief in divine control of the universe has caused.

1161	Nunc quae causa deum per magnās nūmina gentīs
1162	pervulgārit et ārārum complēverit urbīs
1163	suscipiendaque cūrārit sollemnia sacra,
1164	quae nunc in magnīs flōrent sacra rēbu' locīsque,
1165	unde etiam nunc est mortālibus īnsitus horror
1166	quī dēlūbra deum nova tōtō suscitat orbī
1167	terrārum et fēstīs cōgit celebrāre diēbus,
1168	nōn ita difficilest ratiōnem reddere verbīs.

. . .

1183	Caelī ratiōnēs ōrdine certō
1184	et varia annōrum cernēbant tempora vertī
1185	nec poterant quibus id fieret cognōscere causīs.
1186	Ergō perfugium sibi habēbant omnia dīvīs
1187	trādere et illōrum nūtū facere omnia flectī.

❧ Discussion Questions

1. What sound effects has Lucretius produced in line 1163?

2. What is the effect of the positioning of **est** . . . **īnsitus** in line 1165 and of the placement of **horror**? What effect does the use of **horror** as a synonym for **rēligiō** produce?

3. What to Lucretius seems to be the main activity or focus of religion? Spirituality or ritual?

4. Is Lucretius' use of **perfugium** (1186) ironic?

A dissenting view of the relationship between the gods and the heavens as stated by the Stoic, Lucilius Balbus:

The first proposition—that divine beings exist—seems to need no words of mine. For what could be more clear and obvious, when we look up to the sky and contemplate the heavens, than that there is some divinity of superior intelligence, by which they are controlled?

Cicero, *De natura deorum* 2.2.4 (tr. McGregor)

1188   **locārunt**: syncopated perfect = **locāvērunt**.

1189   **per caelum**: the position of the phrase, echoing **in caelō** above, emphasizes the reasoning of
         ancient men: since we do not understand the workings of the sky, the gods must control
         them; since the gods control the workings of the sky, they must live there.
       volvō, volvere, volvī, volūtus, *to roll.*
         volvī: middle in force, *to roll/wheel themselves.*
       vidētur: agreeing with the nearest subject in number, but applying to both **nox** and **lūna**.

1194   **īnfēlīx, īnfēlīcis**, *unhappy, miserable, wretched.*
         īnfēlīx: explained by the **cum** causal clause, the conjunction of which is postponed.
       tālia: accusative plural neuter modifying **facta** (1195).

1195   **tribuō, tribuere, tribuī, tribūtus**, *to grant, attribute* (to).
       adiungō, adiungere, adiūnxī, adiūnctus, *to join, attribute, ascribe* (to).
       acerbus, -a, -um, *bitter, painful, severe, harsh.*
         īrās . . . acerbās: referring to the belief that dangerous natural phenomena, such as thunder
           and lightning, are indications of the gods' displeasure.

1196   **gemitus, -ūs**, m., *lamentation, pain, sorrow.*
       ipsī: nominative plural masculine, modifying the understood subject **hominēs**.
       ipsī sibi: emphasizing the self-inflicted nature of man's suffering.

1197   **pariō, parere, peperī, partus**, *to give birth to, produce, create.*
         peperēre: = **peperērunt**.
       minōribu' nostrīs: referring to those younger in age, i.e., *our descendants.*
         sibi . . . nōbīs . . . minōribu' nostrīs: the misguided religious beliefs of our ancestors have
           created sorrow for all generations of mankind, past, present, and future.

1198   **pietās, pietātis**, f., *dutifulness, devotion, piety.*
       ūllast: = **ūlla est**.
       vēlō, -āre, -āvī, -ātus, *to cover, veil.*
         vēlātum: modifying the understood accusative subject of the infinitive, **hominem**. The
           participle refers to the particularly Roman religious practice of making sacrifice with the
           head veiled. Vergil describes the legendary origin of the practice in *Aeneid* 3.405.
       vidērī: true passive, *to be seen.*

1199   **vertier**: archaic passive infinitive = **vertī**, here middle in force, *to turn oneself.*
         vēlātum . . . vidērī vertier: alliteration.
       ad lapidem: probably with scornful tone referring to the statues of the gods, which are after
         all mere stones, or to **terminus** stones, which were worshiped at boundaries and cross-
         roads.
       omnīs . . . ad ārās: together with **saepe** (1198) giving the impression that there is a certain
         ostentation involved in the man's frequent and visible worship.
       accēdō, accēdere, accessī, accessūrus, *to go/come to, approach.*

1200   **prōcumbō, prōcumbere, prōcubuī, prōcubitūrus**, *to prostrate oneself, bow down.*
       prōsternō, prōsternere, prōstrāvī, prōstrātus, *to throw to the ground; to prostrate.*
         prōstrātum: here with middle force, *having thrown oneself.*
       pandō, pandere, passus, *to spread out, open.*
       palma, -ae, f., *palm* (of hand).
         pandere palmās: the worshiper stretched out his hands with the palms turned upwards.
           prōcumbere . . . prōstrātum . . . pandere palmās: the repetition of the prefix **prō-** and
             the alliteration perhaps mocks what Lucretius believes to be the mindless ceremony
             of Roman religion, which relied on very exact and detailed performance of its rituals.

1201   **ārās**: object of **spargere** (1202).

1188	In caelōque deum sēdīs et templa locārunt,
1189	per caelum volvī quia nox et lūna vidētur.
	. . .
1194	Ō genus īnfēlīx hūmānum, tālia dīvīs
1195	cum tribuit facta atque īrās adiūnxit acerbās!
1196	Quantōs tum gemitūs ipsī sibi, quantaque nōbīs
1197	vulnera, quās lacrimās peperēre minōribu' nostrīs!
1198	Nec pietās ūllast vēlātum saepe vidērī
1199	vertier ad lapidem atque omnīs accēdere ad ārās
1200	nec prōcumbere humī prōstrātum et pandere palmās
1201	ante deum dēlūbra nec ārās sanguine multō
1202	spargere quadrupedum nec vōtīs nectere vōta,
1203	sed mage plācātā posse omnia mente tuērī.

Velleius the Epicurean on false opinions of the gods:

The poisonous honey of the poets, who present us with gods afire with rage or mad with lust, and make us the spectators of their wars, their battles, their violence and wounds; of their hates, quarrels, altercations; and also of their births and deaths, their complaints and lamentations, their lusts erupting into excess of every kind, adultery, captivity, and intercourse with human beings, so that mortals may have gods for parents. . . . Anyone who considers how rash and foolish are all these beliefs ought to admire Epicurus and to include him in the list of those divine beings whose nature we are discussing.

Cicero, *De natura deorum* 1.16.42–43 (tr. McGregor)

As long as a single drop of blood pulses in her world-conquering, absolutely free heart, philosophy will continually cry out to her opponents, with Epicurus: "The truly impious man is not he who destroys the gods worshipped by the multitude, but he who affirms of the gods what the multitude believes about them."

Karl Marx, doctoral dissertation, *The Difference between Democritus' and Epicurus' Philosophy of Nature* (1841), Preface

---

1202	**spargō, spargere, sparsī, sparsus**, *to strew, sprinkle.*
	quadrupēs, quadrupedis, m., *four-footed animal, quadruped.*
	sanguine multō spargere quadrupedum: Lucretius has made his attitude toward sacrifice eminently clear in two earlier passages: the horrific sacrifice of Iphigenia (1.84–101) and the pitiful mother cow who mourns her sacrificed calf (2.352–66).
	vōtum, -ī, n., *prayer.*
	nectō, nectere, nexī, nexus, *to string together, link x [acc.] to y [dat.].*
1203	**mage**: = **magis**, adv., *rather.*
	sed mage: understand the phrase **pietās est** from above (1198); having depicted in detail the rigmarole of normal Roman religious practice, Lucretius now elegantly and simply describes true piety, which is the tranquillity (*ataraxiā*) which allows one to contemplate the true nature of the blessed gods, as shown in 3.18–24..
	plācātus, -a, -um, *calm, tranquil, peaceful.*
	mēns, mentis, f., *mind.*
	tueor, tuērī, tuitus sum, *to see, observe, perceive.*

1392   **inter sē**: *in groups.*

prōsternō, prōsternere, prōstrāvī, prōstrātus, *to lay on the ground.*

    prōstrātī: nominative plural masculine with middle force, *lying on the ground;* modifying the understood subject *early men.*

grāmen, grāminis, n., *grass.*

1393   **propter aquae . . . arboris altae**: the tranquil picture of the tree-shaded picnic by the riverside is enhanced by assonance, particularly of the vowel *a.*

1394   **ops, opis**, f., *power; wealth.*

    opibus: here, *cost,* thus **nōn magnīs opibus** as ablative of price, *not at great cost.*

iūcundē corpora habēbant: *they gave pleasure to their bodies;* i.e., they refreshed themselves; paraphrasing **corpora cūrant** (2.31); the change of verb has been made to fit the past tense of the passage (**cūrābant** would add a syllable by avoiding elision).

1395   **praesertim**, adv., *especially.*

tempestās: here, *weather.*

annī: genitive singular with **tempora** (1396).

1396   **tempora**: here, *season.*

pingō, pingere, pīnxī, pīnctus, *to paint.*

viridāns, viridantis, *green, verdant.*

herba, -ae, f., *grass.*

1397   **Tum . . . tum . . . tum**: anaphora, perhaps emphasizing the contrast with modern man.

ioca: Lucretius uses a neuter form of **iocus** in the plural.

dulcis, -is, -e, *sweet.*

1398   **cōnsuēscō, cōnsuēscere, cōnsuēvī, cōnsuētūrus** + infin., *to become accustomed/used* (to).

    cōnsuerant: syncopated pluperfect = **cōnsuēverant**; the *u* is vocalic here.

        esse . . . cōnsuerant: pluperfect in imperfect sense, *were the rule, were customary.*

agrestis, -is, -e, *rustic, rural.*

mūsa: not in the sense of a goddess but abstractly for *inspiration.*

vigeō, -ēre, -uī, *to be active/lively/vigorous; to thrive, flourish.*

1399   **caput**: accusative.

umerus, -ī, m., *shoulder.*

plexus, -a, -um, *woven, braided.*

redimiō, redimīre, redimiī, redimītus, *to wreathe round, encircle.*

    redimīre: dependent on **monēbat** (1400).

1400   **folium, -ī**, n., *leaf.*

    flōribus et foliīs: ambiguous construction: either in apposition to **corōnīs** or ablative of means with **plexīs**.

lascīvia, -ae, f., *playfulness, fun.*

monēbat: here, *urged, prompted.*

1401   **extrā numerum**: *out of step, unrhythmically.*

prōcēdere: dependent on **monēbat** (1400).

membrum, -ī, n., *limb.*

moventīs: accusative plural modifying **hominēs** understood.

1402   **dūrus, -a, -um**, *hard, harsh, heavy.*

    dūriter, adv., *heavily, clumsily.*

        dūriter et dūrō: the enjambement of **dūriter** and the repetition of the root **dūr-** stress the ungainlessness of the primitive dancing; for similar repetition accentuating the hardiness of early man see 926: **dūrius . . . tellūs quod dūra creāsset**.

pellō, pellere, pepulī, pulsus, *to strike, beat.*

    dūriter . . . pede pellere mātrem: the hard alliteration of *d* and *p* imitates the thumping sounds of their dancing.

1403   **dūlcēsque cachinnī**: the repetition of the phrase from line 1397 is unusual, but there is no reason to doubt the authenticity of the line.

1404   **omnia**: modifying **haec**, referring to the new arts such as dancing.

quod: the conjunction has been postponed.

50. Simplicity versus Progress

Lucretius describes the simple pleasures of early men. Lines 1392–96 are a close paraphrase of his praise of the simple life of the Epicurean in the proem of Book 2 (29–33). In this passage Lucretius shows that early man rejoiced in songs and dances that now would be considered crude, yet gave them as much pleasure as the most sophisticated arts today. The new always displaces the old. Human longing for novelty leads to much vain labor.

1392	Saepe itaque inter sē prōstrātī in grāmine mollī
1393	propter aquae rīvum sub rāmīs arboris altae
1394	nōn magnīs opibus iūcundē corpora habēbant,
1395	praesertim cum tempestās rīdēbat et annī
1396	tempora pingēbant viridantīs flōribus herbās.
1397	Tum ioca, tum sermō, tum dulcēs esse cachinnī
1398	cōnsuerant. Agrestis enim tum mūsa vigēbat;
1399	tum caput atque umerōs plexīs redimīre corōnīs
1400	flōribus et foliīs lascīvia laeta monēbat,
1401	atque extrā numerum prōcēdere membra moventīs
1402	dūriter et dūrō terram pede pellere mātrem;
1403	unde oriēbantur rīsūs dulcēsque cachinnī,
1404	omnia quod nova tum magis haec et mīra vigēbant.

. . .

1412	Nam quod adest praestō, nisi quid cognōvimus ante

ℭ Discussion Questions

1.   Is Lucretius' depiction of the rustic pleasures of early man idealized? How does this depiction compare with his description of the life of the first humans in passage 46? Have these more developed humans completely lost their hardiness?

2.   How did early man celebrate? Did their celebrations involve material possessions?

1404   **magis**: *rather*, modifying **nova** and **mīra**, since their comparatives were not in use.
     nova . . . mīra: with causal force, giving the reason for **vigēbant**; *since they were rather new and marvelous.*
       omnia . . . vigēbant: order for translation: **quod omnia haec tum magis nova et mīra vigēbant.**
1412   **quod**: nominative singular neuter, with an antecedent **id** understood.
     praestō, adv., *present, at hand.*
     quid: = **aliquid**, as usual after **nisi**.

1413   **in prīmīs**, idiom, *especially, particularly.*
     polleō, pollēre, *to be valued, esteemed.*
       prīmīs placet et pollēre: note the alliteration.

1414   **posterior**: with adverbial force, *later.*
     rēs: Lucretius changes from the neuter to **rēs** for *thing.*
     ferē, adv., *generally, usually.*
     illa: probably accusative plural neuter, *those (earlier) things,* object of **perdit** (1415), but the construction is ambiguous.
     reperiō, reperīre, repperī, repertus, *to find, discover.*

1415   **perdō, perdere, perdidī, perditus**, *to ruin, spoil.*
     posteriorque . . . reperta / perdit: reorder for translation: **ferē melior rēs posterior reperta illa perdit.**
     immūtō, -āre, -āvī, -ātus, *to modify, alter.*
     sēnsūs: here, *feelings.*
     ad: here, *with regard to, towards, for.*
     prīstinus, -a, -um, *old, ancient.*
     quisque, quaeque, quidque, *each, each one.*

1416   **odium, -ī**, n. + gen., *hatred* (for), *dislike* (of).
     glāns, glandis, f., *acorn.*
       glandis: cf. 939–44 for early man's diet.
     illa: nominative plural neuter, modifying **cubīlia** (1417).
     relicta: with **sunt** (1417).

1417   **sternō, sternere, strāvī, strātus**, *to strew.*
     cubīle, cubīlis, n., *bed.*
     frōns, frondis, f., *leaf, foliage.*
     aucta: perfect passive participle of **augeō, augēre**, here, *augmented, heaped, piled high.*
       illa relicta /. . . frondibus aucta: the interwoven word order and chiasmus of **strāta . . . herbīs et frondibus aucta** make the passage difficult to translate. Reorder: **illa cūbilia strāta herbīs et aucta frondibus relicta sunt.**

1418   **pellis, pellis**, f., *hide, skin.*
       pellis: genitive singular, modified by **ferīnae.**
     item, adv., *likewise, similarly, in turn.*
     contemnō, contemnere, contempsī, contemptus, *to despise, scorn.*
       contempta: predicative with **cecidit**, *fell into contempt, became despised.*
     ferīnus, -a, -um, *of a wild animal.*

1419   **quam**: the antecedent is **vestis.**
     reor, rērī, ratus sum, *to think.*
       quam reor: introducing a grimly humorous imagined incident to illustrate man's lust for anything new.
     invidia, -ae, f., *jealousy, envy.*
       invidiā tālī: ablative of attendant circustance with **esse repertam**, *was found with such envy,* i.e., *aroused such envy.*
     tunc, adv., *then, once.*

1420   **lētum, -ī**, n., *death.*
     lētum: accusative, object of **obīret.**
     īnsidiae, -ārum, f. pl., *ambush.*
     quī gessit prīmus: this clause acts as subject of the sentence; understand **is** as antecedent and **vestem** as direct object.
       gessit: here, *wore.*
     obeō, obīre, obiī, obitus, *to meet;* with **lētum**, *to meet one's death, to die.*

1421   **et tamen**: *and yet,* introducing the description of the futility of the attack.
     eōs: referring to those who attacked the first hide-wearer.
     distrahō, distrahere, distrāxī, distractus, *to pull apart, pull to pieces.*
       distractam: modifying **vestem** understood as subject of the indirect statement.

1413	suāvius, in prīmīs placet et pollēre vidētur,
1414	posteriorque ferē melior rēs illa reperta
1415	perdit et immūtat sēnsūs ad prīstina quaeque.
1416	Sīc odium coepit glandis, sīc illa relicta
1417	strāta cubīlia sunt herbīs et frondibus aucta.
1418	Pellis item cecidit vestis contempta ferīnae;
1419	quam reor invidiā tālī tunc esse repertam,
1420	ut lētum īnsidiīs quī gessit prīmus obīret,
1421	et tamen inter eōs distractam sanguine multō
1422	disperiisse neque in frūctum convertere quīsse.
1423	Tunc igitur pellēs, nunc aurum et purpura cūrīs
1424	exercent hominum vītam bellōque fatīgant;

‭CB‬ Discussion Questions

1. What earlier character has Lucretius shown who was unable to enjoy present pleasures? (1412–13)

2. What is Lucretius' attitude towards progress? Is innovation always good? (1412–35)

3. Analyze the grim humor in this passage.

4. If Lucretius were writing today, what modern innovations might he include in his list of things that trouble humans who struggle in rivalry for them? (1423–24) Do these innovations appreciably improve our lives and alleviate pain and suffering?

The passion for wealth, unless limited by satisfaction, is far more painful than extreme poverty; for greater passions create greater needs.

Democritus, *Fragment* 219 (tr. Freeman)

1421	**sanguine multō**: ablative of attendant circumstance, *with . . .*
1422	**dispereō, disperīre, disperiī**, *to perish; to be ruined/destroyed.*
	frūctus, -ūs, m., here, *enjoyment, profit.*
	convertere: here intransitive with **in**, *to develop into, turn itself to, lead to.*
	queō, quīre, quīvī or **quiī, quitus**, *to be able.*
	quīsse: contracted form.
1423	**pellēs**: nominative plural as first subject of **exercent** (adjust the tense to **exercēbant**).
	purpura, -ae, f., *purple* (the color which indicated high rank).
1424	**exercent**: here, *vex, trouble.*
	fatīgō, -āre, -āvī, -ātus, *to weary, tire out.*

1425　**quō**, adv., *for which reason, therefore.*

　　in nōbīs: in us as modern men.

　　opīnor, -ārī, -ātus sum, *to think, believe.*

　　resīdō, resīdere, resēdī, *to settle, lie, remain.*

　　　　resēdit: perfect, *has come to rest, has rested.*

　　　　　　quō magis in nōbīs . . . culpa resēdit: we are more worthy of blame for being influenced by greed, since, being no longer primitive, we should have recognized the dangers of materialism.

1426　**frīgus, frīgoris**, n., *cold.*

　　nūdōs: modifying **terrigenās** (1426).

　　excruciō, -āre, -āvī, -ātus, *to torture, torment.*

1427　**terrigena, -ae**, m., *one born of the earth* (referring to the theory that men were born from wombs in the earth); in pl., *the first men on earth.*

　　nōs: accusative.

　　nīl: here adverbial, *not at all.*

　　carēre: subject of **laedit** and governing the ablative.

1428　**purpureā**: enjambement introducing a line describing the unnecessarily extravagant clothing.

　　signīs: here, *figures, designs.*

　　aptus, -a, -um + abl., *fitted* (with), *adorned* (with).

　　　　aurō signīsque ingentibus aptā: referring to clothing embroidered with massive designs of gold brocade. **Aurō signīsque** is a hendiadys, since the figures are made of the gold.

1429　**dum**: here + subjn., *provided that, as long as.*

　　plēbēius, -a, -um, *common, ordinary, everyday.*

　　　　plēbēia: modifying **vestis** understood; the vowels *ēi* scan as one long syllable by synizesis.

　　quae: introducing a relative clause of characteristic; the antecedent is **plēbēia vestis**.

　　dēfendere: supply **nōs** as direct object.

1430　**ergō**, conj., *therefore.*

　　incassum, adv., *without aim/purpose.*

　　frūstrā, adv., *in vain.*

　　　　incassum frūstrāque labōrat: the heavy spondees produce the effect of laboring. The phrase **frūstrāque labōrat** has been found earlier in the context of love (4.1099).

1431　**semper**: the enjambement is emphatic.

　　cōnsūmō, cōnsūmere, cōnsūmpsī, cōnsūmptus, *to destroy, consume, waste.*

　　inānis, -is, -e, *empty, groundless, foolish.*

　　aevum -ī, n., *life.*

1432　**nīmīrum**, adv., *without doubt, certainly.*

　　quia, conj., *because.*

　　cognōvit: the subject is still **genus (hominum)** (1430).

　　habendī: genitive gerund, *of possession.*

1433　**fīnis**: here feminine, *limit.*

　　omnīnō, adv., *at all*; take with **nōn cognōvit** (1432).

　　quoad, interr. adv., *to what extent, how far.*

　　　　quoad: introducing a second indirect question; a monosyllable, since the vowels *oa* scan as one long syllable by synizesis.

　　crēscō, crēscere, crēvī, crētūrus, *to grow, increase.*

1434　**id**: i.e., our ignorance of the limits of possession and enjoyment.

　　minūtātim, adv., *gradually, little by little.*

　　prōvehō, prōvehere, prōvexī, prōvectus, *to carry forward, convey out* (to sea).

1425   quō magis in nōbīs, ut opīnor, culpa resēdit.
1426   Frīgus enim nūdōs sine pellibus excruciābat
1427   terrigenās; at nōs nīl laedit veste carēre
1428   purpureā atque aurō signīsque ingentibus aptā,
1429   dum plēbēia tamen sit quae dēfendere possit.
1430   Ergō hominum genus incassum frūstrāque labōrat
1431   semper et in cūrīs cōnsūmit inānibus aevum,
1432   nīmīrum quia nōn cognōvit quae sit habendī
1433   fīnis et omnīnō quoad crēscat vēra voluptās.
1434   Idque minūtātim vītam prōvexit in altum
1435   et bellī magnōs commōvit funditus aestūs.

␄ Discussion Questions

1.   What words does Lucretius use to characterize human activity? (1430–31)

2.   What earlier passage depicted men struggling in a sea of troubles? (1434–35)

Cheerfulness is created for men through moderation of enjoyment and harmoniousness of life. Things that are in excess or lacking are apt to change and cause great disturbance in the soul. Souls which are stirred by great divergences are neither stable nor cheerful. Therefore one must keep one's mind on what is attainable, and be content with what one has, paying little heed to things envied and admired, and not dwelling on them in one's mind.
    Democritus, *Fragment* 191 (tr. Freeman)

The animal needing something knows how much it needs, the man does not.
    Democritus, *Fragment* 198 (tr. Freeman)

A contrary view of technological progress:
    Discoveries carry blessings with them, and confer benefits without causing harm or sorrow to any.
        Sir Francis Bacon, *The New Organon* (1620), 124

1434   **altum**: here substantive, *the deep*, i.e., *the sea*.
        vītam prōvexit in altum: metaphor. **Vīta** is the ship of life, which is borne into a sea of troubles (**altum**). This vivid image may continue the imagery that closes Book 2, if the reading **ad scopulum** (2.1174) is correct there (cf. passage 29).
1435   **commōvit**: here, *has stirred up*.
        funditus, adv., *from the bottom*.
        aestūs: here, *surges, tides, tumults*.
        bellī magnōs . . . aestūs: continuing the marine metaphor of the previous line.

1448   **nāvigium, -ī**, n., *ship.*

     nāvigia: accusative plural introducing a series of accusatives, many in rapid asyndeton, all dependent on **docuit** (1453).

   cultūra, -ae, f., *tilling, cultivation.*

     agrī cultūrās: the plural perhaps indicating the various methods of cultivation; note the formation of our English word *agriculture.*

   lēx, lēgis, f., *law.*

1449   **vestīs**: probably referring to elaborate garments such as that described at 1428, since clothing itself would be considered a necessity.

   hōrum: unusual use of the genitive rather than **hōc**, probably for metrical reasons.

1450   **praemium, -ī**, n., *reward, prize.*

     praemia: with **vītae**, referring to material pleasures beyond what is absolutely necessary.

   dēliciās, here, *luxuries.*

   funditus, adv., *utterly, absolutely;* here with **omnīs**.

1451   **carmen, carminis**, n., *song; poetry.*

   pictūrās: *paintings.*

   daedalus, -a, -um, *variegated, skilful, inventive;* here, *cleverly made.*

   signa: here, *statues.*

   poliō, -īre, -īvī, -ītus, *to polish, give a finish to.*

     polīre: infinitive as accusative noun, concluding the series.

1452   **ūsus, -ūs**, m., *practice.*

   impiger, impigra, impigrum, *active, energetic, quick.*

   experientia, -ae, f., *inventiveness.*

1453   **paulātim**, adv., *gradually, little by little.*

   docuit: the singular verb indicates that **ūsus et . . . experientia** is a hendiadys, since practice (trial and error) and inventiveness are inextricably connected.

   pedetemptim, adv., *step by step.*

   prōgredientīs: modifying **hominēs** understood.

     paulātim . . . pedetemptim prōgredientīs: alliteration with *p*, which continues in the next line.

51. Invention by Necessity and Reasoning

In the conclusion of Book 5 Lucretius summarizes man's achievements, both practical and artistic. Compelled by necessity to invent, man then used trial and error and his exceptional intelligence to bring his new creations to the peak of refinement.

1448	Nāvigia atque agrī cultūrās moenia lēgēs
1449	arma viās vestīs et cētera dē genere hōrum,
1450	praemia, dēliciās quoque vītae funditus omnīs,
1451	carmina pictūrās, et daedala signa polīre,
1452	ūsus et impigrae simul experientia mentis
1453	paulātim docuit pedetemptim prōgredientīs.

∞ Discussion Questions

1. How does Lucretius' attitude toward technical innovation here compare with that in the preceding passage?

2. How realistic is Lucretius' description of the process of invention? How does his version compare with Prometheus' claims below?

Hear what troubles there were among men, how I found them witless and gave them the use of their wits and made them masters of their minds. . . . I showed them the rising of the stars, and the settings, hard to observe. And further I discovered to them numbering, pre-eminent among subtle devices, and the combining of letters as a means of remembering all things, the Muses' mother, skilled in craft. It was I who first yoked beasts for them in the yokes and made of those beasts the slaves of trace chain and pack saddle that they might be man's substitute in the hardest tasks; and I harnessed to the carriage, so that they loved the rein, horses, the crowning pride of the rich man's luxury. It was I and none other who discovered ships, the sail-driven wagons that the sea buffets. Such were the contrivances that I discovered for men. . . . Greatest was this: in the former times if a man fell sick he had no defense against the sickness, neither healing food nor drink, nor unguent; but through the lack of drugs men wasted away, until I showed them the blending of mild simples wherewith they drive out all manner of diseases. . . . One brief word will tell the whole story: all arts that mortals have come from Prometheus.

Aeschylus, *Prometheus Bound* 441–82 (tr. Grene)

1454   **ūnumquicquid**: accusative, *each single thing.*

      prōtrahō, prōtrahere, prōtrāxī, prōtractus, *to drag forward or out; to bring into the open.*

      aetās, aetātis, f., *time; age.*

          aetās: equivalent to **ūsus** (1452), *practice over time.*

1455   **in medium**: with **prōtrahit** a metaphor that imagines drawing each development into the center of the group for all to see and share. Similarly, in 1.409 truth was drawn out (**prōtrahere**) from its lair.

      ratiō: equivalent to **impigrae . . . experientia mentis** (1452).

      in lūminis . . . ōrās: the formulaic phrase, first seen in 1.22 in the context of creativity.

      ērigō, ērigere, ērēxī, ērēctus, *to raise, lift up.*

1456   **alid**: = **aliud**, accusative as subject of the accusative and infinitive construction.

      clārēscō, clārēscere, clāruī, *to become clear.*

      corde: here = **animō** or **mente**.

      vidēbant: the subject is **hominēs** understood.

1457   **artibus**: probably archaic dative for genitive of possession with **cacūmen**, but possibly ablative of means.

      dōnec: the linking conjunction is delayed until mid-line.

      vēnēre: alternate third plural perfect = **vēnērunt**.

      cacūmen, cacūminis, n., *peak, pinnacle.*

          artibus ad summum . . . vēnēre cacūmen: referring to Lucretius' own time as the pinnacle of artistic achievement. Most generations after him have claimed the same for themselves.

1454   Sīc ūnumquicquid paulātim prōtrahit aetās

1455   in medium ratiōque in lūminis ērigit ōrās.

1456   Namque alid ex aliō clārēscere corde vidēbant,

1457   artibus ad summum dōnec vēnēre cacūmen.

❧ Discussion Questions

1.   What do you think of Lucretius' claim that the arts had reached the **summum cacūmen**? (1457)

2.   Would Lucretius agree with Sophocles' praise of man's inventiveness in his famous ode to man in *Antigone* (below)?

Many the wonders but nothing walks stranger than man.
This thing crosses the sea in the winter's storm,
making his path through the roaring waves.
And she, the greatest of gods, the earth—
ageless she is, and unwearied—he wears her away
as the ploughs go up and down from year to year
and his mules turn up the soil.

Gay nations of birds he snares and leads,
wild beast tribes and the salty brood of the sea,
with the twisted mesh of his nets, this clever man.
He controls with craft the beasts of the open air,
walkers on hills. The horse with his shaggy mane
he holds and harnesses, yoked about the neck,
and the strong bull of the mountain.

Language, and thought like the wind
and the feelings that make the town,
he has taught himself, and shelter against the cold,
refuge from rain. He can always help himself.
He faces no future helpless. There's only death
that he cannot find an escape from. He has contrived
refuges from illnesses once beyond all cure.

Clever beyond all dreams
the inventive craft that he has
which may drive him one time or another to well or ill.
When he honors the laws of the land and the gods' sworn right
high indeed is his city; but stateless the man
who dares to dwell with dishonor. Not by my fire,
never to share my thoughts who does these things.
    Sophocles, *Antigone* 332–72 (tr. Wyckoff)

58   **quī**: the antecedent **eī**, *these people*, has been suppressed.

    didicēre: alternate third plural perfect = **didicērunt**, from **discō, discere**.

    aevum, -ī, n., *life*.

     agere aevum, idiom, *to lead, spend life*.

59   **tamen**: the people involved have not truly understood the nature of the gods, since they would not then wonder about their involvement in natural phenomena.

    quā ratiōne: *in what way*.

60   **quisque, quaeque, quidque**, *each, each one*.

    quaeque: nominative plural neuter, *each thing*.

    praesertim, adv., *especially*.

61   **superā**: = **suprā**, here a preposition.

    cernō, cernere, crēvī, crētus, *to see, discern, perceive*.

62   **referuntur**: the subject is the same as **(eī) quī** above (58).

    rēligiōnēs: probably referring to belief in the gods' universal power, which Lucretius has discredited (5. 1183–97), as well as to some of the rituals of ancient religious practice that Lucretius has disparaged (5.1198–1203). Particularly memorable is his description of the sacrifice of Iphigenia (1.84–100).

     rūrsus . . . referuntur rēligiōnēs: note the alliteration and the pentasyllabic ending.

63   **adscīscō, adscīscere, adscīvī, adscītus**, *to adopt*.

    omnia posse: accusative and infinitive construction with **quōs** as subject; understand **facere** to govern the object **omnia**.

64   **quōs**: the relative has been delayed.

    miserī: nominative plural masculine, modifying the subject, *misguided men*.

    ignārus, -a, -um, *ignorant, not knowing*.

     ignārī: nominative plural; the verbal idea introduces a series of indirect questions.

    queō, quīre, quīvī or **quiī, quitus**, *to be able*.

65   **quid nequeat . . . terminus haerēns** (66): these two lines are repeated from 1.76–77 where they concluded Lucretius' triumphant announcement of Epicurus' victory over religion and ignorance. The principle of natural limits for all things, as stated here, is one of the most fundamental in Epicurean physics.

    nequeō, nequīre, nequīvī, *to be unable* (to).

    fīnītus, -a, -um, *limited*.

     fīnīta: predicate adjective modifying **potestās**; reorder this clause: **dēnique quānam ratiōne cuique potestās sit fīnīta**.

    dēnique, adv., *in short, indeed*.

    cuique: dative of possession.

66   **quīnam, quaenam, quodnam**, interrog. adj., *what kind of, what indeed?*

     quānam . . . ratiōne: *in what way, how*.

    altē, adv., *deeply*.

    terminus, -ī, m., *boundary post/stone*.

     terminus: supply **sit**. Here Lucretius creates a very Roman metaphor, which shows concern for property rights. By this image he conveys the idea that all things are bound by natural limits.

    haerēns: *(deeply) clinging*.

67   **quō**, adv., *for which reason, therefore*.

    errantēs: modifying the subject, *misguided men*.

    caecus, -a, -um, *blind*.

     caecā ratiōne: *blind reasoning*, equivalent to **falsā ratiōne**, but suggesting the blindness of the misguided men who do not see the truth.

      errantēs . . . feruntur: for a similar description of misguided men see 2.9–10: **passimque vidēre/errāre atque viam pālantīs quaerere vitae**.

CB BOOK 6 &

52. True Piety

Even those who have learned the truth about the tranquil life of the gods can sometimes relapse into the old religion through lack of understanding of mysterious natural events. The harm of such a relapse is not that the gods' peace can be disturbed by us, but that we, in our fear, cannot be at peace in our contemplation of them.

58	Nam bene quī didicēre deōs sēcūrum agere aevum,
59	sī tamen intereā mīrantur quā ratiōne
60	quaeque gerī possint, praesertim rēbus in illīs
61	quae superā caput aetheriīs cernuntur in ōrīs,
62	rūrsus in antīquās referuntur rēligiōnēs
63	et dominōs ācrīs adscīscunt, omnia posse
64	quōs miserī crēdunt, ignārī quid queat esse,
65	quid nequeat, fīnīta potestās dēnique cuique
66	quānam sit ratiōne atque altē terminus haerēns;
67	quō magis errantēs caecā ratiōne feruntur.

CB Discussion Questions

1. What natural events in particular cause men to relapse into fearful worship of the gods?

2. What is Lucretius' cure for man's ignorance about natural events?

3. Why does Lucretius describe men as **miserī** in line 64?

The principal disturbance in the minds of men arises because they think that these celestial bodies are blessed and immortal, and yet have wills and actions and motives inconsistent with these attributes.
Epicurus, *Epistle to Herodotus* 81 (tr. Bailey)

68 **Quae**: accusative plural neuter, referring to false beliefs about the gods.
   respuō, respuere, *to spit out, reject.*
   respuis ex animō: a very vivid image.
   remittis: here with the infinitive **putāre** (69), *banish thinking, cease to think.*

69 **indignus, -a, -um** + abl., *unworthy of.*
   indigna: accusative plural neuter picking up **Quae** (68), *(these) things (that are) unworthy.*
   putāre: infinitive acts as object of **remittis** (68), *thinking.*
   aliēnus, -a, -um + gen., *unsuitable* (to), *alien* (to).
   aliēna: accusative plural neuter, modifying understood *thoughts.*

70 **dēlībō, -āre, -āvī, -ātus**, *to mar, diminish, infringe.*
   deum: = **deōrum**.
   per tē: stressing personal responsibility for the situation.
   tibi: dative with **oberunt** (71) emphatically echoing **per tē**.
   nūmen, nūminis, n. *divine power, will; majesty.*
   dēlībāta deum per tē tibi nūmina sāncta: note the harsh alliteration of *d* and *t* followed by the soft sounds of **nūmina sāncta**.

71 **obsum, obesse, obfuī** + dat., *to be a hindrance* (to), *to harm.*
   dēlībāta deum ... saepe oberunt: initially a surprising statement in the context of Lucretius' denial of the gods' power over men. In the following lines Lucretius clarifies how divinity is sullied and what harm ensues.
   quō, here, *in that, because.*

72 **possit**: Lucretius regularly uses the subjunctive when giving a rejected reason.
   imbibō, imbibere, imbibī, imbibitus, *to thirst.*
   poenās petere imbibat ācrīs: possibly alluding to the Furies, goddesses of vengeance, who tried to suck dry the blood of those who had committed heinous crimes.

73 **quia**, conj., *because.*
   tūte: emphatic form of **tū**, *you yourself.*
   tūte tibi: repetition as in line 70, again indicating that the troubles are self-inflicted.
   quiētōs: modifying **deōs** understood, subject of indirect statement with **cōnstituēs** (74).

74 **cōnstituēs**: showing that man himself, without any sound evidence, has chosen to believe in divine wrath.
   volvō, volvere, volvī, volūtus, *to roll.*
   flūctus, -ūs, m., *wave, billow.*
   magnōs īrārum volvere flūctūs: a metaphorical picture of fury in complete contrast to the gods' real state described in the preceding line: **placidā cum pāce quiētōs**.

75 **dēlūbrum, -ī**, n., *temple, shrine.*
   placidō cum pectore Lucretius intentionally echoes the phrase that described the gods (73), since the Epicureans believed that man could live a god-like life.
   dēlūbra ... adībis: contrary to the common misconception that the Epicureans were atheists, Epicurus himself is said to have attended religious ceremonies regularly. We may suppose he was worshiping the gods, not in their Olympian guise, but as beings enjoying the Epicurean goal of perfect tranquillity. Line 75 should be interpreted in the context of lines 76–78 in which by reference to the **simulācra** of the gods Lucretius indicates that he is not advocating traditional worship, but contemplation of the mental images we receive from the gods.

76 **dē corpore ... sānctō**: of the gods. Since only matter and void exist, the gods must be corporeal. Since they live in the calm area between worlds, they are not so affected by the constant blows that strike us, who live in a greater density of matter.
   quae: nominative plural neuter introducing the relative clause **dē corpore ... feruntur in mentīs hominum**; preceding its antecedent **simulācra**.
   simulācrum, -ī, n., *image.*
   simulācra: accusative, object of **suscipere** (78); the shells or outer layers that all physical things constantly shed. As Lucretius explained in Book 4, we see an object when its **simulācra** strike our eyes, or we think of it when they strike our mind.

68	Quae nisi respuis ex animō longēque remittis
69	dīs indigna putāre aliēnaque pācis eōrum,
70	dēlībāta deum per tē tibi nūmina sāncta
71	saepe oberunt; nōn quō violārī summa deum vīs
72	possit, ut ex īrā poenās petere imbibat ācrīs,
73	sed quia tūte tibi placidā cum pāce quiētōs
74	cōnstituēs magnōs īrārum volvere flūctūs,
75	nec dēlūbra deum placidō cum pectore adībis,
76	nec dē corpore quae sānctō simulācra feruntur
77	in mentīs hominum, dīvīnae nūntia fōrmae,
78	suscipere haec animī tranquillā pāce valēbis.

☙ Discussion Questions

1. How does Lucretius create an effective contrast between reality and imagination in lines 73–74?

2. How does Lucretius emphasize the personal involvement of the reader in lines 68–78?

3. Of what does Epicurean worship consist and what benefits can it provide?

---

77 **nūntium, -ī**, n., *message, communication*; originally a term from augury.
  dīvīnae nūntia fōrmae: the phrase is in apposition to **simulācra** (76).
78 **suscipiō, suscipere, suscēpī, susceptus**, *to take up, receive.*
  haec: resumimg **simulācra** (76).
  animī tranquillā pāce: the Epicurean goal of tranquillity (ἀταραξία).

1090   **ratiō**: here, *cause.*
      ratiō quae sit: indirect question dependent on **expediam** (1093).
   morbīs: here, *epidemics;* dative of possession, *what cause epidemics have.*
   repente, adv., *suddenly, unexpectedly.*

1091   **mortifer, mortifera, mortiferum**, *death-bearing, fatal, deadly.*
   clādēs, clādis, f., *calamity, disaster, ruin.*
   cōnflō, -āre, -āvī, -ātus, *to blow into flame, ignite;* + acc. and dat., *to arouse/stir up* (something against someone).
      cōnflāre: the verb conveys the swiftness and virulence of an epidemic and may also allude to one of the symptoms of the Athenian plague, a terrible burning sensation.
        clādem cōnflāre coorta: note the alliteration.

1092   **morbidus, -a, -um**, *causing disease, unhealthy, sickly.*
   hominum generī pecudumque catervīs: datives with **cōnflāre**; note that the plague affected both humans and animals. For a similar instance, see Vergil's *Georgics* 3.478–566.

1093   **expediō, expedīre, expedīvī** or **expediī, expedītus**, *to explain.*
      expediam: note the enjambement, which allows **expediam** immediately to precede the actual explanation.
   sēmen, sēminis, n., *seed; atom, particle.*

1094   **suprā**: in lines 769–80, which have been omitted in this text.
   sint: subjunctive in a relative clause in indirect statement.
   vītālia: here, *healthful.*

1095   **quae**: introducing a relative clause that precedes its antecedent **multa** (1096).
   morbō mortīque: predicative datives, *for disease and death,* i.e., they bring disease and death.

1096   **multa**: accusative plural in accusative and infinitive construction serving as the subject of **necessest** (1095); understand **sēmina**.
   volō, -āre, -āvī, -ātūrus, *to fly.*
      volāre: emphasizing the point that these are airborne particles, a very advanced idea. See also below **caelum** and **āēr** (1097).
   Ea: supply **sēmina**.
   cum: *when.*
   cāsū . . . forte: a typical Lucretian redundancy serving to stress the random nature of such occurrences.
   sunt: with **coorta**

1097   **perturbō, -āre, -āvī, -ātus**, *to upset, disrupt, disturb.*
      perturbārunt: syncopated perfect = **perturbāvērunt**.
   āēr, āeris, m., *air.*

1138   **quondam**, adv., *formerly, once.*
   aestus: here, *emanation, miasma,* referring to the deadly air.

1139   **fīnibus**: here, *territory, lands.*
   Cecrops, Cecropis, m., *Cecrops* (mythical first king of Athens).
   fūnestus, -a, -um, *fatal, deadly.*
   reddidit: here, *caused to turn out, rendered, made.*

1140   **vāstō, -āre, -āvī, -ātus**, *to make desolate, leave without signs of life.*
      vāstāvit viās: alliteration.
   exhauriō, exhaurīre, exhausī, exhaustus + abl., *to drain, empty* (of).

1141   **penitus**, adv., *from within;* take closely with **fīnibus**.
   fīnibus: here, *territory, country;* ablative of source with **ortus**.
   ortus: from **orior, orīrī**, modifying **aestus** understood from line 1138.

1142   **āera**: Greek accusative singular of **āēr, āeris**, m., *air.*
   permētior, permētīrī, permēnsus sum, *to traverse.*
   campōsque natantīs: poetic phrase for the sea.

53. The Plague at Athens

The earth contains many particles that are harmful to humans. When these particles collect, the atmosphere becomes deadly. Lucretius gives an account, based on the historian Thucydides (2.47–52), of the great plague at Athens in 430 B.C. during the Peloponnesian War. After a detailed catalogue of the horrific symptoms (1145–1214), Lucretius paints a picture of corpse-strewn streets and temples in a city where the tremendous suffering caused the abandonment of religion and normal social customs.

Lucretius opened his epic with the springtime fertility and peace of Venus; he now closes it with a balancing picture of extreme destruction.

1090	Nunc ratiō quae sit morbīs aut unde repente
1091	mortiferam possit clādem cōnflāre coorta
1092	morbida vīs hominum generī pecudumque catervīs,
1093	expediam. Prīmum multārum sēmina rērum
1094	esse suprā docuī quae sint vītālia nōbīs,
1095	et contrā quae sint morbō mortīque necessest
1096	multa volāre. Ea cum cāsū sunt forte coorta
1097	et perturbārunt caelum, fit morbidus āēr.

. . .

1138	Haec ratiō quondam morbōrum et mortifer aestus
1139	fīnibus in Cecropis fūnestōs reddidit agrōs
1140	vāstāvitque viās, exhausit cīvibus urbem.
1141	Nam penitus veniēns Aegyptī fīnibus ortus,
1142	āera permēnsus multum campōsque natantīs,

ᘒ Discussion Questions

1. How does Lucretius use alliteration and word order to set the tone of the passage in lines 1090–97?

2. How does Lucretius indicate the balance between the forces of creation and destruction in lines 1093–96?

3. Why does Lucretius emphasize that such disasters happen at random (**cāsū . . . forte**, 1096)?

1143   **incumbō, incumbere, incubuī** + dat., *to lie down* (on), *sink/settle* (on).
       incubuit: after a succession of words of motion, this stationary verb in enjambement arrives with a dreadful finality.
       Pandīon, Pandīonis, m., *Pandion* (a king of Athens).
          Pandīonis: perhaps this particular king's name was chosen as an ironic pun with **omnī**, since in Greek the root **pan-** means *all*.

1144   **catervātim**, adv., *in large numbers, in heaps.*
       morbō mortīque: repeating the elements from line 1138: **morbōrum et mortifer**.
       dabantur: plural with understood subject *the Athenians*.

1256   **exanimus, -a, -um**, *dead, lifeless.*
       super, prep. + abl., *on top of;* postponed in anastrophe.
       exanimāta: the near repetition separated by the delayed **super** paints a pathetic scene of complete devastation.

1257   **possēs**: past potential subjunctive, *you would (see).*
       retrō, adv., *in the reverse order, conversely.*

1258   **mātribus et patribus**: ablative with **super**, which is again displaced.
       ēdō, ēdere, ēdidī, ēditus, here, *to give out, breathe out.*

1267   **Multaque**: accusative plural neuter modifying **languida . . . membra** (1268), but separated for initial emphasis.
       passim, adv., *everywhere, in every direction.*
       prōmptus, -a, -um, *readily seen, plainly visible.*
          per populī passim . . . prōmpta: note the alliteration.
             per . . . viāsque: reorder **passim per prōmpta loca viāsque populī**, with reference to public areas such as the agoras and stoas, which were filled with refugees from the war.

1268   **sēmanimus, -a, -um**, *half-alive, half-dead.*
       vidērēs: past potential subjunctive, *you would see.*

1269   **horrida**: here, *rough.*
       paedor, paedōris, m., *dirt, filth.*
       pannus, -ī, m., *rag.*
       cooperiō, cooperīre, cooperuī, coopertus, *to cover completely, cover up.*
          horrida paedōre . . . pannīs cooperta: chiasmus.
       perīre: infinitive with **membra** (1268) in accusative and infinitive construction (dependent on **vidērēs**, 1268), which has arrived after an extraordinary number of descriptive words.

1270   **inluviēs, -eī**, f., *filth, foulness.*
       inluviē: ablative of means.
       pellis, pellis, f., *hide, skin.*
          pellī super ossibus ūnā: ablative of description or ablative absolute, using a proverbial expression, *with only skin over the bones,* i.e., *only skin and bones.*

1271   **ulcus, ulceris**, n., *sore.*
       taeter, taetra, taetrum, *foul.*
       prope iam: take with **sepulta**.
       sordēs, sordis, f., *dirt.*
          sordē: long *e* in the ablative singular also occurs elsewhere for metrical convenience.

1272   **Omnia**: accusative plural neuter agreeing with **dēlūbra**.
       dēnique, adv., *indeed; furthermore.*
       deum: = **deōrum**.
       dēlūbrum, -ī, n., *temple, shrine.*
       repleō, replēre, replēvī, replētus, *to fill up, fill.*
          replērat: syncopated pluperfect indicative = **replēverat**.

1273   **mors**: death is personified as the active agent with the verb **replērat**.
       onerātaque: nominative plural neuter modifying **templa** (1274); predicative in force, *(remained) burdened.*

1143   incubuit tandem populō Pandīonis omnī.

1144   Inde catervātim morbō mortīque dabantur.

          . . .

1256   Exanimīs puerīs super exanimāta parentum

1257   corpora nōnnumquam possēs retrōque vidēre

1258   mātribus et patribus nātōs super ēdere vītam.

          . . .

1267   Multaque per populī passim loca prōmpta viāsque

1268   languida sēmanimō cum corpore membra vidērēs

1269   horrida paedōre et pannīs cooperta perīre

1270   corporis inluviē, pellī super ossibus ūnā,

1271   ulceribus taetrīs prope iam sordēque sepulta.

1272   Omnia dēnique sāncta deum dēlūbra replērat

1273   corporibus mors exanimīs onerātaque passim

☙ Discussion Questions

1.   What is the effect of the placement of **omnī** in line 1143?

2.   What relationship does Lucretius emphasize in his description of the dead and dying?

Thucydides' description of the plague:

At the beginning the doctors were quite incapable of treating the disease because of their ignorance of the right methods. In fact mortality among the doctors was the highest of all, since they came more frequently in contact with the sick. Nor was any other human art or science of any help at all. Equally useless were prayers made in the temples, consultation of oracles, and so forth; indeed, in the end people were so overwhelmed by their sufferings that they paid no further attention to such things.

The plague originated, so they say, in Ethiopia in upper Egypt, and spread from there into Egypt itself and Libya and much of the territory of the King of Persia. In the city of Athens it appeared suddenly, and the first cases were among the population of Piraeus, so that it was supposed by them that the Peloponnesians had poisoned the reservoirs. Later, however, it appeared also in the upper city, and by this time the deaths were greatly increasing in number. As to the question of how it could first have come about or what causes can be found adequate to explain its powerful effect on nature, I must leave that to be considered by other writers, with or without medical experience. . . .

Terrible, too, was the sight of people dying like sheep through having caught the disease as a result of nursing others. This indeed caused more deaths than anything else. For when people were afraid to visit the sick, then they died with no one to look after them; indeed, there were many houses in which all the inhabitants perished through lack of any attention. When, on the other hand, they did visit the sick, they lost their own lives, and this was particularly true of those who made it a point of honor to act properly. Such people felt ashamed to think of their own safety and went into their friends' houses at times when even the members of the household were so overwhelmed by the weight of their calamities that they had actually given up the usual practice of making laments for the dead.

Thucydides, *The Peloponnesian War* 2.47–48, 51 (tr. Warner)

(See next page for another passage for comparison.)

1274   **cadāver, cadāveris**, n., *dead body, corpse.*

     caelestis, -is, -e, *coming from heaven, celestial.*

        caelestum: substantive, genitive plural; *of the sky-dwellers*, i.e., *of the gods.*

           cūncta cadāveribus caelestum: note the alliteration and the jarring juxtaposition of **cadāveribus** with **caelestum**. The gods never looked on death, and the dying were usually forbidden entrance to temples. Thus here we see that normal social and religious customs had broken down. Moreover, presumably the dying prayed fervently to the gods for help, which the gods could not and did not provide.

     manēbant: the imperfect indicates that no one even took care to remove the corpses from the temples.

1275   **hospitibus**: an odd and probably ironic word for these refugees from war who were soon to die from the plague. Some have seen a grim humor here, since the worst thing a guest could do would be to die in a host's home.

     quae: the relative has been postponed.

     complērant: syncopated pluperfect indicative = **complēverant**.

     aedituēns, aedituentis, m., *temple-keeper.*

1276   **dīvum**: = **dīvōrum**.

     nūmen, nūminis, n. *divine power, will; majesty.*

     magnī: genitive of value with **pendēbantur** (1277).

1277   **pendō, pendere, pependī** + gen. of value, *to regard as of* (much) *value, to think* (much) *of, to value* (much).

     enim: the explanatory conjunction has been severely postponed.

     exsuperō, -āre, -āre, -ātus, *to overcome, outweigh.*

        exsuperābat: the direct objects are **religiōnem** and **nūmina** supplied from the previous line.

1278   **sepultūra, -ae**, f., *disposal of human remains, burial.*

        mōs ille sepultūrae: though the language itself implies burial underground, it is clear from the description both here and in Thucydides that cremation was the normal practice. The words implying burial are simply broadened to include any disposal of the corpse.

1279   **quō**: *with which*, ablative singular neuter relative pronoun, the antecedent of which is **mōs**.

     cōnsuēscō, cōnsuēscere, cōnsuēvī, cōnsuētūrus, *to be accustomed/used* (to).

        cōnsuērat: pronounced as three syllables; syncopated pluperfect = **cōnsuēverat**.

     humō, -āre, -āvī, -ātus, *to bury, inter, dispose of a body.*

1280   **perturbātus . . . tōtus**: modifying **populus** understood.

1281   **quisque, quaeque, quidque**, *each, each one.*

     suum: i.e., *his own family member.*

     prō rē: *as circumstances allowed.*

     compostum: a textual suggestion in an otherwise incomplete line; contracted form = **compositum**, *laid out, arranged.*

     maestus, -a, -um, *sad.*

1274   cūncta cadāveribus caelestum templa manēbant,

1275   hospitibus loca quae complērant aedituentēs.

1276   Nec iam rēligiō dīvum nec nūmina magnī

1277   pendēbantur enim: praesēns dolor exsuperābat.

1278   Nec mōs ille sepultūrae remanēbat in urbe,

1279   quō prius hīc populus semper cōnsuērat humārī;

1280   perturbātus enim tōtus trepidābat, et ūnus

1281   quisque suum prō rē compostum maestus humābat.

The bodies of the dying were heaped one on top of the other, and half-dead creatures could be seen staggering about in the streets or flocking around the fountains in their desire for water. The temples in which they took up their quarters were full of the dead bodies of people who had died inside them. For the catastrophe was so overwhelming that men, not knowing what would happen next to them, became indifferent to every rule of religion or of law. All the funeral ceremonies which used to be observed were now disorganized, and they buried the dead as best they could. Many people, lacking the necessary means of burial because so many deaths had already occurred in their households, adopted the most shameless methods. They would arrive first at a funeral pyre that had been made by others, put their own dead upon it and set it alight; or, finding another pyre burning, they would throw the corpse that they were carrying on top of the other one and go away.

In other respects also Athens owed to the plague the beginnings of a state of unprecedented lawlessness. . . . No fear of god or law of man had a restraining influence. As for the gods, it seemed to be the same thing whether one worshiped them or not, when one saw the good and the bad dying indiscriminately.

       Thucydides, *The Peloponnesian War* 2.51–53 (tr. Warner)

[On a similar occurrence: the Noric plague]: On this land from the sickened sky there once came a piteous season that glowed with autumn's full heat. Every tribe of cattle, tame or wild, it swept to death; it poisoned the lakes, it tainted the pastures with venom.

       Vergil, *Georgics* 3.478–81 (tr. Fairclough)

1282   **Multaque**: accusative plural neuter with **horrida** (see note below).

      paupertās, paupertātis, f., *poverty*.

         paupertās: many of those in Athens were poor farmers from the countryside; also, the frequency of funerals would have quickly depleted any savings for funeral expenses.

      horrida: here, *grim/dreadful things*; accusative plural neuter as substantive modified by **multa**.

1283   **cōnsanguineī, -ōrum**, m., *blood relations, family members*.

      aliēnus, -a, -um, *of another, another's*.

         aliēna: accusative plural neuter modifying **exstrūcta** (1284), here *of a stranger* (not one of the family); epithet transferred from **rogōrum** to **exstrūcta**.

           cōnsanguineōs aliēna: note the oxymoronic juxtaposition.

1284   **īnsuper**, prep. + acc., *on to the top of, upon, on*; its object is **aliēna rogōrum** (1283) . . . **exstructa**.

      exstructa, here, *structures, piles*.

         aliēna rogōrum . . . exstructa: transferred epithet; **aliēna** logically applies to **rogōrum**.

1285   **subdō, subdere, subdidī, subditus**, *to apply underneath*.

      facēs: here, *funeral torches*.

         subdēbantque facēs: the pyres were kindled at the bottom by lighted torches.

           Namque suōs (1283) **. . . locābant subdēbantque facēs**: this behavior was specifically forbidden by the Twelve Tables, the earliest written Roman code of law.

1286   **potius quam**: governing the subjunctive.

      dēsererentur: *be abandoned, neglected*. This third pentasyllabic ending in 12 lines (1275 and 1277) perhaps adds solemnity to the close of the poem.

         multō cum sanguine . . . dēsererentur: the final lines show how deeply ingrained are religious beliefs and practices and how through religion men pointlessly trouble and harm themselves. This scene depicts people actually brawling over the disposal of corpses. The futility of their actions is obvious: the still-living are injuring themselves over corpses, and, in the Epicurean view, the corpses themselves cannot possibly care about proper burial.

1282   Multaque rēs subita et paupertās horrida suāsit.

1283   Namque suōs cōnsanguineōs aliēna rogōrum

1284   īnsuper exstrūcta ingentī clāmōre locābant

1285   subdēbantque facēs, multō cum sanguine saepe

1286   rixantēs potius quam corpora dēsererentur.

ᬇ Discussion Questions

1.   As the epic closes with the grim picture of natural destruction, how significant does the human race seem?

2.   Many have argued that the epic is incomplete and that Lucretius did not intend to conclude it with this horrific scene of destruction. What do you think?

❧ VOCABULARY ☙

❧ A

ā or **ab**, prep. + abl., *from, by*

abhinc, adv., *ago, previously; hereafter; from this place, hence*

absum, abesse, āfuī, āfutūrus, irreg., *to be away, be absent, be distant*

ac, conj., *and; than*

accēdō, accēdere, accessī, accessūrus, *to go or come to, approach*

accendō, accendere, accendī, accēnsus, *to set on fire, kindle*

accidō, accidere, accidī, *to fall on, to strike*
  accidit, accidere, accidit (impersonal), *it happens*

accipiō, accipere, accēpī, acceptus, *to accept, get, receive, welcome*

ācer, ācris, ācre, *keen, fierce, bitter*

acerbus, -a, -um, *bitter, painful, severe, harsh*

Acherūns, Acheruntis, m./f., *Acheron (a river in the underworld, thus the underworld itself)*

Acherūsius, -a, -um, *of the underworld; hellish*

ad, prep. + acc., *to, toward, at, near; for*

addō, addere, addidī, additus, *to add*

adeō, adv., *so much, to such an extent*
  usque adeō: idiom, *to such an extent*

adeō, adīre, adiī, aditus, irreg., *to come to, approach*

adhibeō, -ēre, -uī, -itus, *to apply, direct to*

adimō, adimere, adēmī, adēmptus + dat., *to take away (from)*

admixtus, -a, -um, + dat., *mixed in, intermingled in*

adsistō, adsistere, adstitī, *to take up position, stand, stop*

adstō, adstāre, adstitī, *to stand near, stand by*

adsum, adesse, adfuī, adfutūrus, irreg., *to be present, be near*

adventus, -ūs, m., *approach, arrival*

adversus, -a, -um, *unfavorable, adverse*

aedēs, aedis, f., *room, pl., house*

aeger, aegra, aegrum, *ill; anxious*

Aegyptus, -ī, f., *Egypt*

aequor, aequoris, n., *sea; level place; plain*

aequus, -a, -um, *equal, even, fair; untroubled, calm*

āēr, āeris, m., *air*

āerius, -a, -um, *existing in air, airy*

aerumna, -ae, f., *trouble, hardship*

aestus, -ūs, m., *heat*

aetās, aetātis, f., *time, age*

aeternus, -a, -um, *eternal, immortal*

aether, aetheris, m., *ether, sky*

aetherius, -a, -um, *heavenly, ethereal*

aevum -ī, n., *life*

afficiō, afficere, affēcī, affectus, *to affect*

ager, agrī, m., *land, field*

agnus, -ī, m., *lamb*

agō, agere, ēgī, āctus, *to do, drive; to discuss, debate*
  age!, *come, come on!*

ait, aiunt, *he/she says, said; they say, said*

aliēnus, -a, -um, *of another, another's; unsuitable to*

aliquī, aliquae or **aliqua, aliquod**, indef. adj., *some*

aliquis, aliquid, *someone, something; anyone, anything*

alius, alia, aliud, *another, other, one . . . another*
  aliī . . . aliī . . ., *some . . . others . . .*

almus, - a, -um, *kindly, gracious, nurturing*

alō, alere, aluī, altus, *to feed, nourish, rear*

alter, altera, alterum, *a/the second, one (of two), the other (of two), another*

altum, -ī, n., *the deep, the sea*

altus, -a, -um, *tall, high; deep*

alvus, –ī, f., *womb*

amābilis, -is, -e, *lovable, pleasurable*

amāns, amantis, m./f., *lover*

amārus, -a, -um, *bitter*

āmittō, āmittere, āmīsī, āmissus, *to lose*

amnis, amnis, m., *river*

amor, amōris, m., *love*

an, conj., *or*

angor, angōris, m., *anguish, anxiety*

anima, -ae, f., *soul, spirit*

animal, animālis, n., *living thing, animal*

animālis, -is, -e, *living, live, of a living creature*

animāns, animantis, m., f., n., *living thing, animal.*

animus, -ī, m., *mind, soul, spirit*

annus, -ī, m., *year*

ante, adv., *previously, before*

ante, prep. + acc., *before, in front of*

anteāctus, -a, -um, *past, gone before*

antequam, conj., *before*

antīquus, -a, -um, *ancient*

appāreō, -ēre, -uī, -itūrus, *to appear*

appellō, -āre, -āvī, -ātus, *to call, name*

aptus, -a, -um, *tied, fastened, bound;* + abl., *fitted* (with)

aqua, -ae, f., *water*

āra, -ae, f., *altar*

arātrum, -ī, n., *plow*

arbor, arboris, f., *tree*

arbusta, -ōrum, n. pl., *trees, woods, orchards*

ārdor, ārdōris, m., *heat*

arma, -ōrum, n. pl., *arms, weapons*

armenta, -ōrum, n. pl., *herds, cattle*

arrīdeō, arrīdere, arrīsī, arrīsus, *to smile, be favorable*

ars, artis, f., *skill*

artus, -a, -um, *close, tightly-fastened*

artus, -ūs, m., *limb*

arvum, -ī, n., *plowed field*

aspergō, aspergere, aspersī, aspersus, *to sprinkle, splash, spatter*

assiduus, -a, um, *incessant, constant*

at, conj., *but*

atque, conj., *and, also, and so*

auctō, -āre, āvī, -ātus, *to increase, cause to grow.*

audeō, audēre, ausus sum, semi-deponent + infin., *to dare* (to)

audiō, -īre, -īvī, -ītus, *to hear, listen to*

auferō, auferre, abstulī, ablātus, irreg., *to carry away, take away*

augeō, augēre, auxī, auctus, *to increase*

aura, -ae, f., *breeze*

aureus, -a, -um, *golden*

auris, auris, f., *ear*

aurōra, -ae, f., *dawn*

aurum, -ī, n., *gold*

aut, conj., *or*

    aut . . . aut, conj., *either . . . or*

autem, conj., *however, but, moreover*

auxilium, -ī, n., *help, aid*

aveō, avēre, *to be eager; to desire, wish*

āvertō, āvertere, āvertī, āversus, *to turn away, divert*

avidus, -a, -um, *greedy*

avis, avis, gen. pl., **avium**, m./f., *bird*

āvius, -a, -um, *pathless, out of the way, unfrequented*

∽ B

bellum, -ī, n., *war*

bene, adv., *well*

bibō, bibere, bibī, *to drink*

blandus, -a, -um, *charming, alluring, enticing*

    blandē, adv., *in a coaxing/winning manner; charmingly*

bōs, bovis, m./f., *ox, cow*

brevis, -is, -e, *short, brief, small*

∽ C

cachinnus, -ī, m., *laughter*

cadō, cadere, cecidī, cāsūrus, *to fall*

caecus, -a, -um, *blind; unseen, invisible, hidden; impenetrable*

caelestis, -is, -e, *coming from heaven*

caelum, -ī, n., *sky, heaven*

calidus, -a, -um, *warm*

campus, -ī, m., *plain, field*

canis, canis, m./f., *dog*

canō, canere, cecinī, cantus, *to sing*

capiō, capere, cēpī, captus, *to take, catch, capture, seize*

caput, capitis, n., *head*

carcer, carceris, m., *prison; stall*

careō, carēre, caruī, caritūrus + abl., *to need, lack*

carmen, carminis, n., *song; poetry*

casa, -ae, f., *hut, cottage*

castus, -a, -um, *virtuous, chaste*

cāsus, -ūs, m., *fall*

    cāsū, *by chance, accidentally*

caterva, -ae, f., *crowd, herd*

causa, -ae, f., *reason, cause; case*

    genitive + **causā**, *for the sake of, for*

caveō, cavēre, cāvī, cautus, *to be careful, watch out for, beware*

cēdō, cēdere, cessī, cessūrus + dat., *to yield to, give in to*

cēlō, -āre, -āvī, -ātus, *to hide, conceal*

cēnseō, cēnsēre, cēnsuī, cēnsus, *to think, suppose*

Cerēs, Cereris, f., *Ceres* (goddess of agriculture)

cernō, cernere, crēvī, crētus, *to see, discern, perceive*

certāmen, certāminis, n., *contest*

certō, -āre, -āvī, -ātūrus, *to strive*

certus, -a, -um, *certain, fixed*

    certē, adv., *certainly*

cēterī, -ae, -a, *the rest, the others*

cibus, –ī, m., *food*

cieō (or **ciō**), **ciēre** (or **cīre**), **cīvī, citus**, *to move, stir, rouse*

circum, prep. + acc., *around*

circumdō, circumdare, circumdedī, circumdatus, *to put/place around; to surround*

cithara, -ae, f., *lyre*

cīvis, cīvis, m., *citizen*

clādēs, clādis, f., *calamity, disaster, ruin*

clāmor, clāmōris, m., *shout, shouting*

clārus, -a, -um, *bright, illustrious; clear-sounding, clear*

classis, classis, f., *fleet*

clueō, cluēre, *to be called, be named; to be*

coepī, *I began*

coetus, -ūs, m., *union*

cognōscō, cognōscere, cognōvī, cognitus, *to find out, learn;* in perfect, *to have learned, to know*

cōgō, cōgere, coēgī, coāctus, *to compel, force*

colligō, colligere, collēgī, collēctus, *to gather together, collect*

collis, collis, m., *hill*

colō, colere, coluī, cultus, *to cultivate; to dwell in, inhabit*

color, colōris, m., *color, tint*

comitor, -ārī, -ātus sum, *to accompany*

commemorō, -āre, –āvī, -ātus, *to mention, comment on, recount*

commodus, -a, -um, *pleasant*

commoveō, commovēre, commōvī, commōtus, *to move, upset*

commūnis, -is, -e, *common*

compleō, complēre, complēvī, complētus, *to fill, complete*

compōnō, compōnere, composuī, compositus, *to compose*

comprimō, comprimere, compressī, compressus, *to curb, constrain, suppress*

cōmptus, -ūs, m., *hair, tress*

concēdō, concēdere, concessī, concessūrus, *to admit, concede; yield*

concelebrō, -āre, -āvī, -ātus, *to fill with living things, enliven; to throng, crowd*

concidō, concidere, concidī, *to fall down*

concilium, -ī, n., *meeting, union*

concipiō, concipere, concēpī, conceptus, *to conceive*

concursus, -ūs, m., *meeting* (by collision)

concutiō, concutere, concussī, concussus, *to shake violently, agitate*

condō, condere, condidī, conditus, *to found, establish, compose; to hide*

cōnferō, cōnferre, contulī, collātus, irreg., *to confer, bestow; to compare*

cōnficiō, cōnficere, cōnfēcī, cōnfectus, *to accomplish, finish*

cōnfirmō, -āre, -āvī, -ātus, *to strengthen, confirm*

cōnfiteor, cōnfitērī, cōnfessus sum, *to confess, admit*

cōnflō, -āre, -āvī, -ātus, *to blow into flame, ignite*

congerō, congerere, congessī, congestus, *to heap up, pile up*

congressus, -ūs, m., *meeting*

cōniciō, cōnicere, coniēcī, coniectus, *to throw, throw together; to guess*

coniungō, coniungere, coniūnxī, coniūnctus, *to join*

cōnor, -ārī, -ātus sum, *to try*

cōnscius, -a, -um, *inwardly aware, conscious* (of), *conscious of guilt*

cōnsequor, cōnsequī, cōnsecūtus sum, *to catch up to, overtake*

cōnsilium, -ī, n., *plan*

cōnsimilis, -is, -e, *similar, like, alike*

cōnsistō, cōnsistere, cōnstitī, *to halt, stop, stand; to remain fixed, stand firm; to be, exist*

cōnspiciō, cōnspicere, cōnspexī, cōnspectus, *to catch sight of, see, perceive*

cōnstituō, cōnstituere, cōnstituī, cōnstitūtus, *to decide*

cōnstō, cōnstāre, cōnstitī, *to stand together, consist, remain constant, remain fixed, be, exist*

cōnsuēscō, cōnsuēscere, cōnsuēvī, cōnsuētūrus, *to be accustomed or used (to)*

cōnsūmō, cōnsūmere, cōnsūmpsī, cōnsūmptus, *to destroy, consume, reduce to nothing*

contemnō, contemnere, contempsī, contemptus, *to despise, scorn*

contendō, contendere, contendī, contentus, *to compete, contend*

contineō, continēre, continuī, contentus, *to confine, hold, constrain, dominate*

contingō, contingere, contigī, contāctus, *to touch; to defile, pollute*

contrā, adv., *in return ; in opposition; on the other hand*

contrā, prep. + acc., *against, opposite, in front of, facing*

conveniō, convenīre, convēnī, conventūrus, *to come together, meet, assemble*

convertō, convertere, convertī, conversus, *to turn (around)*

convīva, ae, m., *guest (at a banquet)*

convīvium, -ī, n., *feast, banquet*

coorior, coorīrī, coortus sum, *to rise up, arise*

cōpia, -ae, f., *supply; opportunity*

cor, cordis, n., *heart*

corōna, -ae, f., *garland, crown*

corporeus, -a, -um, *consisting of body, corporeal, material, physical*

corpus, corporis, n., *body*

corripiō, corripere, corripuī, correptus, *to seize, grab*

crēber, crēbra, crēbrum, *frequent, repeated*

crēdō, crēdere, crēdidī, crēditus + dat., *to trust, believe*

creō, -āre, -āvī, -ātus, *to create, make*
crēscō, crēscere, crēvī, crētūrus, *to grow*
Crēta, -ae, f., *Crete* (large island southeast of Greece)
culpa, -ae, f., *fault, blame; flaw*
cultus, -a, -um, *cultivated*
cum, conj., *when, since; although*
cum, prep. + abl., *with*
cūnctus, -a, -um, *the whole of, all*
cupīdō, cupīdinis, f., *longing, desire* (for)
cupidus, -a, -um, *eager, keen, desirous*
cupiō, cupere, cupīvī, cupītus, *to desire, want*
cūr, interr. and relative adv., *why?*
cūra, -ae, f., *care*
cūrō, -āre, -āvī, -ātus, *to look after, take care of*
cursus, -ūs, m., *running, rapid motion; charging*
curvus, -a, -um, *curved, bent*
custōs, custōdis, m., *guard*

✼ D

daedalus, -a, -um, *variegated, skillful, inventive*
dē, prep. + abl., *down from, from, concerning, about*
dea, -ae, f., *goddess*
dēbeō, -ēre, -uī, -itus, *to owe;* + infin., *ought* (to)
decet, decere, decuit, *it is becoming, fitting; one should*
dēclīnō, -āre, -āvī, -ātus, *to change direction, deviate, swerve*
dēcursus, -ūs, m., *descent, downward rush*
dēdicō, -āre, -āvī, -ātus, *to make clear, proclaim, declare*
dēfendō, dēfendere, dēfendī, dēfēnsus, *to defend, protect*
dēferō, dēferre, dētulī, dēlātus, *to award, grant*
dēfessus, -a, -um, *tired*
dēgō, dēgere, *to live, spend* (one's time)
deinceps, adv., *in turn, next*
deinde, adv., *then, next*
dēlectus, -a, -um, *select, picked for excellence*
dēlībō, -āre, -āvī, -ātus, *to mar, diminish, infringe*
dēliciae, -ārum, f. pl., *delights*
dēlūbrum, -ī, n., *temple, shrine*
dēmum, adv., *at last, finally; indeed*
dēnique, adv., *in short, indeed; at last, finally; furthermore*
deorsum, adv., *downwards*
dēpōnō, dēpōnere, dēposuī, dēpositus, *to lay down, put aside, set down*
dēsertus, -a, -um, *deserted, uninhabited*
dēsīderium, -ī, n., *desire/longing for, grief for*
dēsinō, dēsinere, dēsiī, dēsitus, *to stop, cease*

dēterō, dēterere, dētrīvī, dētrītus, *to wear away*
deus, -ī, m., nom. pl, **dī**, dat., abl. pl. **dīs**, *god*
dēvincō, dēvincere, dēvīcī, dēvictus, *to conquer thoroughly, subjugate, subdue*
dexter, dextera, dextrum, *right*
dextra, -ae, f., *right hand*
dīcō, dīcere, dīxī, dictus, *to say, tell*
dictum -ī, n., *saying, word*
diēs, diēī, m. or f., *day*
differo, differre, distulī, dīlātus, *to scatter, disperse.;* intrans., *to differ*
difficilis, -is, -e, *difficult*
diffīdō, diffīdere, diffīsus sum, semi-deponent + dat., *to lack confidence in, distrust*
diffugio, diffugere, diffūgī, *to scatter, disperse*
diffundō, diffundere, diffūdī, diffūsus, *to spread widely, diffuse*
digitus, -ī, m., *finger*
dignor, -ārī, -ātus sum + infin., *to consider worthy, to deign* (to)
dignus, -a, -um + abl., *worthy of, deserving*
dīmittō, dīmittere, dīmīsī, dīmissus, *to send away*
discēdō, discēdere, discessī, discessūrus, *to go away, depart*
discidium, -ī, n., *separation, sundering, dissolution*
discō, discere, didicī, *to learn*
discutiō, discutere, discussī, discussus, *to dispel, scatter*
dispōnō, dispōnere, disposuī, dispositus, *to order, arrange*
disserō, disserere, disseruī, dissertus, *to set out in words, discuss*
dissimilis, -is, -e, *dissimilar*
dissoluō, dissoluere, dissoluī, dissolūtus, *to break up, dissolve; to release, free*
distō, distāre, *to differ, be different*
dīus, -a, -um, *with the brightness of day, bright, divine*
dīva, -ae, f., *goddess*
diverberō, -āre, -āvī, -ātus, *to cause to part by hitting, to cleave, split*
dīversus, -a, -um, *different, in a different direction, apart*
dīvidō, dīvidere, dīvīsī, dīvīsus, *to divide*
dīvīnitus, adv., *by divine agency, power; divinely*
dīvīnus, -a, -um, *divine*
dīvus, -ī, m., *god*
dō, dare, dedī, datus, *to give*
doceō, docēre, docuī, doctus, *to teach*
dolor, dolōris, m., *grief; pain*
dominus, -ī, m., *master, owner*
domus, -ūs, f., acc. pl. **domōs**, *house*

dōnec, conj., *until*

dōnō, -āre, -āvī, -ātus, *to give; to present somebody* (acc.) *with something* (abl.)

dōnum, -i, n., *gift*

dubitō, -āre, -āvī, -ātus, *to be in doubt; to hesistate*

dubium, -ī, n., *doubt*

dūcō, dūcere, dūxī, ductus, *to lead, take, bring*

dulcis, -is, -e, *sweet*

dum, conj. + subjn., *until; provided that;* + indic., *while*

duo, duae, duo, *two*

dūrus, -a, -um, *hard, harsh*

♔ E

ē or **ex**, prep. + abl., *from, out of*

ēdō, ēdere, ēdidī, ēditus, *to give rise to, cause, produce*

efferō, efferre, extulī, ēlātus, irreg., *to carry out, bring out*

efficiō, efficere, effēcī, effectus, *to bring about, accomplish;* with **ut** plus subjn.

effugiō, effugere, effūgī, *to flee, run away, escape*

effundō, effundere, effūdī, effūsus, *to pour out;* pass., *to spill*

egeō, egēre, eguī, + gen. or abl., *need*

ego, meī, mihi, mē, mē, *I, me*

elementum, -ī, n., *basic principle, element*

ēmergō, ēmergere, ēmersī, ēmersūrus, *to come forth, arise, emerge*

ēmittō, ēmittere, ēmīsī, ēmissus, *to send out*

enim, conj., *for*

eō, īre, iī or **īvī, itūrus**, irreg., *to go*

eō magis, adv., *all the more, by this*

epulae, -ārum, f. pl., *banquet, feast*

equus, -ī, m., *horse*

ergō, conj., *therefore*

ēripiō, ēripere, ēripuī, ēreptus, *to snatch from, away*

errō, -āre, -āvī, -ātūrus, *to wander, be mistaken*

ērumpō, ērumpere, ērūpī, ēruptus, *to burst forth, out*

et, conj., *and, also; than, as*

etenim, conj., *for*

etiam, adv., *also, even, again*

etiam atque etiam, *again and again*

etsī, conj., *even if, although*

exanimātus, -a, -um, *paralyzed; lifeless, dead*

exanimō, -āre, -āvī, -ātus, *to kill*

excellō, excellere, excelluī, *to be pre-eminent, excel*

exeō, exīre, exiī or **exīvī, exitūrus**, irreg., *to go out*

exerceō, -ēre, -uī, -itus, *to exercise, train, keep at work*

eximius, -a, -um, *outstanding, exceptional*

eximō, eximere, exēmī, exēmptus, *to remove*

exitium, -ī, n., *destruction, death*

exōrdium, -ī, n., *starting point, beginning*

exorior, exorīrī, exortus sum, *to rise up, come to birth, come into existence, spring to life, arise*

expediō, expedīre, expedīvī or **expediī, expedītus**, *to explain*

expellō, expellere, expulī, expulsus, *to drive out, expel*

experior, experīrī, expertus sum, *to test, try*

expleō, explēre, explēvī, explētus, *to fill*

expōnō, expōnere, exposuī, expositus, *to set forth, expound, explain*

exprimō, exprimere, expressī, expressus, *to press out, express*

exsistō, exsistere, exstitī, *to come into being, emerge, arise*

exsolvō, exsolvere, exsoluī, exsolūtus, *to unloosen, release, unravel*

exstō, exstāre, exstitī, *to exist, be found*

exstruō, exstruere, exstrūxī, exstrūctus, *to build*

extrā, prep. + acc., *outside*

extrahō, extrahere, extrāxī, extractus, *to drag out, take out*

extrēmus, -a, -um, *at the end, uttermost, extreme*

♔ F

facilis, -is, -e, *easy*

facile, adv., *easily*

faciō, facere, fēcī, factus, *to make, do*

factum -ī, n., *deed*

facultās, facultātis, f., *power, ability*

fāma, -ae, f., *fame, report, story*

fascēs, fascium, m. pl., *rods (symbols of office)*

fateor, fatērī, fassus sum, *to concede, admit*

fatīgō, -āre, -āvī, -ātus, *to weary, tire out; to criticize, assail*

fātum, -ī, n., *fate*

fax, facis, f., *torch*

fēcundus, -a, -um, *fertile, rich, prolific*

fēlīx, fēlīcis, *lucky, happy, fortunate*

fēmina, -ae, f., *woman*

fera, -ae, f., *wild beast*

ferē, adv., *generally, usually*

fermē, adv., *quite, entirely; invariably, always*

ferō, ferre, tulī, lātus, irreg., *to bring, carry, bear, endure; to say*

ferrum, -ī, n., *sword; iron*

ferus, -a, -um, *fierce, rough, harsh*

fervō, fervere, fervī, *to move quickly, seethe*
fessus, -a, -um, *tired, weary*
fēstus, -a, -um, *festival/feast* (day)
fētus, -ūs, m., *fruit, produce; offspring*
fidēlis, -is, -e, *faithful*
fidēs, fideī, f., *good faith, reliabiity, trust*
figūra, -ae, f., *shape, size*
fīlum, -ī, n., *thread*
fingō, fingere, fīnxī, fictus, *to fashion, devise, imagine*
fīniō, -īre, -īvī, -ītus, *to finish, limit, bound*
fīnis, fīnis, m. (f.), *end, limit; border*
    fīnītus, -a, -um, *limited*
fīo, fierī, factus sum, irreg., *to become, be made, be done, happen*
flābrum, -ī, n., *gust, blast*
flammō, -āre, -āvī, -ātus, *to flame, blaze*
flectō, flectere, flexī, flexus, *to guide, steer, direct*
fleō, flēre, flēvī, flētus, *to weep, cry*
flōreō, -ēre, -uī, *to flourish*
flōs, flōris, m., *flower*
flūctus, -ūs, m., *wave; turbulence, trouble*
flūmen, flūminis, n., *river, stream, flow*
fluvius, -ī, m., *river*
foedus, -a, -um, *filthy, disgusting, foul*
    foedē, adv., *foully, basely*
folium, -ī, n., *leaf*
fōns, fontis, m., *spring, the water of a spring*
forās, adv., *outside*
fore, alternative form of **futūrum esse**
forīs, adv., *outside, abroad; from without, from outside*
fōrma, -ae, f., *form, shape, appearance*
formīdō, formīdinis, f., *fear*
forte, adv., *by chance*
fortis, -is, -e, *brave, strong, mighty*
fortūna, -ae, f., *fortune* (good or bad)
frangō, frangere, frēgī, frāctus, *to break*
frīgidus, -a, -um, *cool, cold, chill*
frīgus, frīgoris, n., *cold*
frondifer, frondifera, frondiferum, *leaf-bearing, leafy*
frōns, frondis, f., *leaf, foliage*
frūctus, -ūs, m., *fruit; enjoyment, profit*
frūgēs, frūgum, f. pl., *produce, crops, fruit*
fruor, fruī, frūctus sum + abl., *to enjoy*
frūstrā, adv., *in vain*
fugiō, fugere, fūgī, fugitūrus, *to flee*
fulgōr, fulgōris, m., *glitter, brightness, gleam*
fulmen, fulminis, n., *thunderbolt*
funditus, adv., *from the bottom, utterly, completely*

fundō, -āre, -āvī, -ātus, *to base, found, establish; to ground*
fundō, fundere, fūdī, fūsus, *to pour out/forth*

𝕭   G

gaudium, -ī, n., *joy*
generātim, adv., *by species, according to kind/race*
genetrīx, genetrīcis, f., *mother*
genitālis, -is, -e, *concerned with creation, growth; generative*
gēns, gentis, f., *family, race; pl., peoples*
genu, -ūs, n., *knee*
genus, generis, n., *race, stock, nation; type, kind*
gerō, gerere, gessī, gestus, *to wear; to carry on, perform, do*
gignō, gignere, genuī, genitus, *to create*
globus, -ī, m., *sphere*
glōria, -ae, f., *fame, glory*
Grāius, -a, -um, *Greek*
grāmen, grāminis, n., *grass*
grandis, -is, -e, *aged, old*
grātus, -ā, -um + dat., *pleasing (to) dear (to) grateful; pleasant*
gravis, -is, -e, *heavy, serious*
gremium, -ī, n., *lap*
gubernō, -āre, -āvī, -ātus, *to pilot, control, govern*
gutta, -ae, f., *drop*

𝕭   H

habēnae, -ārum, f. pl., *reins*
habeō, -ēre, -uī, -itus, *to have, hold*
haedus, -ī, m., *kid, young goat*
haereō, haerēre, haesī, haesūrus, *to stick*
haud, adv., *not*
herba, -ae, f., *grass*
Herculēs, Herculis, m., *Hercules (Greek hero)*
hīc, adv., *here*
hīc, haec, hōc, *this, the latter*
hinc, adv., *from here*
homō, hominis, m., *man*
    hominēs, hominum, m. pl, *people*
honor, honōris, m., *honor; political office*
horribilis, -is, -e, *fearful, dreadful*
horridus, -a, -um, *shaking with fear, quaking, trembling; rough*
horrifer, horrifera, horriferum, *frightening, dreadful*
horror, horrōris, m., *bristling; dread, fear; awe, wonderment*

hospes, hospitis, m., *guest*
hūc, adv., *here, to here*
hūmānus, -a, -um, *human*
humī, *on the ground*
humō, -āre, -āvī, -ātus, *to bury, inter, dispose of a body*

❧ I

iaceō, -ēre, -uī, -itūrus, *to lie, be lying down*
iaciō, iacere, iēcī, iactus, *to throw*
iactō, -āre, -āvī, -ātus, *to toss about, drive to and fro*
iactus, -ūs, m., *the action of throwing*
iam, adv., *now, already; soon*
ibi, adv., *there*
īciō, īcere, īcī, īctus, *to strike*
ictus, -ūs, m., *blow*
īdem, eadem, idem, *the same*
igitur, conj., *therefore*
ignis, ignis, m., *fire*
ignōrō, -āre, -āvī, -ātus, *not to know, to be ignorant of*
ille, illa, illud, *that; he, she, it; the former; that famous*
imber, imbris, m., *rain*
imbibō, imbibere, imbibī, imbibitus, *to drink in; to thirst*
immānis, -is, -e, *huge, immense*
immēnsus, -a, -um, *infinite, boundless*
immortālis, -is, -e, *immortal*
impediō, -īre, -īvī, -ītus, *to hinder, prevent*
impello, impellere, impulī, impulsus, *to strike or beat against, stir*
imperium, -ī, n., *empire, power, authority*
impetus, -ūs, m., *attack*
impius, -a, -um, *irreligious, impious*
in, prep. + abl., *in, on, among*
in, prep. + acc., *into, against*
ināne, inānis, n., *empty space, void*
inānis, -is, -e, *empty, groundless, foolish*
incassum, adv., *without aim or purpose, in vain; fortuitously*
incertus, -a, -um, *not fixed, uncertain*
incipiō, incipere, incēpī, inceptus, *to begin*
incitus, -a, -um, *set in rapid or violent motion, roused, stirred up*
inclutus, -a, -um, *celebrated, famous, renowned, illustrious*
incolumis, -is, -e, *unhurt, safe and sound*
increpō, increpāre, increpuī, increpitus, *to blame or reproach loudly; to chide, rebuke*

incutiō, incutere, incussī, incussus, *to strike, dash (one thing [acc.] on another [abl.])*
inde, adv., *from there, then*
indignus, -a, -um, *unworthy, not deserving*
indūcō, indūcere, indūxi, inductus, *to lead on, urge, entice*
ineō, inīre, iniī or inīvī, initus, irreg., *to go into, enter*
īnfāns, īnfantis, m./f., *infant, young child*
īnferiae, -ārum, f. pl., *offerings and rites in honor of the dead at the tomb*
īnfestus, -a, -um, *hostile*
īnfīnītus, -a, -um, *limitless, infinite*
īnfirmus, -a, -um, *weak, shaky, frail*
īnfrā, adv., *below, beneath*
īnfringō, īnfringere, īnfrēgī, īnfrāctus, *to weaken, impair*
ingenium, -ī, n., *intelligence, ingenuity*
ingēns, ingentis, *huge*
ingrātus, -a, -um, *unpleasant, unpleasing; unenjoyed, unappreciated.*
innumerus, -a, -um, *countless, numberless*
inquam, irreg., *I say*
īnsideō, īnsidēre, īnsēdī, īnsessūrus + dat., *to lie heavy on, beset, trouble*
īnsignis, -is, -e, *conspicuous, glorious*
īnsinuō, -āre, -āvī, -ātus + dat., *to insert by sinuous means, to work one's way in*
īnstituō, īnstituere, īnstituī, īnstitūtus, *to establish*
īnstō, īnstāre, īnstitī + dat., *to stand over, press upon; to set foot on*
īnsum, inesse, īnfuī, *to be present in (or on), to reside in*
integō, integere, intēxī, intēctus, *to cover, cover over*
integrō, -āre, -āvī, -ātus, *to replenish*
intellegō, intellegere, intellēxī, intellēctus, *to understand, realize*
inter, prep. + acc., *between, among*
interdum, adv., *from time to time, sometimes*
intereā, adv., *meanwhile*
intereō, interīre, interiī, interitūrus, *to perish, be destroyed*
interimō, interimere, interēmī, interēmptus, *to destroy*
intervāllum, -ī, n., *gap, interval*
intus, adv., *within, inside*
inveniō, invenīre, invēnī, inventus, *to come upon, find, discover*
invītō, -āre, -āvī, -ātus, *to invite*
iocus, -ī, m.; n. in pl., *joke, funny story*
ipse, ipsa, ipsum, *himself, herself, itself, themselves; very*

īra, -ae, f., *anger, wrath*
is, ea, id, *he, she, it; this, that*
ita, adv., *thus, so, in this way, in such a way*
itaque, adv., *and so, therefore*
item, adv., *likewise, similarly, in turn*
iūcundus, -a, -um, *pleasant, delightful*
iungō, iungere, iūnxī, iūnctus, *to join*
iūs, iūris, n., *right, law, justice*
iuvenis, iuvenis, m., *young man, youth*
iuvō, -āre, iūvī, iūtus, *to please, delight*

✂ L

lābor, lābī, lāpsus sum, *to slip, fall, stumble*
labor, labōris, m., *work, toil*
labōrō, -āre, -āvī, -ātus, *to work*
lac, lactis, n., *milk*
lacrima, -ae, f., *tear*
lacrimō, -āre, -āvī, -ātus, *to weep, cry*
lacus, -ūs, m., *lake*
laedō, laedere, laesī, laesus, *to harm*
laetus, -a, -um, *happy, glad; fertile, productive*
lāna, -ae, f., *wool*
langueō, -ēre, *to be ill in bed; to be faint, weak*
languidus, -a, -um, *drooping*
lapis, lapidis, m., *stone*
largus, -a, -um, *plentiful, copious, abundant*
lātē, adv., *widely, far and wide*
latebra, -ae, f., *hiding-place, lair*
latex, laticis, m., *liquid, water*
latrō, -āre, -āvī, -ātūrus, *to bark*
laudō, -āre, -āvī, -ātus, *to praise*
laus, laudis, f., *praise, fame*
legiō, legiōnis, f., *legion* (a division of the Roman army)
leō, leōnis, m., *lion*
lepos, lepōris, m., *charm, grace*
lētum, -ī, n., *death*
levis, -is, -e, *light*
lēx, lēgis, f., *law*
līber, lībera, līberum, *free*
licet, licēre, licuit + dat., *it is allowed*
līmen, līminis, n., *threshold, doorway*
lingua, -ae, f., *tongue; language*
liquidus, -a, -um, *clear, bright*
liquor, liquōris, m., *liquid*
lītus, lītoris, n., *shore*
locō, -āre, -āvī, -ātus, *to place*
locus, -ī, m.; n. in pl., *place*
longus, -a, -um, *long*
   longē, adv., *far, far from, afar*
loquēla, -ae, f., *speech*
lūcidus, -a, -um, *bright, shining, clear*

lūctus, -ūs, m., *grief, mourning, lamentation*
lūdī, -ōrum, m. pl., *games*
lūdō, lūdere, lūsī, lūsūrus, *to play; to trick, cheat*
lūmen, lūminis, n., *light*
lūna, -ae, f., *moon*
lūx, lūcis, f., *light*

✂ M

mactō, -āre, -āvī, -ātus, *to slaughter, sacrifice*
maestus, -a, -um, *sad*
magis, adv., *more; rather*
magnus, -a, -um, *big, great, large*
maior, maior, maius, gen. **maiōris**, *bigger, greater*
mālō, mālle, māluī, irreg., *to prefer*
malum, -ī, n., *trouble, misfortune, evil*
malus, -a, -um, *bad, evil*
maneō, manēre, mānsī, mānsūrus, *to remain, stay, wait*
mānēs, mānium, m. pl., *spirits of the dead*
   dīs mānibus, *to the spirits of the dead*
manifestus, -a, -um, *clear, visible*
manō, -āre, -āvī, *to flow, drip*
manus, -ūs, f., *hand; band (of men)*
marceō, marcēre, *to be enfeebled, weak; to waste away*
mare, maris, n., *sea*
māter, mātris, f., *mother*
māteria, -ae or **-āī**, f., *matter*
māteriēs, materiēī, f., *matter*
māternus, -a, -um, *of a mother, maternal*
maximus, -a, -um, *biggest, greatest, very great, very large*
medius, -a, -um, *mid-, middle of*
melior, melior, melius, gen., **meliōris**, *better*
   melius, adv., *better*
membrum, -ī, n., *limb*
Memmius, -ī, m., *Gaius Memmius* (the dedicatee of the poem)
mēns, mentis, f., *mind*
meō, -āre, -āvī, -ātūrus, *to pass, travel*
meritō, adv., *deservedly, with reason*
merus, -a, um, *pure, unmixed*
metuō, metuere, metuī, *to fear*
metus, -ūs, m., *fear*
meus, -a, -um, *my, mine*
mīlle, *a thousand*
   mīlia, mīlium, n. pl., *thousands*
mināx, minācis, *menacing, threatening*
minimus, -a, -um, *very small, smallest, least*
minister, ministrī, m., *attendant* (of a priest)
minitor, minitārī, minitātus sum, *to threaten*

minor, minor, minus, gen. **minōris**, *smaller, less*

minuō, minuere, minuī, minūtus, *to lessen, reduce, decrease*

mīrābilis, -is, -e, *wonderful, surprising*

mīror, -ārī, -ātus sum, *to admire, wonder at, wonder*

mīrus, -a, -um, *wonderful, marvelous, strange*

misceō, miscēre, miscuī, mixtus, *to mix*

miser, misera, miserum, *unhappy, miserable, wretched*

misereor, -ērī, -itus sum + gen., *to pity*

mittō, mittere, mīsī, missus, *to send, let go*

mōbilitās, mōbilitātis, f., *speed*

modus, -ī, m., *way, method; limit*

moenia, moenium, n. pl., *walls*

mōlēs, mōlis, f., *mass, huge bulk*

mōlior, mōlīrī, mōlītus sum, *to strive, struggle, try*

mollis, -is, -e, *soft*

mōmen, mōminis, n., *movement, motion; trend*

moneō, -ēre, -uī, -itus, *to advise, warn*

mōns, montis, m., *mountain, hill*

morbidus, -a, -um, *causing disease, unhealthy, sickly*

morbus, -ī, m., *illness, disease*

morior, morī, mortuus sum, *to die*

mors, mortis, f., *death*

mortālēs, mortālium, m. pl., *mortals*

mortālis, -is, -e, *mortal, destructible*

mortifer, mortifera, mortiferum, *death-bearing, fatal, deadly*

mōs, mōris, m., *custom, manner; pl., character*

mōtus, -ūs, m., *motion, movement*

moveō, movēre, mōvī, mōtus, *to move*

muliebris, -is, -e, *womanly, female*

mulier, mulieris, f., *woman*

multimodīs, adv., *in many ways*

multus, -a, -um, *much; pl., many*

    multum, adv., *greatly, much*

    multō, abl., *by much, much*

mundus, -ī, m., *world, earth*

mūnītus, -a, -um, *fortified*

mūnus, mūneris, n., *gift, service, duty*

murmur, murmuris, n., *murmur, rumble*

mūsa, -ae, *muse (goddess of song and poetry)*

mūtō, -āre, -āvī, -ātus, *to change*

mūtus, -a, -um, *silent, mute*

mūtuus, -a, -um, *mutual*

☙ N

nam, conj., *for*

namque, conj., *for, for indeed, for also*

nārēs, nārium, f. pl., *nostrils, nose*

nāscor, nāscī, nātus sum, *to be born*

nātīvus, -a, -um, *having a birth/origin, created*

natō, -āre, -āvī, -ātūrus, *to swim*

nātūra, -ae, f., *nature*

nātus, -ī, m., *son; pl., children*

nāvis, nāvis, f., *ship*

nē, conj. + subjn., *not to, so that . . . not, to prevent, to avoid, lest*

nec, conj., *and . . . not, nor*

    nec . . . nec, *neither . . . nor*

necesse, adv. or indecl. adj., *necessary*

    necesse est, *it must be that, it is necessary*

nēmō, nēminis, m. / f., *no one*

nemus, nemoris, n., *grove, forest*

neque, conj., *and . . . not, nor*

    neque . . . neque, *neither . . . nor*

nequeō, nequīre, nequīvī, *to be unable* (to)

nēquīquam, adv., *in vain*

niger, nigra, nigrum, *black*

nihil, *nothing*

    nīl, *nothing*

nīlum, -ī, n., *nothing*

    nīlō, adv., *by nothing, not at all*

nīmīrum, adv., *without doubt, certainly*

nimis, adv., *too much*

nisi, conj., *unless, if . . . not, except*

niteō, -ēre, -uī, *to be radiant, shine*

nitidus, -a, -um, *bright, shining, gleaming*

nītor, nītī, nīxus sum, *to strive, strain, exert oneself (to)*

nōbilitās, nōbilitātis, f., *nobility of rank or birth*

noceō, -ēre, -uī, -itūrus + dat., *to do harm (to), harm*

nocturnus, -a, -um, *happening during the night*

nōdus, -ī, m., *knot*

nōmen, nōminis, n., *name*

nōn, adv., *not*

nōnne?, *surely (introduces a question that expects the answer "yes")*

nōnnumquam, adv., *sometimes*

nōs, nostrum, nōbīs, nōs, nōbīs, *we, us*

nōscō, nōscere, nōvī, nōtus, *to get to know, learn*

noster, nostra, nostrum, *our*

nōtus, -a, -um, *known*

novem, *nine*

novitās, novitātis, f., *newness, strangeness*

novus, -a, -um, *new*

nox, noctis, f., *night*

nūbēs, nūbis, f., *cloud*

nūbila, -ōrum, n. pl., *clouds*

nūbo, nūbere, nūpsī, nūptūrus + dat., *to marry*

nūdus, -a, -um, *naked*

nūllus, -a, -um, *no, none*

nūmen, nūminis, n. *divine power, will; majesty*
numerus, -ī, m., *number*
numquam, adv., *never*
nunc, adv., *now*
nusquam, adv., *nowhere*
nūtus, -ūs, m., *nod, command*

O

ob, prep. + acc., *on account of*
obeō, obīre, obiī, obitus, *to meet, encounter, come up against*
obsistō, obsistere, obstitī + dat., *to stand before, oppose, resist*
obstō, obstāre, obstitī, obstātūrus, *to stand in the way, obstruct, block*
obsum, obesse, obfuī + dat., *to be a hindrance to, to harm*
obtineō, obtinēre, obtinuī, obtentus, *to hold*
occultus, -a, -um, *invisible, hidden; secret*
occidō, occidere, occidī, occāsūrus, *to fall down, perish, be ruined*
occurrō, occurrere, occurrī, occursūrus + dat., *to run or hurry to meet*
oculus, -ī, m., *eye*
odor, odōris, m., *smell, odor*
offerō, offerre, obtulī, oblatus, *to provide*
officium, -ī, n., *official ceremony, duty, function*
omnīnō, adv., *at all, altogether*
omnis, -is, -e, *all, the whole, every, each*
onerō, -āre, -āvī, -ātus, *to load, burden*
operiō, operīre, operuī, opertus, *to hide, cover*
opīnor, -ārī, -ātus sum, *to think, believe*
opprimō, opprimere, oppressī, oppressus, *to overwhelm, oppress*
ops, opis, f., *power; wealth*
optimus, -a, -um, *best, very good, excellent*
opus, operis, n., *work*
  opus est, idiom, usually + abl., *to be necessary*
ōra, -ae, f., *shore; rim; border*
orbis, orbis, m., *circle*
  orbis terrārum, *the whole circle of the lands, the whole earth*
ōrdō, ōrdinis, m., *order, position*
orior, orīrī, ortus sum, *to rise, arise, come to be*
ōrnātus, -a, -um, *decorated, distinguished*
ōs, ōris, n., *mouth, face, expression*
os, ossis, n., *bone*
ōsculum, -ī, n., *kiss*
ostendō, ostendere, ostendī, ostentus, *to show, point out*

P

pābulum, -ī, n., *pasture; food*
pactum, -ī, n., *way, manner*
palla, -ae, f., *palla (a woman's full-length outer garment)*
pālor, -ārī, -ātus sum, *to wander, stray*
pandō, pandere, passus (or **pānsus**) **sum**, *to spread out, reveal, show, make known*
pangō, pangere, pepigī, pactus, *to arrange, compose*
pār, paris, *equal, matching, fitting, reasonable;* + dat., *equal to, like*
parcō, parcere, pepercī, *to spare; to avoid.*
parēns, parentis, m./f., *parent*
pareō, -ēre, -uī + dat., *to obey*
pariō, parere, peperī, partus, *to give birth to, produce, create*
pariter, adv., *equally, at the same time*
parō, -āre, -āvī, -ātus, *to prepare, get ready*
pars, partis, f., *part, direction, region, degree*
partus, -ūs, m., *birth*
parvus, -a, -um, *small*
pāscō, pāscere, pāvī, pāstus, *to feed, pasture*
passim, adv., *everywhere, in every direction*
patefaciō, patefacere, patefēcī, patefactus, *to make visible, reveal; to open*
pateō, patēre, patuī, *to extend; to lie open*
pater, patris, m., *father*
patior, patī, passus sum, *to suffer, endure, permit, allow*
patria, -ae, f., *nation, native land*
patrius, -a, -um, *of a father, fatherly, paternal; native*
paucī, -ae, -a, *few*
paulātim, adv., *gradually, little by little*
paulum, -ī, n., *a small amount, a little*
pausa, -ae, f., *pause, respite*
pāx, pācis, f., *peace*
pectus, pectoris, n., *chest, breast, heart*
pecus, pecudis, f., *herd, livestock*
pellis, pellis, f., *hide, skin*
pendeō, pendēre, pependī, *to be suspended, hang*
penetrō, -āre, -āvī, -ātus, *to penetrate*
penitus, adv., *from within, inside, deeply*
per, prep. + acc., *through, along; by*
peragrō, -āre, -āvī, -ātus, *to traverse*
percello, percellere, perculī, perculsus, *to strike*
percieō, perciēre, perciī, percitus, *to propel*
percipiō, percipere, percēpī, perceptus, *to learn; to lay hold of, seize*
percutiō, percutere, percussī, percussus, *to strike*

pereō, perīre, periī, peritūrus, *to die, perish*

perferō, perferre, pertulī, perlātus, irreg., *to report; to endure*

perficiō, perficere, perfēcī, perfectus, *to accomplish; to construct, make*

pergō, pergere, perrēxī, perrēctus, *to proceed, continue*

perīc(u)lum, -ī, n., *danger*

perimō, perimere, perēmī, perēmptus, *to destroy*

perpetuus, -a, -um, *lasting, permanent*

perspiciō, perspicere, perspexī, perspectus, *to see clearly, thoroughly; to perceive*

pertundō, pertundere, pertudī, pertūsus, *to bore through, perforate, puncture*

perturbātus, -a, -um, *confused*

pervincō, pervincere, pervīcī, pervictus, *to win a complete victory, prevail*

pervolitō, -āre, -āvī, -ātus, *to flit through*

pervulgō, -āre, -āvī, -ātus, *to make publicly known; to spread abroad, over*

pēs, pedis, m., *foot*

pestis, pestis, f., *destruction, death*

peto, petere, petīvī, petītus, *to look for, seek, head for; to aim at, attack*

pictūra, -ae, f., *picture*

pietās, pietātis, f., *dutifulness, devotion, piety*

pinguis, -is, -e, *fat, rich*

plācātus, -a, -um, *peaceful, calm*

placeō, -ēre, -uī + dat., *to please*

placidus, -a, -um, *quiet, calm, serene*

plāga, -ae, f., *blow*

plēnus, -a, -um + gen., *full*

plērumque, adv., *generally, often*

plūrēs, plūrēs, plūra, *more*

plūrimus, -a, -um, *most, very much*

plūs, plūris, n., *more*

pōculum, –i, n., *cup*

poena, -ae, f., *punishment, penalty*

pollēns, pollentis, *powerful, strong*

pondus, ponderis, n., *weight*

pōnō, pōnere, posuī, positus, *to put, place*

pontus, -ī, m., *sea*

populus, -ī, m., *people*

porrō, adv., *moreover*

porta, -ae, f., *gate, door*

possideō, possidēre, possēdī, possessus, *to hold, occupy, control*

possum, posse, potuī, irreg., *to be able; I can*

post, adv., *after(ward), later*

post, prep. + acc., *after*

posterus, -a, -um, *next, following*

postis, postis, m., *door-post*

postquam, conj., *after*

postrēmō, adv., *finally*

potestās, potestātis, f., *control, power*

potior, potīrī, potītus sum + abl., *to obtain, seize*

potis, indecl. adj. + infin., *has the power, is able (to)*

potius, compar. adv., *rather*

praebeō, praebēre, praebuī, *to display, show, provide, offer*

praeclārus, -a, -um, *distinguished; very bright*

praeclūdō, praeclūdere, praeclūsī, praeclūsus, *to prevent, deny, shut off, bar*

praeditus, -a, -um, + abl., *endowed with, possessing*

praemium, -ī, n., *reward, prize*

praesēns, praesentis, *present*

praesertim, adv., *especially*

praestāns, praestantis, *exceptional, extraordinary*

praestō, adv., *present, at hand*

praestō, praestāre, praestitī + dat. and abl. of measure, *to excel, surpass; to be greater*

praeter, prep. + acc., *except*

praetereā, conj., *besides, too, moreover*

praetereō, praeterīre, praeteriī or **praeterīvī, praeteritus**, irreg., *to go past*

premō, premere, pressī, pressus, *to press*

prīmōrdia, -ōrum, n., *first-beginnings, beginnings, elements*

prīmus, -a, -um, *first*
    cum prīmīs, idiom, *especially, in particular*
    prīmum, adv., *first, at first*

prīnceps, prīncipis, *first*

prīncipium, -ī, n. *first principle; beginning; first-particle, first-beginning, atom*

prior, prior, prius, gen. **priōris**, *first (of two), previous*
    prius, adv., *earlier, previously*

prius (quam), adv., compar., *before, earlier*

prīvō, -āre, -āvī, -ātus + abl, *to deprive of, free from*

prō, prep. + abl., *for, on behalf of; in accordance with*

prōcēdō, prōcēdere, prōcessī, prōcessūrus, *to go forward*

procul, adv., *in the distance, far off, far*

prōdeō, prōdīre, prōdiī, prōditūrus, irreg., *to come forth*

proelium, -ī, n., *fight, battle*

profectō, adv., *indeed, certainly*

prōferō, prōferre, prōtulī, prōlātus, irreg., *to carry forward, continue*

proficīscor, proficīscī, profectus sum, *to set out, leave*

profundō, profundere, profūdi, profūsus, *to flow down or forth, hang down; to pour out*

profundus, -a, -um, *deep, profound; vast, boundless*

prōgredior, prōgredī, prōgressus sum, *to go forward, advance*

prōlēs, prōlis, f., *offspring*

propāgō, -āre, -āvī, -ātus, *to reproduce, propagate, produce, cause*

prope, adv., *near, nearby, nearly*

proprius, -a, -um, *one's own, its own, their own*

propter, prep. + acc., *on account of, because of; near*

prōrsum, adv., *altogether, absolutely*

prōrumpo, prōrumpere, prōrūpī, prōruptus, *to burst forth, out*

prosternō, prosternere, prostrāvī, prostrātus, *to lay on the ground*

prōsum, prōdesse, prōfuī + dat., *to be of use, benefit*

prōtrahō, prōtrahere, prōtrāxī, prōtrāctus, *to drag forward or out*

pruīna, -ae, f., *frost*

puella, -ae, f., *girl*

puer, puerī, m., *boy; child*

pugna, -ae, f., *fight, battle*

pulcher, pulchra, pulchrum, *beautiful, pretty, handsome*

pūnctus, -a, -um, *pricked in*

pūrgō, -āre, -āvī, -ātus, *to clean*

purpureus, -a, -um, *purple*

pūrus, -a, -um, *spotless, clean, pure*

putō, -āre, -āvī, -ātus, *to think, consider*

⁊ Q

quā, adv., *where, in which*

quadrupēs, quadrupedis, m., *four-footed animal, quadruped*

quaerō, quaerere, quaesīvī, quaesītus, *to seek, look for, ask* (for)

quālis, -is, -e, *what sort of, what kind of*

quam, adv., *how; than; as*

quandō, interrog. and relative adv., *when?, since*

quandoquidem, adv., *since*

quantus, -a, -um, *how big? how much? how great?*

quāpropter, adv., *because of which, therefore*

quārē, adv., *by which means, wherefore, therefore;* interrog., *in what way, how, why*

quasi, adv., *as if*

-que, enclitic conj., *and*

queō, quīre, quīvī or **quiī, quitus**, *to be able*

querēla, -ae, f., *complaint, lament*

quī, old abl., *how?*

quī, quae, quod, *who, which, that*

quia, conj., *because*

quīcumque, quaecumque, quodcumque, *whoever, whatever, whichever*

quīdam, quaedam, quoddam, *a certain*

quidem, adv., *indeed*

quiēs, quiētis, f., *rest; resting-place; den*

quiēscō, quiēscere, quiēvī, quiētūrus, *to rest, keep quiet*

quiētus, -a, -um, *peaceful, calm, tranquil*

quīn, adv., conj., *but, but that; that*

    quīn etiam, idiom, *but also, furthermore*

quīnam, quaenam, quodnam, interrog. adj., *what kind of, what indeed?*

quippe, adv., *surely, indeed, for*

quis, quid, interrog., *who, what?;* indefinite, *someone, something, anyone, anything*

quis, sī (see **aliquis**)

quisquam, quicquam, *anyone, anything*

quisque, quaeque, quidque, *each, each one*

quīvīs, quaevīs, quodvīs, *any (one, thing) you like*

quō, adv., *for which reason, therefore; to where*

quōcumque, adv., *wherever*

quod, conj., *because, that, whereas; but*

    quod superest: a formulaic phrase, literally *as to what remains*, simply means *next*

quoniam, conj., *since*

quoque, adv., *also*

⁊ R

radius, -ī, m., *ray*

rāmus, -ī, m., *branch*

rapāx, rapācis, *apt to seize or tear away, tearing*

rapidus, -a, -um, *rushing, tearing, rapid*

rapiō, rapere, rapuī, raptus, *to snatch, seize*

raptō, -āre, -āvī, -ātus, *to drag violently away, sweep or rush along*

ratiō, ratiōnis, f., *reason, explanation; way, working; system, philosophy*

    ratiōnem reddere, idiom, *to give an account/ explanation*

recēdō, recēdere, recessī, recessūrus, *to withdraw*

recipiō, recipere, recēpī, receptus, *to receive, recapture*

rēctus, -a, -um, *right, proper, correct; straight*

reddō, reddere, reddidī, redditūrus, irreg., *to return, go back; explain*

redeō, redīre, rediī or **redīvī, reditūrus**, irreg., *to return, go back*

redūcō, redūcere, redūxī, reductus, *to lead back, take back*

referō, referre, rettulī, relātus, irreg., *to bring back; to reproduce; to refer*

rēfert, rēferre, rētulit, impersonal, *it makes a difference, it matters*

reficiō, reficere, refēcī, refectus, *to remake, redo, restore*

regiō, regiōnis, f., *region, area, direction*

rēgnum, -ī, n., *kingdom*

regō, regere, rēxī, rēctus, *to rule*

rēiciō, rēicere, rēiēcī, rēiectus, *to throw back*

rēligiō, rēligiōnis, f., *religion*

relinquō, relinquere, relīquī, relictus, *to leave behind*

remittō, remittere, remīsī, remissus, *to send back*

reor, rērī, ratus sum, *to think*

reparō, -āre, -āvī, -ātus, *to replace, restore*

repente, adv., *suddenly, unexpectedly*

reperiō, reperīre, repperī, repertus, *to find*

repleō, replēre, replēvī, replētus, *to fill up, fill*

repōnō, repōnere, reposuī, repositus, *to place back, lay back*

requīrō, requīrere, requīsīvī, requīsītus, *to ask, inquire; to need, miss, lack*

rēs, reī, f., *thing, matter, situation, affair*

reserō, -āre, -āvī, -ātus, *to unbar a door, unseal*

resistō, resistere, restitī + dat., *to resist*

resolvō, resolvere, resolvī, resolūtus, *to loosen, unfasten, release*

respiciō, respicere, respexī, respectus, *to look back (at)*

respondeō, respondēre, respondī, respōnsūrus, *to reply*

restō, restāre, restitī, *to stand firm in opposition, resist*

retineō, retinēre, retinuī, retentus, *to hold back, hold, keep*

retrō, adv., *backwards, back*

revocō, -āre, -āvī, -ātus, *to recall, call back*

rēx, rēgis, m., *king*

rīdeō, rīdēre, rīsī, rīsus, *to laugh, smile (at, on)*

rīpa, -ae, f., *bank*

rīsus, -ūs, m., *laugh, smile*

rīvus, -ī, m., *stream*

rīxor, -ārī, -ātus sum, *to quarrel*

rogus, -ī, m., *funeral pyre*

Rōmānus, -a, -um, *Roman*

    Rōmānī, -ōrum, m. pl., *the Romans*

rōs, rōris, m., *dew*

rota, -ae, f., *wheel*

rumpō, rumpere, rūpī, ruptus, *to burst, break*

ruō, ruere, ruī, *to drive headlong, ruin, destroy*

rūrsus (rūrsum), adv., *again, once more, in turn; back*

ℭꝫ S

sacra, -ōrum, n. pl., *religious rites, sacrifice*

saec(u)lum, -ī, n., *age, era, generation; race, tribe*

saepe, adv., *often*

saeviō, -īre, -iī, -ītūrus, *to rage*

saevus, -a, -um, *fierce, savage*

sagāx, sagācis, *keen, sharp, wise*

saltus, -ūs, m., *woodland, glade*

salūs, salūtis, f., *safety; health*

salūtō, -āre, -āvī, -ātus, *to greet, welcome*

sānctus, -a, -um, *holy, sacred*

sanguen (n.) and **sanguis, sanguinis**, m., *blood*

sapiēns, sapientis, m., *wise man*

satiās, satiātis, f., *satiety, surfeit*

satiō, -āre, -āvī, -ātus, *to satisfy, fill*

satis, adv., *enough*

saxum, -ī, n., *rock*

scelerōsus, -a, -um, *wicked*

scelus, sceleris, n., *crime*

scindō, scindere, scidī, scissus, *to cut, split, carve, tear*

sciō, scīre, scīvī, scītus, *to know*

scrībō, scrībere, scrīpsī, scrīptus, *to write*

sē and **sēse**, acc. and abl.; gen. **suī**, dat., **sibi**, *himself, herself, itself*

sēcrētus, -a, -um, *separate, distinct*

sēcūrus, -a, -um, *carefree, unconcerned, safe*

sēdēs, sēdis, f., *seat, center (of some activity)*

sēiungō, sēiungere, sēiūnxī, sēiūnctus, *to separate*

semel, adv., *once*

sēmen, sēminis, n., *seed; atom, particle*

sēmoveō, sēmovēre, sēmōvī, sēmōtus, *to remove, separate*

semper, adv., *always*

senex, senis, m., *old man*

sēnsus, -ūs, m., *sensation, sense*

sentiō, sentīre, sēnsī, sēnsus, *to feel, notice, realize*

sepeliō, sepelīre, sepelīvī, sepultus, *to bury*

sequor, sequī, secūtus sum, *to follow*

serēnus, -a, -um, *clear, bright; tranquil, serene*

sermō, sermōnis, m., *conversation, talk*

servō, -āre, -āvī, -ātus, *to save, protect, preserve*

sī, conj., *if*

    sī quis (= sī aliquis), *if anyone, someone*

sīdus, sīderis, n., *star; constellation*

significō, -āre, -āvī, -ātus, *to indicate, show, make known*

signum, -ī, n., *signal; statue; constellation, stars*

silva, -ae, f., *woods, forest*

silvestris, -is, -e, *woodland-dwelling, wild, rough*

similis, -is, -e + dat., *similar (to), like*

simplicitās, simplicitātis, f., *singleness of nature, unity*

simul, adv., *together, at the same time*

simulac, conj., *as soon as*

simulācrum, -ī, n., *image, statue; film*

sine, prep. + abl., *without*

sinō, sinere, sīvī, situs, *to allow*
   situs, -a, -um, *located, situated*

sitiō, sitīre, *to be thirsty*

sitis, sitis, f., *thirst*

situs, -a, -um, *placed, situated*

sīve . . . sīve, conjs., *whether . . . or*

socia, -ae, f., *ally*

socius, -ī, m., *ally*

sōl, sōlis, m., *sun*

soleō, solēre, solitus sum + infin., *to be accustomed (to), be in the habit of*

solidus, -a, -um, *solid*

sollemnis, -is, -e, *formal, ceremonial; solemn*

sollicitus, -a, -um, *anxious, worried*

sōlus, -a, -um, *alone, only*

solvō, solvere, solvī, solūtus, *to loosen, untie, free*

somnium, -ī, n., *dream*

somnus, -ī, m., *sleep*

sonitus, -ūs, m., *sound*

sōpītus, -a, -um, *lulled to sleep, asleep*

sōrsum, adv., *apart, separately*

spargō, spargere, spārsī, spārsus, *to strew, sprinkle*

spatium, -ī, n., *time, period; space*

speciēs, -ēī, f. , *sight, appearance; face*

spectō, -āre, -āvī, -ātus, *to watch, look at*

spēs, speī, f., *hope*

sponte, ablative, *will*

squāmigerī, squāmigerum, m. pl., *scale-bearing creatures, fish*

sternō, sternere, strāvī, strātus, *to strew, scatter*

stinguō, stinguere, stīnxī, stīnctus, *to extinguish, annihilate, destroy*

stīpō, -āre, -āvī, -ātus, *to compress, pack tight*

stō, stāre, stetī, statūrus, *to stand*

strātum, -ī, n., *sheet, covering; pavement*

studeō, studēre, studui, *to desire*

studium, -ī, n., *enthusiasm, study, pursuit, devotion; desire*

stultus, -a, -um, *stupid, foolish*

suādeō, suādēre, suāsī, suāsūrus, *to urge, induce*

suāvis, -is, -e, *sweet, delightful*

sub, prep. + abl., *under, beneath*

subicio, subicere, subiēcī, subiectus, *to place underneath or below*

subigō, subigere, subēgī, subāctus, *to suppress, subdue*

subitus, -a, -um, *sudden*
   subitō, adv., *suddenly*

suborior, suborīrī, subortus sum, *to be provided*

subter, prep. + acc., *beneath*

suēscō, suēscere, suēvī, suētus, *to be accustomed*

sum, esse, fuī, futūrus, irreg., *to be*

summa, -ae, f., *sum, whole; total*

summittō, summittere, summīsī, summissus, *to send up, put forth; to drop, lower, sink*

summus, -a, -um, *greatest, very great, the top of, highest, supreme*

sūmō, sūmere, sūmpsī, sūmptus, *to take, take up, pick out*

super, adv., *from above*

super, prep. + acc., *over, above*

superbus, -a, -um, *proud, arrogant, haughty*

supersum, superesse, superfuī, superfutūrus, *to remain*

suppeditō, -āre, -āvī, -ātus, *to provide, supply*

suprā, adv., *above, on top*

suprā, prep. + acc., *above*

suprēmus, -a, um, *highest, top (of)*

surgō, surgere, surrēxī, surrēctus, *to rise, arise, spring up*

surripiō, surripere, surripuī, surreptus, *to steal*

sūs, suis, m. / f., *boar*

suscipiō, suscipere, suscēpī, susceptus, *to take up, undertake*

suspendō, suspendere, suspēnsī, suspēnsus, *to suspend, hang*

suspiciō, suspicere, suspexī, suspectus, *to look upwards*

suus, -a, -um, *his, her, its, their (own)*

‎ T

tābēscō, tābēscere, tābuī, *to waste away*

taeda, -ae, f., *torch*

taeter, taetra, taetrum, *foul*

tālis, -is, -e, *such, like this, of this kind*

tam, adv., *so, such*

tamen, adv., *however, nevertheless, yet*

tamquam, conj., *just as if*

tandem, adv., *at last, at length*

tangō, tangere, tetigī, tāctus, *to touch*

tantus, -a, -um, *so great*

    tantum, adv., *only; so much*

tantusdem, tantadem, tantundem, *just as much*

tardus, -a, -um, *slow*

Tartara, -ōrum, n. pl., *Tartarus* (the infernal regions, the underworld)

tegō, tegere, tēxī, tēctus, *to cover*

tellūs, tellūris, f., *earth*

tēlum, -ī, n., *spear, shaft, missile; weapon*

tempestās, tempestātis, f., *storm; season, weather*

templum, -ī, n., *temple*

temptō, -āre, -āvī, -ātus, *to try, test; to assail, attack*

tempus, temporis, n., *time; season*

tenebrae, -ārum, f. pl., *darkness*

teneō, tenēre, tenuī, tentus, *to hold*

tener, tenera, tenerum, *tender, delicate, soft*

terminus, -ī, m., *boundary post/stone; limit*

terra, -ae, f., *earth, ground, land*

terror, terrōris, m. *fear, terror*

tertius, -a, -um, *third*

timeō, -ēre, -uī, *to fear, be afraid of/to*

    timendus, -a, -um, *to be feared*

timor, timōris, m., *fear*

tollō, tollere, sustulī, sublātus, irreg., *to lift, raise*

torreō, torrēre, torruī, tostus, *to scorch, burn*

tot, indecl. adj., *so many*

tōtus, -a, -um, *all, whole*

tractō, -āre, -āvī, -ātus, *to try, investigate, practice*

trādō, trādere, trādidī, trāditus, *to hand over*

tranquillus, -a, -um, *calm, quiet, tranquil*

trānseō, trānsīre, trānsiī or trānsīvī, trānsitus, *to go across, cross, go through*

tremulus, -a, -um, *trembling, unsteady*

trepidō, -āre, -āvī, -ātus, *to be alarmed; to tremble*

trepidus, -a, -um, *fearful, perilous, restless, anxious*

tribuō, tribuere, tribuī, tribūtus, *to grant, attribute (to)*

trīstis, -is, -e, *sad; bitter*

tū, tuī, tibi, tē, tē, *you*

tueor, tuērī, tuitus sum, *to see, observe, perceive*

tum, adv., *at that moment, then*

tumultus, -ūs, m., *uproar, commotion*

tunc, adv., *then*

turba, -ae, f., *cause of confusion/turmoil; disturbance*

turbō, -āre, -āvī, -ātus, *to confuse, disturb, stir up, alarm*

turbō, turbinis, m., *whirl, whirlwind, tornado*

turpis, -is, -e, *foul, base*

turpō, -āre, -āvī, -ātus, *to pollute, defile*

tūte, emphatic form of tū, *you yourself*

tuus, -a, -um, *your*

C3 U

ūber, ūberis, n., *udder*

ubi, adv., conj., *where, when*

ūllus, -a, -um, *any*

ūmor, ūmōris, m., *moisture, liquid*

umquam, adv., *ever*

unda, -ae, f., *wave*

unde, adv., *from where*

undique, adv., *on all sides, from all sides*

unguentum, -ī, n., *ointment, perfume, oil*

unguō, ungere, ūnxī, ūnctus, *to anoint, smear with oil*

ūnus, -a, -um, *one*

    ūnā, adv., *together*

urbs, urbis, f., *city*

urgeō, urgēre, ursī, *to press, insist*

usquam, adv., *anywhere*

usque, adv., *all the way (to), as far as*

    usque adeō, idiom, *to such an extent*

ūsūrpō, -āre, -āvī, -ātus, *to call habitually, to name, term; to perceive*

ūsus, -ūs, m., + abl. + form of sum, *to need*

ut, conj. + indic., *as, like, when;* + subjn., *so that, that, to*

uter, utra, utrum, *which of the two?*

uterque, utraque, utrumque, *each (of two), both*

ūtilis, -is, -e, *useful*

ūtor, ūtī, ūsus sum + abl., *to use*

utrimque, adv., *on both sides*

utrum . . . an . . . , conj., *whether . . . or . . .*

uxor, uxōris, f., *wife*

C3 V

vacuus, -a, -um, *empty; free (from)*

valeō, -ēre, -uī, -itūrus, *to be strong, be well*

validus, -a, -um, *strong, powerful*

vapor, vapōris, m., *steam, heat*

variō, -āre, -āvī, -ātus, *to be different, to vary*

varius, -a, -um, *different, various, varied*

vās, vāsis, n., *vessel, vase*

vāstus, -a, -um, *vast, desolate*

vātēs, vātis, m., *prophet, seer*

-ve, enclitic conj., *or*

ve(he)mēns, ve(he)mentis, *violent, strong*

vēlō, -āre, -āvī, -ātus, *to cover, veil*

velut, adv., *just as*

veniō, venīre, vēnī, ventūrus, *to come*

ventus, -ī, m., *wind*

Venus, Veneris, f., *Venus, the goddess of love*

verber, verberis, n., *blow, blast*

verberō, -āre, -āvī, -ātus, *to beat, whip*

vereor, verērī, veritus sum, *to be afraid of, fear*

vērnus, -a, -um, *occurring in spring, vernal*

versus, -ūs, m., *verse*

vertō, vertere, vertī, versus, *to turn, overturn*

vērum, adv., *but*

vērus, -a, -um, *true*

    vērō, adv., *truly, really, indeed*

    vērum, -ī, n., *the truth*

vēscor, vēscī + abl., *to feed (on)*

vēstigium, -ī, n., *track, footprint, trace*

vestis, vestis, f., *clothing, garment, clothes*

vetus, veteris, *old*

vetustās, vetustātis, f., *old age*

vexō, -āre, -āvī, -ātus, *to annoy, harry, harass*

via, -ae, f., *road, street, way*

vicissim, adv., *in turn.*

victor, victōris, m., *victor, conqueror*

victōria, -ae, f., *victory*

videō, vidēre, vīdī, vīsus, *to see*

    videor, vidērī, vīsus sum, *to seem, be seen*

vigeō, -ēre, -uī, *to be active, lively, or vigorous; to thrive, flourish*

vigilō, -āre, -āvī, -ātūrus, *to stay awake, be alert*

vincō, vincere, vīcī, victus, *to conquer, win*

violentus, -a, -um, *violent, savage*

violō, -āre, -āvī, -ātus, *to do harm*

vir, virī, m., *man, husband*

vireō, virēre, viruī, *to be green with vegetation, to be vigorous, thrive*

virgineus, -a, -um, *of a maiden, virgin*

virgō, virginis, f., *maiden*

viridāns, viridantis, *green, verdant*

viridis, -is, -e, *green*

virtūs, virtūtis, f., *strength, excellence*

vīs, acc. **vim**, abl. **vī**, nom pl. **virēs**, *force, power; amount;* pl., *strength, military forces*

vīscera, vīscerum, n. pl., *vital organs*

vīsō, vīsere, vīsī, vīsus, *to go to see, visit; to look upon, see, behold*

vīta, -ae, f., *life*

vītālis, -is, -e, *of life, vital*

vītō, -āre, -āvī, -ātus, *to avoid*

vitulus, -ī, m., *calf*

vīvidus, -a, -um, *lively, virorous*

vīvō, vīvere, vīxī, vīctūrus, *to live*

vīvus, -a, -um, *live, alive*

vix, adv., *scarcely, with difficulty, only just*

vocō, -āre, -āvī, -ātus, *to call, invite*

volō, -āre, -āvī, -ātūrus, *to fly*

volō, velle, voluī, irreg., *to wish, want, be willing*

volucris, volucris, f., *bird*

voluntās, voluntātis, f., *will*

voluptās, voluptātis, f., *pleasure, delight*

volvō, volvere, volvī, volūtus, *to roll*

vōmer, vōmeris, m., *plowshare*

vōx, vōcis, f., *voice*

vulgus, -ī, n., *crowd, common people*

vulnus, vulneris, n., *wound*

vultus, -ūs, f., *face, expression*

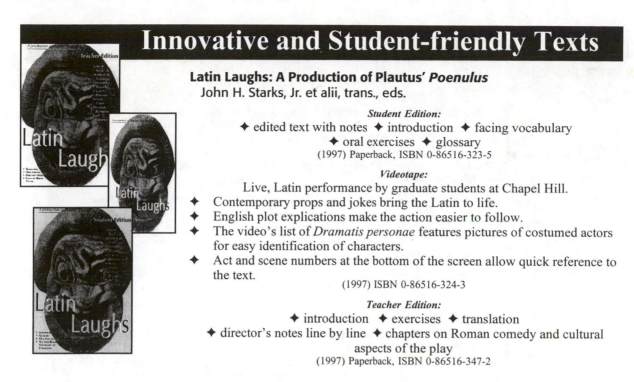

Innovative and Student-friendly Texts

Latin Laughs: A Production of Plautus' *Poenulus*
John H. Starks, Jr. et alii, trans., eds.

Student Edition:

✦ edited text with notes ✦ introduction ✦ facing vocabulary
✦ oral exercises ✦ glossary
(1997) Paperback, ISBN 0-86516-323-5

Videotape:

Live, Latin performance by graduate students at Chapel Hill.
✦ Contemporary props and jokes bring the Latin to life.
✦ English plot explications make the action easier to follow.
✦ The video's list of *Dramatis personae* features pictures of costumed actors for easy identification of characters.
✦ Act and scene numbers at the bottom of the screen allow quick reference to the text.

(1997) ISBN 0-86516-324-3

Teacher Edition:

✦ introduction ✦ exercises ✦ translation
✦ director's notes line by line ✦ chapters on Roman comedy and cultural aspects of the play
(1997) Paperback, ISBN 0-86516-347-2

To stage Plautus in Latin, and professionally ... was already a major achievement. But Starks and Company have gone further. With their Poenulus *videotape and instructional booklet, they have taken Plautus on the road, where he belongs: into schools and colleges, where young and old, students and teachers alike, can be initiated into the incomparable delights of quarreling, competing, worrying, lamenting, brawling, and lovemaking in the comic mode. Our "dead language," it seems, is very much alive!*

— **Kenneth J. Reckford,** University of N. Carolina

Ovid: Selections from Ars Amatoria, Remedia Amoris
Graves Haydon Thompson

In print continuously since 1952, this selection from Ovid's *Ars Amatoria* and *Remedia Amoris* continues to appeal because of Professor Thompson's jovial appreciation of Ovid's sophisticated and urbane humor: "Let no one be deceived by the serious pose Ovid adopts at the beginning of his poem," Thompson warns in his Introduction. "He is Professor Ovid, M.A.—*Magister Amoris*, Master of the Art of Love. His is a didactic or teaching poem, like Lucretius' *De Rerum Natura* or Vergil's *Georgics*, but a burlesque one. He dons the horn-rimmed spectacles of the classroom, sets them well down on the end of his nose, and gazes in mock solemnity upon his pupils. The reader must join in the fun in the same spirit."

✦ Text ✦ Commentary ✦ Vocabulary

I am delighted to learn that your Selections from the Ars *will be reprinted soon. Reflecting on my use of it as both student and teacher, I find it still an excellent text, the product of your obvious sound scholarship...I delight in re-reading your introduction and notes, full of wit and gentle humor. Now that the AP exam includes Ovid, I should think that your text would be quite popular at schools boasting strong programs in classics.*

— **Auguste J. Bannard**

168 pp. (1952, corrected 1958, sixteenth reprint 1997) Paperback, ISBN 0-86516-395-2

BOLCHAZY-CARDUCCI Publishers, Inc.
orders@bolchazy.com

Latin Grammar & Composition

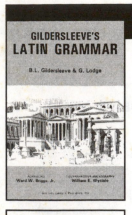

Gildersleeve's Latin Grammar
B.L. Gildersleeve & G. Lodge

The classic Latin grammar favored by many students and teachers with two new addtions:
♦ Foreword by **Ward W. Briggs, Jr.**
♦ Comprehensive bibliography by **William E. Wycislo.**

"Rightly interpreted, grammar is the culmination of philological study, and not its rudiment ... No study of literature can yield its highest result without the close study of language, and consequently the close study of grammar."

Basil L. Gildersleeve, *Selected Classical Papers*

"Compare his work with any other treatise hitherto in use, and its superiority will be manifest."
Southern Review

613 pp. (1895, third ed., reprint with additions 1997) paperback, ISBN 0-86516-353-7

New Latin Grammar
Charles E. Bennett

New Latin Grammar uses specific examples from primary sources to help students learn the inflections, syntax, sounds, accents, particles and word formations of the Latin language. It also includes a history of the Indo-European family of languages, the stages of the development of the Latin language and sections on prosody, the Roman calendar, Roman names, and definition and examples of figures of syntax and rhetoric.

xvi + 287 pp. (1908, Reprint 1995) paperback, ISBN 0-86516-261-1

New Latin Syntax
E. C. Woodcock

This book gives a historical account of the chief Latin constructions, aiming to equip students to interpret texts as well as to write correct Latin. The index of passages quoted makes it useful as a reference work for teachers. This is a necessary reference and an indispensable vademecum for teachers and advanced students.

xxiv + 267 pp. (1959, Reprint 1987) Paperback, ISBN 0-86516-126-7

New Latin Composition
Charles E. Bennett

In *New Latin Composition,* Bennett draws examples, vocabularies, and exercises from two of the most widely-read Latin authors: ♦ Caesar in Part I ♦ Cicero in Part II. Also includes sections on sentence composition, passage composition, oral composition, and the value of oral communication in Latin, which has only recently begun to be recognized.

ix + 292 pp. (1912, Reprint 1996) paperback, ISBN 0-86516-345-6

Latin Prose Composition & Key to Latin Prose Composition
M.A. North & A. E. Hillard

This book is aimed at helping students to enhance their command of Latin grammar and vocabulary with exercises structured in a manner that gradually enables students to build their Latin prose skills.

A book that has well stood the test of time.

— **R. S. Kilpatrick,** Queen's University of Kingston

Latin Prose Composition: xix + 300 pp. (Reprint 1995), Paperback, ISBN 0-86516-308-1
Key to Latin Prose Composition: (Reprint 1996), Paperback, ISBN 0-86516-307-3

Graphic Latin Grammar
James P. Humphreys

Four double-sided pages containing all your Latin grammar charts on sturdy card stock ready for insertion in a 3-ring notebook.

(1961, Reprint 1995) Four 3-hole-punched laminated reference cards, ISBN 0-86516-111-1

BOLCHAZY-CARDUCCI Publishers, Inc.
orders@bolchazy.com